"Begi ning with the ill-starred arrival in 1873 of a lone Irishman from Newr rket, County Cork, to be a policeman, followed by twenty more from e same town, and ending with the death of the last man in 1950, this g undbreaking book is a story of life, death, and crime in colonial Hong Kong. It is also an account of an important part of Hong Kong's popul ion that has eluded most historians: the European working class. With arsenal of previously untapped materials in Ireland, Britain and Hong Kong, Patricia O'Sullivan, granddaughter and great-niece of two of th policemen, tells the remarkable tales of the families who over eigh ive years built their own 'little Ireland' in Hong Kong."

– John M. Carroll, Dept. of History, University of Hong Kong, author of *A Concise History of Hong Kong*

" *Hong Kong – An Irish History* is a fascinating account of how Iri played a key role in building the modern-day Hong Kong Polic rce and indeed modern-day Hong Kong. Patricia O'Sullivan gives id account of how Irish emigrants, including her own family, sought out a better life, and thrived in an environment and culture totally different from their own childhoods in rural Ireland. It is a very good read."

– Eoin O'Leary, Irish Ambassador to the People's Republic of China

"We get white-collar crime, blue-collar crime, corruption, gambling, disease, typhoons and plagues, but also the daily grind of ordinary people going about their work. ... O'Sullivan has an encyclopaedic mind and she engages with her subject with razor-sharp zeal."

– *Books Ireland* magazine

Policing Hong Kong – An Irish history

Patricia O'Sullivan

BLACKSMITH BOOKS

To the memory of Murty Ned and Dan O'Sullivan of Barnacurra, Newmarket, Co. Cork, and of Ann O'Brien, née O'Sullivan, who between them all started me on this journey.

Policing Hong Kong: An Irish history
ISBN 978-988-77927-3-4

Published by Blacksmith Books
Unit 26, 19/F, Block B, Wah Lok Industrial Centre,
37-41 Shan Mei Street, Fo Tan, Hong Kong
Tel: (+852) 2877 7899
www.blacksmithbooks.com

Edited by Samuel Rossiter
Layout by Pete Spurrier

Second printing 2018

Contents

Royal Asiatic Society Hong Kong Studies Series is designed to make widely available important contributions on the local history, culture and society of Hong Kong and the surrounding region. Generous support from the Sir Lindsay and Lady May Ride Memorial Fund makes it possible to publish a series of high-quality works that will be of lasting appeal and value to all, both scholars and informed general readers, who share a deeper interest in and enthusiasm for the area.

Other titles in RAS Hong Kong Studies Series:

Ancestral Images: A Hong Kong Collection Hugh Baker

Cantonese Society in Hong Kong and Singapore Marjorie Topley, Jean De Bernardi (ed)

Custom, Land & Livelihood in Rural South China 1750-1950 Patrick Hase

Dragon and the Crown. Hong Kong Memoirs Stanley Kwan with Nicole Kwan

Early China Coast Meteorology. The Role of HK 1882-1912 Kevin MacKeown

East River Column. Hong Kong Guerrillas in the Second World War and After Chan Sui Jeung

Escape from Hong Kong: Admiral Chan Chak's Christmas Day Dash, 1941 Tim Luard

For Gods, Ghosts & Ancestors Janet Scott

Forgotten Souls: The Social History of Hong Kong Cemetery 1845-1918 Patricia Lim

Governors, Politics and the Colonial Office Gavin Ure

Hong Kong Internment 1942-45. Life in the Japanese Civilian Camp at Stanley Geoff Emerson

Portugal, China and the Macau Negotiations 1986-1999 Carmen Mendes

Public Success, Private Sorrow. The Life and Times of Charles Henry Brewitt Taylor Cyril Cannon

Reluctant Heroes. Rickshaw Pullers in Hong Kong and Canton 1874-1954 Fung Chi Ming

Resist to the End. Hong Kong 1941-1945 Charles Barman, Ray Barman (ed)

Scottish Mandarin. The Life and Times of Sir Reginald Johnston Shiona Airlie

Six Day War of 1899. Hong Kong in the Age of Imperialism Patrick Hase

Southern District Officer Reports. Islands and Villages in Rural Hong Kong John Strickland (ed)

The Lone Flag. Memoir of the British Consul in Macau during World War II John Reeves

The Peak: An Illustrated History of Hong Kong's Top District Richard Garrett

Watching Over Hong Kong. Private Policing 1841-1941 Sheila Hamilton

Acknowledgements

This book has only come about because of the interest, help, support and friendship of many people over a considerable period of time. As the Epilogue makes clear, I am deeply indebted to the two people who, respectively, made my first visits to Hong Kong possible and shared with me material already unearthed and taught me my way around the intricacies of researching Hong Kong history. Since then their continued faith in me and in the value of the project has helped keep me motivated. Thank you so much, Dennis and Richard.

I am very grateful for the generous specialist help from, amongst others, Stephen Verralls, Stephen Davies, Nigel Wodehouse, Louis Ha, Christine Thomas, John Carroll and the late Gregory McEwen. Jill Fell spent numerous hours 'toothcombing' the manuscript to rid it of many errors, whilst Christopher Munn's advice and support throughout the process has gently steered me along better paths than I would have chosen for myself. In Newmarket Raymond O'Sullivan has been an indefatigable source of local historical knowledge, and Barbara Anslow's memories of the pre-War and internment years have been very helpful. Annemarie Evans, May Holdsworth and Geoffrey Emerson have been fantastic 'critical friends' of the project, and I owe so much to David Bellis and the Gwulo community.

The support and encouragement of Chief Superintendent Kerry Carew and members of the Hong Kong Police Force has been of great value, as has that of the Peter Ryan, Irish Consul General and the staff of the Irish Consulate. The Royal Asiatic Society, Hong Kong Branch and the Ride Fund early gave me generous support to help my research. I am, of course, very grateful to Pete Spurrier and Blacksmith Books for their encouragement and support, and for being such easy and open people to work with.

I have made ample and frequent use of various institutions in the course of the research for this book, and would record my gratitude to Mr. Bernard Hui and the staff of the Public Records Office in Hong Kong; the staff and management of The National Archives, Kew, London; Mr. C. M. Sum and the Police Museum in Hong Kong; the Librarians and staff of Hong Kong Central Library and the Committee and Librarians of the Helena May Library, Hong Kong.

The descendants of people mentioned in this book have been enormously generous, providing me with photographs and information of their relatives, and frequently welcoming me – until that point an unknown relative of theirs – into their homes and lives. My profound thanks are due to Patricia and Clare O'Driscoll, the late Marjorie Davitt, Kevin Murphy, Moonyeen Du Conte, Anne Hardy, Paul Murphy and family, Joy Hodgens, Carmel Beatty, Caroline Feenan and Patrick Haugh for their generosity.

Of my immediate family, I am indebted to my aunt, Ann O'Brien, cousins Dan and Murty Ned O'Sullivan and Aidan Keane, all sadly no longer with us. I would like to say a great thank you to cousins Mary O'Keeffe (Buzz Kenneally), Conor O'Brien, Mary Collins Walsh and Cristine Deasy for ferreting out family photographs and putting up with a myriad of questions from me, over such a long time.

Finally, I would like to thank the Council, residents, members and especially the lovely staff of The Helena May, who have provided me with an excellent home during my frequent visits to Hong Kong.

Note: Places and streets in Hongkong have, since the beginning of the British presence, been known by both Chinese and English names. However, some changes have occurred over time. The author has opted to employ some of the terms that were standard in the period before 1945, e.g. using the single word Hongkong, rather than the separate syllable/word rule that would apply now. Thus in the text, this term refers to the British colony, whilst Hong Kong will refer to the contemporary place, the Special Administrative Region of China.

Introduction

From its inception in 1841 the Hongkong Police Force mirrored the racially divided structure of the rest of the British Empire, with career civil servants commanding an organisation comprising contingents of Chinese, Indian and European men. Not until 1920, and gaining momentum after the Asia-Pacific War (1941-1945) were local men integrated into the inspectorate and above. In the years before, the British constables held the superior position over their Indian and Chinese counterparts, but they were just ordinary working class men motivated by the chance of a pension and a more financially rewarding job than they could hope for back home. For many, acquaintance with the Far East lasted just the one five-year term before they returned to the 'real life' of British towns and cities, marriage and family.

In contrast, over a period of more than eighty years, men came to the colony from one small Irish town, making their careers in the Police Force and their home in this borrowed city. Newmarket, Co. Cork numbered about 1,200 residents in the first decades of the twentieth century. At that time in Hongkong, at least twelve of her men were police officers and their family connections numbered nearly one hundred. Providing a somewhat unique community for these men, this situation also yields a rich seam of material for the modern researcher, or at least a great number of avenues to explore. Thus whilst these men and their families are the focus of this study, the aim is also to shed light on the life and work of the European constable in an era of which there are few traces in today's Hong Kong.

The Europeans

The role and life of the working class European in Hongkong, through the period of the colony's growth from a small, rather insignificant, outpost of the British Empire to international entrepôt and commercial centre, is one that has been largely overlooked by the standard histories. Always a tiny percentage of Hongkong's population, these westerners, 'Europeans' in the terminology of the time, stood primarily for those from the British Isles, but also included Americans and Canadians, Germans, Italians and others. Over the period covered by this study the population of the island of Hongkong grew from 121,000 to over a million in 1940, the growth fuelled, naturally, by the great numbers coming from the Chinese mainland to seek work and livelihood in the colony.[1] The Europeans generally accounted for about 3% of the total, with another 2% from other non-ethnic Chinese groups.[2]

Of these westerners perhaps one quarter occupied senior positions in commerce, trade or the Administration, wealthy enough to live on the higher roads or up on the Peak. In the absence of the great land-owning families of the motherland, these men with their families formed the self-appointed élite of the colony. Forming a 'middle class' were the accountants, solicitors, engineers, highly skilled mechanics and the like whose education and occupation gave them a certain independence, usually with sufficient funds to return home should they wish.

The working classes

The majority of the Europeans, however, were not so free to come and go, for it could take three or four years of assiduous saving to amass passage money. Some, such as the police, were bound to their employers for a set period, and, akin to the army, would have to purchase their discharge if they wanted to be released before the set date. Recruited by advertisement, or through their employers, a trickle at the outset turning into a steady stream by the beginning of the twentieth century, rank and file British men were brought out from 'home' to attend to the clerical routine of commerce, banking, trade, shipping and insurance businesses, and to run

---

1 In 1940 there were also estimated to be three quarters of a million refugees from the north. During the period of the Japanese occupation the population dropped by around 50%, but thereafter began the explosive growth that would characterise the rest of the century.

2 Held in the National Archives, at Kew, London, the census records appear in annual *Blue Books* series CO133.

the day to day administration of the Governor and his Councils. In large part these men would stay for between five and twenty-five years, for by forty-five a man was sapped of much of his vigour and strength. The enervating climate in the days before air conditioning and refrigeration, together with exposure to the diseases of the tropics before effective cures and vaccines, took its toll on all but the hardiest of constitutions. For most, return home was the goal, with a small pension and some savings, probably to find some less demanding work for later life.

While British men were in Hongkong they occupied a predominantly masculine world, with only a minority in the position to support a family, let alone successfully persuade a woman of their acquaintance in Britain to take on the challenge of being a colonial wife.[3] Unyielding racial and class prejudices combined to mean that only those of particularly strong character, or near the bottom of the social scale would consider taking a local Chinese wife, although no such scruples existed about forming less permanent connections. But this lack of family-based European society reflected the situation for most of the majority Chinese population too, for whom Hongkong was a workplace and not a home, wives and children staying in their villages of the southern region of the mainland.

Thus most of these British men were separated by six-week ship journey, and more in the early years, from their own people. Ties of friendship, occupation, mess, clubs, church, lodge and sporting teams had to stand in place of domestic life. For those who did return from leave with a new bride, the perennial shortage of married quarters led them to look for accommodation in the ethnically mixed parts of the town, but this rarely involved any integration into the local community. Women generally restricted their social contacts to others in their spouse's occupation group, e.g. the police wives mixing with those from other government departments only when a man had transferred there, and was therefore already known. There is little evidence to suggest that when service in the

3 In 1864, the start of the period studied here, the adult European population numbered 1100 men and 432 women, however, the latter figure includes an undisclosed number of wives of the men of the garrison since they lived in private quarters in the town. The garrison, numbering around 1250 was not included in the population figures.

colony finished, the friendships made between the families continued to a great degree.

Passing references to the lower-paid Europeans appear in the general histories of Hongkong (Cameron, Endacott, Sayer, Welsh *et al.*), but H. J. Lethbridge's article *Conditions of the European Working Class in Nineteenth Century Hong Kong* is one of the few specific treatments of the subject.[4] Lethbridge presents a bleak picture of the lives of the majority of Europeans in Hongkong in the second half of the nineteenth century: his thesis is that the working class lived continually on the periphery of society, both European and Chinese, in a 'no-man's land' between the communities. He attributes their continued presence in Hongkong largely to a familiarity with discipline and hierarchically imposed order for the many discharged soldiers amongst their number, and secondly to the poor level of wages attainable in Britain at the time.

Studies are beginning to appear on the Chinese working class. In English these are represented notably by David Faure's work on the *'common people'*.[5] Some interest has emerged in exploring the commonalities between those dependent on the weekly or monthly pay packet within the different ethnic groups, acknowledging that as much as the cultures kept themselves apart, often through entirely mutual disdain, there is a greater history, full of examples of the interdependence of the peoples.

The Irish

The Scots, from Taipans to clerks, might have dominated trade in Victorian Hongkong, but the senior ranks of the Administration were more broadly representative of the British Isles. Of pre-1941 governors, eight were Irish and two more had Irish parentage, and all, bar John Pope Hennessy, from the Anglo-Irish Protestant ascendancy. The Civil Service examinations were the route for many an educated, middle class Irishman, be he a member of the Established Church or Roman Catholic, to gain his advancement in society, even if that then meant a period of service in the colonies. The Catholic Church had been early

4 Lethbridge, *Hong Kong: Stability and Change.*

5 Faure *The Common People in Hong Kong History* in ed. Lee *Colonial Hong Kong and Modern China.*

present in the newly emerging colony along with the troops and sailors that secured it. But although they were ministering to large contingents of Irish soldiers, the mission was mainly staffed by Italian priests from the neighbouring Portuguese Macao, later joined by a growing number of locally ordained men, and French and Italian nuns with a particular care for the many abandoned baby girls (Chinese) and orphans of the colony. The first years of the period covered were also the tail end of post-famine emigration from Ireland, but this had little impact on the population here. The preferred destinations of the hundreds of thousands fleeing the dire conditions of the mid-century were, of course, the United States and later Australia, from which a return journey for retirement was not envisaged.

The Police

The police became the subject of this study following the discovery that not only had the author's grandfather and great uncle been members, but that they were related to a group of men whose service spanned almost a century, and whose numbers were out of all proportion to the size of the little place whence they all hailed. Initially, that discovery called for just an unearthing of their particular stories, but the remit gradually widened over time to encompass their work, environment, families and society, i.e., the European working class policeman's life. That said, if one approached the subject from the general outlook rather than the particular, it would be hard to find a better group of men on whom to focus. For the most part (from 1872 onwards) their arrival in Hongkong was officially arranged, they joined an organisation that was well documented and with a stable leadership, if they progressed in the Force their individual careers would be noted in annually produced records, and they are often mentioned by name in the newspapers of the time. Compared with, for example, those working for the banks or shipping firms, or even in other branches of the civil service, these are men with a visible presence in the community, which translates to some measure into a presence for the researcher.

But only to a certain measure. As noted, the police exist in government records, largely because copies were routinely sent to London, and went in the course of time into the National Archives. The occupation by Japanese forces from the last days of 1941 until 14th August 1945 was a profound rupture in Hongkong's history. Documents that had been assiduously kept were destroyed, either by the British to save them from falling into enemy hands, by the Japanese during the occupation or by white ants and mould in the years afterwards, when the need to reconstruct the ruined city overwhelmed all other considerations.

History in general has quite an uphill task in a place as focussed on achieving progress as contemporary Hong Kong. The present Hong Kong Police Force have had little contact with their history in comparison to many forces in the United Kingdom, although recently material on its earlier story has appeared on its website alongside a series of articles about its more recent past. The small Police Museum on Coombe Road, once the Wanchai Gap Station, is staffed by the Museums Department of the government, and holds a large number of artefacts, arranged to tell the story of earlier days and more recent issues on a thematic basis, but little in the way of documented history. However, the Special Administrative Region is increasingly integrating its time as a British colony into its wider history and identity, and the stories of organisations and people of that time are becoming less the preserve of the expatriate community, as much as an acknowledged part of the common heritage of Hong Kong residents.

An interesting parallel to the fate of Hongkong's police history can be found in that of the Irish Republic. For most of the period of this study, Ireland was, of course, administratively, politically and economically part of the United Kingdom. Only since independence and the establishment of the Irish Free State in 1923 has its police force, An Garda Síochána, answered to Irish masters, rather than those in London who controlled its predecessor, the Royal Irish Constabulary. Like Hongkong, documented history in Ireland comes up against problems: many of the centrally held records were destroyed in the attack on the Four Courts in 1922, whilst the identification of the RIC as an enemy force meant that local records were often also destroyed in the early 1920s. Ireland, too, has a Force Museum in Dublin Castle, staffed by serving police, and alongside many artefacts has a good library of material, albeit mostly relating to the post-1923 period.

It has already been mentioned that the European police often appear by name in the newspapers, and it is largely from this same source that a rich trove of stories emerges, building a picture of the work a constable or inspector might expect to do, the people with whom he would deal with and the problems he would encounter. This has been supplemented by verifiable accounts from children and grandchildren of the men, which have been most generously shared with the author throughout this project. One story, though, is of greater significance to this group than any other, and was the reason that this whole journey started. At the beginning of 1918, shortly before the disastrous Happy Valley Racecourse fire, Inspector Mortimer O'Sullivan, along with four other policemen, lost his life in a bloody and violent incident in a tenement in Wanchai. It was to uncover the facts about this dimly recalled event in family history that the initial enquiries were made. All the rest has grown from there, and whilst this book attempts to reflect all aspects of the colonial policeman's life, it will also serve to show that, then as now, and the world over, ensuring a secure and peaceful existence for the community requires a police force whose individual members face risks the rest of society would find unacceptable.

The Men from Newmarket, Co. Cork

The group of men – and women – who are the subject of this study had rather a different experience of colonial Hongkong to that outlined earlier, and stand in sharp contrast to Lethbridge's view of the working man as a mere pawn of the state. Of twenty men, all bar five were born in the small town of Newmarket or its surrounding townlands (hamlets) in north County Cork, Ireland, and the remaining were connected by marriage. The trail of men began with two individuals, who arrived independently of one another, almost a decade apart, and who caused, for the most part directly, fourteen more men to journey from Newmarket and join the Hongkong Police Force. Only one man, the second of the original pair, had previous police experience, in the London Metropolitan Police Force. Whilst two transferred to other government departments, and four served just one five year term, the majority of men made their career in the Force. Not all were to see Ireland again, four dying during their police careers.

Newmarket (Áth Trasna), like so much of Munster (the south western quadrant of Ireland) is known for dairy farming, and it was thus that the men were engaged before commencing their new lives. No working farmer's life is one of ease, but a combination of good soil, amenable climate, a benevolent landowner and good infrastructure helped most of the farms in the neighbourhood to prosper. The large families of the time did mean that there were sons to spare, but the manner in which these men were recruited (by successfully established fellow Newmarket men), and the fact that it was often elder sons who answered the call suggests that their choice was made not by dire financial necessity but by real prospects. This was no 'last resort', but a rare opportunity to rise in the world for men whose future would otherwise not be one of poverty, but would be rather predictable.

Brother following brother, or cousins arriving one after the other was not unknown by any means, and, albeit less frequently, son followed father into the Hongkong Police Force. However, so far as can be discovered, the size of the group of men connected with Newmarket does seem to be unique in the Force's history, and perhaps in Hongkong at the time too. At one point, around 1912-13, there were ten, possibly twelve Newmarket men serving in the Force, out of a total of about 170 European policemen. But it was precisely because this kinship group existed, reinforced and broadened by the descendants of the two pioneers, that these men <u>could</u> persevere in their careers. As noted, these men had no police experience, no experience of making a life away from home and family, and Hongkong was then, much more so than today, the ultimate break from the apron strings. Others had to find their sense of belonging in clubs, masonic lodges, billiards teams, shooting parties etc: the Newmarket men had a "little Ireland in the East" to affirm their identity. But alongside that creation of a discrete community, and acting as counterbalance, it can be seen that those men whose careers took them away from the colonial Police Force developed much stronger links with the local community, particularly the Portuguese in Hongkong.

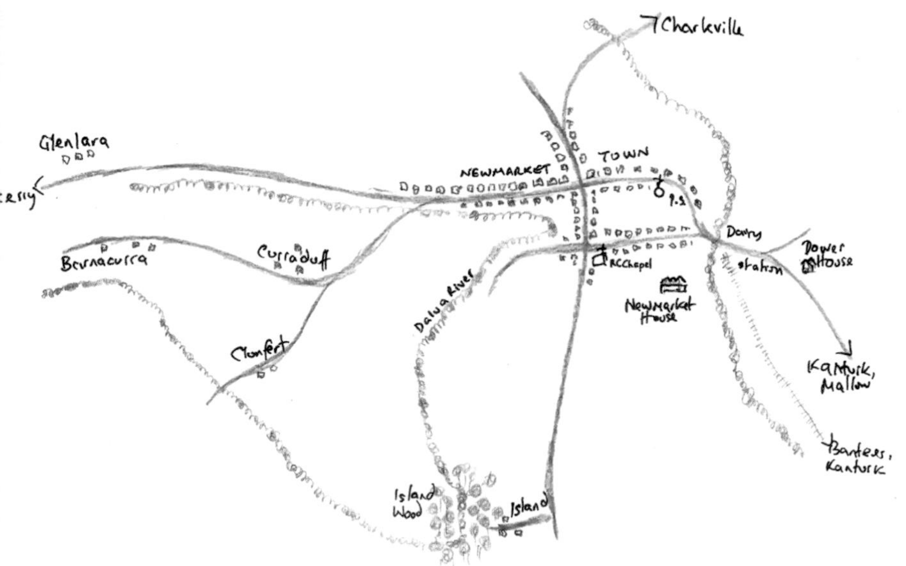

Newmarket area of north County Cork (Duhallow), above, within Ireland (below).

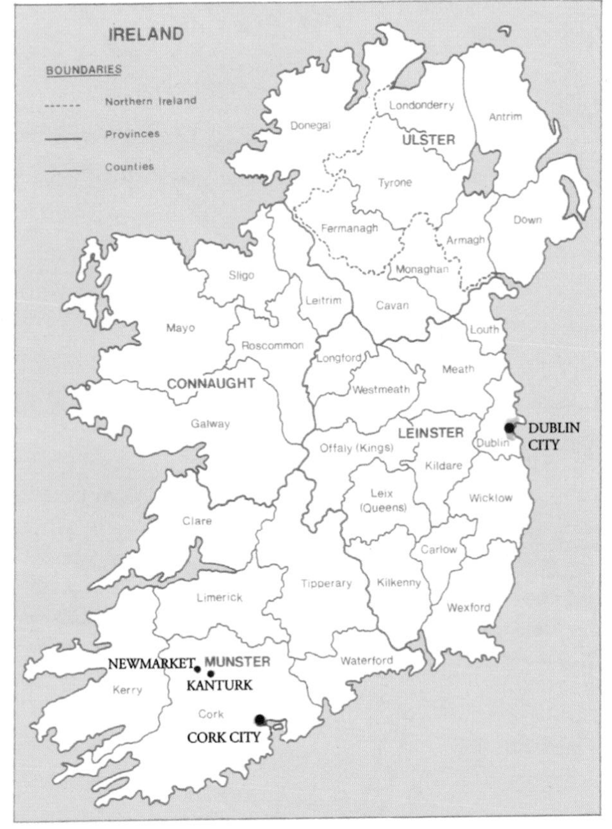

MOUNT GOUGH
LEWKNOR
MOUNT GOUGH
CRAIGRAY
BROCKHURST
THE RIDGE
ABERGELDIE
HAZELEY
FUNGSHUI
TJANDI
HILDEN
TANDERAGEE
ARDSHEAL
BELVEDERE
THE CLIFFS
FINDLAY ROAD
PLANTATION ROAD
CAPSUMUN
THE COTTAGE
TANYALLON
PEAK HOSPITAL
PEAK HOTEL
FORMOSA
THE FARM
GLENSHIEL
THE BUNGALOW
RICHMOND HOUSE
ALTADENA
CRAGSIDE
MARTINHOE
ROAD
VICTORIA HOSPITAL
QUARTERS
LYEEMUN
DUNEDIN
BARKER
THE CROW'S NEST
INVERDRUIE
PEAK TRAM WAY
PEAK ROAD
MAY ROAD
LADIES RECREATION GROUND
SERVICE TANK
ALBANY FILTER BEDS
TRAMWAY STATION
MAGAZINE GAP RD
MAGAZINE
GAP RD.
THE FIRS
BOWEN RD
OFFICERS' MESS
LAURISTON
QUEEN'S
STATION
PEAK
MACDONNELL ROAD
GLENCOE
KINGSCLERE
ALBANY
ROBINSON ROAD
BOWEN ROAD
MILITARY HOSPITAL
THE GROVE
BRAESIDE
UNION CHURCH
KENNEDY ROAD
STATION
VACCINE INSTITUTE
ST. JOHN'S CHURCH
BOTANICAL GARDENS
UPPER ALBERT RD
GLENEALY
MACDONNELL ROAD
KENNEDY RD.
MILITARY QUARTERS
SCHOOL
GOVERNMENT HOUSE
ST. PAUL'S COLLEGE
PEAK TRAMWAY STATION
DETENTION BKS.
LOWER ALBERT RD
VOLUNTEER HEAD QUARTERS
ICE HOUSE ST.
DUDDELL ST.
WYNDHAM ST.
KENNEDY
ROAD
CATHEDRAL
P.W.D.
MURRAY BATTERY
BATTERY PATH
PARADE GROUND
VICTORIA BARRACKS
HEAD QUARTER HOUSE
SCANDAL POINT
MURRAY BARRACKS
R. E. WORKSHOP
BANKS
CITY HALL
PRINCE'S BUILDING
HONGKONG HOTEL
QUEEN'S RD
DES VOEUX
MILITARY STORE
WELLINGTON BARRACKS
NAVAL YARD
CRICKET GROUND
SUPREME COURT
ROAD
QUEEN'S
YORK
KING'S
PEDDER ST.
GENERAL POST OFFICE
CHATER
CONNAUGHT
NAVAL YARD
H.K. CLUB
JACKSON ST
WARD
QUEEN'S STATUE WHARF
KOWLOON FERRY
BLAKE PIER
NAVAL DOCK
V.R.C. MURRAY PIER

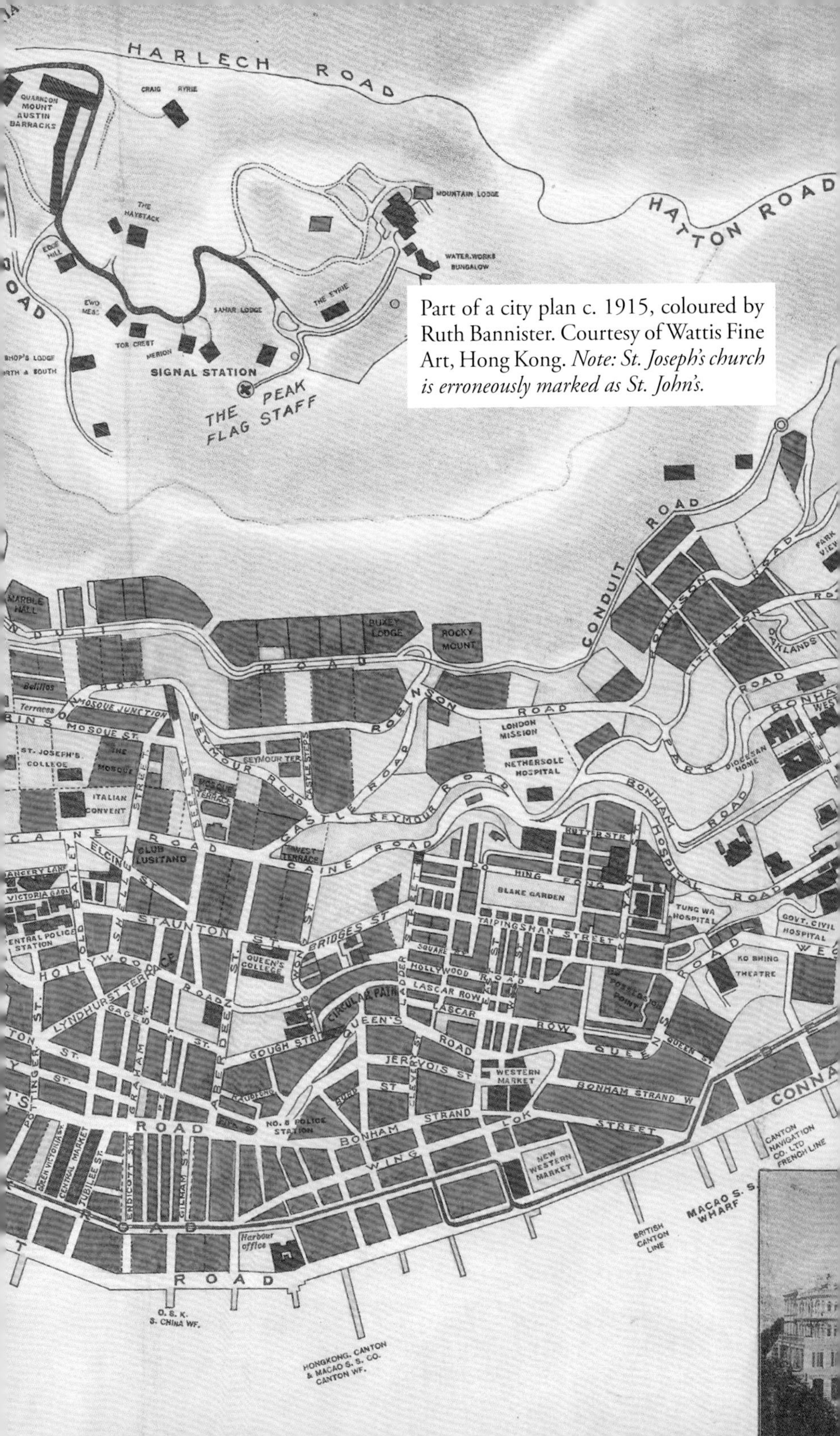

Part of a city plan c. 1915, coloured by Ruth Bannister. Courtesy of Wattis Fine Art, Hong Kong. *Note: St. Joseph's church is erroneously marked as St. John's.*

Clockwise from top left: Inspector Patrick O'Sullivan, Nora O'Sullivan (née Ahern), Amah, Ellen O'Sullivan (née Kenneally), daughters of Mortimor and Nora: Hannah (Joan) and Catherine (Kathleen) O'Sullivan. This studio portrait was taken in the summer of 1918, some months after the death of Inspector Mortimor O'Sullivan. It was not uncommon for women here to change from dark mourning clothes after just a few months, especially with the approach of warmer weather.

Wedding of William Davitt and Margaret Hennessy, 25th February 1908. Front row, l. to r.: Maria O'Sullivan, Nora Lysaught (with Margaret Lysaught in front), Margaret Hennessy, William Davitt, Thomas Francis O'Sullivan, May Nolan (with Marie Nolan in front). Behind, l. to r.: Edmund O'Sullivan, Nicholas George Nolan, John Joseph Lysaught, Mortimor O'Sullivan, Fr. Augustine Płacek, Tim Murphy, John O'Sullivan. (Courtesy Marjorie Davitt and O'Sullivan family)

The Praya East showing No. 2 Police Station and Wanchai Road (r.) c. 1910. (Postcard, courtesy of the Police Museum, Hong Kong)

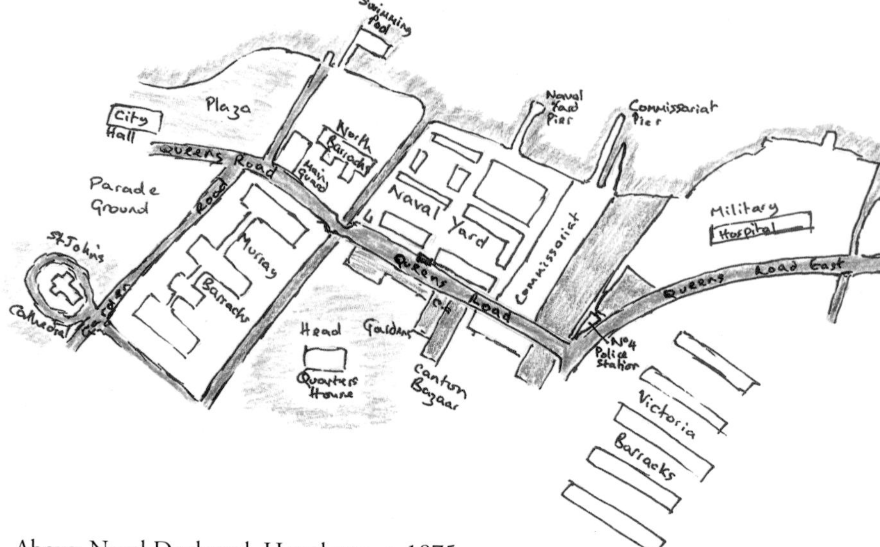

Above: Naval Dockyard, Hongkong, c. 1875.
Below: Central Police Station, Magistracy & Victoria Gaol, c. 1870.

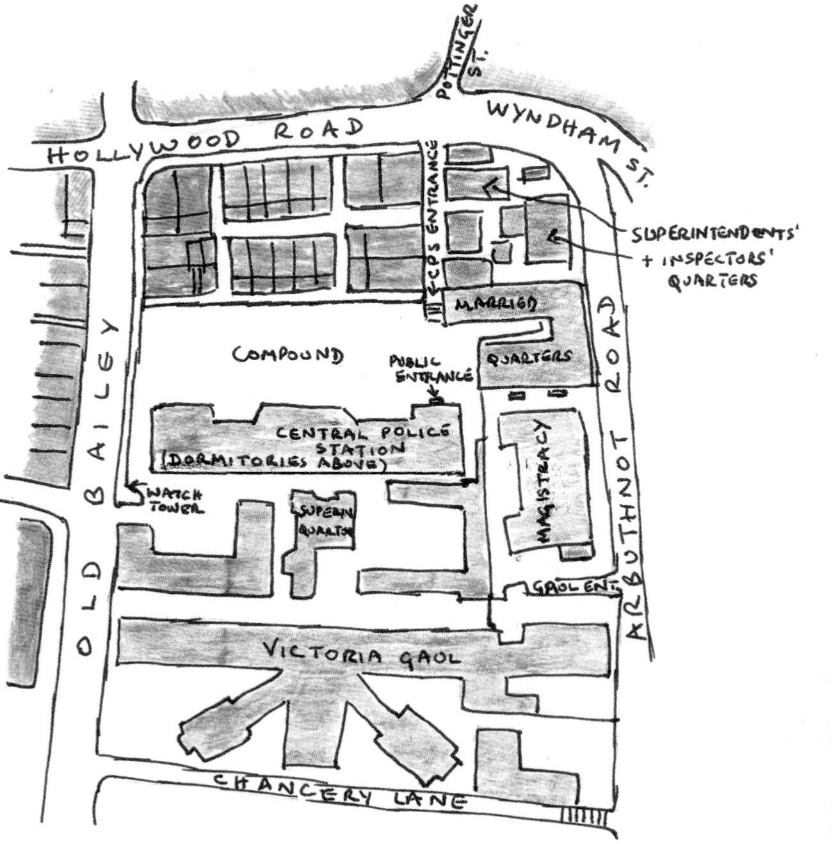

POTTINGER ST.
HOLLYWOOD ROAD
WYNDHAM ST.
CPS ENTRANCE
SUPERINTENDENTS' + INSPECTORS' QUARTERS
OLD BAILEY
MARRIED QUARTERS
COMPOUND
PUBLIC ENTRANCE
CENTRAL POLICE STATION (DORMITORIES ABOVE)
MAGISTRACY
ARBUTHNOT ROAD
WATCH TOWER
SUPERN QUARTS
GAOL ENT.
VICTORIA GAOL
CHANCERY LANE

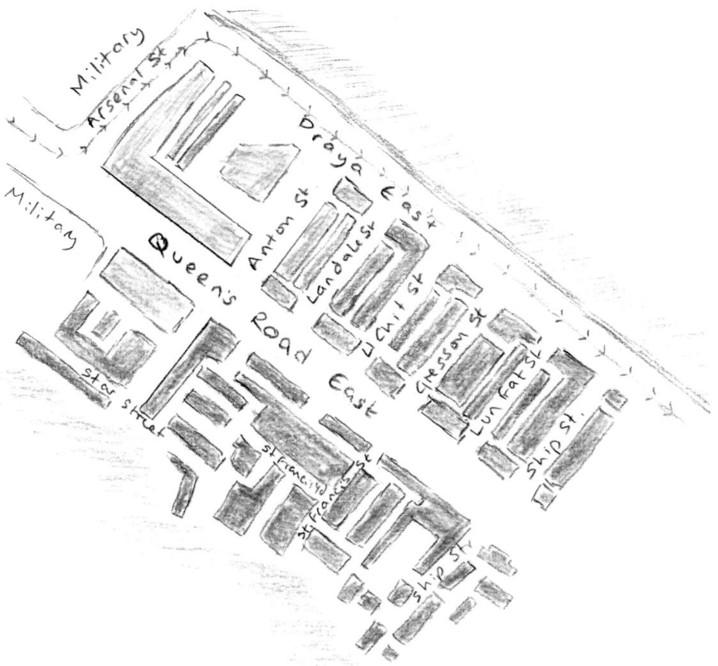

Above: Gresson Street area, Wanchai, c. 1918.
Below: Wanchai Road area, c. 1900.

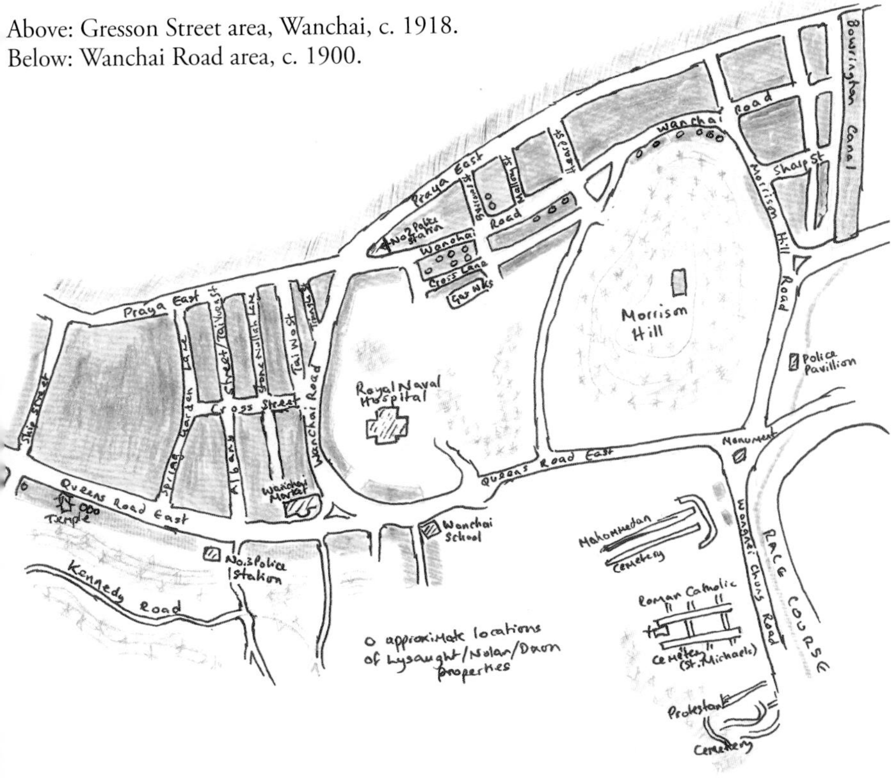

Bringing out the bodies from 6 Gresson Street, 22nd January 1918. The many uniformed and plain clothes police are joined by police reserves and other government officials, whilst the throng of onlookers is held back at the Queen's Road East entrance to Gresson Street. In this reproduction, the shop signs and verandahs can also be seen. (courtesy of O'Sullivan family)

The experience of life and work in Hongkong had profound effects on all the families who returned, and for most this was transformational. None of the men returned to farming, except in very part-time ways, almost none to their home town, even when the political situation in Ireland made that possible.[6] Children went to university, entered professions, rose to prominence in the government, church, army and medical professions amongst others. Yes, children from Irish farms were starting to have more opportunities at this time, but colonial service provided these families with an enviable head start.

Inevitably, and by its nature, this study sees Hongkong through almost exclusively European eyes. The paternalist, intolerant and frequently prejudiced attitudes of these European visitors to a Chinese island were little questioned then, but grate roughly upon contemporary understanding and sensibilities. However, as part of the history that is here recorded, there is little that can be done but to acknowledge that they belong only to a time now long past. This book does not attempt to justify or account for the British hegemony of the period: it is left to far better qualified writers to examine the impact of colonial rule here. Class, and its divisions, was given close attention by the insecure Hongkong European community, and it is used here as a convenient shorthand for the backgrounds and expectations of different sectors, without challenging the late nineteenth-, early twentieth- century concept. Finally, this study neither claims nor aims to be a definitive history of police in Hongkong, but to give small, almost domestic, snapshots to illustrate an otherwise neglected part of Hong Kong's heritage.

6 The author's grandfather kept cows for a time, which he grazed in Phoenix Park, Dublin.

Chapter One

An inauspicious beginning

"We are brought out here to be treated worse than prostitutes!"

Six weeks, the men were told, would see them at their destination, and so their relief at finally arriving over nine weeks after boarding in Liverpool was tempered by exhaustion, boredom and hunger. Their morale had been affected by the rumours that circulated through the group and, as their hardship increased through the voyage, this dampened the natural excitement at seeing for the first time their destination: this island that was both part of the British Empire and yet China. Nor was the island itself producing much of a display for these twenty young policemen. The mist had only just lifted, and Hongkong harbour was still cold and dank on the morning of 10th March, 1873, with the hills behind barely visible though the grey cloud.[7]

Some of the more senior among them tried to muster their colleagues into order and to set a cheerful tone, but they battled against the odds as the press of life, both human and animal, swirled around and, together with cargo and luggage, filled the deck, the narrow gangway and the wharf to overflowing. Having endured lengthy delays at each stop *en route*, the men were understandably disgruntled as the ships officers harried the passengers, for the captain perversely wanted to leave Hongkong for Shanghai within twenty-four hours.

The ships' reports carried by the Hongkong newspapers told how crossings that winter had been hard and hazardous: the Atlantic and the Bay of Biscay had, throughout the early weeks of January, seen a succession of the most violent storms. The men had sometimes feared for

7 Meteorological data in Report of Colonial Surgeon for 1873, published in the *Hongkong Government Gazette* 4th April 1874, and weather reports in newspapers of the week.

their lives. One Irish policeman, George Hennessy, had wryly claimed a small lifebelt emblazoned with the ship's name, *SS Ajax*, as a memento. The *Ajax's* sister ship, the *SS Antenor*, having left Liverpool ten days later on the same route, had been compelled to put into Lisbon for a few days to repair damage.[8] But the *Ajax* had not even managed to leave British waters before it hit trouble, crashing into one small craft, which in turn shunted another. These two smaller vessels, the *SS Kelloe* and the *SS Holmside* were both damaged, and the undamaged *Ajax* was obliged to pause its journey whilst reports were made. An extended stop of four days at the Suez Canal further delayed the vessel, and similar lack of haste at Penang and Singapore did not help.[9] Then, just as the men felt that the end of their ordeal was in sight, a monsoon struck the vessel after it left Singapore, meaning that this last leg took a full eleven days, over the six it might take on more favourable seas. The ship had, moreover, been short on supplies of food and water, making the long crossing of the Arabian Sea and Indian Ocean yet more arduous for those in the cramped and uncomfortable cabins.

The twenty men of the London Metropolitan Police Force who had answered, with varying degrees of willingness, the advertisement for duty in the Hongkong Police Force had been engaged by Charles Vandeleur Creagh, the Deputy Superintendent of Police, who was coming to the end of his eighteen-month leave of absence from the colony.[10] He had returned to Hongkong travelling by train to Venice, thus avoiding the notorious Bay of Biscay, and changing at Bombay to the *SS Australia,* a ship more than twice the size of the *SS Ajax,* for a more comfortable journey to Hongkong.[11] With hindsight, the Colonial Office might have regretted the necessary economies which sent the new recruits on the cheaper vessel, and especially without an experienced member of the Colonial force among them. For it was rumour, rather than substantiated

8 *Hongkong Daily Press* 11th March 1873.

9 Leaving Liverpool on 6th January, the ship then left Port Said on 23rd, and Suez on 27th. It reached Penang on 21st February, leaving two days later, and arrived at Singapore on 25th, departing for Hongkong on 28th February. *Hongkong Daily Press,* 11th March 1873.

10 *Metropolitan Police Orders* 6th December 1872.

11 *Hongkong Daily Press* 10th February 1873.

information, that circulated amongst the men during those cooped-up weeks.

The men were leaving the largest police force in the world, some 9,600 men strong, looking after an area of 620 square miles. The Metropolitan Police was divided into many divisions and sections, and then subdivided again around individual police stations. The twenty engaged for Hongkong came from a variety of stations and thus few of them knew each other before their voyage out, bringing with them hearsay and gossip from their former colleagues concerning their new posting. One such rumour was that there was a medical examination on a monthly basis, to which the men would have to submit. No ordinary check-up, the purpose of this inspection was to ascertain whether they had any venereal disease. Some men had heard that such examinations had once existed in the army, but nothing like it had been known in a civilian police force in the British Isles, so far as they had heard tell.[12] The problem, as far as the men saw it, was that Creagh had not had a copy of the regulations with him. There had been mention that permission to enlist extra men had come through in something of a rush and so the men had not been able to see the terms to which they were signing up. Some thought that he ought to have obtained a copy from the Colonial Office, but others were prepared to put their trust and hope in his assertion that the rules were just the same as those in the Metropolitan Police. Thus these twenty men had signed papers resigning their positions there and engaging themselves to travel, at the Government's expense, to Liverpool and thence to Hongkong, where they would be duly sworn in for duty as colonial policemen for the next five years.

Despite Creagh's assurance, anxiety about this disgusting examination festered, so that all were keen to know the truth. When, at long last on *terra firma*, and with their luggage safely around them, Barrack Sergeant William Gair met them, the men's mood was not sanguine. Gair asked after their voyage, and received a spirited description, understanding that

12 The Contagious Diseases Acts 1864 and 1866 made provision for examination of troops in garrison towns, which seems to have been sporadically enforced, but soon abandoned on the grounds that it affected the morale of the soldiers.

the men felt themselves "most shamefully treated and half starved"[13]. He advised them to take it up with Captain Superintendent Deane, and see what could be done, but the men had other concerns, too. P. C. George Briarly, one of the more forthright of the group, asked Gair about the truth of the examination rumour. On learning that indeed they would face this each month, Briarly turned to his colleagues in disgust and exclaimed: "We are brought out here to be treated worse than prostitutes!"[14]

The new Hongkong men

The twenty men were a disparate group, with little more than their police service in common. Most were sons of skilled or semi-skilled men, a storehouse man, a railway worker, a waiter etc., few with trades to pass on to their sons. There was a belief at the time that Metropolitan Police recruits generally came from farm-labouring families, but tracing these men through the census records of 1861 and 1871 suggests that this was not the case for most of this group. Many had a large number of younger siblings still with their parents in 1871 who would benefit from any little contribution that the man could send home from his wage. The Metropolitan Police was developing a recruitment system to support its expanding need, thus this group of men hailed from many parts of England and from Ireland. A few came from the home counties and Middlesex, but a number were from the west of England: Wiltshire, Dorset and at least two from Cornwall.

Some of the men had Irish parentage, and at least three had been born in Ireland: George Hennessy, Joseph Corcoran and George Briarly. The last came from the midlands of Ireland and was born in 1845 in Tullamore, Kings Co., (Co. Offaly) into a Royal Irish Constabulary family. As the eldest son he followed his father and brother in law into the force at nineteen, with his brothers joining in subsequent years. He would have known from his father how difficult it was to progress in this force. Indeed, the very low pay and military-like conditions of service proved too much for the young man, who resigned six years later and went to

13 W. M. Deane, Captain Superintendent to The Hon. C. Clementi Smith, Acting Colonial Secretary, 1st May 1873 CO129/163 p 258.

14 Ibid.

London.[15] He seems to have given himself a six-month holiday, and then joined the Metropolitan Police in June 1871. Although he had valuable experience already, he does not seem to have fared well in this force, being passed over for promotion, and acquiring a crop of disciplinary marks against him.[16] When the call for volunteers for the Hongkong Force came, he was serving in T division, which covered the Kensington area and included Hammersmith Police Station, where he had been on the census night in 1871.

Less is known of Corcoran's antecedents. He was born in 1850 in Co. Galway, in the west of Ireland, and had joined the London police three years before sailing out east. As P. C. 243 he served in No. 1 District, G Division, Finsbury, and came to notice when he signed the petition for increased pay in September 1872, representing his Division at the meeting in October that year.[17]

Of the same age as Briarly, but coming from a very different background, George Hennessy had left his family's small home in Glenlara, just outside the farming town of Newmarket, Co. Cork on 10th April 1866 to seek work in London. His father worked for his farmer landlord, and without any tenancy to inherit, and a bevy of sisters to help support, Hennessy perhaps felt obliged to find employment that would allow him to send money home. Passages for this journey were relatively cheap even at this time, and such a journey was often thought of as migration rather than emigration.[18] Neither Hennessy's Rough Book – his own title for his scrapbook of personal details, newspaper cuttings and 'model letters' – nor the Metropolitan Police records indicate how he spent the next two years.[19] However, as a tall young man, (his pension records, some 30 years

15 Herlihy, *The Royal Irish Constabulary* and records of the R.I.C. held at the National Archives, London, at HO 184/16.

16 *Metropolitan Police Orders* 12th December 1872.

17 MEPO 2/146.

18 Clear, *Social change and everyday life in Ireland, 1850-1922,* p.66 ff., discussing migration for both seasonal agricultural and construction work, generally to England and Scotland.

19 This scrapbook was kept from late 1880s and is in the possession of Hennessy's family, with some pages in the Police Museum in Hongkong. Many of the details, especially of his earlier life, are from this source. Entries by him continue until about 1896, thereafter with notes made by his wife and younger daughter.

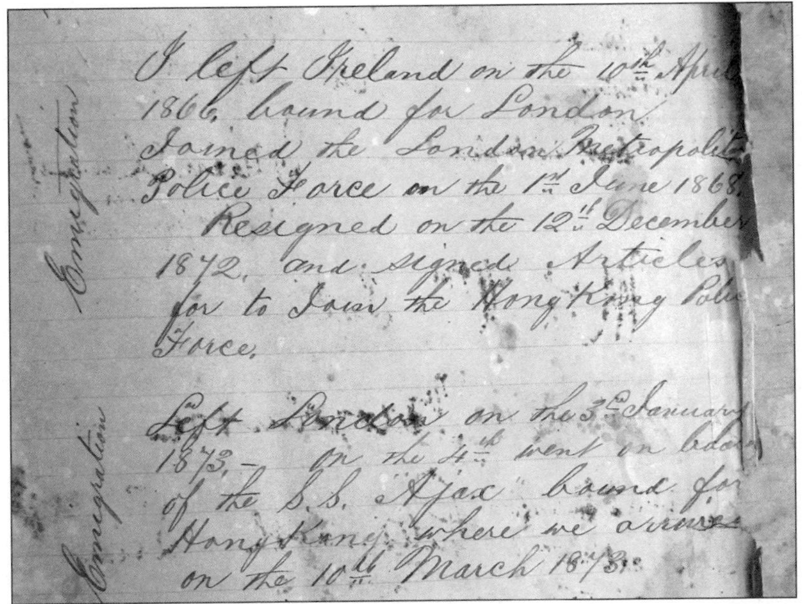

Emigration

I left Ireland on the 10th April
1866, bound for London.
Joined the London Metropolitan
Police Force on the 1st June 1868.
Resigned on the 12th December
1872, and signed Articles
for to Join the Hongkong Police
Force.

Emigration

Left London on the 3rd January
1873. — on the 4th went on board
of the S.S. Ajax bound for
Hongkong where we arrived
on the 10th March 1873.

Detail from Rough Book of George Hennessy (courtesy Hennessy family)

later, record his height as six foot and his build, then, as 'stout') used to the hard work of a small farm, he would not have had too much difficulty securing work in the rapidly expanding London of the 1860s.

On 15th June 1868 he was sworn in to the Metropolitan Police and given the Warrant number 50579. Initially based in Kilburn, north London, as was usual then, he received little formal training, learning his police-craft 'on the job' from his more experienced colleagues. Early in 1870 he was moved to "A" Division, serving the Whitehall (Central London) area. Here he moved steadily up the ranks to a 2nd Class Constable, also taking on Reserve duties, which would have attracted an additional allowance.[20] On the census night in 1871 he was stationed at Wellington Arch Police Station on Constitution Hill, along with an inspector, a sergeant and thirteen other constables, in what was reputed to be the second-smallest police station in the world.

The Police Order (notice) that came round about Hongkong on 6th December 1872 asked for men with three years' service and under

20 I am indebted to Christine Thomas for details of Hennessy's Metropolitan Police career.

thirty-two years of age. A term of engagement for five years was required. The men had to take a lot on trust, with little idea of where Hongkong was, let alone the conditions there. But the pay compared favourably with London, for the men were to receive $40 per month, equivalent to £100 p.a., and a pension of one quarter salary after just ten years' service, which would have been an attraction even to a young man. In the autumn of 1872 London police pay had just been increased in the wake of disturbances and unrest in the Force, and most constables earned between £1 7*s* and £1 16*s* a week, £70 to £93 p.a.

The men, under the command of a Metropolitan Police sergeant, were mustered at Euston Station, and put on the train for Liverpool. In Hennessy's words:

> *Left London on the 3rd January 1873 – on the 4th went on board of the S.S. Ajax bound for Hongkong, where we arrived on the 10th March 1873.*[21]

Victoria, Hongkong 1873

However ambivalent these men were about their arrival, the colony had no mutual misgivings. Aside from the people around the Praya (waterfront) waiting to meet the regular passengers, (a handful of Europeans along with a large number of Chinese, the latter who had joined the boat a few days earlier at Singapore), a crowd had gathered to see and greet the new 'London Men'. The only precedent for such a large group of policemen arriving was that of the forty Scottish men who had been brought out the previous year, and who had already caused a deal of trouble to the miscreants who saw the colony as a place of easy money. The press noted these arrivals and the reports give the impression that there was a readiness to believe that the state of law and order in the colony would at last resemble their image of that in the motherland.[22]

Pedder Wharf, named after the colony's first Harbour Master, was, in 1873, the main landing stage for the town, but was really quite inadequate for the scale of the traffic the harbour attracted. So, disembarkation was probably initially to a lighter or small vessel in the harbour, which then

21 Hennessy's Rough Book.
22 *Hongkong Daily Press,* 11th March 1873.

transferred them to the wharf. Thus after this hurried, chaotic procedure the new arrivals found themselves jostled by passengers from the cross-harbour ferries, along with the cargo and boatmen of a multitude of small boats and junks. However, they had landed in the very heart of Victoria, as the town of Hongkong Island was then known, with Queen's Road, the main thoroughfare, lying only one street back. The men would have had little time to remark on the crowds and their welcome, or register more detailed first impressions as they marched, and then climbed, up Pedder Street, past the landmark Clock, along Queen's Road, noting the Post Office and Court Building on the north (harbour) side, and then up stone slabs of Pottinger Street to the Central Police Station on the Hollywood Road, their baggage carried by a team of Chinese coolies.

Entering the compound of the Central Police Station for the first time, the men encountered a parade ground enclosed on all four sides. In front of them to the south was the imposing three-storey building that housed both the headquarters and the barrack accommodation, while behind them was the blank wall separating the compound from the terraced houses which fronted onto Hollywood Road. To the west stood, as it does

Central Police Station (1862), photographed 2011

now, the high wall onto Old Bailey Street, but with stables below, whilst opposite were the buildings of the Magistracy and the accommodation for senior officers. The main building stretched almost the full width of the compound, some 230 feet, and was built of red brick with cement rendering. Long colonnaded balconies and a Chinese tile roof added to the Colonial style. The central section was flanked by two slightly recessed wings, each with a projecting section at the end. On the ground floor this area was devoted to the offices of the Chief Superintendent, the Coroner and the clerks, with a staircase to either side of these. The recessed wings provided dormitory accommodation for constables, the west end projection housing sergeants, with slightly larger individual rooms available for married men. The upper floors were entirely given over to accommodation; dormitories stretched the entire length of the top floor, with day rooms occupying the middle section of the second. On each end of these floors were more rooms for married and single sergeants. The plans of 1862 show sleeping space for 222 constables, five single and five married sergeants, with an additional room for a married man in the watch tower beside the west end of the building.[23] Behind the ground floor, and built separate from the Headquarters were the police cells, almost subterranean because of the gradient of the site, and behind this the high wall of Victoria Gaol.

A problem to be remedied

From the outset, some thirty and more years earlier, the Europeans who presented themselves for the Force were, on the whole, a motley lot, ill adjusted for the hard regular land life. Often they were sailors who had been discharged or absconded or loafers who had found themselves in the colony, living hand to mouth. The Chinese were only engaged for the Water Police, where they would spend more time and energy rowing the Police Launch than policing the waters. Even here, recruitment of good Chinese candidates had been unavailing, as much because of the local contempt for both British policing and British justice, as through the dismissive views of the poor value of employing Chinese constables held by Charles May, the long time Superintendent of Police (1845-1862)

23 Originally in CO129/86 now held as MPGG 1/118/1-5.

and thereafter influential magistrate. The force's numbers had been made up by drafting men *en masse* from various Indian regiments, often with little regard as to the suitability of the particular regiments, and only adding to the incomprehension, Babel-like, between police and policed. In 1862 an Ordinance had been passed which tried, amongst many other issues, to address the low retention rates and the reliance of constables on their non-official earnings from bribery and 'squeeze', by raising the pay of a European constable from £60 to £70 p.a., and introducing a pension scheme after ten years' service.[24] The Indian and Chinese rates of pay were also raised, although remaining approximately one half (Indian) and one third (Chinese) that of the Europeans, with the constables of the two contingents now receiving £32 10*s* and £20 respectively.[25] The accommodation provided did improve considerably when the Central Police Station was built in the same year, but $27 per month was still scarcely enough for a man to live on.[26] Eight years later vacancies in the European contingent were still running at 50% p.a., mainly through death or dismissal, alcohol usually being the root cause in the latter case and not infrequently in the former.[27]

The poor state and inefficiency of the police force in Hongkong had been a continual headache for successive Governors and a source of anxiety and dissatisfaction for the colony's rate payers. True, some able soldiers purchased their discharge from the Army whilst on the China Station and joined the Police Force, and occasionally adventurous travellers would enlist, but it was primarily the very poor pay that would make them swap their posts for more lucrative one in other Departments in the colony or the nearby treaty ports as soon as possible. An *Enquiry*, prompted by the largest public meeting Hongkong had seen, held in September 1871, had called for a substantial pay increase for the European contingent, a more modest rise for the Chinese, together with continued recruitment to this contingent, and efforts to be made requiring non-Cantonese speakers to

---

24 Ordinance No. 9 of 1862, together with Police Regulations, *Hongkong Government Gazette*, 6th September 1862.

25 Up from averages of £25 and £18 5*s p.a.*.

26 Taking $1= 4 shillings 4 pence.

27 Report of Captain Superintendent of Police, 1870, *Hongkong Government Gazette* 24th June 1871.

learn the language spoken by 95% of the population. Governor Kennedy requested experienced police officers from home, and a group of forty-five men were recruited from Scottish forces. When this was then repeated the following year, with the Metropolitan Police agreeing to allow the recruitment of twenty men from within its ranks, the contingent had seventy-seven constables paid at the new £100 p.a. rate (including all the new men) and fourteen of the lower paid men from 1871. The change in the constitution of the European section of the force was thus considerable, as can be seen by the following chart:

Strength of the Hongkong Police Force 1862 & 1873[28]

	Inspectors	Sgts & Acting Sgts	Constables
1862			
European	10	6	47
Indian	-	18	310
Chinese	-	18	85
Total strength	494[29]		
1873			
European	11	8	91
Indian	-	11	161
Chinese	-	17	181
Water Police (Chinese)		9	136
Total strength	625[30]		

28 *Blue Books CO*133/19 1862 and *CO*133/30 1873. '*Blue Books*' was the colloquial term for annual government returns of the Administration, sent back to London, detailing, amongst other data, all the personnel employed with dates of engagement and salaries paid etc. Sets of the originals can be found in a number of libraries and institutions, most accessibly at the National Archives in London, where they are categorised in the Colonial Office series - CO133.

29 Including twelve Chinese Sergeant Interpreters.

30 Including one Indian Jemadar and one Interpreter, and fifteen Chinese Interpreters.

A new job and a new home

Initially, it seems, all the new men were quartered at the barracks of the Central Station, which conveniently, if rather claustrophobically, shared a site with the Magistracy (Police Courts) and Victoria Gaol. The buildings were on a grander scale than Police Stations and barrack-like 'police houses' of the Metropolitan Police, which usually accommodated fifty to one hundred men. The London men went into their new place of employment by the workday entrance at the east end, in through the reception area and charge room, then along the corridor leading to the central section and the Superintendent's office. Maybe they were shown then to their quarters, and allocated their bed space. Lunch would have been of refreshingly familiar fare for the importation of European-style foodstuffs, and local manufacture modified to accord with British tastes, was well established by this time, and the different sections of the force kept largely to their national cuisines. After this, much of the first afternoon was taken up with the practicalities of their new home.

What little time remained before nightfall at 6.30 p.m. gave the men an opportunity to explore the town. Out of the Station, in the coming days the men would be perhaps thankful for the heavy winter uniform of blue serge tunic with buff-coloured facings, and trousers of the same material, a cape for wet weather, thick leather belt, heavy boots and a cap for the head, since they might not have been expecting a fairly cool 60° to 65° F (15-18° C) with a wind that could be quite blustery after the heat they had experienced in the latter part of their voyage. The skies remained overcast, but with no rain to speak of and no suspicion of sun, one of their first impressions outside the compound may have been of the towering Peak and the surrounding hills massed over them. The Central Station was one of the tallest buildings at the time, so the verandahs and windows of the upper storey gave them a panorama both of the town and the harbour, which, as the colony's *raison d'être*, was continually busy. And maybe they commented on the bareness of the rocky island they had come to, for in 1873 the forestation of the Peak and the hills of Hongkong island was still decades away, and trees were not plentiful.[31]

31 A. B. Freeman-Miford, *The Attaché at Peking,* quoted in White, *Hongkong: Somewhere between Heaven and Earth,* p. 67.

Passing down the little lane that connected the compound with the town, the men came out first to the Hollywood Road and then descended to Queen's Road, with colleagues of longer standing pointing out the amenities they might immediately need: a barber, good at cutting European hair; a tobacco shop selling imported brands; and laundries that could be trusted to produce clean, well pressed results. There was also the matter of purchasing a camphor-wood uniform box. Usually there would be plenty already in the Central Station that could be recycled from previous owners, but with so many recent recruits, it was necessary for the London men to go to the makers, whose shops, mostly on the Praya, saw a healthy trade, since it was one of the few methods of storage that could prevent the worst effects of the humidity. It was said that a uniform tunic, hung up overnight, could have a complete coating of white mould spores by the next morning in the most humid months. No doubt inns and taverns, whose clientele would make work for them would also be noted, but they would not be of personal interest to the men, such places being out of bounds to the force, and the beer and spirits on sale in the day rooms of the Headquarters being usually of a more reliable quality. As the days went past the men began to understand the town's layout. Around the headquarters stood a mix of commercial and financial establishments, European and Chinese shops, taverns and brothels. To the west were the densely inhabited Chinese quarters, of which Taipingshan was the most notorious, with houses built into the side of the hill and thus below street level at the rear. Two or three storeys tall, a scant twenty foot wide but sixty foot in depth, each floor was subdivided into cubicles, and, if possible, also divided vertically with a cockloft. Thus each storey frequently accommodated fifty people, who would all have to use the six foot square cookhouse, without stove or chimney. Needless to say, there was neither mains water nor sanitation to these properties, and, due to their design, little fresh air. The streets running north and south off the western end of Queen's Road and the shanty areas by the shoreline were little better, for the residents here had to make maximum use of the lower slopes and the small amount of level ground.

The few imposing granite houses on the Peak, spaciously laid out along winding, climbing roads and tracks, stood in sharp contrast to the situation below. The military cantonment to the east of the Police Headquarters, extending to the harbour in one direction and close to Kennedy Road and Government House up the hill in the other, effectively split the town in two, with the mixed population of Wanchai really only accessible through the bottle-necked artery of Queen's Road.

In some of the correspondence between Hongkong and the Colonial Office in London there are hints that perhaps some of the men had taken a degree of persuasion by their superiors to agree to come out to Hongkong. As already noted, in the months before their recruitment there had been unrest amongst the constables of the Metropolitan Police, with a large petition and a meeting of approximately one third of the Force held on 17th October 1872 calling for better pay and conditions.[32] In the aftermath of this, one of the organisers was punished by dismissal, which prompted a strike of about 180 men. They were summarily dismissed, although in time most were reinstated. The meeting itself was such a major show of discontent that the nervous Home Office swiftly made arrangements to increase the pay and shorten the duty hours.[33]

When the advertisement appeared in the London Police Stations for recruits for Hongkong on 6th December 1872, it stated that the Defaulters Book record had to accompany any application to join, but since there was no list of who had actually attended the October meeting, this could not have been held against them. That Joseph Corcoran was a signatory to the petition does appear on his record, and it is tempting to speculate that some men, perceived by their immediate superiors to be a little more prone to agitation than others, were 'encouraged' to apply. Despite the stipulation in the advertisement that only men with a good character, presumably, eligible for the force's 'Good' (2) grade or above would be accepted, this requirement seems to have been overlooked. Perhaps there were insufficient volunteering, since the twenty men selected included

32 Documents relating to the strike and protests are found in MEPO 2/146.

33 Emsley *The English Police* p. 97.

two with lower conduct grades: Sullivan, 3, and Briarly, 4, the latter being the lowest grade before dismissal became likely at grade 5.[34]

Their new rank of first class constables was a big promotion for all the men, with the increased salary it attracted, but they might not have realised that, with this fixed in dollars, if sterling gained in strength, their pay would suffer. When the colony had been established, the traditional 'international' currencies, the Mexican and Spanish 8 reale (dollar) were generally used, alongside Indian rupees and Chinese 'cash'. Efforts were made to impose sterling, and then a locally produced dollar, but without success, and the silver dollar prevailed. Bank notes were issued, but these took time to establish themselves as legal tender, and it was the early 1860s before they were widely accepted. In the meantime, the colony's currency was particularly susceptible, since although linked to the silver standard with its income predominantly in this form, its expenditure was mainly in sterling, tied to the gold standard. However, the situation regarding the pension a man might claim after ten years was more reliable, as the rate here had been fixed the previous year at 4s/2d to the dollar, and compared favourably to that of the home forces, where pensions were haphazardly and somewhat reluctantly bestowed, and usually only after very long periods of service. But the men might not have heard, nor paid too much attention to cynical voices warning them that the Colonial Office could afford to offer such a pension since many gave up or died before reaching even ten years out East.[35]

Creagh, and later Inspector Grey, pointed out to the men who came to enrol just how much better their promotion opportunities would be, since the size of the Hongkong Police Force, and more particularly its European contingent, was so very much smaller than that of the

---

34 Little is known about Constable Maurice Sullivan. Not from Newmarket, Co. Cork, he appears in the Metropolitan Police records as present on police manoeuvres in Blandford, Dorset in 1872. Named later as a potentially insubordinate man, he was however swiftly promoted to Sergeant and served as Assistant Foreman in the Fire Brigade in 1875. However, he resigned "On private affairs" in January 1876.

35 For the years 1870-1872 with approximate average contingent sizes of Europeans - 100; Indian - 300; Chinese 200 the number of deaths for the three years was 9 Europeans, 6 Indians and 6 Chinese.

Metropolitan Police. In London, with its three classes of constable above the recruit, it could often take a man twenty years or more to arrive at sergeant. By contrast, the Police Force in Hongkong, now being able to recruit better men than hitherto, was phasing out the different grades of constable. Thus if a man was resolved to stay in the service there, he might find himself a sergeant within a very few years.

It is possible that some of the men who would eventually board the *Ajax* had seen the lively correspondence in the Scottish newspapers resulting from various letters sent by members of the 1872 intake from the Edinburgh, Glasgow and other forces north of the border. One anonymous policeman had started it off by writing to the *Edinburgh Daily Review* telling of their dreadful passage over, the callousness of their accompanying senior officer (Inspector Grey), and the general conditions of near-anarchy in Hongkong which they were expected to police.[36] One can imagine that it was through alarmed relatives back in the men's hometowns that the other Scottish police in Hongkong heard of his assertions, which some then vigorously refuted, until it reached the Inspector himself. Grey weighed into the argument, which continued in the Scottish papers, and his side was supported by testimony quoted from letters received by relatives. These presented a different picture: of a passage out that, although not one of comfort, was not distressing, and, at six weeks in one case, was also swift.[37] The life of the Hongkong policeman was portrayed as very much 'softer' than that of a man patrolling the streets of Glasgow. Here he only needed to carry a baton, and if a man was apprehended too drunk to walk, coolies could be engaged to carry him in a chair to the Station.

> *There is little danger of one getting his head broken in a row here, for disturbances are few and far between.*[38]

---

36 Quoted in *Hongkong Daily Press* 16th January 1873.

37 The forty-five men strong Scottish contingent came out in two batches, the first 20 leaving Liverpool on 2nd December 1871 on the *Sarpendon* and arriving at Hongkong early in February; the second consignment on the *Glacus*, leaving Liverpool on 23rd December and accompanied by Inspector Grey, arriving on 11th February 1872.

38 From a letter, quoted in *Hongkong Daily Press* 16th January 1873.

Despite some fluctuation in the value of the men's pay during the 1870s, there was the chance of saving money, whether for later years or, more usually, to send home to support family. Having been used to weekly pay, and thus making most of his purchases by cash, now it was necessary for a man to budget for the monthly pay packet, and keep a tally on the shops and services that had allowed him credit. In London they had received a bounty of fifteen pounds on joining, "to acquire an outfit", presumably for the voyage and the warmer climes of Hongkong.[39] For those who had not spent too much of it, this and any savings from their London salaries would have required a safe home in this new and unfamiliar environment. Many would be prompted to open bank accounts, something most unusual amongst their class of men back in London. Doubtless they consulted with their more experienced colleagues as to which banks might provide reasonable security, for they may well have heard how easy it was for banks to collapse in the colonies, and none of those here would have been familiar names to them. However, each provided links with London banks, for example the Hongkong and Shanghai Banking Corporation was allied to the London and Counties Bank, and their relative longevity and substantial holdings would have given reassurance. Constable George Hennessy, from Newmarket, Co. Cork, did just that, recalling later that on 11th March he opened an account at the Hongkong and Shanghai Bank and deposited one hundred dollars.[40] Later the men would take a trip to the General Post Office, where one particular section, the Money Order Office, saw busy trade as men arranged to send some of their earnings home to parents back in the British Isles.

Back in the Headquarters on that first evening, the men would have been welcomed with a lively and convivial party, as had happened the previous year for the Scotsmen, and would continue as tradition into the 1880s and beyond, when further groups from Scotland, as well as from Bristol, Plymouth and Liverpool arrived. For the Londoners this was their first real opportunity to interrogate the more experienced men

39 Crown Agents to Governor MacDonnell, 7th October 1871. CO 129/154 p 37.

40 Papers in connection with Wa Lane gambling scandal, 4th September 1897, CO 129/277 p. 176 ff.

on the unfamiliar aspects of life and work in their new home, although in the days before easy travel, it is tempting to imagine that some of the unfamiliar Scottish accents made for an unanticipated communication problem for the new arrivals. Notwithstanding, it was here that Briarly and others most alarmed by the ship-board rumours sought out more about the unwelcome examination. They heard how recent ones had been very rough indeed; that men were marshalled through with no attempt at privacy; and that sometimes the Surgeon even had convicts, and not even British ones at that, but Indian and Chinese to help him. The new men could not tell, of course, which reports were the unalloyed truth, which had a gilding of exaggeration and which relied too heavily on stories from earlier times. The mixture of good-natured ragging with genuine help unfortunately served to harden the attitude of some of the men against their superiors, with dismal consequences.

The first couple of days must have been both busy and bewildering. They had been equipped with their uniform, which was not necessarily new, and had to be made to fit as best it could. The Stores Sergeant had also distributed bedding, linen, cooking and eating utensils, for which the men had paid a deposit. Evidently, some articles of bedding were in short supply, since the money for the purchase of such items came from the Police Fine Fund, which was proving inadequate for current requirements. By the end of the year the Government had allowed such purchases to be made from the Police budget.[41] From a tour of the building they found that the kitchens and washrooms were not within the barracks itself, but, in contrast to the substantial main building, were shacks and lean-tos, making use of space on the east side of the building (kitchens) and beside the Old Bailey Street wall (washrooms). The original plans had included an elegant three-sided colonnaded building behind the main building, linked by a walkway, which was to include stables and coolie accommodation as well as the kitchens and bathrooms, but the Gaol had taken over the space, and this was never built.[42] In consequence, and for years to come, all these offices had to be accommodated in make-shift

41 Report of the Captain Superintendent of Police, 1873, *Hongkong Government Gazette*, 21st February 1874.

42 Plans formerly CO129/86 now held MPGG 1/118/1-5.

fashion, to the detriment of all. Just four water closets, simply labelled "Private" on the 1862 plans, served each floor, and were also shared by the families occupying the married sergeants' rooms.[43]

Also unfamiliar, but of course, not unexpected, would have been the large number of Indian and Chinese constables. The Central Station housed mainly Indian and European constables since the majority of the Chinese constables were married, and so lived in the town with their families or in one of the houses in the surrounding area rented by the Police, with only the youngest recruits occupying one dormitory in the Station.[44] But in the cramped barracks, whilst the different contingents had separate dormitories, these were frequently reached by going through that of another, and this close proximity mirrored the conditions for many of the working classes in the colony's wider community. At this time even London policemen would have had little contact with people of nationalities from outside Europe. (Despite the power of the British Empire in India and Asia in general, during the third quarter of the nineteenth century, only in the dock areas of Poplar and Limehouse might they have met with people from Asia: mainly Lascar, Japanese and Chinese sailors.) Fraternising between the races was not encouraged, so collar numbers, rather than names, were the usual method of identifying and addressing constables of every race, and these were recycled as men left, died or were promoted to inspectors.[45]

The abundance of cheap Chinese labour meant that even the parsimonious Colonial Office provided a large team of coolies for the

---

43 In his Report for 1870 (*Hongkong Government Gazette*, 26th April 1871), Deane stated that the Central Police Station still lacked a proper cookhouse and latrines, etc., whilst Edward Willcocks, the Police School Master-in-Chief, reported that whilst the rooms provided for their use were light and airy, the stench from the nearby out-offices could be sickening.

44 For example, No. 23, Wyndham Street was owned by A. Jorge but rented for Police accommodation. Rate Book for 1872, HKRS 38-2-12.

45 In the Metropolitan Police men had two identifying numbers: a collar number up to three digits long, which would be similarly recycled, and an unique engagement number, by this time into five figures. The smaller force of Hongkong needed just the collar number. The system continues today, with shoulder numbers providing a convenient way of identification, particularly for constables and sergeants with the more common Cantonese surnames.

barracks, and so the men's experience would again parallel that of other working class Europeans in the colony who were now attended by any number of servants. Few of the families from which these men came had any servant living in, though some may have had a daily girl to help with the heavier domestic chores. In their police house accommodation, the wife of the Inspector in charge sometimes had oversight of domestic matters, but the servant girl occasionally found listed in the census records would almost certainly have worked for the Inspector's family, and had little to do with the men barracked there. The constables, and particularly the most junior, were expected to do all necessary work under the supervision of a barrack sergeant, who also took charge of the messing arrangements. In Hongkong the Barrack Sergeant's role was a semi-official one, and it appears that the responsibility for the canteen was given to another sergeant, with similar posts held in the Indian contingent. The system of messing may well have been familiar, but here each contingent (nationality) of the force used a different kitchen and meals were brought through the side entrance and up the into the day room or dormitories.

In their free time on succeeding days they would have wandered down to the harbour, where a myriad of small boats, sampans, junks, ferries and barges were continually busy. Each day an average of five or six larger vessels arrived, still both steamers and sailing ships at this time, hailing from all round the China coast, the Straits Settlements and further afield. San Francisco, South America, Australia, India as well as Europe all had lines that connected regularly to the important trading hub of Hongkong. The large parade ground, with the cricket pitch alongside, all belonged to the military cantonment and occupied the central part of the foreshore. The sporting scene, as ever in a British colony, was lively, with teams being recruited from firms and businesses, as well as the stationed regiments and the police in a wide variety of games and sports. Football matches between the police and army were taken particularly seriously, and keen sportsmen in the latest intake would have found an enthusiastic welcome from their colleagues. The parade ground in the Police Compound served as an admirable practice pitch on a regular basis. Level ground being at a premium, football and rugby matches were frequently held at Happy Valley, far out to the east of the city. An area that had been a notoriously unhealthy malarial swamp in the colony's early years, the paddy fields had long been filled in, and now it was exclusively used for recreation, especially horse racing, the drilling of large contingents of troops - and for the burial of the dead in the cemeteries of each religion.

Overlooking the town and the barracks was the spacious Government House, the residence of the Governor and his family for all but the hottest months, when they retired to the Peak. Between this and the military parade ground below stood St John's Cathedral, white plastered stone on a granite base. The entire European contingent were required to be present at Sunday worship, according to their individual traditions, and so long as their police duties permitted, with their attendance checked by one of the Inspectors. The Military Chaplain held early morning services for the troops at St John's, to which the Anglican (Church of England) of the Police would go, whilst Presbyterians attended the Union Church on Staunton Street. The numerically largest Christian denomination in Hongkong at the time, however, was the Roman Catholic Church, partly because of the presence of so many people of Portuguese extraction, with the proximity of Macao, but also because the soldiers stationed in Hongkong were predominantly Irish. Further up the lower slopes of the Peak stood St. Joseph's Catholic Church, on a garden site, where the parish priest was chaplain to the soldiers and the church was also thought of as the 'Police Church', in preference to the (much closer) Catholic Cathedral on Wellington Road.

Entertainment outside the Police Headquarters was harder to find. As in London, disreputable (and thus barred) theatrical and musical shows predominated over more respectable offerings, and the latter frequently sold out early. The well-meaning efforts of religiously inclined ladies to provide bible reading and mission evenings fell on rather stony ground. This lack of alternative leisure time occupation was one factors that made alcoholism so prevalent as to be almost the norm in the earlier days of the colony, and common in subsequent decades.

Down to work – the policeman's job

Naturally, as experienced policemen, the new recruits were anxious to find out how the duties expected of them would compare to those of the Metropolitan Police, the types of crimes they could expect and the sorts of behaviour that should elicit their interest. They would not have been surprised to find that the colony was increasing the proportion on night duties. In this it reflected the Metropolitan Police, which, in the course of the 1860s saw 60% of men walking their beat between the hours of 10 p.m. and 6 a.m. With the more uniform hours of darkness in Hongkong, Captain Superintendent Deane and the Colonial Government found the need to employ a similar proportion of men between 6 p.m. and 6 a.m., including as many as possible of the European contingent. The previous year the Scottish recruits had been kept solely on night duty during the warmer months and had come through with remarkably little sickness, therefore the practice was repeated with the London men.[46]

They were to be on the alert for some of the same nefarious activities as they had met in London: larceny, theft and street fighting amongst them. The diverse nature of the population accounted for some particular problems, for example, the many foreign seamen, and sometimes the stationed soldiers made trouble when 'in their cups', with the cheap rough liquor always available. Disputes between chair coolies (those who carried sedan chairs or pulled the wheeled rickshas that were replacing chairs) and their passengers were frequent, whilst accusations of theft on one side, and abuse on the other between masters and mistresses and servants, seem to come to court in greater numbers than in London. The new constable would have to be introduced to some offences that were specific to Hongkong, or were brought to the magistrates far more frequently than back home. Infringement of licence and pass regulations were one such, for example, those in contravention of the regulations originally made in 1857 requiring all Chinese abroad in Victoria between 8 p.m. and the morning gun to carry a police pass and a light.[47] Other, frequently victimless, crimes, such as being a rogue and vagabond, or

46 Annual Medical Report for 1872, *Hongkong Government Gazette*, 17th May 1873.
47 *Hongkong Government Gazette*, 18th July 1857.

a suspicious character were used as much to control the fluid Chinese population of the city as to prevent crime. This use of policing resulted in extraordinary high levels of prosecution and conviction, which the Governor, John Pope Hennessy, saw as unprecedented in any British colony. Of the population of 140,000, almost 7.5% (10,426) were brought up on a charge, of which 5.7% (7,998) were convicted.[48] Some offences, common in London, would be encountered far less frequently, though. The individual prostitute would come only rarely into contact with the constable (in his official capacity), since the system of registered brothels had ensured that street-walking was all but eliminated.

The segregation of brothels by the race of the user, whereby those for European clients were in the east of the town, those for Chinese clients towards the western end, further controlled the situation. Aside from the detection and closure of sly (i.e. illegal) brothels, and the occasional fracas between their clients, in Hongkong prostitutes gave little trouble to the average constable on the beat, a situation not without irony as the story of the London men unfolded. However, kidnapping, especially of girls, often for domestic labour or prostitution, was not uncommon, although it would be some years before this crime and the related *Mui Tsai* system really came to public notice.[49] Opium smoking was common, and permissible, but convictions were regularly brought for the possession or trading of illicit opium. More notorious and pervasive throughout the Chinese communities was gambling, and the opportunities for corruption that it brought were numerous at all levels of society, including amongst the Europeans. These three aspects of life in Hongkong: prostitution, opium smoking and gambling, were among those where over the years the Colonial Office's insistence on home values produced problematic

---

48 John Pope Hennessy to the Legislative Council of Hongkong, 17th September 1877, *Hongkong Government Gazette* 22nd September 1877. The use of policing is explored in greater depth in Munn, *Anglo-China,* especially p. 329 *ff.*

49 *Mui Tsai* was the tradition of sending young daughters to an adoptive family, usually for a financial consideration, where the girl would be educated according to the station of the new family. Almost inevitably, though, it was a system open to abuse, with many young girls sold into domestic servitude or prostitution.

situations in the colony. In the case of the last of these, Britain's prohibition of all forms of gambling for the working man (of whatever race) collided with the pursuit of luck, a search deeply embedded in the culture of the Chinese. Governor MacDonnell's earlier pragmatic attempt to control the corrupting effect that illegal gambling had on great numbers of his Police Force had been squashed by London, and Hongkong reverted to a state where gambling and lotteries were similar to a smouldering slag heap, breaking out in one place as soon as it was doused in another.[50]

The environment and the nature of the town gave rise to other problems that the police would encounter, e.g., the narrow streets and alleys meant that the offence of 'obstruction' by people trying to claim from the footpath or road a little more space for themselves or their trades, appears almost daily in the magistrate's court at the time. Polluting the watercourses by washing or using as a latrine, or by depositing debris, 'night soil', or even corpses, was regarded with particular opprobrium in a city where the water supply was often erratic and almost invariably inadequate. Connected to this, but an offence in its own right, was the cutting or destruction of trees or large shrubs on the slopes that still deserved the 'Barren Rock' soubriquet.

Soon after his arrival in 1867, Deputy Superintendent Creagh had been instrumental in the introduction of regular drill practice to ensure an improved degree of discipline and *esprit de corps* within the body of men. The results had been good, but it proved hard to maintain as a regular fixture on the timetable because of the flexibility needed in order to fill all the required beat duties. Sickness was almost constantly inflicting depredations on the number of men available, running as it did at this period at 100% when comparing the yearly hospital admissions with the strength of the Force. When the Scottish contingent arrived, and in an effort to really unify the force, Creagh decided initially on an hour's drill

---

50 In 1867, through being buried deep in an Ordinance for Order and Cleanliness (No. 9 of 1867, *Hongkong Government Gazette* 22nd June 1867), eleven licenses had been given for gambling houses, resulting in huge profits for the licensees, together with a large revenue for the Administration, and a reduction in crime. However, through Parliament's distaste for any sanctioning of gambling, three years later London succeeded in having these licenses revoked, and impounded the revenue made from them.

three evenings a week, although after a few months this was reduced to one session of twenty to thirty minutes every Friday evening, particularly to ensure that equipment was kept in order.[51] It seems reasonable to assume that the London men were obliged to attend frequent drills, especially in the light of the events that unfolded in the subsequent weeks, but that for them, too, these eventually became cursory weekly fixtures.

Alongside their share of the duty roster, the constables were expected to attend the Police School, which had recently been restructured by School Master Edward Willcocks, along with general efforts to raise the status of the force. Advancement in all ranks, previously dependent on 'good conduct, activity and ability' alone now also required passes in examinations, the subjects of which for the Europeans were chiefly reading, writing, arithmetic and geography. Learning Chinese was optional for this contingent, but without a certificate of competency in the language, it was not possible for a man to be promoted to sergeant. However, attendance of the Europeans was not good at this time, whether through disinclination or because duties made it difficult to give the time.

On 12th March, two days after arriving in Hongkong the men were formally sworn in as Constables for the Force, although copies of the regulations were still not available for them. When, on 16th March, they were summoned to the Captain Superintendent's office to have the rules read to them, these were finally distributed together with the duty rota, and they dispersed to their various posts. All were stationed initially in the Central Station, it is apparent that they continued to form a close group, perhaps being housed in the same dormitory.

For many of the men, therefore, their first experience of active policing was during their third night in Hongkong, and a strange one it must have seemed. The constables took alternate months of duty, from 6 p.m. to 12 midnight, and from midnight to 6 a.m., so aside from half an hour or so at the beginning of the earlier shift, the whole period of duty would have been spent in darkness. One imagines that few would have had opportunity to find out the 'lie of the land' of their particular section earlier in the day, and so would be very dependent on the more

51 *Hongkong Daily Press*, 16th January 1873.

experienced man who accompanied them, particularly the Scots, as records show that by the end of 1873, these two groups accounted for 64% of the European constables. The European constable had charge of a 'section' of the city, which comprised around half a dozen 'beats', which were taken by an Indian constable. The European had to patrol round, directing and taking regular reports from the Indians, and, if possible, assist in any arrests the latter made.

With approximately an area the same as that of the City of London (1.2 sq. miles, the 'Square Mile') but with rather a different shape, the city of Victoria was, in the 1870s, almost four miles long but only 800 yards deep at most, and had a population of close on 106,000.[52] Here was a town that appeared to be almost entirely built on a hillside so steep that logic, it might be thought, should preclude such construction. The piecemeal sale of land leases in 'lots' or sections made for a maze of small alleys and passages between buildings which outdid even those in the oldest parts of London, just as the number of Chinese residents squashed into each building exceeded that achieved by the greediest landlord in Britain. Gas lighting was gradually coming to the streets, but naturally the poorer ones were the last to benefit. Perhaps the most striking contrast, though, between London and Hongkong at night was the very absence of people. Teeming by day, the streets were strangely quiet after 8 p.m., those (Chinese) abroad risking imprisonment or a fine, in accordance with the Night Pass Ordinance.

The offensive examination

Dissatisfaction about the examination issue continued amongst the men. On the evening of 15th March, Acting Chief Inspector Horspool, a former Metropolitan Police man, met a group of eight of the London men including Briarly, coming off duty. They questioned him further about the medical examination, and said that they wanted to be exempted from it, since they had had no inkling of it when they signed papers in

52 Census returns for 1865, *Hongkong Government Gazette* 10th February 1866 and *Historical and statistical abstract of the Colony of Hongkong, 1841-1930,* Hongkong, Noronha & Co., 1932 quoted by Sayer *Hongkong 1862-1919* p. 138-9. Population figures throughout this study have been taken from this source.

London. Horspool advised them to make an application to that effect to Superintendent, and to get some of the older men to sign it in order to add weight to their case. The mood of the men was not helped by finding that some of the reports they had received from their Scottish colleagues were in fact true, and that the previous inspection had been particularly rough and lacking in proper regard for privacy. The norm for these inspections seems to be that they were conducted in the day room or perhaps the dormitories of the Central Police Station, either of which could be on the thoroughfare to the kitchens and washing facilities etc. Why the London men did not take their objection to Captain Superintendent Deane remains unclear, although their Scottish colleagues may have told them that the petition they had made the previous year to have this rule rescinded had been fruitless.

Inspector Thomas Grey (also formerly of the Metropolitan Police) knew of the disaffection the regulation was causing, and sent for three of the men who had been especially recommended to him by a former colleague in London. Grey tried to persuade the men not to be led away by the hot-headedness of a few, especially since they would have such a good chance of promotion in this force. However, his words fell on deaf ears. On the evening of Wednesday, 26th March the men were told to report for the medical inspection the following morning, and, as a body, they vigorously expressed their unwillingness. Briarly was reported as saying to the Barrack Sergeant: "You won't find any of us there".[53] And indeed, come the event, none of the new men were present.

Shortly after noon that Thursday all the men were called to appear before Deane, who told them that they should have informed him earlier if they had objections to the examination. Briarly again acted as the spokesman for the group when they were ordered to comply with the regulation. Upon his saying that none of them would attend, a furious Deane rounded on Briarly and had him arrested. The remaining men were sent away to 'kick their heels' until the next day, when they again refused to submit to the degradation of the loathed inspection. The next afternoon, after two days confined to the barracks, all the men crossed

53 W. M. Deane, Captain Superintendent to The Hon. C. Clementi Smith, Acting Colonial Secretary, 1st May 1873, CO129/163 p 272

over to the Magistracy where their colleague was brought before the Police Magistrate, charged with insolence and insubordination. A bullish Deane wanted the Magistrate to rule immediately on what he claimed was a clear case of disobeying orders, but Mr. F. W. Mitchell, finding that Briarly had not been made aware of the charges that were to be brought against him, much less having had time to obtain representation, ordered an adjournment.

Briarly appeared again before Mr Mitchell the next morning, represented by Mr Hayllar. The men, he went on to explain, did not primarily object to the examination itself, but the way it was conducted, and the fact that had they known of it, they would not have consented to join the Hongkong Police Force in the first place, since such a rule was not part of the regulations of their previous force. Mitchell clearly thought that the charge stood on somewhat shaky grounds, but advised the men to submit, promising in return that Deane would present their case to higher authorities. After consulting his colleagues, Briarly agreed, but said that they wanted to make known how strongly they wished the matter to be put to the Governor. Mitchell, obviously relieved to have this awkward case over, pronounced himself very glad not to have to resort to the full sanctions of the law, and Briarly was fined $5. The men returned to their duties, and the examinations were conducted without any further incident a couple of days later.

The monthly examination of the men had been enshrined into the Orders and Regulations of the Police Force, which were made under Ordinance No. 9 of 1862. The same Orders prohibited a constable from "frequenting" a brothel, under the threat of dismissal, but required that "when becoming so infected" he report immediately to the Colonial Surgeon for medical aid.[54] However, whilst the latter requirements applied to all three contingents, in practice only the Indian and European contingents were liable for examination. The segregation of brothels, along with the married state of many of the Chinese constables, meant that the Administration could quietly ignore the health of this section of the Force.

54 Orders and Regulations for the General Government of The Hongkong Police Force, *Hongkong Government Gazette,* 6th September 1862.

In 1857 the Venereal Disease Ordinance permitted brothels to exist if they were registered, for which a fee was due, and putting the keeper or mistress under the obligation to ensure all women working therein were medically examined every ten days, and provide a weekly list of the health of each.[55] If found to be infected, a woman would then be removed to the Lock Hospital, with the brothel keeper liable for the fees of such treatment. The legislation applied both to brothels for Chinese and non-Chinese clients, although in practice those for the former were excluded.[56] Such registration was almost without precedent in the British Empire, but the grounds given for such a measure, the cripplingly high level of infection on ships that had visited the port, and amongst the garrison, were felt to provide ample justification. However, since brothels were, alongside opium dens and gaming houses, another opportunity for officials, and in this case particularly the poorly-paid and ill-disciplined police, to extract bribes, then bringing them under official control would quieten some of the complaints of corruption and divert such monies into the Government's coffers.[57] This Ordinance, however, made scant inroads into either police corruption or infection. Five years on, 31% of the Police Force were affected, and the Colonial Surgeon reported that the average length of treatment required was then forty-three days.[58] Early in his term of office, Governor MacDonnell reckoned that over half of the inspectors in the Force were in receipt of monthly 'allowances' (some of which were from brothel-keepers), often in excess of their salaries.

The legislation had predated the Contagious Disease Ordinances that were in force in British garrison towns by some seven years, but it was replaced by the Ordinance of 1867, which owed much to that of the homeland, and targeted the individual prostitutes far more than the

---

55 Ordinance No. 12 of 1857, *Hongkong Government Gazette,* 28th November 1857.

56 This exclusion, justified on the basis of the Chinese' reluctance to engage with western medicine, or to have their women examined by British doctors, was equally about the inability reluctance of the colony to address the health needs of the majority population.

57 See Munn, *Anglo China* p. 297.

58 Figures and information (to 1869) in this paragraph taken from The Report of the Colonial Surgeon for 1869, Government Gazette, 14th May 1870.

earlier law, which had 'registered' the individual women only in so far as their medical records.[59] The effect of the measure was a great reduction in infection rate and treatment time both amongst the prostitutes and their clients. In the Police it had fallen to 16.66% by 1869 and was below 10% in 1873, although in terms of admissions to hospital the general sickness rates in the force was still running at about 80%, divided fairly evenly between the three contingents.[60] The possibility of releasing the police from the 'objectionable examination' does not appear to have been discussed in the light of their improved health; indeed, MacDonnell would not have wanted to relinquish this control over the Force.[61]

And so, apart from the promised report on the men's grievance against the distasteful examination sent to the Governor, the whole story might have ended. However, Deane was still dissatisfied, and used his report to the Executive Council on 3rd April to make his case against Constable 115 Briarly in particular, but also Constables 20 Penn, 111 Corcoran, 123 Costello, and 37 Harvey, as mutinous. Constables 54 Hooper and 117 Sullivan he believed *'to be inclined to become contumacious'*, but not to be as mutinous as the others or a danger to the group. Deane was called for questioning at that meeting of the Executive Council and told the Council that Briarly was *'a most turbulent and insolent man, and it would be unsafe to leave him in the Force'*, and added that Harvey, who had spoken in an insolent manner to him, should also be dismissed.

With such a damning report and the Governor's support for Deane, the Council, then, had little choice but to recommend Briarly's dismissal, which the Governor duly endorsed and communicated his decision to Deane later that same day.[62] The other men named were put on notice.

---

59 Ordinance No. 10 of 1867 for the better Prevention of Contagious Diseases, *Hongkong Government Gazette*, 27th July 1867.

60 Report of the Colonial Surgeon for 1873, Government Gazette.

61 The control of prostitution by the administration of British and other colonies has been examined by a number of recent writers, notably for this study Howell and Levine, the latter arguing from a feminist perspective, whilst the former's geo-historical examination of the situation in Hongkong gives an understanding of the racial segregation at the heart of the legislation. However, neither address the equally patriarchal control of their clients, men of the lower orders of society, especially those men directly under government orders.

62 Briarly, thus required to leave Hongkong, but without the means to purchase his passage, was rescued by the strength of public opinion in his favour, when the

Noting that similar regulations for the Army had already been rescinded, the Council resolved to do away with the regulation for the police, but should a man become sick with a venereal disease and not report himself to the Colonial Surgeon he would be both put on full stoppages whilst in hospital and also fined.

Early years on the beat in Hongkong

With their experience of police work right in the centre of London, once they had settled in and learnt their way around the town, many aspects of the job must have seemed very familiar to the new men, even if now conducted in a warmer and much more humid environment. The constables were involved in preventing disorder and law-breaking in the crowded streets and being a deterrent as much by their presence as by their actions. The myriad of petty crimes that came before the magistrate each week would be part of their daily, or rather nightly occupation. Stealing bricks; breaking down branches at the back of a police station; being a suspicious character with intent to rob drunken sailors; causing a disturbance around a brothel; being a rogue and vagabond; throwing stones at a boat with intent to damage; stealing eggs from a child; causing an obstruction in the street, these were all offences that the constable encountered on a frequent, often weekly basis.[63] As a constable, he would rarely be involved in the court appearance of the miscreant or hear the result. Most resulted in a fine, ranging from a few cents to $20, with the option of time in Victoria Gaol in lieu. Street gambling in Ship Street, a recurrent offence, brought a more visible punishment: the guilty undergoing a term in the stocks, which he had to carry from the gaol

---

Daily Press collected a fund for him, which quickly grew. It would appear that, on leaving London in January 1873, Briarly had also left behind a sweetheart, for he married shortly after he arrived back, on July 2nd to Mary Elizabeth Francis. Having failed in his attempt to restart his police career in London he first became a tramcar conductor, and then subsequently joined the Lambeth Waterworks Company where he became an Inspector and lived with his family in Stockwell, south London. Mary died in 1889, having borne him one son and four daughters, whilst Briarly, after retiring on pension, remarried in 1900 and moved to Luton, Bedfordshire, where, after a short time as a publican, died in 1913, aged 69.

63 *Hongkong Daily Press*, 7th, 10th and 11th March 1873.

to Ship Street and back, after which he would stay in the Gaol for three months.[64] Some of the crimes themselves might have a peculiarly 'Eastern' feel, but for the large part, the constable's routine duty essentially differed little here from that in London.

However, the year following their arrival gave the London policemen quite a new experience. On the night of 22nd September 1874, Hongkong sustained the most severe typhoon in its recorded history up until that time, the storm beginning in the early evening and reaching its zenith in the hours after midnight. By the next morning, it was conservatively estimated that two thousand people had lost their lives, primarily by drowning, as the sea surged into the town to a level of three or four feet in places. The insubstantial dwellings that hugged the seafront and the many small junks and boats in the harbour stood no chance from the vicious winds and huge waves. The Colonial Surveyor estimated that 96% of all buildings in Hongkong suffered some damage, with hundreds of houses being either destroyed or rendered unfit for habitation. Fearing that he would lose too many men, Captain Superintendent Deane ordered the police to stay securely inside their barracks until the storm had abated, much to the ire of the public, who felt that, with the much-vaunted efforts to raise the reputation of the force, and the increasing proportion of the Police Rate paid by the local Chinese community, they were entitled to help from this quarter. By his refusal to allow his men to give assistance during the storm, Deane had effectively allowed free rein to the fires that sprang up in many parts of the town, since the Fire Brigade was, with the exception of a small number of permanent Chinese firemen and coolies, staffed by the Police. In the aftermath, the newspapers, of course, had much to say on the issue, and dissatisfaction with Deane's management of the event went as far as the Legislative Council. Indeed, certain members put forward a motion that the Captain Superintendent should be publicly censured and his pay should be reduced. However, perhaps fortunately for the overall health of the force, Deane had an ally in the Governor, who vigorously defended him in the submissions to London on the events of that night. The Police, did, however, play a large part in the clearing of the wreckage of both human life and property

64 *Hongkong Daily Press,* 10th March 1873.

subsequent to the storm, and were kept busy containing the looting that followed. Life was not comfortable for them when off duty either, as the Police Barracks had lost a section of its roof and most of the external woodwork, whilst the officers' quarters were badly damaged by the loss of both the roof and the chimneys.

Although bringing a level of experience and energy to the European contingent, the great home recruitment scheme had not been a substantial success for the residents of Hongkong, who were looking for a stable and efficient police force. By the end of 1876, when the Scottish men were coming towards the end of their five-year term, Deane reported that only fourteen of the original forty-five would be staying on. Of the twenty London men, just half were still in the force. The Scottish group had fared worse in terms of sickness, with six of their men dying in the period, together with seven dismissals. The five dismissals from the London men included James Harvey and Frederick Hooper, who, having been identified by Deane during the examination debacle, had, perhaps not surprisingly, been dismissed for insubordination in October, whilst another of the marked men, John Costello, followed the next year.[65]

George Hennessy, the Newmarket man, in common with his colleagues, had lost three days pay over the medical inspection affair, but otherwise, apart from one caution upon being late for duty by half an hour, did not fall foul of his superiors, and proved the correctness of Horspool's prediction of advancement when he was amongst the first of the London group to be promoted to Sergeant on 1st August 1876.[66] Ironically, Corcoran, one of the three in Deane's firing line who did not lose his post, made even swifter progress, receiving his sergeant's stripes soon after the dismal saga had played out, and being confirmed in his acting role as

65 The case of Harvey and Hooper, however, was rather different, and perhaps shows that Deane's reading of his men's characters was not entirely wrong. They had applied for release on a series of minor issues, the real problem being that service in the Hongkong Police was not what they had expected, and they did not think they would do any good there, as they could not refrain from grumbling and making discontent. Their special error was to apply directly to the Governor, rather than going through their superior. It would appear that their colleagues really were out of patience with these two men, and there was no cry of any injustice when they were dismissed.

66 Hennessy's Rough Book.

Inspector in November of 1876. Sergeant Hennessy, though, thus gained a increase in his pay to £112 10*s* p. a., which became $540 when all the police salaries started to be recorded in the *Blue Books* in dollars in 1878, at a rate of about four shillings to the dollar. He gained a Fourth Class Good Conduct medal in January 1878, and the Third Class medal the following year. Medals, usually for significant courage or initiative shown in bringing criminals to account, were infrequently given in these years, but unfortunately, there is no record of the particular actions that earned Hennessy his. The holder of a medal was also entitled to an extra allowance of $30 p.a. per class of medal, which brought Hennessy an extra $5 a month. He also served for a period as Telegraph Clerk. Such extra responsibilities were often eagerly snapped up by constables and sergeants keen to progress and to make a little extra money, as all had small allowances attaching to them.

Together with some others of the Metropolitan men, Hennessy joined the Fire Brigade on 1st January 1874, and served until he had to resign on his appointment as an Inspector on 15th April 1886.[67] Like fellow Londoners, John Cleaver and Joseph Flynn, he moved up from fireman to Assistant Foreman. Hennessy received his promotion in December 1876 when a Police Sergeant, earning an additional $72 to his annual salary.[68] The allowance, though, could be hard earned, for only men stationed for police duties within reach (and earshot) of the Fire Station, attached to No. 5 Police Station, at the junction of Wellington Road and Queen's Road West were eligible, and had to hold themselves ready to turn out at any time when they were not on police duty. Formed some ten years earlier, the Brigade was reliant on the response of off-duty policemen hearing the alarm bells, and the hiring of street-coolies to pull the unwieldy fire-engines through the streets. When fighting the fires that quite regularly occurred, they were hampered by the difficulty of getting engines into the narrow side streets, the length of hose then required to reach the fires and the erratic supply and pressure of water, which had to

67 A certificate of Fire Brigade service is one of the items from Hennessy's family, now in the Police Museum.

68 *Blue Books* 1880 *CO*133/37.

be lifted from the harbour by the steam pump, which itself could take almost half an hour to get a sufficient head of steam going.

Hennessy, together not only with all the Brigade, but the whole force and hundreds of soldiers, sailors and men of the merchant fleets and civilians, played his part in fighting the fire on the night of Christmas Day 1878. A huge part of the central area of the city was engulfed in the flames, which were believed to have started in a chandler's shop in Endicott Lane.[69] The highly flammable nature of all the buildings and their contents in this and surrounding lanes ensured that, with the wind buffeting first one way and then the next, no sooner had the engines reached one street, when the fire had hopped over to the next. The heat reached inferno levels, with houses combusting into flames through the radiant heat from fires on the opposite side of the road. Although the Fire Brigade was nominally led by Deputy Superintendent Creagh, there was no real 'chain of command'. Creagh's two assistants were a senior clerk in the Treasury and the Acting Harbour-master (and Naval officer). The Engineer and his assistant were civilians, the former the manager of the "Novelty Iron Works". The engine drivers were police constables and the two foremen formerly so, now Inspectors in the Sanitary Department. The spread of the fire was inexorable by any standard means and it became quickly obvious that there was no strategy for dealing with anything on this scale. In previous serious fires, the only solution had been to destroy buildings and blocks of houses by bombing, so as to create a void over which, it would be hoped, the fire could not jump. It was largely thus that any progress was made with this fire, which was still burning fiercely the next morning. However, the command for the Army to start these detonations had been delayed, as no-one was willing to take responsibility for the decision. The Governor, John Pope-Hennessy, had not been woken and informed of the fire until 3 a.m. Whether it was he who finally gave the Army their orders is unclear.

In addition to the obvious problems, this was the one night when it could be reasonably assumed that a large proportion of the European male community had consumed more than their usual amount of alcohol, as

69 The following paragraphs owe much to Nebbs, *The Great Fire of Hongkong.*

proved to be the case. The morning light brought no abatement of the fires, but a clearer picture of the destruction already wrought: great areas that the previous day had been thriving lanes and streets of shops and tenement housing were now just so much smouldering ash. Meanwhile, the fire was crossing roads and threatening even the Central Police Station and the Gaol. The Civil Hospital, which had been destroyed by the 1874 typhoon, had taken over buildings on Hollywood Road, behind which lay the Police Compound. Patients were quickly evacuated as it became clear that this building would soon be in flames. Fears were expressed that the Catholic Cathedral on nearby Wellington Road would catch light. As the highest building in the area, if its steeple were to blaze, there would be no stopping the spread of the fire. However, by prompt action this was averted and nor did the fire spread southward beyond that one section of Hollywood Road.

The fires burned for over sixty hours, causing over $1 million worth of destruction. It had spread over 10.5 acres, rendering hundreds if not thousands of Chinese homeless. In the immediate aftermath the police had to help organise the clearance of roads, relief for those left without shelter or possessions and suppress the widespread looting that took place in the area. What was not investigated, and perhaps the police would not have been equipped to make such enquires, were the numerous claims that were submitted to fire insurance companies subsequently. The suspicion was raised that much of the damage claimed had been at least exacerbated by owners keen to cash in.

Life in the colony returned to normal in the months that followed, but fires, mercifully not again on the scale of that Christmas night, whether suspicious or entirely accidental, would remain a constant feature of the work of those Police who did duty in the Brigade. Sergeant Hennessy would find himself regularly in charge of the pumps or the hoses, as on the afternoon one year later when a small two-storey house in Second Street, dangerously close to the new Civil Hospital, caught fire. The blaze had probably started in the cookhouse at the back, but took the occupants completely by surprise. Fortunately, the civilian volunteer brigade, led by one Mr Senna, were quickly on the scene, followed by the regular brigade, led by Sergeant Hennessy. With two nearby hydrants providing a good head of water, the blaze was quenched within the hour *and the firemen finished and went home.*[70] The residents, though, must have been less happy, for their house was completely gutted.

70 *Hongkong Daily Press*, 3rd January 1880.

Chapter Two

Down in the Yard

The Naval Dockyard Police and its Irish inspectors

To the north and west the rural north Cork town of Newmarket is girded by a semicircle of hills, but south of the town is only one small upland of any size rising from the pastureland, a mile or so away. The townland, a hamlet, that sits atop this hill takes its name from the Island Wood, which itself tumbles dramatically down to the River Dalua. The Wood has long been the playground of the people who live around Newmarket. In the spring the whole area is alive with new life, whilst in summer the woods ring to the sound of children swinging on branches, jumping in and out of rock pools and racing down the steep inclines. In autumn all turns to russet and gold, and, dappled with late sunlight, presents aspects to vie with the prettiest Wicklow glades. By winter the townland is left to itself, the cottages seeming to hunker down to extract what protection they can from the bare trees, only the highest branches of which come up as far as the roofs, as the wind and driving rain sweeps across the hill-top.

In the middle of the nineteenth century much of the land in this region belonged to the Aldworths, an ascendancy family, who were known as relatively compassionate landlords. The farms around Island were small, especially when compared to those along the roads west and north of Newmarket town, being mostly less than fifteen acres. They were not especially subdivided and sublet, as happened in poorer areas of the country by this time, but they did not provide much comfort in the living for the twenty or so families whose small holdings appear in the returns in Griffith's Valuation. However, the woods and river held a tempting additional source of food, provided the Aldworths' gamekeeper could be dodged. At twenty-four acres, James Lysaught's farm was a little larger, whilst closer to the wood their neighbour, John Murphy, had just seven acres.[71] Griffith's Valuation Tables, which were compiled in 1854-6 in this part of Co. Cork, give, in the absence of comparable surviving records to the 1841-1891 English census returns, a unique insight into the residence of families and their relative prosperity (or lack of it).

James Lysaught had married Mary O'Riordan and had just one son, the eldest child, William, who was baptised on 7th April 1835, followed by a succession of at least five daughters.[72] Little is known of their early years, until the stories of the departure of William for foreign parts. According to folk memory, both he and his father were called "The Poacher". Various understandings of this exist: that, indeed, they were poachers, and that William escaped with his life from the hanging that the Assizes could impose by fleeing, or being hurried off, to the USA. Others will tell you that when a man bore that title it actually meant the opposite: that they were the gamekeepers for the Aldworth's, protecting the Island Wood from local two-footed predators. Feeling would run high against such men, especially if they were the instruments by which their neighbours were too frequently brought to justice, and it might have been expedient to give up the prospect of the family farm to evade that. There is also a suggestion that the term relates to bully boy tactics used by father and son to remove distressed tenant farmers from their smallholdings for either their own benefit or (more likely) that of their superior landlord. This,

---

71 *Griffith Valuation Tables* of 1856. These Valuation Tables were created between 1848 and 1864, itemising all the farms, houses and buildings, from the grandest hall to the meanest shack, with the names of the tenant and the immediate landlord given, and the amount of land (if any) in order to establish the rates due by each person to the local Poor Law Union towards the maintenance of workhouses and the local poor. Alongside each table a highly detailed map was prepared showing the position and extent of lands, and, in the case of towns, the layout of houses along the streets, etc. Richard Griffith, who conducted the survey, was also instrumental in building the Cork-Killarney road, which greatly improved the communication and the prosperity of the region.

72 In the time before compulsory registration of life events, not everyone was as meticulous about recording dates as George Hennessy and his Rough Book. The baptismal date here comes from the Newmarket Parish Register, but Lysaught gave his date of birth as 30th March,1836. The simplest explanation is that he was either given the wrong date by his mother at some point, or, once away from his family, just forgot.

admittedly contentious reading, has been met with some scepticism, partly because it is felt locally that a man engaged in any such activity would have been called something 'a lot worse than "poacher"!' Whatever the reason, the younger Lysaught disappeared from the Newmarket scene early in the 1860s, with the farm eventually passing to Daniel Murphy, who married the youngest Lysaught daughter, Hannah, in 1875. Daniel was the eldest son of farmer Timothy Murphy (brother of neighbour John) in Clashykinleen, a townland some five miles west of Newmarket, and probably the home of Mary Riordan.

The first Newmarket man in Hongkong

Why William Lysaught travelled across America to the western states is not known. In later decades of the century Newmarket had an established community around the Klamath Falls area of Oregon, where many of these emigrants kept connections with their hometown, even to the uncommon extent of visiting back. But since there is no record of any connection with the area in the 1860s, it could be conjectured that Lysaught had heard of the (now spent) gold-rush in California, and headed west in search of a fortune. He is known to have been in California before coming to Hongkong, and it could be that in San Francisco he encountered the Chinese community and learnt of opportunities in the British owned colony. A regular steamer service operated from San Francisco to Hongkong and it was from one such ship that he landed in Hong Kong during 1864. There he would remain, and, in contrast to the majority of residents of all races and men, he never returned to his homeland, which might, of course, say something about the extent of his need to leave it in the first place.

Now twenty-seven or twenty-eight years old, with a fair education and a variety of skills from a decade or more of running a farm with his father, he was no beachcomber or discharged sailor, and yet neither was he of the class that would travel out to the colony to take up a position in a firm. The large commercial firms, and to these Lysaught, with his later proven business acumen, would surely have turned, would look askance on a man without credentials for any but the lowest posts. The junior clerical positions were usually filled by Portuguese, and there were ample

The Praya and waterfront c. 1860

numbers of discharged Indian soldiers and West Indian seamen to take the watchman jobs. However, the Government departments, such as the Public Works Department, the Police and the Gaol were ever in need of steady, industrious British men, although Lysaught would have soon learnt that the remuneration here was not going to lead him to make his fortune. But any job was better than none, and like so many before him, he would then be well placed to explore more lucrative opportunities. Such seems to be his thinking when by chance he made acquaintance with the fellow Irishman, Henry Dixon, the Inspector of the Dockyard Police.

Lysaught's early weeks and months in the colony are almost lost to view: family 'memory' is that he joined the Naval Dockyard Police Force upon arrival. It is more probable that he followed the usual route and applied to the regular police, was accepted and from here was moved swiftly to the Dockyard, perhaps at Dixon's request. The transience of all Hongkong's population tends towards a rather ephemeral grasp upon history at the time: only twelve years later the authorities had trouble tracing the development of the Naval Yard Police Force, using terms such as '*at an earlier time*' and '*at some point past*'. It is safe to say that until 1869 there was a certain 'sharing' of manpower, and that the Naval Commodore and later the Dockyard Police Inspector could apply to the Captain Superintendent for new constables as needed.

The Naval Yard from the harbour

The Naval Dockyard and its Police Force

With the accession of a permanent base in the region, Naval Stores were amongst the first structures erected by the British arriving in Hongkong, in April 1841.[73] These initially were just sheds, out of the way of the commercial and military part of the town, but soon more substantial buildings in the newly acquired shore base in Central were added, that would later assume the role of Naval Yard. By 1859, because of the ongoing hostilities, the Navy reorganised this to become a Victualling Yard and a Dockyard, the latter holding the machinery and parts to keep the ships in fighting condition.[74]

As the size of the Yard increased so, of course, did its personnel, with posts gradually appearing in the *Navy Lists,* probably some years after they had come into existence.[75] Thus in 1861 a Master Attendant of the Yard,

73 Harland, *The Royal Navy in Hong Kong since 1841* p.5.

74 *Navy List, 1859.*

75 The biannual *Navy List* initially names only the Commodore and Master Attendant of the Stores and the Accountant (also the Naval Paymaster), but later starts to include lists of clerks and the senior engineers, whilst the commercially

and an Accountant are listed, with the commander of the receiving ship becoming first "Naval Officer in Charge of the Naval Establishment" and then simply "Commodore, Hong Kong" in 1866. These were supported by teams of engineers, boatbuilders, carpenters and fitters, writers, clerks and coolies.

The commercial firms provided their dockyards with armed, drilled guards in military style uniforms, who were often discharged soldiers from Her Majesties Indian regiments. The Naval Dockyard, in common with the Governor's residence, the Gaol and the Mint were normally guarded by serving members of the Army, frequently supplemented by a few men from the Police Force, particularly when sickness swept through the garrison. The costs relating to the protecting the Yard were then met by the Naval Storekeeper.[76] Towards the end of the 1850s the military were no longer able to spare men, and since the precedent in the British Isles was for the Dockyards to be protected by a civilian police force, reflecting the civilian nature of most of those working therein, a similar plan seems to have been envisaged for Hongkong.[77]

In addition to covering for the army at times of necessity, the police force in Hongkong was accustomed to providing inspectors and constables for special duties. Thus the 1860 *Blue Book* records, working for Charles May, the Police Superintendent, and his deputy, just two Deputy Inspectors. But there were also two Deputy Inspectors of Markets and ten (Indian) Market Constables, two Inspectors of Nuisances and one Inspector of Brothels.[78] The salaries of these seconded men were initially 'chalked up' to the force, whose ledger then showed a corresponding credit entry from other departments of the Government. However, there is no mention of men employed at the Dockyard, probably because the *ad hoc* nature

---

produced *Chronicle and Directory of China* provides further information. Towards the end of the century volumes of the *Chronicle* give names of the Naval Dockyard Police Force Inspector and Sergeants, and the number of constables employed.

76 Governor Bonham to Earl Grey, 24th August. CO129/25 pp. 227-246.

77 By an Act of Parliament (Cap CXXXV) of 28th August 1860 the head of the (London) Metropolitan Force had been authorised to arrange the policing of all the Royal Dockyards by his men.

78 *Blue Book* for 1860, CO133/17 p 164-167.

of the system was never formalised. In 1850 this all-European force had consisted of two sergeants and twelve constables. Eleven years later Governor Robinson sought permission to put the arrangement on a more permanent footing, and he was authorised to enlist one inspector, three sergeants and fifteen constables. Still the Dockyard men do not appear in the *Blue Book* lists and indeed later correspondence would suggest that they were not considered to be part of the colonial Police Force by this time, although men were still transferred as needed. The men collected their pay from the Naval Paymaster, and, operating exclusively on Naval property, they were not the colonial Administration's responsibility.

The Government records for the colonial (town) police force do not list individual men below inspector rank, and so only if a man reached that position can one reliably trace his career back through official documents. In the case of the Yard force, detail is yet more obscure, for no regular records have emerged at all during the nineteenth century. There is just one surviving (complete) list of men in this Force which was sent back to London from this century. Nor do the men often appear by name in reports of court proceedings at this time. The explanation for this lies partly in the nature of their work: theirs was a rather hidden Force, and the press reporters would have had little opportunity to get to know these constables. But perhaps more significantly, relatively few cases from the dockyard came before the Magistrates. It seems probable that, in the semi-closed community of the Dockyard, most petty offenders would have been dealt with by the Inspector or the Commodore.

In a letter of 1862, Governor Robinson bemoans the fact that the average length of service for a European Constable is just three months in the regular force.[79] The Dockyard Police recruited from the same pool of discharged soldiers, and occasional seamen and adventurers, together with a few beachcombers, and since there was some early sharing of men, the Town constables' wage of £60 to £70 p.a. ($25 to $30 per month) most probably applied here. With the requirement for men to live in Yard premises in rather makeshift barrack accommodation around the police offices, good men must have been just as hard to secure. Perhaps the relatively small scale of the dockyard, and duties that were essentially

79 Robinson to Duke of Newcastle 6th May 1862. CO129/86 p 46.

those of guarding property, rather than keeping the peace and dealing with the mass of Hongkong's humanity, persuaded some men that this would be less arduous employment than in the town police. However, with less contact with the local population, there was also less chance of making a little supplementary income by 'squeeze' or bribery than their Town colleagues might have.

Henry Dixon – the Yard's first Inspector

One man who does emerge from the shadows here is the first Inspector, one Henry Dixon.[80] Born to William and Maria Dixon of Rathdowney, Queen's County (now Co. Laois), Ireland, like many young men without prospects, he had joined the British Army. The 59th Regiment of Foot had been stationed in Ireland, and Dixon had sailed east with his regiment in 1849. Hongkong was the garrison for the great majority of the British troops engaged in the China wars, whether on the island at Victoria Barracks, or at those at Stanley or Deep Water Bay, or in cramped hulks: troop ships moored semi-permanently in Victoria Harbour. Only with the accession of British Kowloon in 1860 did the garrison acquire more space, if not more facilities. Dixon served in this regiment for some nine years, taking part in the storming of the walls of Canton, with the rather quiet 'capture' of that city which followed in December 1857, for which he gained a medal. The following year, with the 59th scheduled to move to South Africa, Dixon decided upon a career in the colony that was beginning to show signs of prosperity. The young man had seen far more of his colleagues die of disease than through military action, and at a higher rate than in the civilian population of Hongkong, and so his chance both of survival and prosperity were obviously better in the town than in the camps. Thus, along with a number of others from his regiment, on 16th November 1858 he purchased his discharge, and joined the colonial force. Here he soon rose to sergeant, and then became the first Inspector of the Dockyard Police under the reorganisation initiated by Governor Robinson and the Commodore in 1861, taking charge of a

80 Biographical information comes from his son's letter of 24th March 1895, CO129/268 pp 693-98, church marriage records noted in the Carl Smith cards and medal record cards WO100/41 p 116.

team of fifteen constables and three sergeants, whose duties consisted primarily of watching over the stores and workshops, particularly at night time.

Bishop Raimondi

On 9th April 1863 Henry Dixon married Isabella Roza Pereira at the Catholic Cathedral on Robinson Road. Elizabeth, the anglicised version of her name preferred by her husband, was the twenty-two-year-old daughter of Antonio and Antonia Josepha Pereira, described in the church register as being of Macao. The family, with at least two elder daughters and two sons, lived, however, in Hongkong, and had some years earlier been able to buy property along the Hollywood Road and in Square Street. It may be reasonable to assume a level of affluence that would see Isabella bring a dowry with her, for the will of Isabella's widowed mother, Antonia Pereira, proved in 1884, left her unmarried daughters sufficient enough for each to purchase a newly built house.[81]

Dixon, a Catholic, would be seen as an eligible catch for young Isabella, for although not highly paid, his position ensured respectability for the couple. He had secure work in the Yard, which was not in the overcrowded sections of the city, and might have the possibility of advancement into the Colonial Administration. (If his salary matched those of his town counterparts it would be between £125 and £175 per annum.) It is most likely that they spent their married life occupying the Inspector's room at the Naval Yard, but, since the Yard had no married quarters, the Inspector would be permitted to reside outside, so they may have taken rooms in nearby Ha Wan, the name then given to the westernmost part of Wanchai.

81 The will of Antonia Pereira. HKRS 144-4-755.

Their first child was born in the summer of the next year, but both mother and child were ill, and the priest, Fr. Raimondi was summonsed to baptise the boy, '*in danger of death*', on the twenty-sixth of August.[82] The boy was given the name Joseph, more likely by the priest than by his mother, but died three days later. Isabella recovered, however, and bore her second child exactly one year later, on 19th August, 1865. This boy was named Henry William, after his father and paternal grandfather, whilst his brother, born two years later, was called William Henry.

It was about the time of the birth of Dixon's first child that William Lysaught arrived in the colony, when Hongkong had just 'come of age', and was feeling the benefit of increasing independence from the controlling hand of the Colonial Office in London. Its coinage had been accepted by London, who had given permission for the Administration's accounts to be presented in dollars. There had been an attempt at establishing a mint for the territory and the postal service was running well, as regular shipping services emerged between Hongkong and most of the other world ports. Local banking houses were coming into being, the Hong Kong and Shanghai Banking Corporation Ltd., the foremost of these, started in 1864. Meanwhile the government oversaw the extension of road building, a Government School for both European and Chinese and the laying-out of that great British institution, the Public Gardens. But despite the extensive wharves and godowns of Dent's and Jardine's, Hongkong was in the early days of its prosperity, and as such, not yet the magnet for all who hoped to escape the rural poverty of so much of its nearest neighbour. The population of the colony, which had risen, in part with the acquisition of British Kowloon, from 85,000 in 1859, stood at about 120,000 when Lysaught arrived in 1863, but then changed little in overall numbers, although with a constant coming and going of Chinese from Canton, for the next decade. Indeed it was not until near the close of the 1870s that numbers started to climb, and the year-on-year growth that would so characterise its future commenced. However, one group of people who were already feeling Hongkong's magnetic force were the criminal underbelly, the very many small-time thieves who could find

82 Fr. Raimondi would later become the first Roman Catholic bishop of Hongkong.

rich pickings, and scant discouragement in the 'soft' English judicial system. Throughout the early 1860s crime started to escalate, organised robberies and gruesome murders were not infrequent and Triad influence was often suspected, although rarely proved. Any sea voyage always risked the peril of abduction by pirates, who were both plentiful and vicious. In response, the Government established harbour offices around the island and on Kowloon to dissuade the more audacious brigands, and brought in measures, as seen, attempting to improve the quality of the Police Force and efforts to keep criminals off the streets at night. Armed watchmen protected the private businesses, which were seen by its civilian population as Hongkong's *raison d'être:* the full godowns and warehouses of a port that was rapidly becoming the most important free-trade port in Asia.[83]

Hongkong proposes but London disposes

But amidst all this commercial development, Hongkong was the Navy's primary base in the region. With the greater mechanisation of ships, especially the growing dominance of steamships in the Royal Navy, the Yard's role could only increase and its security become ever more crucial. The Dock Yard Police was a small team and had, rather against the odds, apparently been a relatively stable one. However, towards the end of 1866 the Commodore and the Inspector had been obliged to put up with a most inconvenient depletion of the Force when a number of men who had breached discipline had absconded or resigned at a moments notice, and there was no recourse to sanction or punish.[84] A flurry of correspondence between the interested parties: Commodore Jones; Vice Admiral Kepple; Governor MacDonnell and Captain Superintendent Deane followed. The Attorney General and Deane realised that the Police Ordinance of 1862 (which had replaced the first such as the authority under which constables were recruited and enrolled in the colony) had made no provision for

83 Perhaps the most organised and highly regarded of these private security police were those of Jardine Matheson's at East Point, where a team of Indian sepoys, often referred to as Special Constables were employed. Hamilton p.33ff.

84 W. G. MacDonnell to Duke of Buckingham, Secretary of State for the Colonies, 10th June 1867, CO129/133 p 313.

such as the Dock Yard Police. Therefore men joining after this date might have been sworn in, but under no Ordinance to give them the authority of constables. Men joining before 1862 remained constables by virtue of the 1844 Ordinance, which had not been repealed, but the more recent recruits were not, and, as Deane phrased it, were

> *"on precisely the same footing as armed sepoys employed by Messrs. Jardine Matheson ... to guard their premises at East Point."*[85]

That a few of the men did legally have standing as constables was almost incidental: the majority of the men were mere watch-men.[86] Fortunately for the legal system of Hongkong, it does not seem to have crossed their minds to question the validity of any arrests made by these non-constables.

Vice Admiral Henry Kepple was concerned that the Commodore should have the authority to punish miscreant members of the force. The Governor wished to see a simple and complete transfer of these men to the Naval Authorities, severing all and any connection to the Colonial Police Force. Deane, on the other hand, wanted to ensure that the men would have the proper authority to do their job. It seems reasonable that he would not want to agree to a police force in the same territory that was entirely out of his jurisdiction, and so he set about to make detailed suggestions as to how the system could be regularised.

The men currently employed should be sworn in, he proposed, with the regular Police Force, but detailed for duty only at the Yard. They would serve the remaining period of their five year terms, with service to date counting for their pensions. The constables' pay being similar to that of the town Force, they would continue to be barracked at the Yard, with all the costs of their pay and upkeep being paid monthly, he suggested, by the Admiralty to the Government. If it was necessary to replace men, he would endeavour that it would be with men of similar length of service, so as to avoid altering the pension situation for the Admiralty. Deane was a strong advocate for a six-hour working day for the European

85 W. M. Deane to Plumer, Acting Naval and Victualling Accountant, 27th February 1867, CO 129/122 pp 150-154.

86 Inspector Dixon had been asked by Mr. Deane to draw up a list of those men who had enlisted before the 1862 Ordinance (CO129/133 p 298 27th February 1869). Sadly this list has not come down to us.

members of his force, considering this the maximum length of time men should be outside in the summer heat and humidity. Since the present shift length was some eight hours, and as the Dockyard force was solely European, the Commodore was asked to consider how many additional men he would require to allow for this change, and to agree to their enlistment.[87] A further sergeant and 8 constables were thus engaged, with the Naval Authorities in Hongkong taking on the additional costs and agreeing to Deane's proposed payment scheme. Indeed, throughout the correspondence at this stage there is a real sense of the Governor, Captain Superintendent and Naval establishment all working to resolve the issue with efficiency and alacrity.

But as so frequently was the case, Hongkong might decide upon one course of action, but those in offices ten thousand miles away seemed almost to delight in their ability to introduce 'spanners'. On this occasion, although it took the best part of two years to run its course, the problem was two-fold. MacDonnell had necessarily gone forward with the Ordinance required rather swiftly and it had passed through the Legislative Council before it had been officially sanctioned by the Colonial Office.[88] London had objected to the Ordinance, since it was not in line with the provisions in other parts of the British Empire, and therefore the oaths taken by the men who had been sworn in under it were now invalid. Secondly, and more decisively, the Admiralty baulked at the idea of pensions for these men, especially as they were in line with those of the Town force, eligible after ten years' service, and the piqued Colonial Office were in no mood to fight them on Hongkong's behalf. Thus the Governor had a group of men who had been promised pensions which now might have to come from the colony's coffers. So to avoid a situation when these men might, *by a side wind eventually claim Pensions from this Colony for services rendered to the Admiralty*[89] he proposed that all should be required to resign from the Colonial Police Force. With much

87 Figures and information (to 1869) in this paragraph taken from The Report of the Colonial Surgeon for 1869, Government Gazette, 14th May 1870.

88 Correspondence relating to the Ordinance, 1869, CO 129/136 pp 261-375. It should also be remembered that, before telegraphic connections, a round of correspondence took a minimum of twelve weeks.

89 *Ibid.*

regret, he explained to the Commodore that should men not so resign claims to pensions, he would have no option but to dismiss them.

The Colonial Office formally disallowed the Ordinance, and the Admiralty produced Acts of 1839 and 1860 relating to the Metropolitan Police (who provided the Naval Dockyard Police in England at this time), which stated that the pensions of these men were paid not by the Admiralty but by the Police Superannuation Fund. Pensions currently ran at about £24 per man per annum, and, of course, Hongkong had no such Fund.

At the end of 1868 and prior to the disallowance of the Ordinance, Dixon and the Commodore's Secretary and right hand man, F. A. Carter, gained wind of the way the Admiralty were thinking. They therefore drew up one list of those who were prepared to sign an agreement relinquishing all claims to a pension, but remaining under all other conditions, and another of those who, at the men's own suggestion, would release the colony from any such claim, but required an agreement that they could claim their discharge at one month's notice, rather than wait for the expiration of the usual five year term. This request does not seem unreasonable, for with no half-pay leave, no pension and scant promotion prospects, there was little advantage in being part of this force. This proposal would bring them into line not only with the guards and watchmen of the commercial firms, but also with the other civilian employees of the Yard. Perhaps surprisingly, the men divided equally between the two options, but with four of the five sergeants preferring to take their discharge swiftly if opportunities presented. Possibly some of the men who opted to remain on the five year term were coming close to the end of a period of service. It would appear that the men's situation was held in abeyance that winter, waiting for further communication from London and the Admiralty.

Whilst there can be no doubt that the Governor was relieved that the situation had been resolved, he was still galled that London had ridden roughshod over his Administration and the people who served it. In a letter to Commodore Oliver Jones on 18th February, 1869, he complained:

> *"The members of the Naval Dockyard police will thus be simply relegated to their original status and will once more constitute a force entirely separate from and independent of the Colonial Police. I am however very anxious personally that Inspector Dixon and all the men serving in the Naval Dockyard Police should clearly understand that I take this step reluctantly and merely from the necessity of freeing the Colony from a legal liability which no one wishes to attach to it, namely that of giving pensions for services not rendered to the Colony. I understand from Mr. Deane, that the Reports against the men of the Naval Yard Police have been few and that their general conduct has been satisfactory during his brief nominal connection with them.*
>
> *"I have therefore been particular in recording the reasons for the action, which this Government has been compelled to take in the matter, because I would be sorry that any member of the Naval Yard Police should for a moment imagine that his discharge from the Colonial Force implied the slightest imputation against his character."*[90]

The correspondence ends at this point, or at any rate, any subsequent discussion between the parties in Hongkong has not survived. There had been no question of agreeing to the request for free movement from the Force, and in cases later in the press it is apparent that men would still have to agree to a five-year term. For those who chose to re-engage the length of time already served was carried over, and from the careers of men that can be traced, it appears that the majority of men abided by their first decision upon the general discharge at the end of February 1869. Thus, having established what this Force is not, there is no record of any attention given of the powers of the inspector and his men, nor how it would be known. Later that year Dixon, writing his will, describes himself as the 'Inspector of Naval Yard Watchmen',[91] which is how the men were described in newspaper report of an incidents in April of that year, when Police Magistrate Charles May asked *"if the constables at the*

90 *Ibid.*

91 Will of Henry Dixon, 21st July 1869. HKRS144-4-206.

Naval Yard are called watchmen now".[92] There is little consistency, though, as three days later a 'Dockyard Constable' is referred to as witness to a case of furious driving (whipping a scrawny pony into a frantic speed along Queen's Road Central),[93] and then three months later they become 'special constables' when Inspector Lysart *(sic)* brings up one William Whyte on the charge of absconding from the Force.[94] By the middle of the next decade they are back to being regularly referred to as the Dockyard Police or Naval Dockyard Police Force, throughout which time their power to make arrests has not been questioned, suggesting that it was more a case (not unprecedented) of being able to report to London that the right moves had been made, and then getting on with business as usual.

A Dockyard Family

The sickness that had stalked Dixon, first in his regiment, then in his own home, caught him as the administrative saga was playing out its last chapter. By spring of 1869 the only recourse was to send him home to try to recover. Dysentery and 'remittent fever' (malaria) were the two biggest killers amongst the foreign community, but gradually, with the improvement in the hospital and the water supply, and the development, albeit rudimentary, of sanitation in some parts of the town, the mortality level in this group was dropping. Whatever ailed Henry Dixon, he was first cared for on board the Navy's Hospital Ship the *SS Melville,* but it became apparent that the best hope for recovery would be for the patient to be removed to more temperate climes. Thus the Naval Surgeon booked a passage for him on the next available ship to the United Kingdom, which, a few months before the opening of the Suez Canal, was scheduled to take the route around the Horn of Africa. The longer journey on this Naval ship would be preferred, as much of the journey would be in somewhat cooler seas and would avoid the trying overland journey through Egypt, in addition to which he would be under the care of the ship's doctor. Dixon bade farewell to his wife and children,

92 *Hongkong Daily Press* 24th April 1869.
93 *Hongkong Daily Press* 27th April 1869.
94 *Hongkong Daily Press* 6th July 1869.

for, since she was not a British citizen in her own right, and with her mother living in Hongkong, the Admiralty would not consider paying for additional passages for them. Isabella and her children duly moved out of the Inspector's quarters, and went to live with her mother in Hollywood Road. Dixon's condition worsened however, and he was considered too sick to continue with the voyage, and thus, when he was taken off at the British Naval base at Simonstown, Cape of Good Hope, and transferred to the Naval Hospital, he was dependent on the kindness of strangers. In hospital, it was the Anglican chaplain, Rev. Stephen Jacob RN, who persuaded him to make his will on 21st July.[95] A preprinted form was completed by the chaplain thus:

> Royal Hospital at Cape of Good Hope
> In the name of God, Amen.
> I, *Henry Dixon late Inspector of Her Majesty's Naval Yard Watchmen at Hong Kong* now a Patient in the Naval Hospital Simons Town being of sound mind, do hereby make this my last Will and Testament: I give and bequeath unto my *Wife, Elizabeth Dixon residing at Hong Kong the sum of One hundred and twenty six pounds sterling in the Commercial Bank London and also* all such Wages, Prize Money, Allowances, and other Sum or Sums of Money, as now are, or hereafter may be due to me for my service on board the said Ship, or any other Ship or Vessel, of the Royal Navy, together with all other my Estate and Effects whatsoever and wheresoever.
> And I do hereby appoint *The Reverend Father T Raimondi, Catholic Cottage Hongkong* executor of this my last Will and Testament, and hereby revoking all former Wills by me made; I declare this to be my last Will and Testament. In witness whereof I have at "the Naval Hospital Simonstown": hereunto set my hand, this *twentysixth*[96] *day of July* in the year of our Lord One Thousand Eight Hundred and *Sixty Nine*:

95 HKRS144-4-206 21st July 1869.

96 Although the Archive records the date as 21st, the author's opinion is that the correct reading is 26th July.

Henry Dixon
Witnesses *John Newman (?) Bernard staff surgeon RN*
S.H. Jacob Chaplain, RN

Dixon, who had been out east for many years, had not used the emerging banks in Hongkong for his precious savings, preferring the security of a London firm (which incidentally merged in 1871 with the Westminster Bank, a forerunner of the present NatWest Bank plc). For an executor he had, like many a dying soldier in Hongkong, cited his friend and the best-known cleric, to both Catholics and non-Catholics alike. Dixon's signature is neat and with well-formed characters.

He died just a day or two later, and is recorded in the church records as having been buried in Hongkong the next month. His grave is now lost, and although it is not unprecedented for a body to be transported so far at that time, preserved in alcohol for later burial, it would have been both unusual and expensive. Before the telegraph had connected Hongkong to other parts of the British Empire and beyond, the news of her husband's death likely accompanied a 'token' of him, suitably encased. No doubt it fell to Fr. Raimondi both to break the sad news to Isabella, and to arrange the funeral, which took place at the end of August. At her mother's home, with her husband's outstanding pay and the money from the London bank, Isabella and her family were not destitute, and left in a better position than many widows in the years before the Widows' and Orphans' Fund.

Lysaught, who had joined the force in 1864, had become a sergeant before five years had elapsed. At the time, prior to the establishment of the Police School for language training in 1869, promotion in the regular Force was largely a matter of length of service allied with a rudimentary examination in police procedure. However, with the high turnover in the personnel of the Force, and the generally poor quality of the men that it could recruit, a man with a fair education and who was not too fond of the bottle might reasonably expect to be promoted from constable early into his second term of five years. His rise from there to Inspector, however, would usually be a longer journey. In the Dockyard, however, Lysaught succeeded to his friend's position with a short period, probably only a few months, of service as a sergeant behind him. He had been the only man of that rank to agree to the full terms of the Government, and to be bound to his five year terms of service, and thus now the only sergeant of any experience in the Yard. Was there any element of calculation when he opted to waive the 'right' to leave at a month's notice? Whether that was the case or not, "The Poacher" had quickly, by default, become very much the "Head Gamekeeper" in his little empire.

Although there is no way of confirming such, Henry Dixon may well have asked his junior man to 'mind' his family in his absence and Isabella/Elizabeth would naturally have turned to her husband's successor in the Yard for help with the will, and with gaining access to his money. The money from London, which may well have been part of her dowry, (for otherwise it is difficult to imagine how a former private in the army would have amassed such a sum) would have to be realised. Up until the last years of the century young widowhood was not an unusual state in which women in the colony found themselves, but because this was a predominantly male environment, finding a second, or occasionally, third husband was generally possible even though they brought children from the earlier marriage with them. Unions were not infrequently contracted between European sailors and Chinese women, but there seem to be more marriages between discharged soldiers and women from the (Catholic) Portuguese community, reflecting the predominance of Catholic Irishmen in the regiments stationed around China. However, the police and members of other Government departments who hoped to rise in their careers were expected to find their brides back home while on leave. Even as late as 1870, there was a casual assumption made that unprotected western women in the colony would be 'no better than they ought to be'.

In contrast to British India, in the nineteenth century, Hongkong was not a destination of choice for the '*fishing fleet*'. There is no evidence to show that young unmarried women came out in any number either to marry a British official by prior arrangement or, more speculatively, to stay with an established European family and find a husband while she was there. The lists of arriving passengers and hotel residents in that century rarely include more than one or two unattached Misses. Indeed, it is difficult to see that any young women, whose family had raised the fare to send her out, would choose to travel for an extra twenty to twenty-five days beyond India or Ceylon. Hongkong was still, in the mind of the British newspaper reading public at any rate, frontier land, without the very well established society that major Indian towns and stations could offer, no members of the aristocracy to lend glamour and with a far smaller number of British families to whom to entrust the girl initially. Examples exist of young women, usually escorted by a Government employee returning from leave, travelling to marry in Hongkong, but generally these marriages had been at least mooted back home, when the intended bridegroom was there on leave. Even at the beginning of the next century the wedding would often have to take place almost as soon as the ship bringing the bride arrived and certainly before it departed for Shanghai or Kobe, as she would have no home in Hongkong until she moved to her husband's.

Mrs. Dixon was, of course, by no means 'unprotected', either before her marriage or in 1870, coming from a Portuguese family well established in Hongkong. For Lysaught this was, perhaps, just the first instance when he would benefit from the freedom that his particular position gave him, especially when he started to visit Isabella at her family home, for had he, or Dixon before him, been in the regular police, their marriages would not have found favour with Captains Quin or Deane. Since it was not until the next century that the northern section of Pottinger Street was subsumed into the Compound, the annual Rate Books at this time usually locate the Central Police Station as being in this street, although occasionally its address is given as No. 10, Hollywood Road. The Pereira family lived at No. 8, so Lysaught's frequent visits could not have passed unnoticed.

The Inspector was genuinely fond of the two fatherless little boys, and the twenty-nine-year-old woman suited him well. Isabella, as she became known from this point, reverting back to her birth name, knew life in the Yard, and what was expected of an Inspector's wife. Dixon's will was finally proved at the end of May 1870, which, with his assets in Hongkong, some back pay due and the money released from London came to a little under $1000. Lysaught would have been alive to this, and the Pereira family's quite comfortable circumstances wouldn't have gone unnoticed either.

Little record exists of Isabella's father, Antonio Carolus Pereira, other than he came from Macao, but had lived for many years in Hongkong. His wife, Antonia Josepha, whose native language was Portuguese, was illiterate and spoke little English, but seems to have had her own money, since in 1882, (before the Married Women's Property Act, passed in Hongkong in 1885) she states that in 1857 she purchased I.L. 255a, a corner plot with openings onto Hollywood Road and Square Street.[97] The vendor had been the former Japanese sailor turned printer, Adonia Rickomartz, whose story, with that of his milliner wife Henrietta, is recorded in Susanna Hoe's *The Private Life of Old Hong Kong.*[98] The majority of the Pereira's children had been born in Macao, two sons finding work as clerks, but not rising to any great height or fortune before their early deaths, whilst the two daughters, Maria Antonia and Clara Maria, who did not follow Isabella into marriages, later benefitted from their mother's will and used their inheritance to acquire substantial properties in the much more desirable Rednaxela Terrace.

The pair were married on 31st August, 1870, once more at the Cathedral in Wellington Road, just as Isabella came out of her year's mourning for her first husband. Well established in the colony, Lysaught chose for his witnesses his sergeant in the Dockyard Police, John Jones, and two men from the regular Force.[99] Alvah Hazlett was the Inspector of Nuisances, a type of sanitary inspector, before the establishment of the Sanitary Department, having the full powers of a police inspector but paid for by the Civil and Lock Hospitals. The third man was James Livingstone, another 2nd class police inspector, but also with special

97 Will of Antonia Pereira, made 15th October 1882 and proved 28th April 1884. HKRS 144-4-519. I.L. = Inland Lot, the parcelling of land, all of it Government owned (aside from that of the Navy and Army), the leases of which were put up for auction and could be then subsequently resold.

98 Hoe, *The Private Life of Old Hong Kong,* pp. 91-92.

99 John Jones, a constable on the 1868 list, was the one man who 'changed his mind' and opted to stay in the Dockyard Force.

duties. Livingstone was paid for by the Registrar General's Department, and was Hongkong's Inspector of Weights and Measures.[100]

The arrival of their first child, two days after Christmas of same year, might have caused some comment and so one can imagine that Isabella's relative seclusion from the wider Hongkong society, tucked away in the Dockyard Station, would be some comfort, although one suspects that Isabella returned to her mother's house on the Hollywood Road for the actual birth. Maria Antonia Lysaught was christened on 4th January, taking the name of her godmother, Isabella's eldest sister, and of Lysaught's mother. The church records state that she is 'Anglo-Chinese', for the normality of inter-racial marriage in Macao meant that there was a tendency to assume that all Macanese were necessarily of mixed blood, but whatever their actual ethnicity, the Pereira family regarded themselves as Portuguese. Over the course of the next twelve years, Isabella bore at least eight or nine more children, with some uncertainty due to the lack of correlation between the Latin translations given by the Italian priests in their baptism and confirmation records and the names by which the children were actually known. Of those who would survive into adulthood, Elizabeth, Lillian, John Joseph, Margaret, James and Caroline, were joined, in 1889, by the couple's last child, Kathleen.

Life in the Naval Dockyard Police Force

The eighteen seventies saw growth and developments in the capacity and capability of the Yard. The largest structure was the great Steam Factory, described by the press as having an almost 'ecclesiastical' aspect, with forges and steam hammers.[101] The Turnery and Fitting Shop contained the huge lathes and drilling machines required to work on ships' engines, while a small steam engine, that was said to be the first machine made in Hongkong, drove the fans in the Foundry. The Boiler shed was by far the noisiest area, with the coppersmith's and the blacksmith's shop adding

100 These two inspectors were among the first of the Force to gain the benefit of a pension. Having served for 10 years they both retired in 1874, at 43 and 35 respectively and both received about 25-28% of their salary for more than forty years.

101 The details of the buildings in the Yard comes from a description in *China Mail* 11th July 1878.

their share to the immense din. The harbour-side was bounded by a new concrete sea wall, slipway and pier. The Yard was rightly proud of the great shear-leg, a static scissor-legged crane, that had been made on site and, installed near the end of the pier, was capable of lifting the engines in and out of the largest steamships, up to 50 tons in weight.[102] The store houses, both naval and victualling and the various offices, for the Commodore, the Master Attendant, the storekeepers and the many clerks and writers were mostly around the edges of the yard, while interspersed were lawns and flowerbeds, beds of ferns and even a tennis court. Above the offices was the accommodation for many of the British and Portuguese who were employed there. The Chinese came into work at 7am each morning through the imposing new iron gates, the only entrance from Queen's Road, and set into a palisaded high wall that ran the width of the Yard. It was the job of the police to ensure that only those hired entered the yard, and that all were searched as they left at the end of the day. It is unclear what facilities the station held: presumably, aside from the Inspector's room(s), a charge room and a cell would have been essential, but whether the police mess, for the single men, was attached to the police offices is unknown. It would appear that from the time of the increase in the Force numbers, some married constables had been recruited and were permitted to reside in the town. Some of the professions in the Yard maintained their own messes, hence the reference to the Engineers' Mess in 1870 which employed its own servants and coolies, but the Police had the running of a general canteen, which all those employed in the Yard could use.[103] In return for taking charge of this, any small profit the canteen made was put towards the Police Mess fund.[104] All these men could also use the facilities of the Royal Naval Canteen, an imposing building occupying some of the Blue Buildings, on the Praya, east of Arsenal Street.

It was this compact, noisy and increasingly busy world that the Dockyard Constables had to know inside out. With so many workshops

102 The largest shear-leg (2015), capable of lifting 8,700 tons, is in the Netherlands.

103 *Hongkong Daily Press* 5th July 1870.

104 *China Mail* 14th October 1881.

to patrol in and around, the Yard was divided into half a dozen beats, with constables responsible for individual beats and the sergeants taking reports from each regularly during their shift. At a later date it is recorded that men took six-hour shifts, alternating between the night watches and the day duties every two weeks.[105] 'Watchman' Gale, one of those brought in to replace the dozen or so who had left at the end of February 1869, presented his case to Magistrate Charles May in the April of that year, when he charged three men, one employed on a Government lighter and two boatmen of the Yard, with the theft of eight pounds of copper nails.[106] Before giving all three the choice of a month in gaol or an eight dollar fine, May, perhaps not *au courant* with the intricacies of the Force's recent history, having asked about their status, suggested that these men be sworn in as Special Constables to give them a little more power. Copper, brass and lead, which could find a ready and lucrative market in the town, were frequently found to be missing, maybe because those who chose to steal it became more inventive in ways to get it past the gate police. Naval Yard Sergeant Kerr charged Dockyard employee U-a-on with stealing two and three-quarter pounds of copper piping by hammering it flat and then concealing it in his shoes, whilst another man had four and a half pounds brass hidden 'in his girdle'.[107] In 1882 two and a half pounds of lead as well as copper was stolen by two men in March, and in October, Sergeant Vanstone and Constable Duffin found copper cut into convenient pieces being 'collected' by Wong Ahung and Cheng Ain.[108]

Other offences that the Force had to deal were issues concerning the resident Europeans and their Chinese servants, as in the case in 1870 where one of the engineers suspected four mess servants and a coolie of being involved in the theft from his chest of $280 and his gold watch and chain.[109] In 1871 John Sandford, described as a Special Constable charged Yep Asing, one of the police mess servants, before Mr May of stealing his silver watch. He sometimes lived in a room in the town, and

105 *Hongkong Telegraph,* 1st October 1891.
106 *Hongkong Daily Press,* 24th April 1869.
107 *Hongkong Daily Press,* 12th July 1877 and 1st August 1881.
108 *China Mail,* 21st March 1882 and 6th October 1882.
109 *Hongkong Daily Press,* 5th July 1870.

having a headache one morning at 11 a.m. despatched Yep there for a glass of 'medicinal' gin. He repeated this at 4 p.m., and then returning himself at 7 p.m. found the watch gone. The young Chinese woman, who described herself as his 'protectress' when he visited the Canton Bazaar house, had been in the room, and missed the watch after the second visit of Yep. Sandford had caught up with Yep in the early hours of the next morning, and, since the offence had not taken place within the Dockyard, had taken him to P.C. 71 to make his charge. The newspaper speculated about the second glass of gin: did Sandford ask for it because the first had proved an effective remedy or because it hadn't, or because another seemed like a good idea?[110] Most of the offenders were men who worked or had some business being in the Yard. The case of Lum Asz, described in the *China Mail* as a servant, but not of the Yard, who somehow got into one of the messes, and stole $90 worth of items from Isaac Adams, a carpenter's mate, is unusual. Lum was apprehended by two of the Yard police before his escape was effected.

Given the nature and size of machinery, there are surprisingly few fatal accidents reported from the Yard, but when these happened the police, as would the colonial force, sometimes had to investigate. One incident, which narrowly avoided being fatal, involved a young messenger getting caught by his queue in the revolving shaft that drove the machinery in the steam factory. Spun round at fifty r.p.m., the unfortunate man's feet battered the ceiling in, so hard was the impact, but luckily the mechanism was stopped in time, and he was found to have no injuries to his head, 'just' requiring his arm to be amputated on the *SS Melville*, the hospital ship.[111]

Men of the Dockyard Police

Ironically, pursuing a solution to the initial problem of desertion gave the Inspector and Commodore Jones a much greater problem of replacement and retention of personnel, since, as expected, when at their own suggestion all had been discharged at the end of February 1869, rather less than half then re-engaged. Such a sudden depletion meant

110 *Hongkong Daily Press,* 4th March 1871.

111 *Hongkong Daily Press,* 6th March 1865.

that Lysaught started his new role by still having to fill posts left vacant, including finding some men with sufficient experience to fill the sergeant positions. Watchman Gale, who was at the hearing when Charles May questioned their designation and John Wood, the Dockyard constable involved in the furious driving case were amongst these newly acquired men. Others are known because they caused more trouble for the Inspector, amongst whom were Joseph Egan and John Power, who were reported by Lysaught for insubordination and fined forty shillings each, or fourteen days in default thereof by Magistrate May.[112] William Whyte, the absconder who had not understood that an initial month's probation conferred an equal obligation on him to stay in the Yard Force for that time was another such man.

Whyte had been fined $10, but the question soon arose as to whether the civil courts had any jurisdiction over men employed by the Navy, given their somewhat ambiguous status. Lysaught did manage to find some reliable men, though, who, along with most of those who continued in the Force beyond 1869, allowed it to continue to function effectively, but one imagines that the Inspector and the Commodore were still frequently frustrated by challenges to their authority. In 1875 Commodore Jones persuaded the Governor to promulgate an ordinance to enshrine that authority in local law. As engagements were about to be renewed, the 'Naval Yard Police Ordinance, 1875' was passed on 16th February that year. Its threefold purpose was to ensure good discipline in the Force, giving the Commodore the same powers as the Captain Superintendent in relation to the men, and, in cases of neglect of duty or ill-discipline, to subject these men to the same penalties and sanctions as the Colonial Police.[113]

Disciplinary matters did occasionally appear in front of the Police Magistrate. Constable Hugh Lewis seems to have been dismissed from the Force when he was given a fine of $10 or three weeks in gaol for hitting his wife of one year.[114] Luckless twenty-two-year-old Constable Frederick Morris was found to be drunk on duty on New Year's Eve 1884, when he

---

112 *Hongkong Daily Press,* 4th July 1870.

113 *Hongkong Government Gazette,* 27th February 1875.

114 *Hongkong Daily Press,* 2nd September 1882.

should have been guarding the Naval Coal Store in Kowloon. Inspector Lysaught, suspecting that his inebriated state had aided the extensive robbery that happened from the Naval Sheds that night, brought him before Mr. H.E. Wodehouse, who gave him fourteen days hard labour in return.[115] A report of a case of embezzlement from the Yard Canteen in 1881 show both the normal procedures for disciplinary matters and the problems regarding the intersection of local and naval administration. Cornelius Conners was the Yard constable with charge of the Canteen at the time, and it appears that when the non-payment of suppliers was noticed, he absconded with $162. After vainly sending out a sergeant to see if he could be found, Lysaught had to report his desertion to the Commodore, who put out a reward for his return. Conners was found and arrested by Constable Northcote of the town police, and brought before the Staff Commander and Master Attendant, where he admitted to misappropriating $161 of canteen funds. The matter was placed before the Magistrate, who remanded him for the Criminal Assizes. However, it appeared that a loophole in the law, probably in connection with private associations (as the canteen was) on Naval property falling between the two administrations, meant that the charge of embezzlement had to be dropped. But in view of not being able to pursue this charge, the Magistrate then felt it necessary to give him the maximum punishment for his three and a half day period of desertion: six months in gaol.[116]

The only other sighting of Naval Yard Policemen in the records that have survived are the occasional listing by name of the inspector and sergeants in the *Chronicle and Directory of China*, and less frequently, in the *Navy Lists*. Comparing lists over the available years, the sergeants served two or three years before moving on, with only one or two remaining for longer periods and helping to give continuity to the force. During the last quarter of the nineteenth century, five, or occasionally six men are listed at this rank, the more permanent men being Nicholas Nolan (1874-1883); J. Vanstone (at least 1883-1889); W. Godwin and J. O'Toole (both at least 1889-1896). Godwin later moved to become the caretaker of a recreation ground whilst Vanstone stayed in a similar

115 *Hongkong Daily Press*, 20th February 1885.

116 *China Mail*, 6th, 7th, 14th and 15th October 1881.

profession and became a watchman at the Hongkong and Whampoa Dock Company.[117] The families of Nolan and Godwin were to intersect later with that of Newmarket's other original export, George Hennessy.

No official record of the pay of men in the Yard has come to light, but in view of their, admittedly intermittent, connection with the colonial force in the early years, it seems most probable that the pay of constables and sergeants was increased in 1862 and 1872 along with that of the larger body. But much later, in October 1891 a letter appeared in the *Hongkong Telegraph* that sought to bring the conditions of this hidden band of men to public notice.[118] Written by '*Truncheon*', in the long established tradition of anonymous letter writing in the Hongkong press, the pay and terms of the men are recorded and compared to that of the Hongkong Police Force. Although Truncheon wants his readers to know of the 'grievances' of these men, the letter is written as if by an outsider. However, that outsider has detailed knowledge. There are 32 men currently in the Force, he explains: 25 constables, 6 sergeants and the one inspector. The constables receive $40 per month compared to the town men's $50, with the same provision of clothes, boots and quarters, whilst the sergeants' pay at $45 per month is ten dollars lower than his Hongkong Police Force colleagues. But here the writer seems to be working with out-of-date information, since the regular Force pay that year had been increased to $60 per month for sergeants. However, he was correct to make the point that the men of the larger force can also receive extra allowances for telegraphic duty, good conduct, language proficiency etc., and have their half pay leave with passage home paid, and a pension to look forward to: not so the Yard men. The constable here may serve as many years as he is able, and still receive only his $40, unless a sergeant's post becomes available, and at the end has only any little he has been able to save to retire upon. Interestingly, Truncheon tells us that the inspector's salary is $100 a month plus free quarters, and thus the same as that of (the highest paid of) his opposite numbers.[119] Truncheon

117 *Hongkong Telegraph,* 15th November 1890.

118 *Hongkong Telegraph*, 1st October 1891.

119 Again, his figures for the town police are inaccurate: the three classes of inspector were paid $80. $91 and $114 per month.

considers that, since the men must be of equally impeccable character, there should be parity between their pay and advantages. It is interesting to speculate who might have written such a letter. It might, of course, be Lysaught himself, or just possibly one of his senior sergeants, but if so, they would surely have followed the more direct and well-trodden course of a petition to the Admiralty via the Commodore. To have access to the pay rates, especially that of Lysaught, as well as the hours of duty, suggests that it must have been an intimate acquaintance of the inspector. But surely the mistake about the new salaries excludes his Hongkong Force peers: more probably it was one of his former colleagues who had moved to a different government department, but signed himself with this soubriquet 'in memory' of his time in that Force. Just possibly, it was written by Lysaught's close business associate and personal friend, J. J. Francis, Q.C., who never shirked from 'standing up for the little man'

Otherwise, until close to Lysaught's retirement in 1894, the Dockyard Policemen disappear from view in correspondence sent back to the Colonial Office or the documents of the local government. Lysaught's team of sergeants changed gradually over the years, and one imagines that the personnel as well as the work of the Force settled into a regular pattern. Inspector Lysaught's duties had a settled routine and it was less than ten years after his arrival in Hongkong that he seized the opportunity the city presented to start to build his family's fortune.

Chapter Three

Inspector Hennessy's world

In the last quarter of the nineteenth century Hongkong grew both in commercial importance and as a city, with many trading companies being formed and the population increasing by 30% in the years 1876-1886.[120] The pressure on space became acute, with complaints being levelled at the government on the one hand against the creation of ghetto-like Chinese districts and equally against the encouragement given by maverick Governor, John Pope Hennessy (1877-82) for the Chinese to occupy more central and mid-level areas thought of as exclusively European.[121] To address this problem more permanently, his successor, George Bowen (1883-85) put in train what would become the Praya Reclamation Ordinance in 1889, and formed the Sanitary Board to attempt to implement the regulations of the Public Health Ordinance, addressing some of the worst living conditions in the colony. For the Police, 1884 saw the opening of the splendid new Water Police Headquarters in Tsimshatsui, but the Fire Brigade were kept busier than ever with an alarming increase in the number of fires in the city, which ensured that the insurance firms advertising daily in the newspapers had plenty of clients.

But for some thoughts were turning homewards: George Hennessy's first term as a colonial policeman had expired back in March 1878. For many this would mean their happy return to their homeland, some useful experience and just a few pounds saved. Then likely would follow

---

120 *Historical and statistical abstract of the colony of Hong Kong, 1841-1930* records the Chinese population growing from 130,168 to 171,290 and the non-Chinese from 8,976 to 10,412 in the period.

121 Arguably the governor least popular with the European community was a Corkman and a Roman Catholic.

re-enlistment into a home Police Force and he would certainly have tales to tell that would ensure he would be stood a drink or two in the mess or in the pub. But alternatively, application could be made to remain in the Force, and if accepted, men could then apply to take a maximum of nine months leave, during which time they would receive half pay and a return passage. It was, however, not uncommon for men who intended to make this their career to remain (working) in the colony instead, for which they received a gratuity of three month's salary. For a young constable, who might be rather 'short' living on half pay and who was not permitted to marry until he reached the rank of sergeant, 'going home' could seem an expensive fool's errand, since for many the prime attraction of home, aside from a respite from the oppressive climate, was the opportunity to find a suitable bride to take back. Hennessy applied and was accepted for a second term, and took the more remunerative option, so that he would look forward to his first home leave becoming due early in 1884.[122] In his Rough Book he records family deaths that had occurred since he had left: the only one of his married sisters who had not emigrated died, along with her husband in the summer of 1879 or 1880, his father in 1881, all known, of course, only via correspondence; his mother was to die on 16th April 1890. Whether he was remitting money home is open to question for there is a 'town memory' that castigates him for leaving his poor mother unsupported, but perhaps he was simply organised and forward thinking, for he managed to save $4000 from his pay by the time of his 1884 leave, an amount on which he could consider setting up a decent home for a wife and being able to educate his children.[123]

With this nest egg and the prospect of further promotion in the near future (he had already had a short period as Acting Inspector, third class, in 1882 when five of the full Inspectors had been on leave) Hennessy looked forward to returning to the colony with a bride and making of a home for her.[124] For him, as with some of the men who were intent on a career in the Force, stability and the chance of a family life held greater attractions

122 When leave was commuted, the nine months then worked did not count towards the next period of five years, although it was pensionable service.

123 From the 1897 documents in *CO129/277* p.226 from Acting Deputy Superintendent Mackie's letter in support of Hennessy.

124 *Hongkong Telegraph* 14th April 1882.

Sergeants Hennessy (right) and Stanton (left) (from Hennessy's private collection, courtesy of the Police Museum, Hong Kong)

than hard drinking in the canteen or the club. But for those less domestically inclined, there was one, probably two Police Clubs, outside the Central Station, as well as more general establishments, including the Cosmopolitan Club in Staunton Street to which sergeants and inspectors could belong, alongside the lure of the brothels reserved for Europeans ('European women's houses', as they were politely known), close at hand in the eastern part of Hollywood Road. Hennessy would later claim, and was able to call on fellow inspectors to testify, that he had kept his liquor tab to below $5 each month and did not visit the brothels.

Hennessy must indeed have been a frugal man. The context of the information about his savings suggest that it was not acquired from 'irregular' earnings or back-handers. For reasons already mentioned, it is difficult to find out exactly what a junior member of the Force earned over a period, but putting the available information together, it would appear that Hennessy's regular pay for the time from his joining to his 1884 leave was $5,780. Add to this his Fire Brigade service, worth $684 and allowances for medals another $345. He received a gratuity of three month's pay as a sergeant in 1878 in lieu of leave, giving him another $135. More speculatively, he is recorded as doing telegraph duty and theatre duty at times. Over the period these might have earned him another $168, and the allowance for his role as Acting Inspector over the years 1882-84 another $84. The total now comes to $7,196 over the eleven year period. Saving $4,000, without the help of any little 'squeeze' money now looks a little more possible, but he would have lived all those years on an average of twenty-five dollars a month.

Back to Newmarket

Hennessy's leave started on 1st April 1884, and he would be due back on 1st January of the following year.[125] Arriving in London six weeks later, after a more comfortable journey than that of ten years earlier, one wonders whether he might first have stopped to 'look up' some of his former colleagues before taking the boat train to Holyhead. After weeks at sea the crossing of six hours in a small steamer passed very quickly, but afforded him the pleasure of the first sight of his homeland on that late spring day, a moment frequently anticipated during long hours on duty. By contrast, the long, slow train journey to Mallow through Maryborough (Port Laois) and Limerick Junction, and then on the Killarney line out to Banteer (actually called Kanturk at the time, but situated near the much smaller town of Banteer) must have seemed frustratingly slow. Compared to the rush and bustle, (although not actual speed) of Hongkong, and the efficiency of trains in England which reached 70 mph and more, the smaller trains on many route in Ireland were much slower (although on eastern and midland routes not the ubiquitously sluggish turf trains). The connecting line to Newmarket was some five years off, so his final nine mile journey would be horse-powered, but if the light held, at least gave the compensation of reminding him of once-familiar landmarks on the final leg of his homeward journey.

Brothers John and George Hennessy, father and uncle to Sergeant Hennessy, are held to be 'blow-ins' to the Newmarket area, some years before the great Famine of the 1840s. Both appear in Griffith's Valuation Tables, renting houses from their immediate neighbour farmers, in townlands to the west of Newmarket. George Hennessy rented a house and a garden from Murtogh Sullivan of Barnacurra whilst his brother John (the policeman's father) had settled in Glenlara after marrying Mary Ann Barry of that townland on 3rd March 1835. A little better placed, Griffith records them having tenancy of a house with garden and 'office' (probably an outdoor privy, or perhaps a shed or cow house) in Glenlara. His immediate landlord was Michael Kinneally, who with his brother, farmed much of the land around. The Poor Law Union were entitled to collect rates of 12 shillings p.a. from the tenant. The two townlands lie

125 Recorded in Police Defaulter's book, *CO*129/277 p.228.

each about four miles to the west of Newmarket, Glenlara being roughly a mile and a half north of Barnacurra. The town of Newmarket itself was, in the mid 1880s, a thriving community, with a high street full of shops, a Post, Money Order and Telegraph office, a branch of the Munster and Leinster Bank, a doctor and a veterinary surgeon, a large Protestant church and a larger Catholic chapel. A new creamery, Newmarket Dairy, took the milk of the surrounding farms, and two large horse fairs each year aside from the monthly cattle market would attract a great influx from all the small villages around, being some of the principle fairs of North Cork. Twenty four and more licensed houses to serve the thirst of the hard working populace would ensure that the members of the Royal Irish Constabulary could not return too early to their barracks near the church on Fair nights.

The Irish summer and autumn gave Hennessy a time to regain his strength, even in the small Glenlara cottage, where he was reunited with his mother, now aged 80, who lived with an unmarried daughter, the other siblings having, by this time, all emigrated to Queensland, Australia. There is no trace of his uncle, John Hennessy or his family by this time but his connection with the older man's former landlord remained, and Hennessy took his share with the work on Murtagh O'Sullivan's farm.[126] He found the work hard going: city life, it seemed, had softened him in unexpected ways. Despite his limitations as a farm labourer, O'Sullivan welcomed him, and in the evenings his stories of the exotic East and of brave police escapades found ready audiences amongst the young family, especially the eldest children: Margaret, Patrick and Mortimor, aged 9, 8 and 7 respectively. It was by introduction to Murtagh O'Sullivan's brother, Thomas, at his farm a mile or so closer to Newmarket, that Hennessy met his future bride. Bridget had been born in Curraduff, Newmarket during the summer of 1855, the second child of Hanora MacAuliffe and Thomas O'Sullivan, and at 29 was relieved by the offer of marriage from a local man who seemed to be making a good career for himself.[127] She married

126 The son of Murtogh Sullivan who had employed John Hennessy. From this period onwards the "O" seems to be established in family records.

127 Parish records Newmarket Church , death notice - *The China Mail,* 25th December 1888 & memorial stone.

Hennessy on 25th September 1884 in Catholic chapel in the town and the couple probably spent the first weeks of their marriage in her family home. They set sail back to Hongkong in the middle of November on the *SS Tasmania,* and amongst their fellow passengers were the publisher of the daily newspaper *The China Mail,* George Murray Bain and his wife and Hennessy's colleague Thomas Campbell.[128] Like so many a new colonial bride, Bridget would have to cope with the rigours of the six week journey, through the Mediterranean and the Suez Canal, then via India, Ceylon and Singapore whilst in the early months of pregnancy. Sadly, we have no account of the voyage from her.

The Hennessy family in Hongkong

Mary Georgina Hennessy, born on 1st July 1885, and known as May, appears in the baptismal records for 13th August. The couple had two further children, both girls, Honoria Agnes, known as Cissie, born 6th September 1886, and Margaret born in 1888.[129] There is a noticeable gap between the births and baptisms of the girls (Honoria was baptised on 4th November, some eight weeks after her birth) which might not have been out of the ordinary in an Anglican or Protestant household, but is unusual in the Roman Catholic tradition, particularly at this time. In the records in Newmarket, where the birth date is recorded, baptism almost invariably takes place the next or following day, for the family would be anxious to have the child christened as soon as possible. A healthy child would be taken straight to the font by the father and a female relation, together with the sponsors (god-parents). Infant mortality being such an ever-present reality, not to have the child baptised would, should it die, doom it to an eternity in limbo. In Hongkong, though, there was greater fear from taking the child out, and exposing it to the unhealthy climate, and 'vapours', which, together with the lack of female relatives to take charge of such matters, seems to mean that it was left until the child's busy policeman father could make the arrangements.[130] Similar delays in

---

128 *The China Mail* 1st January 1885.

129 Calculated from her appearance in the 1911 Census of Ireland.

130 The Chinese traditional belief in illness, especially malaria in Hongkong, deriving from foetid miasmas from newly turned or disturbed soil, which found

baptism have been found in most of the Catholic families in this study, through to the 1920s. Of Margaret, the third daughter, born on 14th December 1888, there is no trace in the baptismal records. It might be speculated that the births of Mrs Hennessy's daughters took place in their quarters, and in particular the last, which would have been at the time the couple were living above No. 2 Station in Wanchai, which was the other side of town from the Government Civil Hospital. That facility, provided specifically for police and civil servants and their families, along with the less than sanitary conditions of the dwellings of the European working class meant that hospital births were not so rare as they were in the rural parts of the home countries at this time. However, there was one European midwife to attend a birth at home, and Bridget would have been supported by the wives of other police, and by her particular friend, Mrs Margaret Nolan, wife of Gaol turnkey Nicholas Nolan.

At what point and how did George Hennessy and William Lysaught become aware of each other's presence in the colony? Sadly, the former's wonderful Rough Book doesn't have an entry of the type "Today, 10,000 ship miles away from home, I met Inspector Lysaught, a man from a farm not five miles distant from Glenlara." There is nothing to show that Lysaught kept in close contact with his family in Co. Cork in those early years, but from Hennessy's record of, admittedly, later correspondence, it is likely that Newmarket knew that he had gone to Hongkong soon after he arrived. So therefore, if the men had not met through their work, and a constable would not have presumed an acquaintance with an inspector, they were likely informed of the other's existence by letters from the Newmarket community. Bridget, living closer to Newmarket than Hennessy's family, almost certainly knew of Lysaught's sister's family, the Murphys of Island, and would be eager to make the acquaintance of the dockyard family when she arrived in Hongkong.

St. Joseph's Catholic Church on Garden Road, the church where the Hennessy daughters were baptised and made their First Communions had a large contingent of Irish amongst its congregation, including the wives of soldiers and police, and with an active St. Patrick's Club, provided a

---

ready acceptance within the European community, including members of the medical profession.

meeting place for the women. Shortly after Hennessy had first arrived in Hongkong, this church had been in the final stages of completion when it was destroyed by the 1874 typhoon, but with the generous support of the community, of many faiths, it was rebuilt within two years.[131] The sponsors of the Hennessy girls are given as Thomas Campbell and Maria Nolan (for Mary Georgina) and Catherine O'Sullivan (for Honoria, known as Cissie). Campbell, a fellow officer in the Police held the rank of sergeant, and unusually, was for some nine years after his official retirement in September 1888, retained as Assistant Engineer in the Fire Brigade, with his pension held in abeyance.[132] Maria was the daughter of friends Margaret and Nicholas Nolan, but Catherine O'Sullivan is a mystery. It may just be a coincidence of surname, or indeed a mistake, but it is tempting to speculate that this may be a sister of Bridget's, brought out to help with the children, and to keep an eye out for a potential husband. The only fragment that remains as family memory of Bridget's life in Hongkong is that it was in 'the garden' that she and Margaret Nolan agreed that her first daughter, then a year old, would be promised to Margaret's son, Nicholas, ten years old at the time. What is meant by 'the garden' is unclear: no plans of either the Central Station or the Gaol provide evidence of a garden, or space for such. If Margaret Nolan lived in the Gaol then it may be that the women were walking in the Botanical Gardens, or the gardens around St. John's Cathedral or St. Joseph's Church. No doubt the term was quite explanatory to them. The Hennessy family moved in early 1888 from the Central Station to quarters above No. 2 Station, on the corner of Wanchai Road and Praya East (now Johnston Road). Here they were close to a number of police and government families, as the area was being developed as the primary residential location for the European working class.[133] Mrs. Hennessy would have been pleased to remove her young family from the crowded and rather dilapidated married quarters of the Central Station. With the

---

131 ed. Ticozzi, *Historical Documents of the Hong Kong Catholic Church.*

132 A curious point here is that whilst his pay as a Sergeant had been some $540 p.a., with an additional $90 good conduct allowance, and pay of $144 as Engine Driver (in 1883), in retirement he was paid the princely sum of $1080 p.a., being $360 more than the (presumably senior) Engineer, Mr Kinghorn.

133 Crisswell & Watson *The Royal Hong Kong Police (1841-1945)* p.80.

harbour to one side and Morrison Hill to the other, it must have seemed a far healthier part of the town in which to live and although the noise from the godowns along the Praya, particularly those to the east, could be incessant during the day, it would not be far to walk to take her little girls to play on grassy slopes.

In late November 1887 an epidemic of smallpox broke out, and initially it was not deemed to be particularly severe by Dr. Ayres, the Colonial Surgeon, with thirty-nine cases being admitted to hospital in the last two months of the year, of which six were fatal. However, fearing worse, a concerted effort was made to ensure that as many of the residents of the colony were vaccinated against the disease as could be managed.[134] At first the project ran aground through lack of available vaccine, and January 1888 was a very bad month for the colony, with hundreds of cases reported. The Smallpox Hospital was straining at the seams with eighty-four patients in that month, whilst many of the Chinese preferred to be treated more traditionally at the (Chinese) Tung Wah Hospital or were hidden at home, and by the time the epidemic petered out in the spring the disease had claimed 470 Chinese and 29 foreign lives. The European contingent of the police had been particularly hard hit, with two Scotsmen dying, and another eight spending periods up to nine weeks in hospital. Amongst these two brothers from Co. Fermanagh, in the north of Ireland, Galbraith and Thomas Moffat were admitted on successive days in January, and between them spent eleven weeks as patients.[135] Dr Ayres noted in connection with this that the dormitories in the Central Police Station were very overcrowded, and it was common

134 Report of the Colonial Surgeon for 1887 *Hongkong Government Gazette* 14th July 1888. Untreated, smallpox generally had a mortality rate around 33%.

135 Colonial Surgeon's Report for 1888, *Hongkong Government Gazette* 13th July 1889. Neither brother was destined to make 'old bones'. Galbraith transferred to the Sanitary Dept. in 1893 as an Inspector of Nuisances. During the 1896 recurrence of the plague epidemic, he caught the disease and died within a few days, infected, it was believed, when he had to move a much decayed plague corpse in the course of his duties (*Hongkong Daily Press*, 15th June 1896). Thomas remained in the Police, where he rose to First Class Inspector, but was retired on medical grounds in March 1900. He appears in the *Blue Book* list of pensions (page I 148) for that year, and the Census of Ireland the following

for infection to spread via blankets and bed linen. Only three Chinese policemen were treated in the hospital, and all recovered.[136] However, when vaccine became more readily available the take up throughout the population seems to have been considerable, likely because inoculation against the disease was in accord with Chinese medicine, and indeed, the practice there predated western scientific discoveries by some centuries. Bridget Hennessy would have been able to have her children inoculated, and would have hurried to do so when Inspector Quincey's five-year-old son caught the disease. The Government made compulsory the vaccination of all infants over six months, and by the time the Colonial Surgeon was writing his 1887 report, in May 1888, all the prisoners in the gaol had been inoculated, and the practice of vaccinating all new policemen had commenced.[137]

But their new quarters could not protect the family from all the perils of life in the tropics. Bridget Hennessy had celebrated the beginning of her new life in Hongkong on New Year's Day, 1885, as they arrived in the harbour on *SS Tasmania*. Sadly she saw only three Christmases in the colony, as a short little note in the *China Mail* on Christmas Day, 1888 recorded:

> *"DEATH On the 23rd inst. at No. 2, Police Station, Bridget Bertha, the beloved wife of George Hennessy, Inspector of Police, aged 33 years and 6 months. Cork papers please copy."*

Bridget, like so many European women in Hongkong at that time, died shortly after the birth of her third child, suggesting that perhaps Margaret's baptism was an emergency one, and was missed from the parish records. Bridget's tombstone, an imposing granite tablet, records

---

April, but not further pension books, suggesting that he died early in 1901, aged 38.

136 It is possible that some of the relatively high figure of ten deaths amongst the Chinese contingent in 1888 were due to smallpox, as the men frequently travelled back to their homes on the mainland when they were sick rather than face treatment in the Civil Hospital.

137 Ordinance No. 1 of 1888, Compulsory Infant Vaccination Ordinance, *Hongkong Government Gazette* 4th February 1888.

the same information as the newspaper notice.[138]

George Hennessy and babies in 1889 (courtesy Hennessy family)

What would have been the options for Hennessy regarding the care of his infant daughters following his wife's early death? Children of families further up the social scale were sent home to relations as a matter of course, for Hongkong was not considered a suitable climate for a child. This was not an option for Hennessy, if for no other reason than his lack of suitably placed relatives at home. It is possible that they stayed in his quarters in No. 2 station and were cared for by an amah: certainly they would have had a nurse whilst their mother was alive, and since the mid-1860s almost all such roles had been occupied by local Chinese women. Of course, if Catherine O'Sullivan was indeed a relative of his late wife's, she may have stayed to keep house for Hennessy and look after her nieces, but this remains speculation and without any foundation in family memory, either. The position of this police station is significant, for further up the Wanchai Road William Lysaught owned property, and his family, with daughters in mid to late teens, may have lived there. Later records show that the two families were on good terms, it is tempting to wonder if the children were cared for there.[139] This becomes a more likely surmise when it is noted from newspaper reports that Hennessy was moved first to

138 Originally in St Michael's Roman Catholic Cemetery, Happy Valley, later moved Chai Wan Cemetery.

139 Henry Dixon to the Postmaster General, 2nd November 1899, CO129/294 p 306-7.

No. 7 Station soon after Bridget's death. The cramped married quarters, directly above the station, were in a very poor state of repair, with a public latrine just below the windows on one side. Hard up against the poorest part of Hongkong, Taipingshan was certainly an unhealthy environment for a young family. Their late mother's friend, Margaret Nolan, was in no position to help with the care of the small girls, aged three and a half, two and a few months, since she had become Matron of the Gaol, i.e. in (sole) charge of the female prisoners, in December 1887. This kept her fully occupied, as she had to attend to anything up to 210 women in any year, and was often managing twenty convicts in the two rooms allocated.[140]

The girls education would have been put in the hands of the nuns of the Italian Convent at Caine Road or the School for European girls run by the French Sisters of St Paul of Chartres in Wanchai, both with boarding sections, into which Hennessy might have persuaded the nuns to take his babies, for his duties would take him out at all times of the day and night, often necessarily into the filthiest parts of town. That they stayed in Hongkong is known not only through family recollections and photographs of the girls at different ages with their father, but also by a little clip from the newspaper of 1895, reporting the Children's Party at the Central Police Station, where the elder two girls won places in the races, and from their presence in the passenger list of *SS Pekin* when Hennessy took leave on 11th April 1895.[141]

Inspector Hennessy's working life

Of Mr Hennessy's career at this time there is more to be gleaned from the *Blue Books* and the newspapers. Initially he was appointed as Acting Inspector, 3rd Class from 15th April, 1886, with the substantive promotion on 7th February 1887, his Fire Brigade Service Certificate recording the earlier date, as, from that time, he had to resign from the Brigade. His pay rose to $840, which, whilst a considerable increase on

---

140 Report of the Superintendent of Victoria Gaol for 1887, *Hongkong Government Gazette* 31st March 1888, and the Gaol and Prisoner Reports published yearly in the *Blue Book*.

141 *Hongkong Weekly Press* 17th Jan 1895 and *Hongkong Daily Press*, 11th April 1895.

his sergeant's salary of $624, lost him the additional $96 that his recent promotion to Foreman in the Brigade had given him.

Towards the end of the century a growing amount of police time had to be spent on traffic management in the narrow and crowded streets. Not only was it almost impossible to persuade the coolies to drive their rickshas only on the left, but pedestrians of all nationalities seemed deaf to appeals to keep to the pavements, great groups of sailors often to be seen, for example, walking six or eight abreast, completely blocking the road to any other users. In November 1888 Hennessy was appointed Inspector of Vehicles, a role that was primarily concerned with the registration and licensing of public rickshas, sedan chairs and the ever-increasing number of animal-drawn trucks, together with their drivers.[142] He was also responsible for controlling the numbers of vehicles permitted and designating stands and waiting areas for the whole colony, a task that must have kept him very busy alongside his normal work as a Third Class Inspector. However, since it came with an extra $120 p.a.allowance, Hennessy was not going to refuse the work.

In their uniform of fine blue cloth suits with white braid on the jacket in winter, and white light duck (canvas/linen fabric) suits in summer, white covered helmets with blue silk puggaries (thin scarves encircling the crown of the helmet and hanging down at the back to protect the neck from the sun) and frequently carrying their swords, the inspectors were easily recognised and certainly held in greater regard by the late 1880s and 1890s than at any time previously. Usually a total of twelve men, as the highest ranking policeman that the public would expect to encounter, the individual men became known to the local community both European and the established Chinese residents. The imposing figure of George Hennessy was a familiar sight both in his district and at the Magistracy, thus ten years later the Hongkong Telegraph recorded his apprehension of a potential house-breaker and known criminal thus:

> *"As Inspector Hennessy was taking a quiet stroll at five this morning in Hollywood Road, he observed a hawker coming along, the abnormal bulk of whose sleeve excited the sharp-eyed Irishman's suspicions.*

142 *Hongkong Daily Press* 2nd November 1888.

> *Desiring to have his suspicions either confirmed or dissipated, he stopped the hawker and proceeded to tap his sleeve, in which he found an apparently harmless piece of cloth, but upon unfolding the cloth, it was found to contain a very respectable stock-in-trade for any one desiring to enter the house-breaking business, namely a small bundle of joss-sticks (to keep the devil off while premises were being burglarised), 6 skeleton keys, two sharp-pointed instruments, and a piece of charcoal. A further brilliant discovery rewarded the early hours of the Inspector, who, on searching the hawker at the Station, found in his purse 2 small keys which had been filed, a box of lucifers, and seven pawn tickets, the lucifers being doubtless intended to strike a light with in case European bed-rooms might happen to be too dark for the burglar's purpose. There is no doubt the enterprising hawker was proceeding on an extensive marauding expedition when he was, so luckily for the community, overhauled by the Inspector. The prisoner, who has been in gaol before, was remanded for a week, upon the application of Mr. Hennessy, to allow him to make further enquiries.*"[143]

This case does not reappear in the papers. The stopping of 'suspicious characters', very often involving a brief chase followed by a scuffle, from which the Chinese man came out the worse, was such a commonplace event as not to get reported in the papers unless there were other factors involved. When a sergeant, back in 1880, a report appears of his stopping a chair coolie named Nam Atse, who claimed to be returning home from supper with a friend at 4 a.m., but since he was without light or pass, Hennessy brought him to the Police Station and arrested him. He was there found to have two former convictions for larceny, the latter, a month earlier, had resulted in him being bound over for the sum of $50 to be of good behaviour. Breaking that lost him the money and gained him a month with hard labour.[144]

The pattern of duty for the four inspectors usually based at Central Police Station in Hollywood Road was designed so that in any twenty

143 *Hongkong Telegraph* 2nd May 1892.
144 *China Mail,* 7th February 1880.

Governor's inspection and parade at Central Police Station, mid-1890s

four hour period one man was on continuous duty in the charge room, receiving reports from the sergeants and constables, submitting requests for warrants for searches and arrests, overseeing the custody of those brought in and determining the course of action needed to keep good order in his district. Another man would be on duty in the Magistracy, or Police Court, to deal with the cases of the previous day, when that inspector had generally been on duty in the charge room and thus knew the background of the case. A further man would be in charge of the whole district during daylight, performing at least a two hour patrol and responsible for the discipline of the men, and the preservation of law and order, with yet another taking over that responsibility between 6pm and 6am. Captain Superintendent F. H. May reported this when giving evidence at the trial of Job Witchell in 1897: this was not an innovation he had introduced, but an established pattern.[145] This routine could roll almost indefinitely, since men, including the inspectors, had just one day off per month. That would be covered easily at the Central Station, and

145 Statement of F. H. May at trial of Job Witchell, *CO*129/276.

in other stations the inspector's place would be taken by a senior sergeant. Wanchai was at the time quite a minor station and appears to warrant only one inspector, since it was a less populous part of the city, really only growing substantially with the land reclamation in the early years of the twentieth century. This inspector would, with the help of his sergeant, take all the roles as best he could. With a usual pool of just twelve inspectors and a chief inspector, the Captain Superintendent could allocate four men to the Central Police Station, one for the Wanchai stations (nos. 2, 3 and 4), one each No. 7 Station (Western) and No. 5 Station (the Fire Brigade headquarters), Shaukiwan, Tsimshatsui and Yaumatei, and one for the Water Police. [146]

However, he would also have to accommodate the one or more who would likely be on leave at any time and any engaged on duties for (and paid by) other departments, such as Public Works, the Harbour Master or the Sanitary Department. The other stations either on the Kowloon peninsula (Hung Hom) or on the south side of the island (Aberdeen, Stanley etc.) were generally run by a resident sergeant.

As Inspector, a flavour of his working life can be found through the reports of the cases in which Hennessy had a hand. The earliest dates from April 1882, when, during his first spell as acting inspector, he took part in a raid on a gambling syndicate known as the 'Innocent Celestials', comprising mainly of chair coolies, and arrested twenty men, who were subsequently all given the choice of fines or a term in Victoria Gaol.[147] Criminals apparently guilty of the more serious felonies might be arrested by the constable on his beat, but it was the inspector who was responsible for collecting the evidence and presenting the case before the magistrate. In September 1887 Hennessy brought to court one Leung Ashin charged with the murder of a coolie over some bits of cotton stuff, and the next year brought to the magistrate a man charged with running an illegal lottery, a serious crime in the eyes of the Administration.[148] Hennessy's Rough Book included, as did so many policemen's scrapbooks, cuttings

---

146 In the years before the development of Kowloon, Aberdeen and Stanley each had a resident inspector, as shown in the Chronicle and Directory of China 1874.

147 *Hongkong Telegraph*, 14th April 1882.

148 *China Mail*, 2nd September 1887, *China Mail*, 5th April 1888.

from the papers relating cases that he conducted. The case, in October 1887, of a murdered five-year-old girl, was one which he investigated right from the outset, and obviously affected him deeply, as it is well represented here.[149] Thomas Henry Legg was a sailor, out of work at the time of the tragedy, living with his Chinese wife Amni and three girls on the second floor of a house in St Francis Street. Amni Legg had adopted all three girls, whether Legg was the natural father to any or all is uncertain. On the evening of Wednesday, 5th October Legg returned home at around 6pm, expecting to find his daughters busy there, but the house was quite dark and silent, and indeed he had to '*break open the door*', having found it closed. Touching the foot of the little girl lying on the bed board in the kitchen did not elicit a response, and putting his hand to her face he realised that it, and the bed around, were wet. He took a lamp, and then found his youngest child, Achan, quite dead, her throat gashed from ear to ear, and a razor resting on her hand, with his eldest daughter, seventeen-year-old Tai Yuk, sitting on the side of her bed, apparently stupefied.

At the police station Hennessy agreed at once to come, and heard the man's story as they returned. Arriving at the house he went first to the older, apparently sick, girl. Whilst it appeared at first sight that she had been drugged, he found nothing amiss with her eyes, no smell of any substance on her breath, and she was quite able to move herself. Her feet was stained with blood on the soles, and there were footprints leading from the murdered girl's bed to where Tai Yuk lay. Achan had been dead some time for the blood from the deep wound in her throat had dried, and the child's body was quite cold. Hennessy summoned an ambulance for Tai Yuk, who was taken to the Government Hospital where she 'came round' when violently resisting the wardmaster's efforts to get her to swallow an emetic to rid her of any drug. She then started to tell her story. She had spent most of the day dozing and sleeping as she had a headache, but had to attend to her little sister from time to time. She was again sleeping when awoken by men demanding entrance. Achan let them in, and the men grabbed hold of the girls and demanded

149 This case was well covered by the local newspapers (*Hongkong Daily Press, Hongkong Telegraph, China Mail*) from 7th October 1887

they tell them where their parent's money was, threatening them with a razor taken from a drawer in the kitchen. Achan was put onto the bed in the kitchen, threatened again and then cut, the second cut killing her. Tai Yuk was then dragged to the bed under the stairs and forced to drink some bitter substance, whereupon a disturbance in the rest of the house caused the men to leave.

Hennessy was not satisfied by the girl's accounts of the events, and over the next few days conducted extensive interviews in the neighbourhood. Together with the medical staff, he was quite sure that Tai Yuk was shamming her drugged state. This was rather confirmed when a neighbour, one Mr Roach, testified to having seen her a couple of hundred yards from her home at 4.30 that afternoon, and he had remarked upon her agitated, excited condition to a companion. She had gone into a shop further along that road, and there purchased a tiny amount of opium, according to the witness of the shopkeeper and two other people. The blacksmith, Yan A Un, who occupied the ground floor, had returned home from work shortly after 4.30 pm and had tried to get Tai Yuk to clear a mess of urine that had dripped from their floor into his room. It was not until 5.15 pm that he saw Tai Yuk on her verandah and was able to get her to come down. Tai Yuk's disposition through the inquest was reported as cheerful and entirely unconcerned, her response to the reports of her being seen was simply that these people must have been mistaken, she was indoors all afternoon, and most of the time she was asleep. Although there seems to have been no concealment that she was being detained on suspicion of having caused Achan's death, and she was cautioned by the Coroner that she need not answer questions, she seemed convinced of her own innocence, and remarkably unworried by the implication of the statements being made, even if that conviction was well founded.

The little Achan had lost her short life in a matter of moments: there were no marks of violence on her, other than the incisions, and no signs of a struggle. Nor had she been drugged before her death. The fatal wound had been made by one deep, swift cut from left to right. In summing up, the Coroner, Mr Wodehouse established the time at which the murder, if committed by Tai Yuk, must have taken place and the sequence of events should that be so. Against this he reminded the jury of the complete absence of motive; of the absence of blood on her clothing; of her demeanour in court and to consider if such a young girl could really commit such a dreadful crime. If both Tai Yuk's story and the evidence of the various third parties was correct, it would seem that the narrow time frame for the murder, less than hour before her father arrived home, would hardly fit with the state of the little child as Hennessy found her at 6.20 pm.

But perhaps Tai Yuk was born under a fortunate star, for after just fifteen minutes the jury returned with a verdict of wilful murder against some person or persons unknown. George Hennessy did not record his reaction to this in his Rough Book, but one rather suspects that he breathed a sigh of relief.

Another of Hennessy's cases where the truth remains elusive is that of West Indian seaman John Delanchi.[150] On the evening of 12th March 1889 Delanchi was brought into No. 7 Station and charged by Hennessy with cutting and wounding a young Chinese man in East Street, Taipingshan. The story was that the seaman had gone into a secondhand clothes shop, asked to see some shirts, then run off with one of them. Cheong Chun, the cook at the shop gave chase, followed by a shop assistant. As the cook approached Delanchi, the latter drew a sheath knife from his hip pocket and drove it into the side of his pursuer's chest. He escaped, only to be caught by the assistant, who received a slight slash on the hand for his efforts. Again Delanchi fled, and threw the knife away but was caught by a District Watchman, who took him into custody. The next morning, just before Delanchi was due to appear before Mr Wodehouse, the news came through that the cook

Magistrate Henry Ernest Wodehouse (courtesy Nigel Wodehouse)

150 Reported in the press from 13th March 1889.

had died in the hospital in the early hours, and the charge was amended to one of murder. Rather like Tai Yuk, Delanchi remained apparently quite unconcerned through the magistrate's proceedings. At one point he was even left unsupervised in the charge room of the Central Police Station, with ample opportunity to escape, but did not bother.

However, Delanchi had one person to testify for him: Joseph Olson, an unemployed fireman, who lived in the same boarding house as the prisoner. His story corresponded with Delanchi's: that they were taking a walk when a Chinese man carrying a cup came and hit Delanchi on the nose with it, drawing blood. Olson persuaded his friend to let it be, and they continued on their walk. On their return, however, they found about ten Chinese, armed with sticks, who set about them. Olson ran off, but Delanchi was caught by the men, and drew his knife, initially to frighten them, but ended up using it in self defence.

The tenor of the newspaper reports indicates that the shop assistant's story was believed over the West Indians'; however, the Defence Counsel's reminder that all the witnesses for the former story came from the clothes shop, or were friends of its proprietor was not lost on the jury. Delanchi was found guilty of manslaughter, and given a term of three years with hard labour, with the judge describing his actions as 'reckless use of a murderous weapon'. The papers had described John Delanchi as a 'rough-looking sort of fellow', with what would now be offensive and unacceptable descriptions of his physical appearance, but the prejudices are not only in the reporting of the case but run right through it, and are shown on all sides with the Chinese taunting of the West Indian, his disregard for the Chinese bystanders. The judicial system perhaps comes out a little better since a three year term was lenient for a manslaughter conviction. But in contrast to the newspapers, beside the pasted-in reports of this case in his Rough Book, Hennessy wrote of Delanchi: *"And he was one whom any woman might be forgiven for loving."*

Inspector Hennessy and the other five hundred men of the Police Force patrolled the streets, lanes, alleys and paths of Hongkong day and night, week after week through the chilly winters and the oppressive humidity of the summers. Respite came only with their long awaited leave: every five years for the Indian and Europeans, annually (for two weeks) for the Chinese. George Hennessy himself might be growing stouter and grey with the passing of years, but the crimes he encountered towards the end of his career differed little from those at the start. Now he would frequently take charge of cases reported to him, but he was still on the beat, apprehending criminals himself.[151] Likewise, he and his colleagues would not infrequently find and tackle fires whilst on their rounds, sometimes coordinating the Brigade's response to more serious conflagrations.[152]

151 For example, a joint raid on an illegal lottery with Inspectors Hanson and Mackie (*China Mail*, 28th November 1894).
152 *China Mail*, 26th September 1896, reporting a small house fire which Hennessy and the occupants of the house successfully extinguished.

Chapter Four

Pride before the fall – a respected force

Twenty years on from their arrival in Hongkong that grey morning in 1873, four of the London men: Joseph Corcoran, William Stanton, William Baker and George Hennessy were still in the Force, and Nicholas Perry had retired as an inspector just a couple of years earlier.[153] All but Baker had already joined the team of 12 inspectors, and Corcoran would become Chief Inspector in 1895. Working alongside them were three men from the Scottish intake of 1872, and one Chinese man, William Quincey, recruited by Captain Superintendent Deane in to the European contingent after a British military education, and in charge of the Detective branch from 1891. Deane himself had retired on 1st November 1891, and after an interim period when the Force was lead by Major-General A.H.A. Gordon, the Assistant Colonial Secretary and former Cadet, Francis Henry May had assumed command on 11th February 1893, aged 32.[154]

153 Having retired on pension through ill health, Perry returned to England, where, when recovered, he rejoined the Metropolitan Police. After the events of 1897, he applied, unsuccessfully, to rejoin the Hongkong Police as Chief Detective Inspector. His pension records (24th March 1891) are in CO129/249 pp 305-322, and his letter of reapplication (27th Oct 1897) is at CO129/280 pp 420-424.

154 Francis Henry May, b. Dublin, 1860, d. Clare, Suffolk 1922, entered the Colonial Civil Service as a Cadet for Hongkong, held posts of Private Secretary to Governor Des Voeux, and of Assistant Colonial Secretary and Acting Colonial Treasurer before his appointment as Captain Superintendent of the Police Force in 1893. In 1902 he became Hongkong's Colonial Secretary, administering the colony a number of times during the absence of the governors. He moved to Fiji in 1911 as Governor, but returned to Hongkong in that role the following year, retiring due to ill health in 1919. A fluent speaker of both Cantonese and Mandarin, whilst a Cadet he co-authored a book on the local language with his

A terrible duty: the Great Plague of 1894

For many in the neighbouring regions (of China), Hongkong was seen as a convenient source of employment. Canton was less than a hundred miles from Hongkong, and a few hours by boat, and with fares kept low through competition between rival steamer firms, the colony regularly saw 11,000 passengers per week disembark from the Chinese city. However, such easy movement between the two jurisdictions meant that it was more than just goods and people that made the journey. A fierce epidemic of bubonic plague, thought to have appeared first in the Yunnan province of China, carried there via the trade routes from India, had arrived at the start of 1894 in Canton. There it had claimed scores of thousands of lives, and early in 1894, after an exceptionally cold and dry winter, a few cases, isolated and without a particular pattern, began to be found in Hongkong.[155]

However, as the temperature rose, so did the frequency of cases, with the very great majority in the notorious Taipingshan. This squalid settlement lay a few hundred yards to the west of the Central Police Station, and some streets in from the shoreline. Densely packed tenements which had no sanitation and little access to light or ventilation proved ideal breeding grounds for the disease, which by May 1894 had reached epidemic proportions. The Colonial Office in London, anxious primarily about the fate of its European subjects and the stability of the colony, telegraphed for a detailed report. Four days later, on 20th June, Robinson replied in full.[156] By this time 2,552 Chinese residents and two British servicemen had succumbed, although the former figure is likely to be well short of the actual total, as it did not include those many who died after fleeing to the mainland, nor those whose presence in Hongkong was merely temporary.[157] Almost *en masse* the response of the Chinese was to leave the island as soon as possible and to return to their home villages, often carrying the disease there. Contemporary estimates, reported by

---

teacher in Canton, and was the first Governor of Hongkong to rise from local Cadet ranks.

155 Pryor, *The Great Plague of Hong Kong*, p.61 ff.

156 Governor W. Robinson to Marquess of Ripon Secretary of State for the Colonies, 20th June 1894. *CO*129/263 pp 457-478.

157 Starling, ed. *Plague, SARS and the story of Medicine in Hong Kong*, p 27.

the Governor to London, were of 80,000 having done so by the time of the Despatch: in the order of half the colony's population. With crippling effect on industry, trade, commerce and shipping, Robinson described the epidemic as *"an unexampled calamity"*.[158]

But, albeit with limited understanding of the origin or transmission of the disease, the Administration had, through lack of preventative action in the earliest days, allowed the plague to take hold. As Elizabeth Sinn, in *Power and Charity: The Early History of the Tung Wah Hospital, Hong Kong*, demonstrates, racial chauvinism prevented the ruling classes taking note of the warnings that were coming both from the north and even from their own Colonial Surgeon, and pay little heed to the damage the influx of 40,000 people into Hongkong for Chinese New Year in March 1894 might do. Seen as essentially a Chinese matter, borne of over-crowding and unwholesome living conditions, only when business interests and European lives were threatened did the administrative response commence. Then it was swift, and to a large degree effective in containing the epidemic. The Sanitary Board met almost daily, addressing the emergency with a directness that brooked no opposition and won general commendation from the Europeans and some of the prominent members of the Chinese community. The Board was given the authority to draft in men from the Royal Artillery, the Royal Engineers and Shropshire Light Infantry to carry the work of finding and burying the dead, cleansing and white-liming, to disinfect, the many hundreds of infected homes. The Police coordinated much of this (with men from both the Chinese and European contingents acting as interpreters), and when temporary accommodation on ships moored off Kowloon was found, had to persuade the residents, who were at best suspicious, and often hostile, to move there whilst their homes were cleansed. Makeshift hospitals had to be established, with the Police struggling to persuade or coerce plague sufferers' relatives to move them there. The affront residents felt for this summary invasion of their homes, the lack of proper burials for their dead, the gulf between traditional and contemporary western medicine, and their intense distrust for the latter, meant that these were no

158 Robinson to Ripon 20th June 1894 paragraph 32. *CO*129/263 pp 457-478

ordinary logistical tasks, but frequently involved conflict and violence.[159] The police managed to control the worst outbreaks, and although they frequently encountered resistance, apparently no complaints concerning their behaviour in these endeavours were lodged.[160]

Plague duty, with its inherent dangers, was not imposed upon the members of the Force. All were volunteers, with some, like Hennessy, working for limited periods as the need arose, whilst others worked through the months May to September. For most, these duties were on top of their usual work, since the labours of the criminals of Hong Kong was one of the few businesses not impaired by the plague, although with such a migration out of the colony, actual levels of crime did drop markedly whilst the epidemic was at its height. Hennessy was now based in the Central Police Station where he occupied one of the married quarters, perhaps with his three girls, for although the rooms were still in a bad state, and funds had been requested for their refurbishment, they were larger and better sited than those at No. 7 Station. With the lack of understanding about the way this disease was spread (indeed, smoking was advocated as one of the best methods of protecting the police and soldiers from infection), he would not have worried unduly that he could bring this "Chinese" disease into his home.

The plague continued to menace the colony through the summer months and in succeeding years until at least 1929, and although not causing the disruption to trade and loss of life on the scale of 1894, its suppression remained a high priority for the government, aided in succeeding years by better understanding of the disease and its spread. In March 1895, the police engaged on Plague duty, some sixty-three in all, from the three contingents, were decorated for their valuable work at a medal presentation attended by the Governor and members of the

159 Although the soldiers' task of white-liming houses took them frequently into the worst of squalor, it can be imagined that they were none too particular as to how the painting was done, and returning residents would find any possessions not removed treated to the same process.

160 *Hongkong Telegraph* 1st March 1895; *Hongkong Daily Press* 2nd March 1895, Report of the presentation of medals to the Police Force. Against this, it could be argued that many of affected: those being moved around, hospitalised etc, were in no position to submit formal complaints.

Plague Committee.[161] A lack of actual medals meant that only five were given on that day. The others, including Hennessy, received theirs some weeks later. His is now on display in the Hong Kong Police Museum on Coombe Road. Members of the Sanitary Board were also honoured for their work: May was appointed Companion of the Order of St. Michael and St. George (C.M.G.), whilst others, including some of the clerks of the Sanitary Dept, received handsome silver mementoes for their efforts. Mr. Francis Q.C., who as one of the non-governmental members, had worked particularly hard, attending almost every meeting during the course of the plague to his own significant cost, through having to neglect his legal practice, had been presented with a silver ink-stand. The local community was greatly surprised by this, feeling him deserving of the same recognition as had been afforded Mr. May, and the latter was also dismayed at the slight to his colleague, and petitioned London for amends to be made.[162] But Francis' outspoken style and frequent spats with government departments on behalf of his clients irritated the Colonial Office in London, who refused to accede, and the barrister's publicly expressed disgust in a typically hot tempered letter to the Governor, which Francis then made public, did not help his claims.[163] Francis duly returned the ink stand to the Government, with instructions that the proceeds should be used for the benefit of the colony.

Creeping progress towards a healthy Hongkong

Fifty years of development of the commercial hub of the China trade had brought some benefits in terms of the overall health of the population, plague and epidemics excepting. The draining of malarial areas, and better treatment of the disease had led to far fewer deaths than in earlier times, although the 1890s had been seen a higher incident of malarial fever

---

161 *Hongkong Telegraph* 1st March 1895; *Hongkong Daily Press* 2nd March.

162 "The Services of Mr. J.J. Francis Q.C. during the Plague in Hong Kong", report by F. H. May 19th June 1895, CO129/270 pp 397-402. May stated that, making allowance for the slackness of business during the time, he had it on authority of solicitors there, that Francis had turned down in excess of $5000 of legal work, his practice being the largest in the colony.

163 Mr. J.J. Francis to Governor Robinson 27th May 1895, CO129/267 p. 510-520.

than the previous decade. Dysentery, diarrhoea and its accompanying fever, caused in large part from polluted food and lack of sanitation, which killed so many of the troops from the earliest times to well into the 1870s was becoming more avoidable. Rudimentary standards of hygiene in food production and sale were gradually being developed, with some control over the abattoirs by the Sanitary Board and the erection of new markets.

However, even with the building and extension of reservoirs to provide a more reliable, clean supply to the island, water remained a precious product, and insufficient to even consider any significant water-borne sewage system. A drainage system had made progress in the intervening period, so that many European-style houses were connected to the main drain to dispose of waste water. However, the poorer areas only had the street drain in the larger roads, and nothing at all in the alleys and lanes which spread, capillary-like, through the town. Some of the European-style properties were built with earth closets, but with the necessary earth having to be brought some distance. Together with the difficulties encountered when boring holes sufficiently deep in to the hard rock of the island, such toilets did not become common, although an invitation to tender for supply of earth to the Central Police Station suggests that, at least for a time, some of the privies here were of this type. For the most part, the time-worn system of 'night soil' prevailed still, and would beyond the middle of the twentieth century, whereby waste was collected nightly from the European and wealthier Chinese properties, twice weekly in the poorer parts of town, and transported to the mainland, where it was sold and used as fertiliser.

The majority of the European population were, to some extent, insulated from some of the hazards that lurked in the congested areas either, in the case of the more prosperous, by living on the higher reaches of the city, or for those of more modest means, in Wanchai or the more spacious Kowloon, and generally in houses with bathrooms and proper, if separate, kitchens. The diseases that Colonial Surgeon Dr. Phineas Ayres classified as due to filth, viz., typhus, cholera as well as outbreaks of smallpox and measles were thus less frequent visitors to their homes, but for the rest of the colony, such ailments were rarely far from the surface.[164] Maximising occupancy and minimising expense were the governing principals for landlords, both Chinese and European, and the doubling of the Chinese population of Hongkong in the years between 1873 and 1896 played into their hands. Ayres was careful to make a distinction here between the condition of the houses and that of its occupants. He recorded that the people living in these dreadful tenements were not *per se* poor, and he had seen in Hongkong no poverty approaching that which he had encountered in London or India. Indeed, many were well clothed, and ate well, but had no option but to be victims of the greed of landlords. Thus all had to share space where rooms were subdivided in to three or four cubicles in the horizontal plane, and into floors and cocklofts, giving additional 'mezzanine' levels vertically. Generally the ground floor of these houses did not have the benefit of any properly constructed floor: at best ill-laid, quickly broken tiles, and frequently just compacted mud served. Ceilings and thus floors for higher levels consisted of timber boards unadorned by plasterwork, but maybe with a mud mix to ostensibly 'seal' the inevitable cracks and joins. Walls, especially those between cubicles, were more flimsy still, providing often only a rudimentary privacy for the occupants. Built usually three or four times deeper than the street face, the tenements often backed directly onto the next street's houses, with only a small alleyway, or at best a tiny yard separating them. Thus, further than the first ten foot or so, light did not penetrate; neither did fresh air. Most had no chimneys: a smoke hole was cut near the back of the property, which relied on gravity and luck to direct the smoke accurately up successive storeys to the roof. In the 1870s most tenements had been just two storeys high: now, twenty years later, Dr. Ayres reported that usually these houses had three or four storeys.

Just as any tenant of a cottage in Ireland would try to find the money to have a pig or two, and maybe a few chickens, even if there was only

164 During his long association with the colony, Dr. Ayres wrote frequently on the state of the town houses. His reports at the time of the plague e.g. Medical Report on the Epidemic of Bubonic Plague in 1894 (*Hongkong Government Gazette* 13th April 1895); Report of the Colonial Surgeon for 1894 (*Hongkong Government Gazette* 17th August 1895) provide vivid accounts of the living situation of the majority of the population.

a mean patch of 'garden' around the place, so did many, especially the families, who had often come from rural life in China. But in Hongkong there were no gardens, so animals, generally pigs, sometimes even cows, were kept indoors, sharing their space with their owners. The lack of effective disposal of human waste from houses in these streets, lanes and alleys caused a grave health risk, when animal waste was added the result was foetid and stinking. One paragraph, typical of many examples Ayres gives in his 1894 report, serves to illustrate:

> *Take another gully with no name, one end opening into Caine Road just below Dr. Adams' house, the other end into Market Street. This gully is floored with a platform of boards raised about two feet above the ground, the earth below is sodden with black liquid filth, and underneath this footway fowls are kept which afterwards go to the markets. Houses here are cramped up little hovels with filthy floors, and the inhabitants are licensed to keep pigs to the number of ten each.*

Ayres continues:

> *An intimate acquaintance in the course of my student life in hospital practice with the worst quarters of Lambeth, Saint Giles, and Somers Town, enables me to say, I do not believe there could be found in London worse places than are to be found in Hongkong, if so bad …*[165]

Since the Building Ordinance of 1889, newly constructed houses did usually have cookhouses, often at the back of the building, yards and alleyways or 'scavenging lanes', and an attempt, only partially successful, had been made to limit the depth to width ratio.[166] As a later report showed, light and ventilation differed little in houses built in accordance

165 Report of the Colonial Surgeon for 1894, *Hongkong Government Gazette* 17th August 1895.

166 *Hongkong Government Gazette*, 2nd February 1889, affecting primarily those well to the west of Victoria or in Wanchai.

with the Ordinance to those of earlier date.[167] The cookhouse was often as tall as the building itself, connected by a bridge across the yard at upper levels and thus the open space between the accommodation of the building was subdivided into spaces too small to bring light or fresh air to the rooms. For the majority of the quarter million Chinese population and some of the Portuguese, Indians and Europeans, 'home' was a dark, small, airless and smelly space, shared with dozens of others, and that was quite impossible to keep clean. They endured floors that could not be washed because of their construction, walls and ceilings that became thick with greasy soot, fluid waste of all descriptions finding its way through cracks or creating noxious puddles for the unwary foot. Even the battle-hardened Dr. Ayres confessed to occasionally being unable to enter a property due to the extreme stench.

Inevitably, the most congested areas were also the location of most crime. Just as inevitably, with the need to attend and investigate here, the police were exposed to disease on a far greater scale than their office-bound civil servant contemporaries, so the risk of encountering this enemy was a far greater threat than any injury they might have received at the hands of Hongkong's criminals. Potentially taking infection back to their overcrowded quarters, some of which reached no very satisfactory level of construction or cleanliness themselves, especially in the toilets and cookhouses, helps account for the rates of hospitalisation of these men. Ayres comments, in successive issues of his Report to the Government, that the police are most frequently afflicted by diarrhoea, various *'febrile complaints'* and bronchial conditions. A policeman could consider himself very fortunate if he completed a year without spending some days of it in hospital.

The plague had claimed the lives of seven policemen, all from the Chinese contingent: five constables; a sergeant and a sergeant-interpreter. The Indians and Europeans of the Force had come through the epidemic fairly well in terms of their health, for unbeknownst to them, it was more likely to be the thick boots and puttees they wore than the smoking of pipes that prevented their infection as they traipsed through plague

167 Report on the Question of the Housing of the Population of Hongkong, *Hongkong Government Gazette Extraordinary*, 10th June 1902.

ridden and rat infested parts of the town to facilitate the work of the disinfecting troops. While the general health of the men was far better than it had been twenty years previous, the Acting Colonial Surgeon in his 1895 report called it a 'remarkably healthy' year for the European contingent, May still had to calculate for significant absence.[168] The Reports do not reveal the numbers of days lost, or the length of hospital stays, but from the 112 men in this section, there were 96 admissions to hospital. Assuming a (probably very conservative) estimate of five days stay per admission, this amounts to 480 days lost to the Force.[169]

The gamblers' grand opportunity

The pattern and relative proportions of crime during the summer of 1894, whilst lower in overall numbers, differed little from any other year. The plague perhaps provided a certain amount of 'cover' and the removal of a small proportion of the Force from their crime prevention and detection duties aided those criminals who forswore their 'annual vacation' for the pickings the unusually quiet city might offer. But one group of criminals had their activity made considerably easier through the unprecedented and sudden availability of empty cubicles, floors and whole houses in the most affected areas.

The deployment of some of the police on plague duty had brought a few changes in arrangement of the European contingent, with Sergeant William Baker becoming an Acting Inspector, and stepping into the gap left by Inspector Aeneas Mann, who, in charge of part of Taipingshan, had used his local knowledge to help co-ordinate the campaign in that part of the city. Acting Inspector Baker, in what would prove in the months to come to be rather a poisoned chalice of a job, took over responsibility for the northern part of this area, and heard reports from his junior colleagues of illegal gambling flourishing in the area between Hollywood Road and Western Market. These streets, just a little north of those most densely packed alleys where the plague was centred, consisted of the usual sort of

---

168 More modestly, the Acting Captain Superintendent called 1895 a '*satisfactory*' year in terms of health in his report, but the previous year, despite the Plague, May had regarded as '*very satisfactory*'.

169 The Acting Colonial Surgeon's Report for 1895.

houses in this part of town, quite flimsily constructed 'shop houses', with a shop or workshop on the ground floor and residential accommodation above. Some floors were occupied by just one family, whilst many others were rented out in the usual cubicle fashion. It was an easy matter to create alternative entrances to any property through the adjoining walls or even via the lofts and roofs, and now the flight of so many Chinese back to the mainland as the plague gripped meant that the gambling dens had the potential of a real warren of space in which to operate - and to evade disclosure.

Despite a series of measures taken by the government against the formation of specifically Chinese gaming clubs, a steady procession of cases came before the courts, and so it was perhaps the one of the Police Magistrates, H.E. Wodehouse or Commander W.C.H. Hastings R.N. who, in 1894, noting how often Baker applied to him for a warrant to search houses hereabouts, alerted Mr. May. Finding that fourteen warrants had been taken out in the ten week period from Baker's promotion until early October for just one road, Wa Lane, May asked for a report. Baker explained how, at Nos. 4 and 6, Wa Lane, he would arrive with his men to find no games in play, and no gamblers on the scene. The empty rooms had strong doors, escape ladders and sometimes some discarded gambling gear, but no one to arrest, the players having made their exit by way of no. 5. The syndicate employed a great many watchmen, who were cheap and easy for them to find now, since the great decline in trade since the epidemic started had put many of those who stayed out of work. These watchmen ensured that the Central Police Station was monitored whilst play was in progress, and kept Queen's Road, Hollywood Rd, Possession Street and Lower Lascar Row under observation, thus creating a cordon of alarums round the gambling dens. He knew that he was watched whenever he emerged from the Central Station, and more than suspected that play stopped the moment he set foot in the direction of Taipingshan. His information was thorough, being able to submit the names of the gambling masters for each house, and recommending their banishment from the colony.[170]

170 The material connected with the Wa Lane gambling scandal of 1897, CO129/276 p. 386ff..

There is no further mention of this problem: the documents in the colonial records appear in connection to events three years later, and May makes no special reference to gambling in his report for the year, nor did Commander Hastings (then Acting Captain Superintendent) when reporting the following year. It would seem that this particular den was broken up to some extent, for after a flurry of fruitless warrants in November 1894, one eventually resulted in the arrest and conviction of seven men late that month, with just a few skirmishes in the first half of the next year.

After the months of plague in 1894 the cooler weather of autumn came as a great relief, and the colony began to emerge from the ravages of disease, only to be battered by a huge typhoon during the daylight hours of Friday, 5th October. According to 'old hands' quoted by the *Daily Press* the next day, this storm was just as fierce, with winds quite as strong as that of September 1874. In fact this proved not to be the case and the difference now was that Hongkong knew of its coming, so *'all the hongs and stores closed their doors before tiffin'* (lunch) and all but *'a few unbelieving natives'* had ensured their small craft were safely moored.[171] There was still considerable damage to property, and some loss of life, but on nothing like the scale of that two decades earlier. On this occasion, the police were much in evidence, with Sgt McIver and Constable Macaulay receiving particular mention, having come to the aid of the *'hapless sampans'* still out in the harbour.

But Hongkong was getting back to normal, and even a typhoon could not deter the gang who, as evening fell and the storm started to subside, chose this excellent opportunity to break into a shop in Jervois Street, (then) just back from the western Praya. Holding the occupants at gunpoint, they committed one of the larger robberies of the year, getting away with $740 worth of jewellery, money and clothing. Captain Superintendent May later complained about the passivity of the victims of this and similar outrages, for despite the assistants in the shop outnumbering the robbers, the latter had a free hand, and then the shop workers were extremely reluctant to help in the identification in any way. Although Triad involvement in the gambling dens was well known, there

171 *Hongkong Daily Press,* 6th October 1894.

is no suggestion here that there was any intimidation of victims, rather, as May saw it, something near a conspiracy to frustrate the workings of (foreign) law and order.[172] He resumed his complaints two years later, with reference to the proliferation of brothels all over the city, following the repeal of the registration ordinance. Lots of grumbling had been heard, but the Chinese community were quite unwilling to pursue their grievances in the Courts. Why, he seems to wonder (in keeping with colonial attitudes), do the Chinese not avail themselves of the huge benefit of British justice? Needless to say, the Chinese point of view was not examined. The following year crime was reported to be up by 85% with only cases of robbery with violence and kidnapping lower than had been reported earlier in the decade; three murders, eighty-one burglaries and over 2000 reported thefts kept the case books full. Although trade had now resumed, the economy and the livelihood of many of the residents had taken a severe blow, and much of the small scale crime had its origins in the straitened means of the returning residents.

The coolie strike

With cases of plague still occurring, although now in much reduced numbers, plans for the registration of all common lodging houses (where the majority of the transient Chinese male population would stay), which had been proposed in 1891 but dropped because of Chinese opposition, were now revived in earnest. An 'information campaign' was attempted to try to allay fears that this was a preparation to impose taxes or in some other way disadvantage both the Chinese lodging house owners and their immigrant clientele. However, when the regulation came into force in March 1895 the lack of any cooperation from the owners showed how unavailing this had been. The government's coercive tactics that followed were met with a stoppage of some dockhands which quickly spread to become a general strike of coal and cargo coolies working in the ports, involving an estimated 20,000 men. Such action could easily paralyse the functioning of the colony, a situation that could not be permitted, especially as trade had suffered so severely the previous year. Thus measures were swiftly taken, with the military brought in to discharge

172 Report of the Captain Superintendent of Police for 1894.

the vessels now lining up in the port, with the police giving protection to them, and to those coolies who could be found to work. Hennessy's former London colleague Inspector William Stanton engaged these latter men, working, as it were, on behalf of the employers. Initially he had to offer the men the high wage of a dollar a day to overcome their fear of the strike gangs, but later, and to the employers satisfaction, was able to bring this down to 75 cents per day. Hennessy, meantime, undertook to procure the services of sufficient launches and cargo boats in place of those 'impounded' by the striking workers. Many of these were crewed by the Water Police and so able to ferry the goods from the ships at their off-shore moorings. Despite continuing intimidation of the newly hired coolies, the abundance of labour meant that the strike was broken, and normal port business resumed early in April, alongside the registration of the lodging houses. Both men were publicly thanked for their services by Captain Superintendent of Police May in his Police Report of the year.[173] More personally, Hennessy received a letter from the Governor William Robinson (dated 11th April 1895):

> *"The Captain Superintendent of Police having brought to my notice the voluntary work performed by you beyond your ordinary Police duties during the recent strike, it is my pleasure to convey to you an expression of my personal thanks for the zeal and energy which you have displayed in furtherance of the public interest.*
> *"I have also noted with much gratification that you voluntarily postponed your departure from the Colony on well merited leave until the strike was terminated."*[174]

A professional force

The epidemic and its aftermath had been the testing initiation of the man who had succeeded Deane as the head of the Force. A more than competent administrator, May's conservative approach was met with general approval of both the Executive Council and the press. The experience gained

173 Report of Acting Captain Superintendent of Police 1895.

174 From Hennessy's Rough Book, although the page with this letter affixed is now in the Police Museum.

him an overview of policing in Hongkong and an understanding of the changing situation of mainland China and the impact of that on the colony. As crime, its detection and prevention, returned to the forefront of his mind, May made efforts to better coordinate the policing of the colony in general.[175]

The District Watch Force had been the successor of measures taken early in Hongkong's history by the Chinese business community to protect their property and enterprises. In the first two decades, aware that the Police Force had little concern for non-European affairs, and distrustful of the efficacy of their methods anyhow, individual firms had, as already seen, employed guards. The need for a specifically Chinese security force was obvious, even to the reluctant members of the Administration, who in 1866 were persuaded to allow its creation primarily because it would be almost entirely funded by the merchants themselves. What emerged was a force that compromised the wishes of both sides, with too much government regulation for the Chinese and too little accountability for the British. However, contrary to the latter's expectations, the District Watch Force, based entirely in the 'Chinese' side of Victoria, west of the Parade Ground, consistently helped the police in the arrest of thieves and robbers. Whilst the early Police Force came under regular attack for their inefficiency, this group met with general regard, especially from the Chinese business community. The area was subdivided into five beats, not especially allied to those of the Police Force, with each beat patrolled by a group of eight men under the charge of a Chief Watchman.[176]

In succeeding years the District Watch Force was to be rather subverted by the Administration into assisting the Sanitary Department, but was later returned to something more akin to its original purpose, although with yet more official control. In 1894 May had joined the District Watch committee, and understood this force to be clearly an auxiliary police force, and although still quite independently funded, he maintained that it should be allied closer to the regular force. This aim he achieved in 1897, when Watchmen were distributed according to police beats, and

175 Report of the Captain Superintendent of Police, 1897.

176 The history of this Force is covered in Hamilton, *Watching Over Hong Kong: Private Policing 1841-1941.*

came under the direct ambit of the sergeants and inspectors supervising those areas.

Meanwhile, under increasing pressure from public opinion in the British Isles, which deplored the invasion of privacy and liberty that enforced inspection of prostitutes suggested, as well, of course, of the apparent sanctioning of immorality, the Administration was forced to rescind the Contagious Diseases Ordinance of 1867, although this had many supporters within the colony, not least amongst 'respectable' brothel owners and the women working there themselves. Initially the inspections continued anyhow, voluntarily attended by the women, until late in 1890 the premises had to be abandoned.[177] The Women and Girls Protection Ordinance of 1889 which replaced the earlier act dealt powerfully with those who attempted to bring females into the colony for the purposes of forced prostitution or concubinage, or traffic them in any way, but it could not address the health of the established prostitutes. Predictably, infection rates rose: Welsh makes the point that among the British troops in India, which saw a similar withdrawal of the Contagious Diseases Act, incidence of the disease doubled, so that by 1890 half of the army was infected.[178] Amongst the Police in Hongkong the rate initially shot up to 21% in 1890 from 4% in 1885. It then dropped to 13% three years later, and 1894 was healthier again in this regard, but then many of the brothels frequented by the police were closed due to the plague.

Late in 1894 May petitioned for a group of trained policemen to come from the home forces, with the result that ten men from the London Metropolitan Police Force arrived on 9th March 1895, and settled well and quickly, except for the poor man who cut his throat a fortnight later. Another eleven men joined the European contingent that year. Eight were locally recruited, of whom six were dismissed at the end of their probationary months, whilst three others were brought out from the British Isles. Two of these would be prominent members of the Detective

177 Phineas Ayres, Colonial Surgeon, remarked in his report of 1891 that the women attended for weekly examination with great diligence, and, when they needed to be admitted, were grateful and cheerful. He recorded how the return from leave of the Lock Hospital matron, Mrs Ackers, was *'much to the delight of her little patients.'*

178 Welsh, *A History of Hong Kong*, p. 265.

Force in years to come, William Murison, later Chief Detective Inspector and Edmund O'Sullivan, of Newmarket, Co. Cork. A younger brother of Hennessy's late wife, the correspondence which preceded his arrival is lost, but it is a reasonable assumption that Hennessy, frequently in contact with Bridget's relations back in Newmarket, should have proposed such a course. According to family memory, Bridget's brothers were quite a 'rum lot', many involved in the political activism of the region, with the exception of Edmund, who was of a quieter and more serious disposition, and remembered as the gentle 'Uncle Eddie'. Edmund O'Sullivan joined on Monday 11th February, and after the customary six week voyage out, was keen to learn his police-craft from his new colleagues, for, like almost all the subsequent Newmarket men, the only training he had received to date was for the life of a north Cork farmer.

When dismissals and resignations (particularly including those at the end of contracts) were taken into account, the European section had just kept it strength intact by recruitment during the first half of that year. But, as the months went by, May, and his deputy, Commander Hastings, realised that there would have to be another application to the London Force and on 28th August 1895 the Governor, William Robinson, requested permission to recruit eight more men, the selection to be undertaken by May, who was to be on leave in London. Whilst the Colonial Office gave their permission, the Metropolitan Police, tired of being used as a nursery for the colonial forces, refused to provide the full number, allowing only five to be spared, thus leaving the Captain Superintendent to recruit as he could, by making personal application to other of the home forces, and perhaps finding a few individual men who would be worth accepting without prior police experience. Robinson had also proposed some changes to the conditions of service, with which May had been involved with before his departure. A few were mere details. e.g., the men were to be given the money to buy boots, rather than these coming from the stores, others included the tightening up of stoppages for hospital stays, but one, much further reaching, attempted to set down an entitlement for the men to have half their pay eligible for the Exchange Rate Compensation Scheme. The home government, however, baulked at the idea of enshrining this last to print, suggesting rather that men were informed of it, and that they would be entitled to this for so long as it applied to Civil Service positions in Hongkong.

Sir Henry May (from Hennessy's private collection, courtesy of the Police Museum, Hong Kong)

As the countries of Europe moved to gold as the measure of value, the price of silver started to fall after 1870. Initially this was no collapse, as its value was kept up both by its continued acceptance in India and a strong demand for silver in the United States, which, although on the Gold Standard from 1873, bent to commercial pressure, and at one point even promoted a bi-metal Standard. However, with the growth of more international financial markets, the decline was inevitable, and the once near-universal silver dollar could not compete. In Hongkong the sterling price of the dollar dropped from 4 *s.* 4 *d.* in 1872 to 3 *s.* 7 *d.* in 1882; 2 *s.* 8 *d.* in 1892 hitting its lowest point in 1902 at just 1 *s.* 7 *d.*.[179] This was just 36% of its price thirty years earlier, and reflected a 60% drop in the price of silver in London.[180] However, for the European residents, who were paid in dollars, fixed by a nominal rate from a sterling salary figure, the effect was not too serious in the first half of this period. 1873 had seen the beginning of a general depression which affected much of Europe and the United States. The latter country climbed out of it to a more stable position by the end of that decade, but in the United Kingdom the period of deflation continued for another ten years and more. For the European community in Hongkong this resulted in a reduction in price of the many imported goods they consumed, which largely offset the reduced value of their dollars.

179 *Historical and statistical abstract of the colony of Hong Kong 1841-1930*, quoted in Sayers p. 143.

180 From 60 *d.* per ounce in 1870 to 24 *d.* per ounce in 1902. Chiang Hai Ding *The Origins of the Malaysian Currency System (1867-1906)* p. 18.

But during the last decades of the century, trade increased with the United States, where prices had levelled and were starting to rise, outstripping the savings made on shorter freight journeys of European-style produce, whilst deflation in Britain gradually turned into inflation and higher import prices in the colony. The Colonial Office had to take notice of the implications for the hundreds on the Government payroll in the Straits Settlements and Federated Malay Straits as well as Hongkong. For example, a man entering employment in 1890 when the dollar stood between 3 *s.* 1 *d.* and 3 *s.* 5 *d.*, had seen the sterling value of his salary cut by a third four years later, when the rate slumped to 2 *s.*. It took the revival generated by the First World War to overturn this slide.

A pay rise of between 14% and 33% in 1891 for all the European civil servants, and others in some departments had eased the problem for a time, but local prices, too, were rising, with rent increases affecting those further up the career ladders who did not have the advantage of barracks or quarters provided. The slide of the dollar impacted on how much money these men could send home. A constable who wanted to send £5 home to his mother and sisters in 1884 would have to save $28 from his pay of $40 a month. Now ten years later, although his monthly pay had increased to $50, he would now need to save $50. His situation on leave was not too bad: he would be grateful to have the unusual benefit of holiday pay, for although he only received half pay, this would be paid in sterling at the favourable rate, with passage paid to his home and back.

In 1894, after negotiations between the Colonial Office and the administration of the Federated Malay Straits and the Straits Settlements, alongside the Governor of Hongkong, a stop-gap solution was sanctioned whereby the difference between half the salary at the prevailing rate and half at 3 *s.* to the dollar was given as 'compensation'.[181] Since the market rate was 2 *s.* for much of that year, this represented a 25% increase in salary for all those for whom 'home' was Great Britain or another gold-using country. The *quid pro quo* for this allowance was that civil servants had to forgo having leave salary paid at the rate promised by

181 From a despatch by the Marquess of Ripon to the Officer Administering the Government of the Straits Settlements 25th September 1893, quoted in *Hongkong Government Gazette* 10.3.1894.

their original terms of service. Not just the police but many departments of the administration only revised their form of contracts when some significant change was required, (salaries being raised most infrequently), hence many had a contractual right to receive their leave pay at an 1872 rate of exchange of 4 *s.* 2 *d.* to the dollar. By reducing this to 3 *s.* (the rate which held during much of 1891), London hoped, in vain, as it was to prove, that the colonies might yet balance this particular part of their books. Since the senior levels of the administration benefitted most from this move, and it enjoyed obvious popularity, few dissenting voices were heard in Hongkong. Indeed, the Exchange Rate Compensation System became a scheme employed by many of the banks and dock companies, along with some of the merchant houses in the region.

Home again, recruiting in Newmarket

Just two weeks after the arrival of his young brother-in-law, Hennessy and his daughters finally sailed on the Peninsular and Orient steamship *Pekin* on Good Friday, April 11th 1895, the Inspector's first leave for eleven years. At not-quite nine years old, his eldest daughter, May, doubtless had to take her share of minding her younger sisters. Nevertheless, Hennessy must have been quite an involved father for the time, since they did not take an amah with them, nor was there another police or civil service family travelling out to help with the girls, although such ships generally had stewardesses and nurses to assist families. After transferring to the *Parramata* in Bombay, the family arrived in London on 18th May, and then took the train to Holyhead to cross to Ireland. Regular trains now linked Newmarket to Dublin, and so the journey took about five hours with a change at Mallow.[182] Little can be said for sure about the early part of his leave in Newmarket. No members of his own family now remained in the area, his widowed mother having died five years earlier. Having continued to correspond with his wife's family, he did pay visits to some of his married sisters-in-law in their farms in the neighbourhood.

182 Improvements in the line meant that the train services out of Dublin reached speeds comparable to those in England. For example, from Bradshaw's timetables of 1895 we learn that the 120 mile journey from London to Bristol took just over three and a half hours. Dublin to Mallow is about 150 miles, Newmarket a further eighteen miles.

George Hennessy and girls, c. 1891 (courtesy Hennessy family)

His own little family may well have stayed in Curraduff, a substantial farmhouse with enough space to accommodate visitors, where his in-laws would be keen to see their granddaughters for the first time, and hear of their son's safe arrival and start as a policeman in Hongkong. Through his association with brothers Murtagh and Thomas O'Sullivan, Hennessy had a network of family in the area. In earlier years the brothers' father, Murtogh Sullivan, a man whose fertile farm had allowed him to prosper despite the famine years, had purchased very substantial farm tenancies for each of his five sons, and his daughters had been able to marry well.

However, since Hennessy was on leave with the object of finding a second wife and step-mother for the girls, all this, especially staying in the house of his late wife, may have become slightly uncomfortable. Family lore has it that Hennessy 'had his eye on' Susan Taylor, who was to become the second Mrs Hennessy, some eleven years earlier when courting Bridget Bertha. Susan, one of the local beauties, came from a large family in Lisdangan, another small townland about a mile and a half to the west of Newmarket, with a thriving farm and connections with many in the neighbourhood. Life on this farm would later be captured and recorded in Alice Taylor's *'To School through the Fields'*, published in 1988.

At twenty-eight years and nine months (as recorded later by her daughter in further pages of the Rough Book), Susan might, like Bridget before, have been glad to find herself a husband, and one who could provide her with an amah and a 'boy' to take care of some of the chores in the home. However, with a (later) reputation as a strong willed and rather feisty woman, she would surely have been under no illusion that taking on a ready formed family would be easy when she would be so far removed from her own community. There seems to have been some problem about the date of the wedding. In the first weeks of September, in correspondence now lost, Hennessy applied for a three month (unpaid) extension to his leave. The Under Secretary of State for the Colonies replied, indicating his agreement but asking for the grounds. A letter from Hennessy in the Colonial Office records of 18th September 1895 states that he is engaged to be married in February 1896.[183] There was initially some carping in London, for Hennessy's return ticket would not be valid, and issuing a new one would cost the colony £21, and that was before the new wife's ticket had been considered. It was felt that perhaps men should sign leave papers agreeing to their return date before they left Hongkong. Happily, a better understanding of the matter was at hand,

183 Hennessy to Under Secretary of State for the Colonies 18th September 1895 CO129/270 p. 307.

and it was found that since the cost of the return portion was not paid to the shipping company until the journey was undertaken, there was only slight extra cost involved in purchasing a new single ticket for a man 'who has had twenty years' service and had not been home for ten.'[184] The Colonial Office do not remark, however, on the unusual length, for an officer on leave, of his engagement. Hennessy had arrived back in Newmarket at the end of May. Perhaps he wanted to give his future bride time, or maybe he was simply enjoying being back in Ireland and, after such an extended period of service, and, wanting a little more time at home, used the wedding as an excuse. For after all that, the wedding took place at 6 o'clock in the evening of Saturday 23rd November 1895, which originally would have been Hennessy's last weekend in Ireland.[185]

A few weeks before this Hennessy had to attend a medical examination to confirm his fitness for another five year term, his fifth, in Hongkong. This was probably conducted at the army garrison in Buttevant, some 18 miles from Newmarket. Around this time he received a telegraph from the Colonial Office in London asking him to find a number of men for his Captain Superintendent to interview for recruitment to the Force, in return for which he would receive half pay for his extra three months holiday. Further details came in a letter from May, whose leave, which subsequently extended even further to 6th October 1896, had seen him recruiting in Scotland, Ireland and London. Knowing well that by the time he returned to Hongkong, a further new batch of men would be required, he obtained permission to engage up to five men in addition to the original ten. Enrolling the help of an experienced inspector currently on leave was standard practice in these circumstances. The letters he wrote to Hennessy, kept in the latter's Rough Book and now preserved by the Hong Kong Police Museum detail the procedure.

Early in January 1896, having received a number of names from Newmarket, he sent Hennessy a copy of the Conditions of Service, and asked him to explain these carefully to the men, stressing that, because of the recently revised terms, they would not get a pension before age 45. He was also to explain the Exchange Rate Compensation system

184 Memo attached to correspondence, CO129/270 p. 305.

185 From Hennessy's Rough Book

to them, emphasising that it was a privilege granted and not a right, and thus did not appear in the Conditions document. May then asked for full particulars of each man, including his physique, educational achievements, and character references he may be able to supply and information about his antecedents. Although May trusted Hennessy to find good men, these being without police training, he wanted to ensure that he found the best, and stressed that he would be taking four at the very most. One man Hennessy had proposed was too young: James O'Sullivan, who had only just turned 18 was a cousin by marriage from Scarteen, one of the five farms tenancies originally bought by Murtagh Sullivan.[186] A replacement was to be found, and so on Hennessy's eventual list were brothers Patrick and Mortimor O'Sullivan, from the Barnacurra farm where he had worked during his previous leave, Michael Lynch from Ballyduane and one of the Murphy brothers from Bluepool, both townlands within a mile or so of Barnacurra.

In the next letter Hennessy is again urged to explain the pension situation to the men, and that how, if selected, they would have to be ready to leave in a fortnight. May arrived in Newmarket on Monday 20th January, traveling by train from Dublin, and interviewed the men at Lane's Hotel in Church Street, Newmarket, and then sent all four for medical examinations. This Michael Lynch and the younger O'Sullivan passed, with May expressing his regret for Patrick O'Sullivan, and reporting the doctor's opinion that an operation would be possible to correct the varicocele found, should he still wish to proceed. The varicose veins in Murphy's legs were such as to render him unsuitable for the life of a policeman. So, with only two of his men going forward at the time, Hennessy canvassed for four new candidates, who he proposed to his superior, including another of the Murphy brothers, but this man, too, was disappointed. On 4th February May responded to Hennessy: he was not now in need of further Newmarket men, as a man recommended by fellow Inspector William Stanton, and two from the Royal Irish Constabulary barracks had been accepted. May explained,

186 Although at this time men were required to be 'under 25', May would not accept men less than 19 years old.

> "*You see, as you were not personally acquainted with the last four men you wrote about I did not care to take them unless I could not get any others. With Lynch and O'Sullivan it is different. You knew them and took the responsibility of recommending them. And it is only on the personal recommendation of a trustworthy officer that I would care to take men who have not been in a police force.*"

Feeling the duties of his position, May rather officiously tells the older man:

> "*I am sure when you go out you will not forget that you are responsible with me for the good behaviour and efficiency of Lynch and O'Sullivan, and that you will do your best to help them to turn out well.*"[187]

However, he concluded by relaying the good news to Hennessy that the building of new married quarters at the Central Station had commenced, and hoped that Mrs. Hennessy would like her new home. There is no record of how Hennessy had explained to his Captain that he was already married, considering that it was on account of his marriage being scheduled for February that he had acquired his leave extension. However, as the Crown Agents received help finding new recruits without having to pay Hennessy any subsistence or travel allowance, perhaps the situation passed unremarked. Patrick O'Sullivan did indeed undergo the necessary operation, and sailed for Hongkong some two months after his brother. It can be presumed that the Newmarket recruits received good guidance and support from their sponsor as May's hopes were realised:

> "*Five recruits were obtained from the London Metropolitan Police, three from the Aberdeen Police Force, and one from the Royal Irish Constabulary. Two recruits were obtained from England and three*

187 May to Hennessy, Dublin, 4th February 1896, original in Hong Kong Police Museum.

from Ireland who had no previous Police service. These men were all enlisted by myself and have given great satisfaction."[188]

188 Report of the Captain Superintendent of Police, 1896.

Chapter Five

The really enterprising Inspector Lysaught

At the beginning of 1869, even with his head for business, Lysaught could not have anticipated Dixon's departure and death and his subsequent promotion to Inspector, and perhaps was still keeping an eye out for a more lucrative position, maybe in the world of commercial shipping. Now, within a short time of his becoming an inspector, he realised that he could use his elevated position to become better acquainted with the business world of Hongkong. With greater autonomy than his brother Inspectors in the regular Force and a workload that compared favourably to theirs, Lysaught was free to investigate ways in which to supplement his income. His natural inclination to acquire property, perhaps dormant so long since his Newmarket days, could now come again to the fore, as he daily saw the area closest to the Naval Yard develop.

Wanchai had become home to many Portuguese from Macao in the 1860s, with western-style houses springing up at great speed.[189] The arrival of more Chinese meant that these were now interspersed with shop-houses, with their deep, cubicle divided floors, the area thus becoming more ethnically and socially mixed than on the western side of the dividing military cantonment. It was also popular with the many Europeans who worked as clerks, assistants, junior engineers etc., and who wanted perhaps to marry and certainly to move out of the bachelor messes they occupied during their first years in the colony. These men could not afford the rents charged in the older and higher parts of the city and moving into the Chinese sections would not have been contemplated. However, here, as the Rate books testify, houses frequently had a Chinese

189 Smith, *Wanchai: In Search of an Identity* in Faure ed. *Hong Kong: A Reader in Social History* p 47ff.

landlord and a British tenant, and vice versa, and the ethnic character of a road would change from Chinese to Portuguese to British and back to Chinese within 30 houses.[190] And for those men who had taken Chinese or Eurasian brides, the amorphous, somewhat less constrained feel of Wanchai fitted their needs better than the conservative, starchier European parts of town.

Two years after his marriage, Lysaught made his first purchase of Inland Lot 297.[191] Just south of Queen's Road East, going up Ship Street, this consisted of four two-storey, Chinese type houses, occupied by a mixture of Portuguese and Chinese families. In 1872, Ship Street, whilst not an affluent or particularly 'respectable' road, was not the byword for brothels it was to become in the course of the next century. The Rate Books of that year record the occupation of some of the residents, and the trade of the shops. There is one brothel, but that is amongst carpenters, rice stores, coolies, bakery and cake shops, a fruit trader etc.[192] It does not record the trades of those living in the houses Lysaught purchased, which seems to imply that they were purely residential, and which might be hoped since the vendor was Rev. John Leong, one of the first Chinese to become a Catholic priest in the colony. The road had been extended across Queen's Road East and up the hillside in 1859, when plots of land leading up to the French convent and hospital were first made available. The price Lysaught paid was $1600, then about £350, but in times before unsecured loans, how did he amass sufficient funds to make this initial purchase? No doubt the residue of Henry Dixon's money formed a part of this, but it must be wondered whether, now that he occupied a high position in

190 The annually compiled Rate Books detail properties in each street by order, within districts of Victoria, the villages of Hongkong island and Kowloon (and later New Territory villages). Information contained includes the superior leaseholder, description of the property & use, rateable value and dates quarterly rates due and paid. Some volumes include Lot numbers, house numbers and head of occupying household. HKRS 38-2.

191 Inland Lot was defined area, the lease of which was originally sold by the Crown, and could then be traded. At this period the size of lots, especially in Wanchai, was substantial, sufficient often to hold a number of houses etc

192 However, Howell, in *Race, Space and the Regulation of Prostitution in Colonial Hong Kong* p. 54 asserts that there were said to be four brothels in Ship Street in 1873, each with seven women and that these were the lowest class of establishments for Europeans, frequented (unsurprisingly given the location) by soldiers and sailors.

the Yard, he might have used his influence in illicit ways to build up a nest egg? However, against this there are a few problems: the amount was too large: even in the town, most bribes and backhanders were more in the nature of a few, perhaps ten or fifteen, dollars and secondly, the Yard was an enclosed world, where such activity, and on such a scale, could not have been concealed from the Naval and civil authorities. Sales of Crown leases were often reported in the newspapers, and so had Lysaught been engaged in underhand practices of this sort then his career as Inspector would doubtless have come to an abrupt end. Although the records of all his transactions have not survived, after the initial purchases there does seem to be a traceable pattern of good rental income and profitable sales financing further purchases and developments.[193] It seems more probable that the initial additional money came from his in-law's family and perhaps it was Antonia Pereira, with some experience of property purchase herself, that encouraged Lysaught into the venture.

In October of the same year, having owned and collected the rents for four months, Lysaught used the property to raise a mortgage of $500. Such was a common transaction, drawn up for one month, but renewable up to a year, by mutual assent of mortgagor and mortgagee, and subject to interest payments monthly, in this case of 12 1/2 %. The mortgagee in this case was local solicitor John Joseph Francis, who would have taken over the right to collect rents for the period of the mortgage. This is the first recorded contact between Francis and Lysaught, in what became a close business friendship between the two men. Francis, who had qualified as a solicitor three years earlier, met Lysaught in the Naval Yard, for one of his early cases concerned the probate for a Yard clerk.[194] There is no record of what the Inspector did with the $500, but it was certainly something that created more capital for him, since eighteen months later in April 1874 he lent $1000 to Hongkong businessmen, Tung Leong Kok and Leon Ng Cheong against the security of the deeds for I.L. 309. The loan was repaid

193 The documents relating to many of Lysaught's property transactions still exist and are preserved in the Public Records Office in Hongkong, but gaps exist. The Memorials are in HKRS 490-28, other documents relating to his land purchases are in the Land Office files HK58-1 series.

194 *Hongkong Daily Press,* 12th May 1869, call for settlement of accounts re. Robert Henry Grant (dec.) late clerk in Naval Yard. Jno. J. Francis, solicitor for executor.

a year later, and about this time he purchased two smaller Lots, adjacent to his Ship Street property and fronting onto Queen's Road East. Selling all three in December 1875 to Tam Cho Seong of Canton and Leong Bew of Hongkong for $2,100 it might appear that, considering he only raised $500 from Francis, Lysaught had been overcharged by Fr. Leong. However, if that was the case, it did nothing to stem his entrepreneurial spirit, and the next year he paid the small price of just $150 for a short lease on a large plot in Kowloon. Given (now rather fancifully) as Kowloon Garden Lot 28, out towards Hung Hom, this had been the property of local chemist J. D. Humphrey. However, it was in March 1877 that he made his most significant purchase to date, from the trustee and brother of Dudley Hanley, who had been in Hongkong but was now confined to a lunatic asylum in Dublin. Lysaught paid $1,600 for the lease on I.L. 53, close to Spring Garden Street giving him a substantial frontage of 100 feet on the south side of Queen's Road East. Carl Smith records that this was one of two lots which had in 1844 been first owned by a firm by the name of Fox, Rawson and Co., who built six Chinese shops and quarters for their junior staff, to prevent undesirable development, since the plot stood opposite another of their properties, that was then used as the Governor's residence. Lysaught raised a mortgage on these properties and rebuilt European style houses with shops below on the site, and sold them to Francis (now qualified and practising at the Hongkong Bar) for $4,100, around £820.

A new home for the family?

Up to this time there is nothing to suggest that Inspector Lysaught had bought property for his own family's use, but the yearly cycle of birth must by then have been placing considerable strain on the capacity of the Inspector's quarters in the Yard. The autumn of 1877 saw both his step-sons, Henry and William attend the newly founded St. Joseph's College, at that time housed in the Mission building in Wellington Road.[195] The eldest two little girls probably went off to the French Convent of the Sisters of St Paul of Chartres on the Praya, close to both the Yard and the Queen's Road properties, rather than to the school run by the Italian

195 Ryan, *The Story of One Hundred Years* ps. 34 & 80.

Sisters, in further off Caine Road. Meanwhile, Isabella was at home with three or four more children, including new-born Caroline Louise. Moving into an apartment on Queen's Road East might have been a great relief to all, and one imagines that the Inspector was now able to find his documents and charge books, free from nappies, toys and the detritus of small children.

It appears, though, that the family would be soon on the move again, for he did not remain owner of these properties long. The incomplete records mean that it is uncertain as to when and for how much he sold the Queen's Road houses and started to buy in Wanchai Road, but it is clear that these represent the point at which his property speculations gained focus. Inland Lot 841, Wanchai Road, auctioned on 12th October 1881 at an upset price of $500 for 2,500 sq. ft. was his first purchase here.[196] This road, which joins the thoroughfare (Queen's Road East) with the Praya in a gentle curve had gradually been extended to run parallel to the waterfront and beneath Morrison Hill, and provided a further access to the businesses that wanted a share in the harbour-side. Soon the value of this road increased greatly, and six years later Lysaught raised a mortgage of $6,000 on this and a neighbouring property to buy a plot on Queen's Road East, near the recently opened Li Chat Street, and opposite St Francis Street. Here he built six European style houses with separate apartments on each floor and quickly sold three of them. In a later letter to the Sanitary Board, asking for an exemption from a recently passed Ordinance which required him to create a greater amount of clear space in the open shaft between the houses and the kitchens at the rear by narrowing the connecting passageway, he explained:

> *"I have built this style of houses (to meet the requirements of a certain class of Europeans who could not afford to pay a high rent, and this gives them clean, well-ventilated, comfortable quarters at a modest rent, and which, apparently, they duly appreciate as the flats are seldom vacant."*[197]

---

196 *Hongkong Government Gazette* Notification 337 24.9.1881.

197 Lysaught's application, in the records of the Sanitary Board, 16th June 1896.

The houses had plastered walls and ceilings, grate fireplaces (a rarity in Chinese houses) and chimneys, and windows and doors to back and front, and to the kitchen. His tenants, he says, prefer to have adequate passage room, and he would have to reduce their rents if he made alterations. Lysaught won the argument, and retained his profit.

Thereafter comes the steady development of a substantial portfolio of property. Important amongst these was the purchase of much of Cross Lane, close to the old steam bakery and Robinson's Piano Factory. Here, before his retirement from the Yard, Lysaught established an engineering factory and godown. The understanding of heavy engineering he acquired through close contact with the workshops of the Yard had shown him Hongkong's need for better access to large machinery, which he both imported from Britain and made on site. It was into this business that his elder son, John Joseph Lysaught, stepped after leaving St. Joseph's in about 1891. Unfortunately there are no records unearthed to date of who he employed in the godowns, but he would have had no problem acquiring good men through his Yard contacts. The business flourished, and in 1899 and 1902 he bought two plots for residential development, on which he built substantial houses, Killadoon and Homeville, nos. 151 and 153 Wanchai Road, which were the largest residences on that road. Into the latter of these properties he moved his family as soon as it was complete, just before New Year, 1900.

Business associates and family relations

None of this would have been possible for Lysaught had, back in 1869, the Dockyard Police become officially part of the colonial force. The ordinance that prohibited government employees to own property other than their residence or to engage in commerce may only have been passed in 1892, but it was merely putting into local law a rule that already existed in the Civil Service 'canon'. Unlike many of the men of commerce, who purchased land and property advantageously and benefitted from the growing prosperity of the city, Lysaught did not realise his assets and retire home to the British Isles with his wife as an affluent man. Reading the large number of documents that exist concerning his business transactions: purchases and sales; loans taken and given; securities underwritten, it becomes evident that he was, to a far greater extent than other Newmarketeers, a Hongkong man, with friends and businesses associates amongst both the Chinese and European communities. But at heart he was ever an Irishman. Almost every one of the Europeans with whom he did business was Irish, from the poor afflicted Dudley Hanley, the widow Mrs. Anne Doyle, who lent him $6000 at 7 1/2% in 1887, through to his many dealings with J.J. Francis, now a Queen's Counsel and a prominent barrister in the colony.

Francis' route to Hongkong ran along similar lines to so many others, purchasing his discharge there in the mid 1860s from the Royal Artillery, in which regiment he had been commissioned. He then pursued a legal career in Hongkong, qualifying as a solicitor in 1869 and quickly building a good practice, he amassed sufficient of both legal knowledge and capital to enrol in Grays Inn, London, in 1874 to study for the bar. He was admitted to the London Bar in 1876 and that of Hongkong a few months later in 1877, swiftly establishing himself as one of the leading counsels, and involved in almost all the major cases, the more so after his elevation to silk (Queen's Counsel) in 1886. It was said at the time that if one had Francis on one's side, then the case was won, although his fiery temper and adversarial attitude were somewhat at odds with the rather sedate nature of the Hongkong courts of the time. Greenwood, whose article in the Royal Asiatic Society's Journal comes as close as there is to a biography of Francis, reflects that "*... he was a man of faith: faithful to his church and religion, to his native country and fellow country men and to his monarch. He was one of the leading Roman Catholic laymen in Hongkong ...*"[198] counting Bishop Raimondi as a much valued personal friend. Francis saw the place of Catholics in Hongkong as generally good, rather better than that at home, but his support of fellow Irishman and Catholic Governor Pope-Hennessy cost him, in the opinion of the leader writer of the *Hongkong Daily Press*, far more than he gained.[199] He was also a great supporter of St. Joseph's College from its inception, and rarely missed a prize-giving, frequently also acting as an examiner at the school,

---

198 Greenwood, *John J. Francis, Citizen of Hong Kong* p 26. The author is indebted to this article for the majority of biographical information on Francis.
199 *Hongkong Daily Press*, 23rd September 1901.

which, given his reputation, must have been rather terrifying for the candidates.

Lysaught might choose with whom he did business, and have friends in the Naval Establishment and the Colonial Police as well as in more ethnically mixed commercial world, but he could not escape some of the rigid proprieties and prejudices of Hongkong when it came to the marriages of his daughters. It might have been assumed that, accustomed to the arranged marriages that were still happening (often very successfully) in rural Ireland when he left, and with that of his son and a niece from Newmarket agreed well in advance, Lysaught would look to the small but constant pool of his countrymen amongst the sergeants and inspectors. But he would also have been aware that no policeman was expected to marry a woman who was not a British citizen in her own right, or more specifically, could not marry a woman who had non-British family in or near the colony. It was feared that the man would be compromised by the interests of his new relations, and that his ability to impartially do his job would be affected. That the Macanese were included in this interdict does not appear to be explicit, but given the general, sometimes incorrect, assumption that all the Portuguese from Macao were Eurasian, with elements of Chinese blood, together with long-standing English bias against southern-European Catholic races, it can be assumed that the prejudice would extend also to them. Thus none of Lysaught's daughters were married to the local constabulary.

In any event, most of the young ladies did not seem to require too much assistance from their parents in this matter. The eldest daughter, Marion, was appropriately the first to marry at 19 years old, Mr. Alfred Formosa Ramsey, an engineer in the Douglas Steamship Company, whilst Lillian married the Milanese pianist and teacher Signor Antonio Cattanoa in 1898, who was prominent in Hongkong's cultural scene. Elizabeth's marriage to Emerson Gibson two years later did bring another engineer into the family business, but Gibson, who had lived before his marriage in the next door Wild Dell flats, had something of a chequered career, with at least one attempted business, a cycle manufacturing firm, failing. The last family wedding was that of the Lysaught's youngest daughter, Kathleen, who married Alfred Walters when she was twenty.

To their father's sorrow, non of these men were Irish, and all but Lillian's marriage had to be conducted after a dispensation from the bishop, since their spouses were not Catholic, but from the report recorded in the papers of Marion's pretty wedding, the more tolerant Italian priests did not impose the strictures on the celebration that the girls would have encountered in Britain. According to the account, given many years later by one of their unmarried sisters, and which is admittedly rather acidic in tone, Lysaught had not thought highly of some of his new sons-in-law. But he looked after all the couples, giving them the tenancies of flats and accommodation in Homeville and his other houses.

Lysaught's later years in the Dockyard

Meanwhile, Lysaught's work in the Naval Yard continued, with the band of men changing from time to time, but generally with one or two of the sergeants with longer service records to help keep some continuity in the force. Towards the end of the century the ever-increasing activity of the Yard seems to have restricted the accommodation available for the employees there, whether engineers, clerks or police. Meanwhile the continued fall in the sterling value of the Hongkong (Mexican) dollar was putting an increasing strain on the wages of these men, particularly those who had families to support. There was not the same embargo on marriage for constables here as pertained in the town force, but married men were finding it all but impossible to make ends meet on just $40 per month, with no additional allowances such as fire brigade, theatre or telegraph duty. Increasingly they were having to take additional jobs, and, it seems, these inevitably conflicted with their duties at times. It was perhaps on account of these conflicts that a number of men had been dismissed, whilst others were not renewing their contracts and some had applied for discharge from their five-year obligation because they needed to earn more in order to keep their families. "*Truncheon's*" letter of 1891 had been followed by a petition from the men to the Admiralty, which, in the words of one paper, elicited a response:

> "... *with an exhibition of promptitude quite new to the department, the Lords Commissioners appear to have gone into the question thoroughly and in a manner which is not likely to give much*

satisfaction to the rank and file of the Force ... the Admiralty will, while slightly augmenting the salaries of some of the men, nevertheless effect a saving ..."[200]

The Force was to be considerably reduced, down to about twelve European constables, and Indian men brought in for the first time to make up the deficit, paid at about half the rate of their British counterparts. European constables pay was to increase to $45 per month, and sergeant's pay went up further, but there is the sense that the Admiralty's main aim was to cut costs.

Thus, in the middle of 1894, with these changes looming, William Lysaught took his retirement from the leadership of the Naval Dockyard Police Force after thirty years service. He might have reflected that his turn at the helm of his little force was only a few months shorter than that of former Captain Superintendent W. M. Deane, who was, and remains, the longest serving head of the Hongkong Police.

Retirement from the Yard, but not from business

As has been seen, there was no pension from the Admiralty, but Lysaught had a comfortable income from rents on his properties. In all, either the documents or detailed notes relating to some twenty six property transactions in his name have been found. However, these do not create the full narrative of his dealings, leaving many gaps which would probably take a similar number to fill. The majority of his purchases were made during his time as an inspector, whilst after his retirement he seems to have concentrated on his engineering business, and the development of his properties in Wanchai Road. He stepped in to run the Wanchai Engineering Godowns after leaving the Yard, and seems to have managed this for the next ten years, when his twenty-nine-year-old son, John, took over.

Of his other sons, Thomas and Charles did not survive to adulthood, whilst James Patrick, born four years after his eldest son, in 1879 does not emerge in Hongkong beyond church records and a mention in Lysaught's will, although he appears as a driver in the census records of California in 1925 and his death is recorded in San Francisco on 23rd October 1947.

200 *Hongkong Telegraph,* 30th July 1894.

His younger step-son, William Dixon first took an apprenticeship in the Naval Dockyard, then worked later in the engineering firm, and also managed his step father's rental properties. An advertisement in the *Daily Press* in 1890 for flats and a shop in Queen's Road East, the top floor of No. 5 Arsenal Street and some of his houses in Wanchai Road directs the enquirer to *W. Dixon, Machinery Godowns, 3 Cross Lane, Wanchai, near No. 2 Police Station.*[201] Later he became an engineer on one of the steamer lines to Macao, and it was whilst thus employed he caught a fever and died in July 1898, aged 31. He had not married, and thus left his money, just a few hundred dollars, to his mother.

Henry Dixon junior and the Post Office

It must have been with pride that Inspector Lysaught, the family man, attended prize-givings at St. Joseph's College, when his elder stepson, Henry Dixon brought credit on himself, winning awards on more than one occasion. On Saturday, 7th February 1880, he led the long list of prizewinners as the recipient, from the donor, of H.E. The Governor's Gold Medal for English.[202] Both Lysaught and young Henry would have been aware of the possibilities within the civil service for an able man, but in the early 1880s further education in preparation for this career was not an option for this class of society. Thus Dixon left school in 1882, just before his 17th birthday, and his step-father used the influence he had to gain him a post amongst the clerks of the Naval Yard. Alike to those of the Yard Police Force, there is only an occasional glimpse of the men working as clerks, but clearly Dixon progressed in these offices.[203] Maybe at first his family connections gave him some prominence in the largely Portuguese manned department, but soon his own merit must have come to the fore and to the attention of the Colonial authorities, for eight years later, aged just 24 he applied for and was accepted as Superintendent of the Money Order Office, of the Post Office Department.[204] This position,

---

201 *Hongkong Daily Press*, 6th September 1890.
202 *China Mail*, 7th February 1880
203 A rare list of the men employed as 'writers' appears in the *Chronicle and Directory for China, Japan, Corea etc.*, for 1883, where Dixon is the last named of a list of ten writers.
204 *Civil Establishment* List in the *Blue Book* for 1890 Section I page 32.

the third highest in the Post Office, with only the Postmaster General and the Accountant above him, paid what must have seemed the enormous salary of $1440 p.a., the same as Chief Inspector Horspool of the Colonial Police, and certainly more than his stepfather.

The vacancy had come about through one of the worst cases of theft from a government department to hit Hongkong up to that date. The amount lost was $50,681, approximately £8,230, just under one quarter of the transactions of the Money Order Office, and it represented a grave attack on an institution that relied completely upon the trust of the general public.[205] The Office had, for the last five years, been the responsibility of Z. M. Barradas, but in March 1890 suddenly, and without notice, he left the colony. At the time the Post Office was hard stretched, with the Postmaster General, Alfred Lister, terminally ill, but still trying to perform his duties, and it had also suffered the death of a senior clerk in February that year. As Lister and his staff then tried to carry on the Money Order business, and prepare the accounts for the preceding year, it became apparent that Barradas had constructed a very complex scheme for recording money passing through the office, and had written up little of the previous six months' transactions. Since all the money collected by that office passed through his hands, he had had ample opportunity to abstract funds to his own use, the rather lax system of oversight playing into his hands. Barradas was apprehended and brought back to Hongkong that summer, where, through the pages of the newspapers, the public keenly followed his trial, which resulted in a sentence of three years' hard labour. A thorough reorganisation of the Office was undertaken, ensuring that enough checks were in place to make any *"reoccurrence of frauds similar to those lately enacted beyond the pale of likelihood."*[206] Dixon, it was said in that same report, was fulfilling his role properly. The Post Office was one department where all but the most senior posts, and often only that of Postmaster General, were filled

205 The amount lost equates to about £1 million at today's value (2016).

206 Report of the Postmaster General for 1891, *Hongkong Government Gazette* 11th April 1891, Statement of Defalcations of Z.M. Barradas and Balance Sheets for Money Order Office, Sessional papers of the Legislative Council 15th September 1890 and trial reports *Hongkong Telegraph*, 23rd and 24th July 1890.

by Portuguese. Dixon stood between the British and Portuguese worlds, and in the nervous aftermath of the embezzlement, this helped allay fears. Like Barradas before him, but whom it had not deterred, he was required to put up $5000 security against misconduct, one of the largest amounts required from any government servant. His choice of his step-father and, more particularly, J. J. Francis, as guarantors of the bond was a calculated demonstration that although young, he was a trustworthy man who valued his integrity.

The working man and his money

For the majority of the young men choosing to work in the colonies, a major factor in their decision was the opportunity to contribute to the upkeep of their families at home through regular remittances from their salaries. Indeed, it would be expected of them, and in small communities it would leave their families open to comment and gossip if it was known that they were not receiving any money order envelopes. But whilst the early banks in Hongkong dealt largely with currency exchange business, they were not the place for a young clerk or constable to go, should he want to send ten shillings or a pound home to his mother. Even with the development of the mercantile banks such as Dent and Company in 1864 and Hong Kong and Shanghai Banking Corporation a year later, and the growth of local high street banks in Britain, the system lacked the integration to cope with multiple small transactions that would ensue if it were to be accessible to the labouring man.

Some years earlier, the Post Office in the British Isles had established a system of Money Orders, to allow the transfer of modest amounts between parties. Then, in 1862, encouraged by the increased reliability of the Mail Ships, this was extended to include the Colonies. Sums up to £10 could be sent by obtaining and filling in an application form, and presenting that, together with a stamped envelope addressed to the Postmaster of the nearest Post Office to the intended recipient, as well as the sum concerned and the commission charge to the local Money Order Office. The commission charge ranged from 18 cents for sums up to £2, rising to 72 cents for £7 and over, the charges being four times those applied to inland orders, reflecting the exchange commission. The

Office then dispatched this, and returned to the purchaser a receipt and any change due. After the arrival of the mail ship six weeks or so later, the recipient would then be sent word that an order awaited them at their post office, and would have to be able to state the name of the sender before payment was made.[207]

The scheme was hugely popular as it proved safe and simple, easy enough for anyone's elderly mother to trot to her village Post Office and receive from her son the few pounds that would make so great a difference to her comfort, or provide the wherewithal for another sibling to buy a passage out of the country. The system was a godsend, too, for those further up the social scale. A man would have to have independent means to keep bank accounts in both Britain and Hongkong, and for many, especially middle-ranking civil servants, the Money Order was the way to pay school fees, to provide for children, and sometimes wives, sent home to stay with relations, and to maintain property they might have. Individuals in Government service were permitted to remit home up to half their salary in this way. When considering the economic impact the Colonies made on the homeland, remittances sent home are, perhaps, not accorded the significance they are due. By 1903, £16,089 was sent back to the UK via the Hongkong Office, and orders to the value of £1400 to other sterling-using countries. What is perhaps more surprising is that £6,239 was received into Hongkong from the United Kingdom.[208] Whilst the majority of its trade concerned transaction to and from sterling, it also saw considerable business in rupees, gold yen and dollars (for the USA and Canada) and in the silver dollars of the Treaty Ports.

On 2nd December 1893, Dixon, then aged 28 and established in his career, married the twenty-year-old Severina (Amy) Maria Dolores Sanchez in Macao Cathedral.[209] Severina's father was in the British Colonial Service in Shanghai, but the family had relatives in both Macao and Hongkong. William Lysaught gave the new couple the tenancy of 135 Wanchai Road, a modest two storey house of European construction and dimensions, and in the centre of a terrace of six built by him. By

207 *China Mail* 12th October 1881.

208 Report of the Postmaster General for 1903, *Hongkong Government Gazette* 13th May 1904.

209 From records of Macao Cathedral, noted in Carl Smith cards.

virtue of the 1891 general pay rise in the Civil Service Dixon's pay had risen 20% to $1728 p.a., or $144 per month.[210] Positions in the Post Office did not come with either free quarters or a rent allowance (set by the Government at $360 p.a. for subordinate officers). The value of the wedding gift can be understood by reference also to an advertisement for houses and flats in the *Hongkong Telegraph* some ten years after Dixon's marriage, which rather unusually gives the cost of rent, claiming to be the cheapest in the colony. A four-room house just round the corner to Wanchai Road, on Morrison Hill Gap Road is $40 per month, whilst flats of 2 or 3 rooms in the Wild Dell Building, between Lysaught's sets of properties on the Wanchai Road, were $25 per month. The couple's first child, Philip Albert, was born in August 1894, to be followed by another son, Dermot Joseph Henry in 1895. The choice of names is rather curious in a period when family continuity was still preserved in the names of the first sons and daughters. Neither Philip nor Albert have obvious Irish or Portuguese connections, nor appear, so far as can be traced, in either family. Dermot, an anglicised version of the Irish Dairmuid, is unusual even in Ireland at the time.

The Exchange Rate Compensation System (E.R.C.S.), ameliorating the effects of the devaluation of the local currency, soon became essential to the Europeans of Hongkong in order to maintain their standard of living against the ever increasing cost of imported goods. When it started in Hongkong in 1895, certain branches of the Civil Service, including the European Police, were granted this *en masse*, but the members of other departments were allocated it according to some measure of racial selection. A number of men in the Post Office and other departments, including Dixon, were not given the benefit of the scheme and accordingly applied to the Governor Robinson for consideration.[211] He, however, on orders from London, refused on the grounds that these men had been born in the colony and did not have a financial link to a gold-using country since their British-born parents were dead. As becomes apparent through the correspondence between London and Hongkong, and the

210 *Blue Book* 1891 Section I 32.

211 The correspondence relating to Dixon's request in 1895 (29th October 1895) is at CO129/270 pp347-351 and (12th November 1895) CO129/268 pp 688-714.

notes that accompany that, the anxiety was that a floodgate would be opened, should these men be granted the allowance, whereby every child of a British father and Chinese or Macanese mother in Government employ would submit a claim. Dixon, together with A.J. Reed, Second Marine Officer, petitioned London, stressing their parentage, for both fathers had fought for country, dying early before they could go back home, and since then the men had not revoked their citizenship. This initially gained them the allowance, but this was reversed when a committee examined each claim. This prompted a second petition from Dixon, in which he pointed out that others in similar circumstances, even one man with German parentage had retained the allowance, and on this occasion stressing his links with the British Isles. Lysaught wrote twice in support of his stepson's application, telling how Dixon's wage had helped maintain his remittances back to the British Isles through contributions to the household expenses, and now, since his marriage, he (Dixon) was unable to put money by to send his son to Lysaught's relatives in Newmarket for his education. However, all were unsuccessful, since to the crucial question as to whether Dixon had any relatives at Home dependent on him, he could not reply in the affirmative.

It would appear that Lysaught had occasionally sent money home, perhaps to Joanna Murphy, his youngest sister and mother to a tribe of young boys. It is highly unlikely that he would falsely claim to have made such remittances when his own step-son would be aware how easy that was for any enquiring authority to check. But there is little to suggest that such transfers were a common occurrence. It was, though, when more communication was established between Newmarket and the Lysaught family on Hennessy's retirement, that the situation altered for Dixon. The difficult situation of some of Lysaught's other sisters called for the families in Hongkong to send relief to their aunts through the Money Order Office. Probably at Hennessy's instigation, and certainly with his help, in the summer of 1899 one of Lysaught's sisters, the widowed Mrs. Ellen McAuliffe, wrote to Joseph Chamberlain to ask that her (step) nephew receive the compensation allowance. The letter, with its formal language, old fashioned even for the period, rather laboured writing and spelling mistakes is a touching testament to the right of each person to put his or her case before the authorities.[212] Mrs McAuliffe received, however, the usual tersely dignified rebuff: Mr Dixon's case had been thoroughly gone into, and would not be reopened. But Lysaught and Dixon got to hear about this, and one can imagine Hennessy writing to him when the reply from the Colonial office was received. Obliged, for the honour of his step father's sister, then to submit yet another petition himself, Dixon explained:

> *"Since the return of Ex-Inspector Hennessy, on pension, to his native place Newmarket County Cork, in the early part of 1898, we were made acquainted with the straitened circumstances of my Aunts, on my Stepfather's side (Mr. W. Lysaught).*
>
> *Not having any living relations on my own father's side, and being the eldest of the family, it is not unnatural that they look to me for some pecuniary support.*
>
> *Since last November I have, therefore, been remitting for the maintenance of one of my Aunts- the poorest, a widow and childless, Mrs. Ellen McAuliffe, of Commons, Newmarket, County Cork.*
>
> *True, my remittances have not been as frequent and regular as I would have wished them to be, but my salary is small and only sufficient for the needs of myself and family."*[213]

This left the Colonial Office with really no option but to grant the Compensation, worth some $432 p.a. to Dixon, reflecting drily that they were hardly likely to come across many more cases similar to this, so there was little risk of setting a precedent.

Further afield

But scarcely had Dixon gained a satisfactory outcome than events would occur causing him further financial difficulties. The Post Offices of the treaty ports around China, and of Shanghai, were under the administration of the Postmaster General in Hongkong, and accounted

212 The communication in 1899 (17th August 1899) is at CO129/296 pp 420-422 and (9th November 1899) CO129/294 pp 303-309.

213 Dixon to Postmaster General, Commander Hastings, 2nd November 1899, CO129/294 p 306-7.

within the finances of that colony. When, in 1900, the elderly Postmaster at Shanghai retired, it was an opportunity for the Administration to bring that office into better order, and to quieten the complaints of inefficiency that were frequently made to Hongkong. However, there were few suitably experienced candidates for the role: certainly the three clerks remaining were not felt to understand what was required. Eventually, William Solly, the senior clerk in the Hongkong office (and formerly clerk in the Police Department) was persuaded to take up the position, which he commenced in June of that year, but, with his first leave in ten years already agreed, it was also necessary to provide him with a good chief clerk who could manage in his absence.[214] Before this had been accomplished two of the three existing men resigning in dudgeon for not being considered for the Postmaster's role. The report Solly made on 13th June, 1900, four days after his arrival, set alarm bells ringing in Hongkong. He told of a situation whereby each of the four man team (himself and three clerks, two of them, of course, newly in post) had so many responsibilities that no job could be satisfactorily completed, each man chasing his tail to attend to whichever task was most demanding at the moment, and so he asked for an additional three clerks for the office. But with the Barradas case not yet forgotten, and perhaps with some reservations about Solly's ability to cope with problems of this magnitude, Dixon was despatched to Shanghai on 8th July 1900, to stay two weeks, ostensibly to sort out the Money Order Office there, but also to make a thorough assessment of the situation. Reading between the lines of Dixon's report made at the end of his sojourn, there was some friction between the men, possibly because Solly resented having the senior man sent up from Hongkong. However, it was Dixon's endorsement of the other's request, and insistence on the need to pay the employees properly in order to attract and retain the intelligent men required that won the day, both with the Administration in Hongkong, and, eventually, with London.

---

214 William Solly had arrived in Hongkong in 1890 and joined the Police Department as a Clerk. With an aptitude for languages, he availed himself of the opportunity to learn Chinese, passing the third and highest examination in less than four years. From here he had, in 1895, been able to move to the Post Office as Senior Clerk, although with little gain on his former salary.

Dixon had also been able to recruit two marine sorters, men who did an initial sort of the mail from abroad whilst it was in transit between Hongkong and Shanghai. However, when Solly took his half pay leave in April the following year, the Shanghai office was still the subject of many complaints: long queues at the counter; mail from abroad not delivered until 12 hours after the steamer had docked; postmen leaving the mail at the foot of staircases to find its own way up, etc. No suitable deputy was in place, so it was a reluctant Henry Dixon who agreed to move north as Acting Postmaster. Whilst the role came with free quarters in Shanghai, Dixon was expected to leave his family in Hongkong, and was offered a small allowance on condition that he did so.

The arrangements and lack of pecuniary incentive for Dixon show the extent to which civil servants were expected to be just that: completely at the service of the colony. In Hongkong Dixon and A.J. Reed, now the Accountant of the Post Office, had been fulfilling their own roles and that of the Assistant Postmaster, since the departure in July 1900 of Commander Hastings, the Postmaster General, on half-pay sick leave. For this the two men were each granted one quarter of the Assistant's salary, an extra $750 p.a. E.C.L. Lewis, who now acted as Postmaster General drew the remaining half of his own salary as Assistant Postmaster and the available half of Hastings'. Thus the Administration covered all roles and met their obligation to Hastings without incurring any extra expense. When Dixon was moved to Shanghai in April 1901 he initially drew just his Hongkong Money Order Office salary of $2,280 p.a., losing the extra Assistant's pay. His role was shared out between three of his subordinates, without any increase in their salaries. However, he successfully petitioned to receive the lapsing half share of the Shanghai Postmaster's salary (amounting to $1,500 p.a.) in August, thus freeing half his salary to be divided between the men taking on his duties back in Hongkong.

But Dixon's own finances were placed under considerable strain, and maintaining two households proved too much, so that he had to take his children out of school in Hongkong, and bring them and Severina to Shanghai. Here the harsher winter weather meant that all the children were ill, and Dixon had to purchase two tons of coal per month for fires in his apartment, as well as sending by wire to London for woollen underwear for all of them. He was forced to apply to his step-father for assistance, knowing that the Money Orders Lysaught sent him would be noticed in his own office in Hongkong. At the end of January 1902 he reluctantly petitioned the Governor, and London, for a gratuity, reckoning that he was already some $500 out of pocket.

It would have been a rare event in Colonial Office history had this request been granted without naysayers, but it really met with little opposition. London had already received an extract from *Boyd's Commercial Guide for China* dated September 1901, speaking of the remarkable and very satisfactory level of efficiency the Shanghai Post Office had been brought to under Mr. Dixon, and the courtesy and speed with which customers were now served. In addition, Mr. Solly had been granted an extension of leave by London, through to October 1902, and so Dixon would be required to stay in Shanghai even longer than anticipated. To add a top dressing of incentive, Hongkong's Acting Postmaster Mr. Lewis made a scarcely veiled threat to the Colonial Office that if Mr. Dixon's gratuity was not forthcoming, he, Lewis, might have to recall him to Hongkong, where he was certainly needed. The gratuity was sanctioned.

On 6th October 1902 Dixon was finally able to bring his wife Severina and their four children back home to Hongkong, grateful not to have to endure the rigours of another cold Shanghai winter. He was now able to enrol his son, Philip, at his old *alma mater*, and renew his activities not only with the St. Joseph's alumni association, but become active once more in the Wanchai chapter of the St. Vincent de Paul Society, a Catholic men's organisation dedicated to the service of the poor. The growing community, both families of his married step-siblings and the recent Newmarket additions was both close knit and supportive and something that Dixon had to rely on when, about a year after the birth of their second daughter Edith Rose, Severina died in July, 1905, aged just 32, leaving behind six children, with the eldest, Philip, only eleven years old.

Chapter Six

Departures and arrivals

"As Hongkong Island is approached by steamer from the South, it is difficult to distinguish it from the mountainous country of the mainland, nor is there any apparent difference in its barren looking appearance, between it and other hilly islands which appear to surround it, except that some houses and building of European style may be observed on the hill side at Pokfulam and the mast on Victoria Peak is signalling the ship to those in the city below … The steamer, … turning East into the harbour discovers a scene of life and activity, as well as natural beauty, which calls forth the greatest admiration. Overlooking the harbour is the city of Victoria, extending along the northern shore of the island for upwards of four miles, its buildings carried back and up the steep slope of the mountain, tier beyond tier, in some cases to charming situations 600 feet above sea level. In the harbour and alongside the wharves at Kowloon are seen steamers of all nationalities loading or discharging cargo."[215]

In 1896 Hongkong presented a very different image to the young Irish recruits than had greeted either Hennessy or Lysaught on their arrivals. The shore side on the island was fully developed, with many of the great buildings in central area, west of the barracks and Naval Yard buildings, now in their second generation. Some of these, such as the imposing Hongkong and Shanghai Banking Corporation building, new a decade earlier, were losing their water-front position as the shoreline was moved forward by more than 225 ft (70 m). Land was claimed from the harbour, the Praya becoming, in 1904, Des Voeux Road and commercial, residential and industrial buildings springing up quickly to fill the space. At the extreme points both east and west residential development masked

215 Shepherd, *The Hong Kong Guide 1893* p. 5

the earlier predominance of the warehouses and refineries, whilst inland the pressure on level ground had spread from the city west of the barracks, which already in 1873 was closely built up, into Wanchai on the east. What had been spaciously positioned properties on individual lots were rebuilt to the maximum dimensions, and Government sales of smaller plots in between encouraged dense infilling.

The city was therefore pushing up the side of Victoria Peak, with the Roman Catholic Cathedral near Caine Road dedicated and opened in 1889, replacing the former church in Wellington Road which was subsequently demolished. In 1888 the Peak Tramway opened up the lower slopes to the moderately affluent and the upper slopes to development by rich Europeans, with roads above Caine Road being cut out of the hillside. The streets were better lit by night, although still just the main thoroughfares and the smaller roads only in more prosperous areas. By the late 1880s Hongkong had boasted over 600 gas lamps and throughout the 1890s electricity was becoming more frequent and reliable, both as a means of street lighting and to individual properties. Kowloon had changed almost beyond recognition, from being almost solely a military camp, with small Chinese villages alongside maritime interests on the harbour front, to a thriving town in its own right, with an increasing choice of both Chinese and European housing.[216]

Mortimor O'Sullivan, who had celebrated his all-important 19th birthday en route, arrived in Hongkong, together with three other recruits: Michael Lynch from Newmarket, Joe Sutton and George Bell on 4th April 1896.[217] His sponsor had arrived with his daughters and new wife the previous day on the swift P. & O. steamship, *Pekin*, onto which they had changed in Bombay from the *Oceana,* the whole journey taking just 5 weeks. The new recruits, on the other hand, were put on the Ocean Steamship Company's *Palinurus* at Liverpool, a smaller and cheaper cargo-carrying vessel, in which they, along with a man who had disembarked at Singapore, had been the only passengers, and had needed

216 The population of the colony had doubled from some 122,000 in 1872, of whom 6,400 were European to 250,000, with almost 13,000 Europeans in the mid 1890s.

217 Crown Agents report, 14th February 1896, CO129/273 pp 484-5.

a full seven weeks to reach their destination. His brother Patrick had, meanwhile, undergone the necessary operation required by the medical officer and, unbeknownst to him at the time, left Ireland on the very day that Mortimor arrived in Hongkong. He sailed on the *Monmouthshire,* leaving London together with Martin Faherty, a recruit from the Royal Irish Constabulary.[218]

Although their second-class fares, which gave them basic but adequate shared cabin accommodation, had been paid by the Colonial Office, these young men travelled to all effects as private citizens, especially those who had no police experience prior to enlisting. On signing papers for Hongkong they too had received the bounty of £15, with which they bought light suits and shirts for the journey. The O'Sullivans' father was a farmer of some standing and prosperity in the local community as his farm of about 175 acres was one of the largest in the neighbourhood, but his sons were unused to having money of their own in their pockets. Remembering the warnings Hennessy had given them about the cost of imported goods in Hongkong, and the expenses they would initially have there, they were careful to mind their remaining money on voyages over. Both were of a quite studious disposition, and not prone to spend nights in the many bars of their hometown, so that during the long stretches between ports, with the unaccustomed inactivity this involved, they had to derive what entertainment they could from the ships' small libraries.

When Hennessy had arrived, although an Irishman by birth, he had come as one of a group of Metropolitan Policemen, who had had ample time to get to know one another on the journey out. Once in Hongkong, they, together with the three dozen or so remaining from the Scottish detachment, had formed the majority of the European contingent, and there was little need to look outside the Force for companions. A generation later this contingent was still largely composed of men from the Scottish and London forces, but with an appreciable number of Irishmen. Now they generally came in small groups, if not individually, and their integration into the society of the Force would start as they gravitated towards others of their own nationality. To a large extent this still meant that they associated primarily with their co-religionists. This

218 Crown Agents report, 28th April 1896, CO 129/273 pp 488-9.

emerges from the newspaper accounts of marriages, for, with only a few exceptions, these show that the Scots police married at the Union (Presbyterian) Church then on Staunton Street, the English at St John's (Anglican) Cathedral and the Irish at St Joseph's (Catholic) Church on Garden Road.

But for the Newmarket men there was also another social group ready to welcome them. The presence of two older family men meant an ever-increasing tally of relatives and their close friends, and it was this that served to support and integrate the O'Sullivan men, and their kinsmen who followed, into a particular section of the European society in Hongkong in a way that was unique certainly amongst the members of the Police Force, and probably in the wider Civil Service.[219] However, Hennessy's world was necessarily the rather closed one of a senior police inspector: knowing the town and its people in his professional capacity, not associating too closely with them, and at the margin of 'Society' as it existed in Hongkong, the more senior members of the Administration and leaders of commerce. Susan Hennessy would have appreciated having others as new to Hongkong as herself, and the opportunity to talk about familiar, but now far distant people and places. The police wives, especially those living in and close to the Central Station were a little community of themselves, but it was not until the early years of the next century that they would be invited to participate in the good works of charity bazaars and 'working parties' that were organised and patronised by the wives of senior officials of the Government. In the highly status conscious world of European Hongkong, Susan would have found her social interactions very limited, and was likely keen to make the acquaintance of the younger Lysaught women, on the other side of town. There tends to be little trace, however, of women's friendships and activities, and in the usual course of events the family's association with Hongkong and the people there would finish with the man's retirement and return to home, with only his pension to remind him of those days. As it transpired, George Hennessy's departure from Hongkong in 1898

219 Although not in commerce, where a number of influential firms, both British and Chinese, would employ generations of men in the senior roles.

did not mark the end of his family's connection with the Force there, which would continue for another half-century.

But William Lysaught, that other Newmarket man, had no such plans (or pension), and it was not just by his marriage that he was closer to being a citizen of Hongkong, if that were not an anomalous term for the time. In fact, he would be described in his obituary as 'an old resident', i.e., a permanent fixture. The eldest of his sons, John Joseph, was the same age as the O'Sullivan brothers, and worked in his father's engineering business, whilst at 30 and 28 years, stepsons Henry and William Dixon were closer in age to Edmund O'Sullivan. Like the Hennessy's, the Lysaught family was also on good terms with Nicholas Nolan, the head Turnkey and his family since the latter's time as a sergeant in the Dockyard Police. Nolan's eldest son, Nicholas George, whose talent for languages had been early recognised, was well established in his career as an Interpreter at the Registrar General's office, and it is tempting to imagine that this 20-year-old man also helped explain some of the mysteries of Hongkong to the newcomers.[220]

The state of the Force, 1896

Hongkong in 1896 might have grown considerably over the previous twenty years, but the Force which policed it was not markedly larger in personnel, a point made by Acting Captain Superintendent Hastings in his 1895 report during F. H. May's absence.[221]

	Inspectors		**Sergeants**		**Constables**	
	1873	*1896*	*1873*	*1896*	*1873*	*1896*
European	13	12	8	12	91	85
Indian	-	-	9	11	161	199

220 *Blue Book* 1896 Civil Establishment p. I 38.

221 Data taken from *Blue Books* 1873 and 1896, and from the Reports of the Captain Superintendent of Police 1873, 1895, 1896. The post of Chief Inspector, introduced in 1875, is included in the inspectors figure for 1896. The figures for sergeants included Acting Sergeant posts in both years, Indian Jemadar or Sergeant Major respectively. 44 Chinese coolies were employed in the Water Police in 1896, maintaining and sometimes operating or rowing the boats.

	Inspectors		**Sergeants**		**Constables**	
	1873	*1896*	*1873*	*1896*	*1873*	*1896*
Chinese	-	-	2	5	181	186
Water Police (Chinese)			9	11	136	69

Unsurprisingly, though, with the doubling of the population the amount of crime that they dealt with had grown and of this serious crime, especially larceny, had particularly increased.

Serious crime[222]	1873	Cases reported: 1,316	Persons convicted: 948
	1896	Cases reported: 2,314	Persons convicted: 1,378
Persons convicted	1873	Chinese: 6,148, European: 1,021, Indian: 102	
(all offences)	1896	Chinese: 7,453, European: 355, Indian: 49	

In 1873 there were 1412 convictions of Chinese which had been made under one of the most resented Ordinances, being abroad at night without pass or light: in 1896 this figure had risen to 3477. Now the hostilities which had necessitated huge numbers of British soldiers in the area were in the distant past, and with the development of commercial steamships, there were far fewer discharged sailors, the European wastrels who had earlier kept the magistrates busy, especially after payday, were greatly reduced in number.

Yaumatei Police Station, built in 1873 on the waterfront Reclamation Street, close to Tin Hau Temple, remained the most northerly station, closest to the Chinese border. At the extremities of the north shore of Hongkong island, new stations were built at Quarry Bay (1891) in the east and Kennedy Town (1892) to the west, thus requiring more men to be posted outside the city of Victoria than formerly. But they still struggled to provide sufficient accommodation for the men, with some of the oldest stations, especially Nos. 3 and 7 (on Queen's Road East and at the junction between Queen's Road West and Pokfulam Road), which had been built before 1860, in very poor state, and declared by the Colonial

222 Serious crime defined as murder, robbery with violence, burglary, piracy, kidnapping, unlawful possession, larceny etc. Drunkenness, gambling, infractions of pass and light ordinance etc. came under the category of minor offences.

Surgeon Phineas Ayres in 1896 to be unfit for habitation.[223] No. 7 station was so small that many of the men had to be housed in No. 8 station, in Hospital Road, Taipingshan, and walk almost a mile to report for duty. The stations in the south of the island were notoriously unhealthy; Aberdeen would not infrequently see one or even two complete changes in manpower in any year, simply because of the number of hospital admissions which it generated. Dr Ayres put this down to the presence of the malarial lagoon to the east of the port.

The main building of the Central Station, which in 1873 had been relatively new, was showing just how the climate of Hongkong could take its toll on all but the most substantial of structures. But because of the inadequacies elsewhere, the majority of the men had to live in there: May's 1897 reports showed that it was the base for 60 Europeans, 127 Indians and 102 Chinese, perhaps with some of the latter contingent in a barrack-house on Hollywood Road. Much of the ground floor dormitory space had been taken over for offices, and a Force library had grown from a small collection to one which needed a room of its own. Little had been done to the building in the intervening years, beyond patching repairs and temporary erections so it was still far from convenient, let alone comfortable, with awkwardly placed cookhouses, inadequate washing and toilet facilities and a roof with a great tendency to leak in the frequent heavy rainfall.

As May had anticipated, but in the event partly due to events, both within and outside the Force which he could not have foreseen, recruitment was to remain a pressing concern for the rest of the century. It was difficult to persuade trained police officers to sign up for a five year term in Hongkong, and the 'call for volunteers' from amongst home Forces rarely yielded a surplus, hence his recourse in 1898 to taking men from the Royal Irish Constabulary list of approved candidates. The group of eight men, who arrived on the steamer *Glenturret* at the beginning of November, added fresh Irish blood to the community already in Hongkong, and their names feature in later family reports of the Newmarket men. Especially so connected Thomas Cashman from

223 Report of the Colonial Surgeon for 1896, *Hongkong Government Gazette* 14th August 1897

Cork and William Davitt from Co. Mayo, who, like the majority of this group, went on to serve long terms in the Force, retiring on pension often after 20 or more years. William Davitt later recalled that he had answered an advertisement for the post, most likely in a constabulary paper to which he had access.

Even given the sliding silver dollar, service in the Hongkong Force did offer pecuniary advantages, especially for men transferring from home forces. At the turn of the 20th century men in the English and Scottish forces were typically receiving £1. 8*s.* per week as constables of a few years' standing, i.e., £72. 16*s.* p.a. From this they would have to find rent, especially should they wish to move out of police barracks and marry. Back in 1872 constables in London were reporting that 5*s.* per week, £13 p.a., went on rent, and this figure had risen in line with other prices in London. In Hongkong men had to wait until they were sergeants to be allowed the privilege of marriage, and more specifically, of married quarters, which were provided free, along with light and fuel as part of his terms of service.[224] For the Irishman transferring from the Royal Irish Constabulary, or removing himself from the roster for that force, the differential was even greater: commencing at just £39 p.a. in 1900 (15 shillings per week), a man would need twenty years' service to achieve the starting salary of a European constable in Hongkong.

Here the young constable's salary, some $600 p.a., understood as around £100 p.a., had benefitted from the increase in 1891, and exchange rate compensation, but by the time he had been in Hongkong a few months he would realise that the $62.50 per month he now received was vulnerable to price and exchange fluctuations. This would not have been too disastrous for the individual constable had Hongkong been self-sufficient in food or able to meet the demands of the Europeans in the colony from other silver-using territories, particularly China. However, in the late nineteenth century it was arguably one of the economies most

224 There being a limited number of married quarters, from anecdotal evidence, it appears that, at times, some sergeants and inspectors, especially those with larger families, lived in privately rented accommodation, either immediately around the Central Police Station or in Wanchai. Still entitled to quarters, the men would receive a rent allowance in lieu, although this is not recorded in the *Blue Books*.

dependent on external trade in the world, indeed, its very existence was to serve that commerce thus many of the foods and other comestibles: tobacco; alcoholic drink; books; cloth etc considered essential to expatriate life had to be imported from home or the United States. A comparison of the Market Tables, published frequently in the newspapers, shows the steady rise in the price of food stuffs. Aside from a lower spending power, the ability of the constables to send money home was affected. The O'Sullivan brothers were no exception to this, for whilst Barnacurra was a well established farm, the family there had no means of making money aside from that which the land brought in. The regular money orders helped, over the years, with the purchase of livestock and machinery, keeping the large farm productive and up to date.

Comparative table of pay in government departments employing European men which did not require specialist skills at the outset of employment.[225]

Police	Constable (80) $600 p.a.	Sergeant (12) $720 p.a.
	+ quarters & allowances ($108-$192 p.a.) for Fire Brigade duty (36)	
Gaol	Warder (21) $660-$768 p.a.	Principal Warder (3) $960 p.a.
	+ quarters	
Sanitary Dept.	Inspector (12) $720-$960 p.a.	
	+ $240 quarters allowance per annum	
Public Works Dept.	Overseer (15) $720-$1560 p.a.	
	no quarters	

The movement of men between departments within the government occurred as frequently as ever, and as the table shows, the possibilities for men able to learn the supervisory roles generally open to the Europeans were often most attractive.

225 Taken from Civil Establishment List 1896, *Blue Book* CO 133/53. Figures in brackets indicate the number of posts available at this scale.

The state of crime – a reemerging problem

Mr. May had returned to the colony at the end of his extended leave, during which he had personally recruited 11 men, on 6th October 1896, and relieved Commander Hastings, taking up once more the demanding round of meetings for the Legislative Council, the Sanitary Board and the Board of Examiners on top of the command of the Police and Fire Brigade. The commercial, functional nature of Hongkong, and its relative immaturity as a British colony meant that here there was no leisured class of Europeans, no 'idle rich', for (almost) all had to earn their living. The Colonial Office in London ensured that the senior levels of the Administration were kept 'lean' in terms of man-power, and thus men in these posts, such as the Colonial Secretary and Registrar General J. H. Stewart Lockhart; Police Magistrate and Coroner H. E. Wodehouse; the Colonial Treasurer N.G. Mitchell-Innes; the Captain Superintendent of Police and the Governor himself worked as hard for their salaries as did their subordinates. Meetings and duties often went on well into the late evening, and rarely included the long tiffins and dinners perhaps seen in later years and feature of life for the privileged in British India.

On his resumption of duties May had, therefore, many calls upon his time and attention, which in his own department included the murders of two of his men, a District Watchman and a Detective Constable, Lai Tak Shing. Although occurring before he had returned, both men had been shot whilst the police were actually arresting the murderers and May was anxious to ensure their better safety. With the abolition of the registration of brothels ordinance, prostitution was giving the police more problems than at any time in the past. The number of brothels, both legal and sly (unregistered) had grown sharply, and with no control over them, were now proliferating in parts of the city where they had formerly been prohibited. The Captain Superintendent's in-tray was thick with complaints from local residents and business owners about this matter, but with little that they could do unless the complainants were prepared to come to Court, the situation was altogether unsatisfactory. On the matter of illegal public gambling, however, he was unfortunately content to accept the opinion of his deputy. May's report for 1896 confidently asserts that, *"There is very little public gambling carried on in the Colony at the present time.*"[226] Perhaps Hastings, with less police experience, might be forgiven for not ensuring better watch was kept on this area, but he was certain that the gambling operation that flitted amongst properties between Taipingshan Street and Lascar Row, i.e., that which Baker had reported on back in October, 1894, had been broken. It is surely not just the hindsight of a century and more that suggests that a convenient development of concealed entrances and exits, an established group of watchmen who would have built up considerable knowledge of the movements of the inspectors and sergeants, and the insatiable appetite of the local population for pitting themselves against loaded chance was too desirable an opportunity to be overlooked by another entrepreneur.

On Wednesday, 16th June 1897, May received a report of gambling in this area on a great scale, not from one of his own men, but from his colleague and fellow-labourer on the Sanitary Board, Mr. Francis, which the latter had written in response to the representation made to him by some aggrieved employees of the gaming houses. The suggestion has been made that there was an element of personal spite directed toward May in Francis' motives, since he still smarted at the perceived insult of the ink-stand incident.[227] However, little, if any sense of this comes across in the letter or their subsequent engagements in the Magistracy and the Court, and it is more than probable that Francis had quietly been informed of the younger man's application to London on his behalf. Francis wrote:

> *16th June 1897 – My dear May*
> *From two different quarters and at different times the following information has been given me and I think it my duty to pass it on to you.*
> *1. There is in Hong Kong a well known gambling house keeper, named Sam a cha and his partner Lum a chee.*
> *2. They have fully organised gambling establishments constantly going in Taipingshan Ngau Lau Ho Street No. 2, a pork fat shop, and the houses in the same street to which they move periodically.*

226 Report of the Captain Superintendent of Police for 1896
227 Lethbridge: *Hard Graft* p. 30

All these houses have special exits into other houses behind and at the sides, especially through a brothel at the back.
3. The Lun Kee sailors slop shop, in a street leading down hill from Taipingshan, is a sort of depot or head quarters and in a large chest to be found in the upper floor of this house are kept the gambling account books, and the watches, rings and other jewellery and valuables from gamblers. This shop is said to be in a street called Tang Kai Hon No.3.
4. The Master Sam a cha lives with his concubines over a medicine shop of which he is supposed to be the master No. 266 Queens Road West. Yuk Ho Him is the name of the shop.
5. There is another gambling house owned by the same lot in Cheong Hin Kai but there, there are five separate houses in and out of which they are constantly moving.
6. The Proprietor Sam a cha and Lun A chee are said to be very wealthy and very influential and to have the Police in full pay. I am informed that Stanton (Detective Inspector William Stanton) *gets $35 a day, a Chinese P.C. Yeung Fat Chi going daily to fetch the money. There is always a man Ho Chen Leng, a short fat man with projecting teeth, on duty, in or about the Central Station to note any movement, and there are always twenty watchmen on duty about the gambling houses. Sergeant Tang Cheong (P.C. 190) is in with Stanton.*
I am assured that any and every move in or about the Central Station is closely watched and promptly reported and that nothing will enable you to break up this gambling organisation, except your own active personal interference. I have tested the accounts brought to me as fully as I know how and am inclined to believe them.
May I suggest a search warrant for opium (or anything) for the Lum Kee sailors slop shop carried out by yourself from say West Point Station, nothing at all being said at Central and I am assured that you will find in the upper floor of that house a box and in that box ample confirmation, especially in the books to be found in it. There you will find, I am told, a long list of people to whom bribes are paid. You may feel inclined to be indignant at any such charge

> *against Stanton, so am I, but you should test every man, and don't forget that he is in the same position as old Caldwell was,*[228] *with a Chinese wife and Chinese connections and he may be a mere tool in their hands,*
> *Yours ever*
> *Jn. J. Francis*[229]

May spent the next few days making discreet enquiries, then on Monday 21st went with Inspector Mackie, his most senior inspector who had earlier replaced Hennessy in Wanchai, and was thus unlikely to be implicated in any wrong-doing, to search the property that Francis had indicated. As predicted, he was successful despite the precautions of the gambling house because his information led him not to the scene of gambling but to the offices where the records of income and expenditure for the houses were kept. Here Mackie seized money, a hoard of jewellery and, more importantly, account books. These books provided meticulous records, detailing not only scale of the gambling income, but also the expenses, 'hush money' paid out to policemen, district watchmen and other government officials to ensure the free operation of the business.

As word got out many of the Chinese connected with the business rapidly disappeared north, including, as it transpired, members of the detective branch. As May and the attorney general, Mr. W. Meigh Goodman, examined the documents he had removed, the web of suspicion caught an increasing number of the Inspectorate, and May decided to suspend those against whom the case appeared strongest, which included Inspectors Stanton, Quincey, Baker, Witchell and Chief Inspector Corcoran. Referring to the policemen on the list, next to each

---

228 Daniel Caldwell, one time Assistant Superintendent of Police and later Registrar General was amongst very few men who spoke Cantonese fluently in the first decades of the colony and thus indispensable for the Administration, but proved to have feet of clay, and too many reprehensible business colleagues, partly through his close association with the Chinese criminal world.
229 Francis to May, 16th June 1897. Enclosure A of the documents connected with the case, CO 129/276 pp. 380-382.

collar number was the amount paid on a daily basis.[230] For the inspectors and sergeants this was generally between $1 and $3, for the Indian and Chinese constables between 30c and $1 50c. The claim was that the money would be made up into parcels every five days or so, and delivered via intermediaries. It was not suggested that the Europeans had directly requested such money from the gambling house proprietor, rather it was through these intermediaries, mostly serving Chinese constables, that the 'requests' had become known. May was aghast to find that a great number of his men were named in these records, and amongst those were many of his most trusted officers. The proportion of the Force implicated could have been devastating for the colony, for on the lists were: 14 of 109 European contingent (12%) including 6 of 12 inspectors; 38 of 211 Indian contingent (18%) and 76 of 191 Chinese contingent (40%).[231]

Over the next few months all the cases were investigated, although finding proof of the exchange of monies proved next to impossible because the main intermediaries had already absconded to China and could not be traced. The primary witness proved to be the gambling house keeper arrested at the scene, Sam Yin ('Sam a cha' in Francis' letter) and later the accountant for the syndicate, and it was evident that neither man knew many of the sergeants and inspectors by sight, let alone to speak to. A system of nicknames, both between the criminals and in the way in which they colloquially referred to individual police, helped obscure the trail by which money had, allegedly, arrived in police hands, but in the case of one man, Job Witchell, recently promoted to Inspector rank, the intermediary was found before he could slip away.

Job Witchell's case

Witchell's appearance at the Magistracy on Saturday 17th July, 1897 certainly provided good copy for the local papers and had much to

230 Inspectors lost their former collar number on promotion to that rank, and the number would be reassigned. However, amongst the Chinese community, they would still be known thus, rather than by name.

231 Report of Captain Superintendent of Police 1897 *Hongkong Government Gazette* 12th March 1898 and *Blue Books* for 1897 and 1898.

interest the reading public.[232] Witchell conducted his own defence. A number of reasons present themselves for this: he had only learnt of the charges against him late the previous afternoon, when he was taken into custody, and even if he had time to consult a lawyer, his bank account, as he would later attest, stood at just $1138 (about £110) for the support of his wife and five children, the eldest of whom was only 14, and would ill cope with the fees of a barrister to match the Crown's representative.[233] Anyhow, vigorously professing his innocence, he could not conceive that his word, that of a European Inspector would be overridden by that of the Chinese involved, albeit that this group included civil servants and former policemen. Appearing for the Crown before Mr. H. E. Wodehouse that morning was none other than Mr. Francis, and with the primary witness for the prosecution being the head of the Force, it could be argued that Witchell's trial could not be objective. The exchanges between Witchell, Francis and May were lively and often heated, with Witchell cross questioning his superior officer, who, although he tried hard not to be drawn on points of police procedure, was caught out on a number of occasions, when his lack of 'on the ground' knowledge was clearly shown. Initially without knowledge of the source of the evidence for his charge, the defendant was keen to show that he had actively pursued illegal gamblers in his section, a point that May was eventually reluctantly forced to acknowledge. There was confusion and disagreement between Francis and May as to when the latter had first received information about the gambling establishments in the Wa Lane area, but later in the proceedings May agreed that he knew of this immediately after his return from long leave, i.e. early October 1896. Both writer and recipient were keen to keep the provenance of the fateful letter of 16th June in the background. At this early point May and the Attorney General were the only people to have examined the account books seized at 3 East Lane, and the former was loath to release the books, or to let Witchell see the entries purporting to be about him. Although he

232 The reports of the Magistrate's trial appear in the papers (*China Mail et al.)* for 17th - 19th July, and those of the Supreme Court trial between 29th July and 4th August 1897.

233 Witchell was one such married officer who lived in the town, his apartment was at 40 Elgin Street, around the corner from the Central Station.

was supported in this by Francis, the defendant had something of an ally in Mr. Wodehouse, who insisted that he should see the material on which he was being charged. Wodehouse appreciated how the balance of power lay, not infrequently checking Francis when he tried to prevent Witchell pursue a particular line of argument, and at one point assuring the latter that he would ensure a fair trial. However, the Magistrate was sometimes as in the dark as Witchell.

Since the books referred to police by their collar number, Witchell questioned whether 'No. 12' really applied to him. As a recently promoted inspector, his collar number had been given to a new recruit the previous year, and by chance the new No. 12 was stationed in No. 1 District. Fortunately for P.C. 12 Patrick O'Sullivan, his lowly rank and recent arrival meant that he would not be seen as a person requiring hush money on this scale, and the suggestion that there could be any case of mistaken identity was not pursued. Francis' contention that the Chinese population continued to call an Inspector by his earlier number received confirmation when Cheng On, the primary intermediary and excise officer in the (Government) Opium Farm was called. In his narrative statement in response to Francis' initial question he explained that he knew nearly all the Inspectors, since he had formerly been in the Police himself, and anyhow came frequently to give evidence at the Magistrate's Court in his present capacity. Inspector Witchell was well known to him, and known as 'No. 12' amongst the Chinese. "I paid him money $12.60 every Monday." Despite Witchell's attempt to discredit Cheng On's testimony, this fluently damning evidence meant that the Magistrate had no option but to send the case to the Supreme Court, where it was heard in August, pushed in before the summer recess. Although he still protested his innocence at this, he was found guilty and sentenced to six months imprisonment. Initially, the Court tried to impose 'hard labour' on the term, but Witchell's defence counsel successfully pointed out that the offence for which he had been convicted, receiving bribes, was not such a one as could attract that additional burden.[234]

---

234 No consideration was given to what should happen to Witchell after his release from gaol. May was keen to ensure that none of the other men implicated stayed in the colony, but Witchell was under no obligation to leave, and, with

Further investigations

Meantime, May, together with Chief Inspector Mackie had been assiduously tracking the huge list of names and/or numerical references to people in receipt of hush money from the two gambling houses. Both the Governor and the Captain Superintendent believed that public confidence and the integrity of the Force should be as little compromised as possible by these revelations, and so were anxious that no taint of corruption should remain. The great faith that May placed in the list was questioned back in London, who were kept well informed of the progress of the sorry business. Lord Selborne, Under Secretary of State for the Colonies and those who advised him noted that in not one of the subsequent cases could Sam Yin's testimony, that he gave money to intermediaries be verified, and that the 'Chief Constable' (meaning Mr May) had a vested interest in maintaining the character of his force, and anyway, "a policeman is always suspicious." No court, it was reckoned, would be prepared to convict on the scanty evidence that could be provided.[235]

But the detailed knowledge of his mens' movements that Sam Yin's statements revealed gives some excuse for May's conviction of the essential truth of the document, and whilst in his dealings with Witchell at the Magistracy there is more of a hint of man who has been piqued that he had missed earlier opportunities to thoroughly eradicate gambling in these streets, May did not possess the rancorous nature of Deane. Although he was a strict, sometimes harsh, disciplinarian, he respected his senior officers, and would not lightly end their careers. There was a mixed reaction in Hongkong between those who felt that he was exhibiting a 'knee jerk' type reaction to the allegations which would be detrimental to the remaining Force, and those who approved of his aim of eradicating all hint of corruption. It could be argued that the racial intolerance that would characterise so many of May's dealings with the

---

less censorious public opinion than in Britain, proceeded to build a successful career in commercial firms and then later as the owner of a popular inn. Indeed, he appears on the Jurors List in 1899. His wife, however, who had been called to give evidence at his trial, died shortly after his release, and Witchell had the sole care of his five children until he remarried.

235 Memo from Colonial Office, December 1897, CO 129/278 p. 63.

Second family of George Hennessy with Susan Hennessy (née Taylor) and children in Newmarket, Co. Cork (courtesy Hennessy family)

Chinese population when governor was less evident at this time, indeed, many of the European officers shared Witchell's outrage at a Chinese man's word being taken over theirs. However, aside from those who had not already fled the colony, many of the Chinese policemen on the list were summarily dismissed, and only in the cases of the Europeans and a few of the Indians do records of 'defences' exist.

Sam Yin, the gaming house keeper was exhaustively interviewed in prison in connection with each officer, the latter who was then given an opportunity to question him. Inspectors Stanton and Quincey and Sergeant Holt of the Detective Branch, together with Inspector Baker, who was in charge of the district where the gaming houses were located were all dismissed for gross neglect of duty in not discovering and reporting the existence of the houses.[236] The rest of the implicated Europeans were

---

236 Inspector Baker's dismissal does seem particularly harsh, since it is evident that at least some of the members of this syndicate were the same as those Baker had pursued two years earlier. However, there was no real examination of the earlier incidents in the light of the more recent revelations.

removed from the Force by variously being asked or "permitted" to retire or resign, or were informed that they would not be allowed to re-engage for a further period. The European men entitled to pensions did receive them, although for some at reduced rates, but only one Indian constable, compulsorily retired, retained his. About 25% of the total force had been 'named' by the documents recovered, but not all of those left the Force immediately. The detective branch suffered the greatest proportionate loss, particularly of many experienced Chinese detectives.[237]

Before reading through each case, the balance of probability suggests the men's guilt, not least because by taking the money they would have been operating in a not entirely dissimilar manner to much of the Chinese and Chinese/British business community of the time, for whom 'gifts' were morally neutral, rather a sign of good faith and sincere intent. In addition, for the Europeans it was precisely at the rank of sergeant and inspector that the chance for a little more income became not just alluring, but almost a necessity, since almost all the men under investigation were married, and suffering from the fall in the value of their incomes. However, individually many of the men make; in so far as they can, convincing and plausible defences, given that the lack of intermediaries leaves them the near-impossibility of proving a negative. But in the end May's solution seems justified: perhaps it was indeed better to have a police force with no taint of suspicion and lose some men who have committed no indiscretions, than, by requiring these same men to continue their regular work, placing them in an untenable position, with suspicion all around them.

The case against George Hennessy

As 'No. 6 Inspector' George Hennessy was one of the few that Sam Yin, the gaming house keeper, actually recognised, for he had seen him passing in the street, and his watchmen had told him which inspector he was. On the list the record "6, dollar, Fat" meant, Sam Yin explained, that one dollar a day was given to intermediary (and Detective Constable) Yeung Fat for No. 6 Inspector. He had been approached by the constable

237 Lethbridge's claim that 'Altogether, the police lost about half their establishment' (*Hard Graft* p. 31) thus seem to be rather wide of the mark.

soon after the gambling house was opened, towards the end of the year of the Great Plague (1894) and instructed to pay something to No. 6, but had remonstrated that he wouldn't pay more than a dollar a day to a man who was not in charge of his area. In his statement he then gives the precise area of which Hennessy had charge. Sam Yin recalled that he had paid Yeung Fat the money for Hennessy up to 18th June 1895, but not after he went home.[238] 'I cannot remember when he came back. I remember it was after the Plague that he left for England. I paid money for several months before he went home. I cannot remember how many months I paid money for him after his return.' Yeung Fat, like the other intermediaries, had absconded early in the investigation.

Hennessy, present during the interview which produced this statement did not have questions for Sam Yin. Indeed, it is difficult to imagine any line that he could have used, other than perhaps questioning why he <u>had</u> continued to pay Yeung Fat when he, Hennessy, had left for home leave, i.e. between 11th April and 18th June. Rather, he stated that he had no knowledge of any such gaming house until the seizure of the books. He added that Yeung Fat was commonly rumoured to have a large amount of money and thus he would not be surprised to learn of him obtaining such money.[239]

May, in the covering letter he provided both the sub-committee of the Executive Council charged to consider the cases and to Joseph Chamberlain, the Secretary of State for the Colonies, confirmed the overall accuracy of Sam Yin's account of Hennessy's postings, commenting that he found this level of knowledge remarkable. It is broadly in line with the level of detail he was able to provide for each of the men under question. Given that Sam Yin was, at the time these statements were made, held in Victoria Gaol and undergoing hard labour and presumably without recourse to any notes of his own, the precision of his accounts indicates that the Police were dealing with a man with an impressive memory. May believed that Sam Yin's very knowledge of Hennessy's movements would

238 Hennessy had left on leave on 11th April 1895.

239 Case against George Hennessy, 4th September 1897, *CO*129/277, p. 176 ff. All the material relating to Hennessy's case appears in this volume; that of his pension in CO129/ 282, pp. 3-16.

have enabled either the proprietor or the Inspector to discover the fraud had Yeung Fat been extorting money in the latter's name, although he did not specify how this might have been achieved. Whilst convinced of the genuineness and veracity of the lists and of Sam Yin's evidence, May had to concede that it was insufficient to require Hennessy's dismissal. However, he was not prepared to allow him to remain in the force, and suggested either that he not be allowed to re-enlist when his term came up for renewal in 1901 (an unlikely event, anyway, since Hennessy, at fifty-one, was considerably older than many retirees already) or that he be asked to retire. The head of the Force made no recommendations as to pension, but noted that he 'could not conscientiously certify his conduct as having been uniformly good.' This point would have a bearing on the amount of pension Hennessy could expect, for a man required a 'uniformly good' mark to be awarded his full pension and anything less would warrant a reduction by 10%, 15% or even 25%. However, since his record in the Police Defaulter's Book records only the absence from medical inspection at the start of his service, and one instance of being half an hour late for duty the following year, for which he received a caution, May's caveat can only refer to the gambling scandal. Indeed, May added at the end of his testimony: 'I would add that Inspector Hennessy is an officer of whom I entertained the highest opinion until the recent revelations.'

Set against this, Hennessy submitted a letter to his superior officer two days later, stating that he had only ever spoken to Yeung Fat in the course of duty, and through an interpreter in the Charge Room. He had found fault with the man on several occasions and considered this the reason that the detective had seemed to avoid him. He then details his financial situation in proof that he was neither in need of money, nor with excess unexplained funds. He had put $100 into the bank five days after his arrival in 1873 and thereafter been able to save between $300 and $500 a year whilst he was single. His various appointments and good conduct medals all gave him additional income, which he claimed never to have spent in brothels or taverns, but kept a very modest liquor account in the canteen, and could call on the manager of the Hongkong and Shanghai Bank, if need be, to corroborate his claims. Some of the men investigated submitted formal sworn petitions to the Government; Hennessy instead attached a statement by Inspector Mackie, by then Acting Chief Inspector, based on the latter's conversations with Inspectors Kemp and Duncan, none of whom were amongst those on the Wa Lane lists. They concurred that they never saw Hennessy and Yeung Fat to be on friendly terms, nor the detective visiting the Inspector's quarters. Mackie himself knew Hennessy to be careful with money, and that when he had gone on leave to marry for the first time had $4,000 in the bank.

Such an extensive purge naturally took a considerable time, as the normal operations of police work had to continue. The investigation of those most closely implicated were pushed through first, and these men all left the Force in the autumn of 1897. Sergeants were then rapidly promoted into the lower ranks of the inspectorate as men percolated upwards to fill the vacated posts. The last months of Hennessy's career must have been rather strained by the suspicion which lay all around the Force, and by the breaking-up of a team that had given the Police a more stable and professional leadership than it had hitherto known. On a personal level, the departure in this manner of colleagues he had worked with, some for almost twenty five years, must have caused much sadness.

Hindsight does not shed further light on his case, or on those of the other men. Akin to some of the cases Hennessy himself had investigated, the truth remains elusive. In the end, as with the others for whom the 'evidence' rested on Sam Yin's statements alone, his pension was not reduced, and nor were the people of Hongkong willing to condemn men whose loyal service had helped render the colony a safer and more pleasant place for all its citizens. The family sailed on 5th March 1898:

> "Messrs. W. Butlin, A. Mann, G. Hennessy, T. Foord and D. Hall, who have retired from the Hongkong Police Force left for home to-day by the P. and O. liner *Coromandel.* They had a very hearty send off from comrades and civilian friends and bag-pipes skirled them a farewell from the Market Wharf. The Chinese testified their good will to the departing officers with a loud and long-sustained firing of crackers."[240]

240 *Hongkong Telegraph*, Saturday, March 5, 1898.

There is a little unresolved mystery over the return of the Hennessys to Ireland. Family memory has it that the ship got into difficulties at some point and the passengers had to be rescued. Susan recalled watching, with her heart in her mouth, as her daughter Cherry Anna, aged eighteen months or so, was handed sailor to sailor down into a lifeboat. However, there does not seem to be a record of the *Coromandel* having problems on this voyage; indeed it is reported to be back in Hongkong just ten weeks later, but nor has it been possible to find records of the return of the party given in the newspaper report to the UK.

But arrive home they did, and the Hennessys returned to County Cork. In some respects it is surprising that George, with his cosmopolitan experience, did not take his family back to London or Dublin. There are occasional examples of inspectors retiring, admittedly usually a little younger than Hennessy, and then taking up a similar post in a British force, but given his circumstances this would not have been possible. Doubtless his wife's ties with her birthplace were still strong, and maybe he was keen for a quieter, slower pace of life. His full pension of £98. 9*s.* 5*d.* p.a., whilst then a good income by rural Irish standards, was considerably less than the family had become used to, and they moved first to Kanturk, a slightly larger town a few miles east of Newmarket, and into a house on Church Street, with the local clergy and a convent for neighbours. The nuns ran a school there, too, but his oldest three girls (now twelve, eleven and nine years old) were sent to the Presentation Convent School in Crosshaven, some fifty miles south, on the Cork coast. No doubt the Miss Hennessys would have been used to a more refined, and possibly more rigorous education in very class conscious Hongkong than would be available in the north Cork schools.

Susan and George went on to have six more children, the first of which, Catherine, born the year after their return, died young; the others all flourished. In the 1901 Census, Susan gives her occupation as a nurse: it is tempting to think that her husband, ever frugal, persuaded her to seek employment in Kanturk. However, they did not stay long here, as George soon found the house of his dreams in Newmarket, 'Snugboro', just outside the town on a rise above the Newmarket dairy. In this solidly built cottage, proportioned much as its name implies but with a good garden around, he enjoyed almost ten further years of retirement, being sixty-seven years of age when he died, on 8th September 1912.

The Police Force recovers – cases for the O'Sullivans

Back in Hongkong, after the predictable fulminating letters to the press, anxieties about the integrity of the Force receded: as with so many other aspects of life 'out east' the public there knew how the intricacies of commerce might be smoothed along by a little 'help', and were not so ready to apply the absolutist principles that might have been appropriate in the British Isles. Thus it was soon business as usual for the men on the beat, with the reputation of the European contingent enhanced by the addition, in the last two years of the century, of over 40 men from home, most with police experience. Satisfactory recruitment to fill the gaps left in the Indian and Chinese contingents proved more difficult, with low pay a perennial complaint. The recurrence of plague in 1898 once more saw the Police at the forefront of operations but this time one Indian constable on plague duty died of the disease, whilst six Chinese constables were also lost.

Like their sponsor before them, the three O'Sullivan men must have cut imposing figures along Hollywood Road and in the maze of streets out to West Point. Back home, amongst his brothers and cousins, Patrick, at six foot, was known as "the little 'un". Their diligence, combined with the opportunities the 'purge' had created meant that all three men were promoted on 1st May 1899, Edmund to Detective Lance Sergeant, Patrick to Lance Sergeant and the youngest, Mortimor, to Acting Lance Sergeant. The first two were based still in Central Station, whilst the latter moved to No. 7 station. Over the last weekend of that same month, both Edmund and Mortimor became involved in cases which saw the first reports of their activities in the press.

An American, one Andrew Marks had arrived a few weeks earlier in Hongkong from the Philippines, where it was thought that he had run a restaurant. Whether he already knew Miss Marie Terrade, from Algiers, before he arrived is not certain, but soon the couple had set up house together. A very argumentative pair, they had eventually agreed to marry, and the service took place at St. John's Cathedral on Monday 22nd May

1899. The couple moved to Queen's Road Central, but marriage had not made them happier, and during the night of 26th/27th May, Marie ran out of the house. Marks traced her the next morning to the house of an Algerian couple, M. and Mme. Guion, in Pokfulam Road. Unfortunately when he arrived, Monsieur Guion was out, and Marks forced his way into the house past the Vietnamese house-boy. The American went into the bedroom where his wife lay almost naked on the floor. Alarmed by his violence, the house-boy followed him, but when Marks ordered him out, he ran round to the window to keep watch, and saw him lift up his wife's head by her hair, and then, calling out to her, lift her onto the bed. Once more ordered away, the house-boy ran to find his master, who went straight to No. 7 Station and made a report to Acting Lance-Sergeant Mortimor O'Sullivan.

The men ran back to the house, but found both Marks and Marie lying dead in the bedroom. Marks was holding a revolver, and appeared to have shot himself through the head. His wife had been shot through the breast and in the face.[241] There were no reports of anyone hearing gun shot, and no one had seen them after the house-boy left. O'Sullivan made a note of the position of the bodies, which he then had removed to the mortuary. The pair, not one week married, were buried early on Monday morning, 29th May. At the inquest later that day witnesses were called to tell how noisy the pair were, but no-one, not even the Algerian couple, seemed to know them to any extent. Their identity seems to have been only established by the marriage licence that was still in Mark's pocket. As to the reason the tragedy had occurred, the violent tempers of each party had, with lack of any alternative theory, to be accepted.[242]

The gain of the New Territories, with its many islands as well as of the relatively vast area of mainland, gave the Police the opportunity to tackle some of the criminals' more secluded haunts and lairs. The islands of Lamma and Lantau had long been famed for these, and, while the tragedy of the newly married couple was playing out in Victoria, Inspector Gillies, based on Cheung Chau, was visited on 23rd May by villagers from Moi Wa (Mui Wo) on Lantau, and told of an attack on

241 *Hongkong Daily Press*, 29th May, 1899.
242 *Hongkong Daily Press*, 30th May, 1899.

the little village by a group of twenty men two days earlier. The gang had shot and wounded a girl of nineteen and an old man, and got away in the direction of Lamma island in two Chinchew junks, with $112 worth of stolen clothing and property. The next morning the head of the Police Force directed the investigation himself, and set out with Detective Sergeants Sim and (Edmund) O'Sullivan, calling first at Moi Wa for the villagers. The party then sailed on to Yung Shü Wan on Lamma, where, incidentally, a Chinese house had already been identified and would become a Station manned by seven Indian constables the following week. The Police had the sense that something was afoot, and Sergeant Sim saw a man behaving furtively, who, when caught proved to have a box of cartridges on him, together with a piece of resin that one of the villagers identified. A search of the house from which this man had come showed that it had been vacated very recently and in a great hurry, for they found a recently-fired pistol along with the majority of the items stolen from the villagers.

In the mean-time, at Aberdeen Station on the south of Hongkong island a fishing-boat couple reported that they had been robbed and their rigging cut by a gang who had disappeared towards Yung Shü Wan. Sergeant Langley used the telephone to contact the Central Station, where Chief Detective Inspector Hanson told him to get over to Lamma island and tell this to Captain Superintendent May. He took the couple with him, and that afternoon the police continued their search for the gang, eventually coming upon a large group of men holed up in a wide shed. The men fled at the approach of the sergeants, so May and a large group of police returned in the early hours of the next day, and roused and rounded up the whole sleeping group who were brought back to the cells of the Central Police Station. The next morning they appeared in front of the magistrate, charged with being rogues and vagabonds, but their defence that they had only arrived from the mainland a few days earlier and were looking for work, with not a dollar between them cut no ice, and all found themselves serving seven days with hard labour in Victoria Gaol.[243]

243 *China Mail,* 26th May 1899, *Hongkong Daily Press* 27th and 30th May 1899.

Li Tso, Chan Tung and Li Kwan, the man that Sim had arrested on the spot and two others subsequently charged, were brought up at the Criminal Sessions on 21st and 22nd June, where they were given a sentence of seven years with hard labour, and twenty strokes of the birch within their first week of imprisonment. As the sentence was passed, the men declared in unison, "*We'd rather die than go to prison!*". However, the judge explained that he could not accede to their request: he too had to act within the statutes of the law. He then commended the police for their energy and skill in bringing at least some of the robbers to justice in this difficult case.[244] George Sim and Edmund O'Sullivan were given a monetary reward for their efforts in capturing the robbers.[245]

Not to be outdone, Patrick O'Sullivan, who the following month took the role of Acting-Sergeant for a few weeks, appeared in the papers, albeit in a very minor role, involved into the investigation of the death of a Bluejacket, an American marine, who had apparently fallen from a balcony of a hotel close to the Central Station.[246] The O'Sullivan brothers were faring rather better than the men with whom they had travelled out to Hongkong. Of Mortimor's three companions, George Bell seems to have served only a single five-year term, but his fellow Yorkshireman Joe Sutton, P.C. 54, died in the Government Hospital on 7th January 1898. The twenty-two-year-old, described by his comrades as a kind-hearted, jolly fellow, had been in hospital for three months with a long-standing lung complaint.[247] Michael Lynch first appears in the newspapers in July of the same year when he is reported as dying in a police cell in Shanghai. He had been picked up by a Chinese constable when found lying on a pavement unconscious, with his head unprotected from the intense sun. He was taken to a police station and, on the suspicion that it was not just the sun from which he was suffering, but that excess alcohol had something to do with it, put in a cell with food and drink at 1.30 in the afternoon. He responded to a police sergeant at 4pm but was found dead an hour later.[248] He had arrived in Shanghai three months earlier.

244 *China Mail* 22nd June 1899.
245 Report of the Captain Superintendent of Police for 1899.
246 *China Mail* 22nd, 24th and 26th June 1899.
247 *Hongkong Telegraph*, 7th January 1898.
248 *Hongkong Telegraph*, 14th July 1898.

Two days later the same paper reported that this was the same man as P.C. Michael Lynch of the Hongkong Police, perhaps a little reverentially adding that he was a 'well respected' member of the force a few months earlier.[249] Patrick O'Sullivan had arrived with Martin Faherty of Knock Spiddall, Co. Galway, who had been a constable in the R.I.C. He had impressed his superiors in Hongkong, who had put him into the Detective Branch, and readily assented when he recommended his younger brother, Morgan Faherty for service in the Force in 1897.[250] However, Martin was not destined for a long career, since he became suddenly very ill and died in Government Hospital on 18th July 1898.[251]

Another Newmarket bride arrives

By the turn of the century, there could have been few amongst the thousand or so residents of Newmarket and its surrounding townlands that were not aware of the locality's connection to 'the Orient'. Emigration from Ireland, although much reduced from the levels seen between during and after the Famine, was still running at 40,000 per year, about one per cent of the population, usually unmarried young people, women and men alike. In common with many villages and small towns, Newmarket had its 'travel agent', a lady who arranged the passage out, and helped ensure the emigrant was provided with the name of a friendly boarding house and the railroad they would have to take to get to the far-west state of Oregon. Two decades later this position would be occupied by the youngest sister-in-law of Patrick O'Sullivan, but the Colonial Office made all the arrangements for new recruits, providing them with passage to Liverpool or London, and their second-class ticket for the voyage. The departure of Miss Hanora Murphy, the second daughter of Daniel and Joanna Murphy of Island, for Hongkong in November 1900 might have presented this lady with a new challenge, but the ticket had already

249 *Hongkong Telegraph,* 16th July 1898.

250 CO129 276 p. 186-187 F. H. May to Colonial Secretary 5th July 1897. Incidentally, the letter notes that Morgan Faherty was 5' 6 1/4" tall, but of powerful build. May considers this short, too short really, but that a man "*vouched for by a deserving Constable*" be taken nevertheless. He requested that other men selected should be at least 5' 9" but noted that there was no standard fixed for the European Force.

251 *Hongkong Telegraph,* 19th July 1898.

arrived in Newmarket, brought over by Sergeant Edmund O'Sullivan, of Curraduff, on his first home leave. It had been supplied and paid for by William Lysaught, fulfilling the arrangement he had made with his sister, that, shortly after Hanora's 18th birthday, she would marry his eldest son, John Joseph, who was by then 25 years old. Whilst not ubiquitous, as some of accounts of Irish rural society would suggest, arranged marriages were still fairly common in Ireland, and were frequently very successful, with the parties to the match often having known each other for many years. Hanora (or Norah, as she was generally known) and John, however, had more to take on trust, since the latter had never been to Ireland. By 1900, though, cousin marriages, which had been not unexceptional in the country, were now frowned on both by civil society and the Catholic Church. Such marriages, as this couple's would be, required a dispensation from the local bishop to proceed, and these were given now with great reluctance. This may have been the reason that young Lysaught did not visit Ireland to claim his bride, although it could equally well have been his father's careful management of money that suggested that providing just one single crossing was far preferable to a return and a single ticket.

Like Bridget Bertha and Susan Taylor, Norah, who would doubtless have consulted the latter, then still living in nearby Kanturk, packed up her few possessions. Her older sister was at the time in service as a maid to the Lysaght family who lived in The Cottage, on the Pound Hill in Newmarket, the dower house of Newmarket House.[252] Mary Anne Murphy would have given Norah advice preparing a suitable wardrobe, and joined her sister and mother in sewing her bridal gown. There is no suggestion that a dowry was sent out with her to their rich Hongkong relatives, and so the family honour of the Murphy's would be represented by Norah herself.

Escorted by Edmund O'Sullivan, on his return to duty, Norah left the farmhouse early on 12th November 1900, taking the Newmarket branch line to Mallow, where they connected to the main Cork to Dublin train, which took them out to the docks. Here they boarded the Holyhead ferry

252 No relation to William Lysaught, this Protestant 'Ascendancy' family were related to Lord Lisle. The head of the Newmarket family, the Hon. Horace Lysaght, was the local Magistrate.

followed by an uncomfortable overnight train journey down to London, and then on to the port. They sailed the following day on the P. and O. steamer, *SS Rome* along with 150 others, about half of whom were families and bachelors staying on the ship until it reached its final destination at Sydney. Of the others, many were men returning to their posts in India, along with a dozen or so single women, quite probably members of the '*fishing fleet*', out to find a husband amongst the motherland's dispersed. The second class ticket, which included a berth in a cabin shared as far as India perhaps with one of these young women, cost a little over £35, far in excess of the 5 guineas (£5. 5*s.* 0*d.*) or so that was the price of a steerage passage to the United States.[253] The class of her travel indicates the beginning of a dramatic change in the pattern of her life. For amongst the Irish travelling to America even those, like Norah, from modest rather than poor backgrounds, would expect to 'rough it'. But when a ship going east had steerage, such passages were largely reserved for other races, and only the most disreputable Europeans are recorded as travelling thus. Just a few passengers changed ships at Bombay, and travelled east rather than south, amongst them Edmund and Norah, who boarded the *SS Chusan*, a steamer about half the size of the *SS Rome*, which was heading for Shanghai. Norah arrived in Hongkong just in time to celebrate Christmas 1900 with her new family.

---

253 CO129/279 pp 43-46 relates the refund of passage money by a policeman who decided to resign whilst on leave. In 1897 a return P. & O. passage Hongkong to London was $500, with a single fare at $315, calculated at 2s/2d to the dollar.

Chapter Seven

Family life at the turn of the century

In the days before her marriage Norah probably stayed with her step-cousin, Henry Dixon and his wife Severina, a few months before their temporary move to Shanghai. There she would be just a few doors down from Homeville and the rest of the Lysaught family, including three of her future married sisters-in-law. Although she had become well acquainted with Edmund on the voyage out, and doubtless heard many tales of police life, these first months would not have brought her into contact with many town police families. She might have attended the Christmas festivities at the Dockyard or at the Royal Naval Canteen on the Praya, but she would not have attended the Police Dance on Christmas night held in No. 8 Station over in Taipingshan.

It might be that she had seen a picture of her intended husband, for with the popularity of photography in Hongkong, it would have been easy for John Lysaught to post one to her, although getting a photograph to send in return would have been more difficult for Norah. Privately owned cameras in country parts of the British Isles were not common, and she would have to travel to Cork, or at least to Mallow, to find a studio. What did Norah make of John's distinctly Portuguese appearance? No doubt she had seen a little more of a cosmopolitan world on the ship, and Edmund would have done his best to prepare her. But Newmarket was not Dublin: she would have encountered few people of other nations and races, and now here she was in this most ethnically diverse and yet divisive society. She could not fail to have recognised how her new family straddled some of these divides: Isabella, her mother-in-law and her sisters, who still spoke Portuguese more fluently than English;[254] Lysaught's

254 The Lysaught and Dixon families maintained close connections with Isabella's relatives, William Lysaught and Henry Dixon managing property sales

daughters, with an international mix of husbands; the Chinese business associates of the Wanchai Engineering Godowns; the French and Italian nuns, and Italian priests who were honoured visitors to the family houses and the many Irish families of the Lysaughts' acquaintance.

The couple were married in St Joseph's, Garden Road on 15th February 1901, a dry but blustery day, with the bride given away by Sergeant Edmund O'Sullivan, and the marriage witnessed by Elizabeth Lysaught's husband, Emerson Gibson, and Lawrence Mallory, a prosperous timber merchant and neighbouring businessman of the Lysaughts.[255] No note of the wedding appears in the papers, unlike that of some of the daughters, giving rise to the idea that the need for a dispensation had been quietly overlooked, but attention need not be drawn, especially since newspapers across the globe copied locally pertinent information. However, Lysaught senior gave three smaller properties, 135, 137 and 139, Wanchai Road to his son, and the couple moved into 139, continuing to let out the other two houses.

Life for the new Mrs. Lysaught could not have contrasted more with her former life on the farm in Newmarket, where even daughters of prosperous farms would be used to hard manual labour. Since she would have helped the hired girl with the wash-day work, looked after the chickens and pigs; shared the seasonal work of the farm; driven the pony and trap down to town for provisions and attended to the constant round of mending and darning, Norah's initial experience must have been one of great time on her hands. At home, there was a common understanding that almost all worked, and there would be no surprise or disgrace at being caught by an unannounced visitor with one's hair tied into a scarf and a pinafore apron over the dress. But now Norah had less use for that coverall apron, and her wardrobe had to expand, as the need to dress well was an everyday occurrence, and then, come the humid months, the depredations of damp and mould took their toll on her clothes. She had her own home to attend to, which would not usually have happened in

---

and mortgages for them, as attested by Rate Book entries (e.g. that of 1895-6 for I.L. 255a in Hollywood Road) and Memorials.

255 Carl Smith notes that he gave his name to the street next to his timber-yard, Mallory Street. *A Sense of History* p. 133

Ireland, where she would likely have moved into her husband's family house. The Hongkong houses did not centre around the kitchen and the hearth since in European houses of this type, the kitchen was generally part of the main house, but situated at the rear, and the greater part of the work in it would be done by the houseboy. She would have to learn which food products were available, and whilst the main European-run shops of the colony imported many familiar items, these would come at a price. Washing, too, was sent out: the Wanchai Steam Laundry was just a few streets away, and, in the winter, the fires that helped to make clothes so dirty would be laid and cleared without her involvement.

Irish Bacon $1.30 2lb tin	Pork sausages 74c lb	Ham – finest York 70c lb	Irish salmon 83c lb
Biscuits: Cream crackers 66c box	Garibaldi 87c box	Ginger nut $1.10 box	Dog biscuits 16c lb
Canadian cheese 50c lb	L.C. butter 83c lb	Nestles baby food 75c lb	Macaroni $1.00 2lb tin
Cadbury cocoa 75c 1/2lb	Keillers marma- lade 25c lb	Sugar 65c 6lb tin	Ceylon tea $1.00 lb
Tinned peas 58c tin	Fresh peas 34c lb	Tomatoes fresh 26c lb	Turnips 33c lb

from the Price List published by Lane, Crawford and Co. 1st September 1894

The older part of Wanchai Road, that which ran down from Queen's Road East alongside Morrison Hill, consisted of smaller lots and properties, but even here with a mix of house styles and usage. The more recently released lots, from the point where the road turned to travel beneath the hill (at the present junction with Johnston Road) were larger, occupying space between some of the oldest factories and warehouses of the colony, and where, sold for residential building, Crown leases frequently stipulated that only European style houses of a certain minimum value were permitted. The usual route for the Lysaughts and Dixons into town would be along the Praya, rather than battling up Wanchai Road, which would often be crowded with people shopping at the many small Chinese stores that were dotted along that section. If Norah was fond of shopping, Queen's Road Central and West would have provided ample diversion, perhaps explored with her new sisters. But to get to those shops, three years before the introduction of trams, being pulled not by a horse but by a man must have been disconcerting. The noise, unfamiliar smells and closeness of the houses, even out as far as Wanchai Road, would have accosted her, as they had each newly arrived European who was not already a city dweller. The nearness of the sea, though, and the great green space of Morrison Hill would have provided some relief, when she felt too confined.

Eighteen months later, in August 1902 the couple's first child, Margaret Mary was born. With a cache of female relatives, their daughter was born at home, perhaps with the attendance of one of the four European midwives. Six weeks later, when the heat of the summer had abated, the little girl was christened in St. Joseph's church, with the ever faithful Edmund O'Sullivan as godfather, and her aunt, Maria Ramsey as the other sponsor. A son, William John, followed a year later, then five more children, the last born just a year before John Lysaught's untimely death in 1918.

A woman's history in Hongkong – Margaret Nolan

The primary written sources for this study are the documents sent to London and preserved in the Colonial Office collection, the literature of the Hongkong Administration (*Blue Books*, *Hongkong Government Gazette* etc.) and the newspapers of the time. In common with almost every aspect of public life during the period, women's voices are rarely heard: when they appear at all in the Government documents, it is generally by reference to their existence as wives of civil servants etc. They appear more frequently in the newspapers, but they tend to be the victims or, less frequently, perpetrators of crime, if not the happy bride of a fortunate man. When their achievements are celebrated, the women concerned are mostly entertainers: singers, actresses and 'respectable' dancers. Thus those documents that do directly concern the individual women of Hongkong are rare glimpses into lives so often unremarked.

One such set of letters and documents concern the application of Bridget Hennessy's friend, Mrs. Margaret Nolan for a gratuity or pension after her husband's death in 1896.[256] Even so, more is learnt from these about the exact career of her husband than that of her situation. Irishman Nicholas Nolan had joined the British Army in 1859, when aged eighteen or nineteen, and subsequently served for almost fifteen years in the 80th Regiment of Foot. The regiment was based first in India, where Nolan gained a medal and clasp for his part in the Gordon Wars, and returned to the British Isles in 1867. He married Margaret Summers in Newtownbarry, Co. Wexford in that year, and after a few years at home, the couple moved with Nolan's regiment out East, arriving in Hongkong late in 1872. Here, Sergeant Nolan met Inspector Lysaught, who persuaded him, without too much difficulty, since conditions for military families in Hongkong were still grim, to resign from the Army and transfer his allegiances to the Admiralty. Nolan became a Sergeant in the Dockyard Police on 1st June 1874, and was one of the most diligent and reliable of Lysaught's officers, serving under him for the next nine years. The Nolans had at least five children, their eldest a daughter, Maria Anna, born in Lancashire in 1868, two boys who died in childhood, and two surviving sons born in Hongkong, Nicholas George (1875) and Thomas Alexander (1877).

It is a fair surmise that money was always short in the Nolan family, and although, by moving to become a Second Class Turnkey at Victoria Gaol on 1st September 1883, Nolan did not see much increase on his sergeant's pay, the post did offer prospect of promotion. Turnkeys were entitled to free quarters, but like the Dockyard, the Gaol was only designed to provide accommodation for bachelors. The plans from the 1860s, when it was built, show dormitories only, although by this point some accommodation might have been adapted. If it was comparable to that of the Central Station, it would be cramped for a growing European family, since a single room of about 156 square feet (about 15 square metres) seems to be the norm.

Leaving the Dockyard, however, did not sever connections between the families of Nicholas Nolan and his former Inspector, William Lysaught.

256 Petition of Margaret Nolan to Joseph Chamberlain, Secretary of State for the Colonies, submitted the Governor, William Robinson, 11th January 1898, CO129/281 pp. 16-27 and additional biographical information from family sources.

These two families and the Hennessys were all on good terms and their names regularly appear as sponsors for baptism and confirmation of each other's children. The boys, about the same age as Lysaught's two, attended St Joseph's College together, and Maria chose Marion Lysaught as her bridesmaid and witness when, in September 1886, she married John Jones.

Maria's wedding was hardly a love match, for her husband was the Warden of the Gaol, and some 35 years her senior. Having been one of Dixon's Dockyard constables, he had moved to the Gaol and progressed rapidly, having early, it seems, changed his name from Patrick Malloy. Now approaching retirement, he cast about for a wife, and having been a frugal man, with a good salary and prospects of a fair pension, was able to hold out the promise of a comfortable existence. It was for this reason, no doubt, that Nolan agreed to Jones marrying his only daughter. The couple stayed in Hongkong another eight years, and then settled back in Co. Cork, near the sea. They had no children and when Jones died in 1910, he left his widow comfortably off with the rental income from properties he had bought in Cork.

Tracing careers through the available documents gives a fair degree of certainty about an individual man's path but with virtually no documentation existing for the women of Hongkong, speculation sometimes becomes the only recourse. The Rate Books for 1885 give the tenant of 4 Queen's Road East as M. Nolan, Storekeeper. This property was opposite the Naval Yard, and beside the Canton Bazaar, one of the specifically Chinese markets. In an area that would soon all become part of the Military Cantonment, then owned by Lapraik, one of the preeminent shipping firms, and which was on the main conduit between Victoria proper and Wanchai, this busy street would have been an excellent site for a European store. Could it be that, during the course of Nolan's time in the Yard and beyond, the family had lived here, whilst Mrs. Nolan had run a shop to help family finances? Before the barracks were built on this site, the house would back onto open parkland around Headquarter's House (now Flagstaff House in Hong Kong Park), providing another possible location for Margaret Nolan and Bridget Hennessy to make their plans for the union of their son and daughter.

By now a man with valuable experience, it is possible that Nolan had been promised promotion as soon as it became available, for on 1st December of the following year, he skipped over a rank, and was given the post of 3rd Head Turnkey, at a salary of $600 p.a., a 25% increase on his previous pay. The Gaol, always struggling to keep adequate manpower, had recruited a team of twenty or so discharged Indian soldiers from the British army as guards, and Nolan's newly created post gave him the management of these men; in the following year he was given a sergeant to help him with the task. Described as a *steady, active and energetic officer,*[257] he was able to keep discipline amongst the guards and the prisoners without resorting violence, and perhaps for this reason often found himself in charge of the chain gang, i.e., prisoners sent out to work on the construction of the Colony's much needed roads.

Later rate books do not show Mrs. Nolan's shop, but at the end of 1887, now forty-five, she took the role of Matron in the Gaol, attending to a hundred or so female prisoners who would pass through its doors each year. This post brought the family an extra $300 p.a., and with her husband's further promotion that same year, to 2nd Head Turnkey, it seems that the family, with just two remaining boys at home, did move into married quarters. A pay increase for most of the staff of the gaol in 1890 did not include the matron, but in 1892 both the Nolans received increases, Margaret to $480 and Nicholas to $1080, the latter being promoted to Head Turnkey. Mrs. Nolan was a gentle and careful Matron: in the 1891 report of the Medical Attendant to the Gaol, Dr LP Marque, praises her work, not only for the sick prisoners:

> *The matron, Mrs. M. Nolan, who acts as a nurse whenever there is any sick female prisoner, is very attentive to her duties, and by her tact has been very successful in persuading the women to obey the rules of the Goal.*[258]

and again the following year

---

257 Reference for Nicholas Nolan from A. Gordon, Superintendent of Victoria Gaol, 19th January 1887, CO129/281 p.24.

258 Report of the Medical Officer in charge of the Gaol, L. P. Marques, attached to the Colonial Surgeon's Report for 1891 *Hongkong Government Gazette* 19th November 1892.

> *There were, amongst the female prisoners, some cases which required great care in nursing. Mrs. M. Nolan, the Matron, has proved to be very trustworthy and kind to the prisoners.*[259]

Two years earlier, in 1885, it had been decided to set aside 47 Wyndham Street, close to the main Gaol, as the Female Prison. The rent was $40 per month, and the Administration spent $500 converting it for this use.[260] It was, though, of very limited size and had no spare room to use as a sickroom. Amongst those she had to attend that year were two women who gave birth: one successfully, with the child flourishing happily whilst the mother completed her sentence, the other who lived only a few hours, born prematurely to a sick woman, only just admitted to gaol. Her work continued to be appreciated, with similar reports in subsequent years. These are probably the only reports on the work of a woman in Hongkong's Colonial Service other than nurses or teachers in the nineteenth century.

A successful son – Nicholas G. Nolan

In the thirteen years of his Gaol service, Nolan and his family took no leave out of the Colony; nor is there evidence that they had done so earlier. Unlike the regular Police Force, these posts did not come with a five-yearly passage home, since many of the Europeans were recruited locally, often directly from the army and tended to stay in Gaol employment only for a few years. Meanwhile, both his sons were doing well at school and showed an aptitude for acquiring languages: it might be imagined that their father's job brought the boys into frequent contact with speakers of the variety of Chinese dialects found in the colony. Thus when he was fifteen Nicholas sat the tests to become a Student Interpreter. This was the Administration's latest attempt to furnish its courts with loyal men able to interpret fluently between Cantonese-speaking populations and the English-speaking judiciary.[261] The new Government post had

259 Report of Medical Officer, as above, *Hongkong Government Gazette* 24th June 1893.

260 *Hongkong Government Gazette,* 26th September and 14th November 1885.

261 An early attempt to recruit potential interpreters from amongst Chinese youth had floundered for lack of candidates. In the 1860s, the Government's

been created eighteen months earlier, and was a three-year studentship competitively open to boys of less than sixteen years of age, after which, as passed students, they would be reserved for interpretation in the courts.[262] It had proved harder than anticipated to find suitable candidates, and young Nicholas was the first.

He started work in the Registrar General's Office in April 1891, at a salary of $40 per month. Nolan was provided with a Chinese teacher, who was paid $10 per month, with whom he was required to study the reading and translating of Chinese texts. As had been the practice with the earlier Cadet interpreter scheme, he was sent to the mainland for intensive study of Cantonese, in his case working in the Legation at Swatow. He had also to master the shorthand notes made by Court writers, the use of a Chinese dictionary, translating Chinese petitions and to improve his understanding of spoken and colloquial Chinese. Eighteen months later his brother Thomas followed him, and the two young men worked together for the next two years. In April 1894 Nicholas was examined at the conclusion of three years study, but failed to pass one or two of the exams, particularly that of translating petitions. He then spent some time in the Police Court, deputising for one of the interpreters who was absent, and impressed the Magistrate, Mr. H. E. Wodehouse, with his fluency, who considered that he just required more experience to ensure his work was idiomatic. Six months later he presented himself before the board of examiners once more, and after a gruelling six exams, the Board, represented by Dr. E. J. Eitel, the Colony's Inspector of Schools, declared themselves satisfied that he had passed all aspects, most 'with great credit' and was suitable for attachment to one of the Government Departments. His only remaining weakness was translating petitions, but Eitel admitted that this was hardly likely to figure in the work he would

---

next plan had resulted in the Cadet scheme, whereby well-educated young British men came from home for a two-year language course. However, the lack of suitable men to fill administrative roles meant their diversion into these posts earlier than had been anticipated. Later on, this was the route by which the colony gained many of its senior administrative officers.

262 *Hongkong Government Gazette*, 4th May 1889.

have to undertake.[263] Curiously, the Administration appeared confident that he would be passed, as on the day he was taking the first of his exams, they voted that his pay should rise to $100 per month, the sum set for fully qualified interpreters.

The student interpreter role proved a useful one to another Hongkong family. Henry Ernest Wodehouse had been one of the first seven cadets recruited in the 1860s, and alone of the group had spent a large proportion of his career in the courts, albeit as the Police Magistrate. Like all government employees, he had seen his salary fall dramatically through the loss of value of the silver dollar, and, in common with many in the upper ranks of the Administration, was committed to considerable expense in Britain, with school fees for his four sons and the occasional renting of a property. There was little prospect of being able to send his sons to university, and by this time, a degree was a prerequisite for a Civil Service cadetship. Since his eldest son, Philip Peveril John Wodehouse, showed no inclination to join the army or the church, the stalwart professions of so many middle-class families, Wodehouse brought him over to Hongkong, where he was able to persuade the Administration to enrol him as a student interpreter.[264]

Pev, as he was known to family and friends, had a facility for languages, but at nineteen was considerably older than the other students when he joined at the beginning of June, 1897. However, Mr. Wodehouse's son could not stay in this subordinate position long, especially as it came with the stipulation that students should not thereafter seek other roles within the Administration, so on 22nd July the post of First Clerk (Acting) in the Registrar General's office was resurrected, and a salary of $1800 p.a. found for him. The start he had made in Cantonese was not abandoned, and he went on to pass the higher qualification for civil servants (not the interpretership examination) two years later, followed by Urdu in 1902 and Punjabi in 1908. Thus with a position and training very similar to that of a cadet, he was moved to the Police Department in 1901 as

263 Report by Dr Eitel on examinations for post of Interpretership, 1st November 1894, CO 129/264 pp 217-24

264 Mr Wodehouse's much more famous son, Pelham Grenville, had to work in the Hongkong and Shanghai Bank in London before embarking on his literary career in earnest.

Assistant Superintendent, and thereafter stayed in the police for the rest of his long career.[265]

No doubt Nicholas and Margaret Nolan were very proud of their son's achievement, even if he, rather like Henry Dixon, was now at eighteen earning more than his fifty-three-year-old father. But the extra income to the family house had to be carefully guarded, because the son knew that he was required, now qualified, to provide surety for himself in the form of a bond. The 1889 regulations had set a sum of $2000 to be given as guarantee in the event of the passed candidate leaving the colony with less than six years' service to recompense the government, but because of his family circumstances, Nolan was given a year to find this sum, and with his parent's help and his own earnings, submitted a bank bond in July 1895. Meanwhile, however, his brother was not faring so well at his studies, and did not manage to pass the six-monthly tests required. He therefore left the Registrar General's Office early that year, turning to the Dockyard, where he became an apprentice, receiving just a small allowance of a few dollars per month.

A few more references to Head Turnkey Nolan exist. He invested some of his savings into the new Hongkong Electrical Company, and was present at one rather difficult shareholders' meeting in 1894, when the company did not show a profit, and could not give the expected dividend. Later he was one of the witnesses called by the Committee of Inquiry, formed to look into the use of flogging at the Gaol, after the death of a prisoner following punishment and the accusations of another, subsequently discharged, whose wounds had become infected.[266] Perhaps in deference to his status, and indicative of the respect in which he was held, Nolan bore this rank until his sudden death on 4th July 1896 aged fifty-five. The papers record that he was a *very old Government servant, having been in the service some thirty-five years.*[267] By this time all the junior ranks in the prison had been rebranded as 'warders', and his successor

265 *Civil Service List*, 1930.

266 *Hongkong Government Gazette*, 11th July 1896 The Report was dated 8th July.

267 *Hongkong Daily Press*, 6th July 1896.

became Principal Warder. Thus Nicholas Nolan was the last Turnkey of Victoria Gaol.

Margaret continued in her post until the end of that year, when ill health forced her to retire and thus also vacate the married quarters, where she had been permitted to remain following her husband's death. It would appear that the couple had decided to buy a plot of land on which to build a house for their retirement, out on Wanchai road close to that of their old friends, the Lysaughts. On 25th February 1896 the lease for I.L. 368 was purchased, costing $910 and with the condition that the transaction would be complete only if at least $1000 was spent on 'improving' i.e., building a house upon the site within the first year. The site nestled at the harbour side of Morrison hill, just beside the 'Toe of the Cliff', as the diagram calls it. Margaret and her sons were thus soon able to move into the appropriately named *Rockview* early in 1897.

With nine years' service she was not eligible for a pension, but the government awarded her a gratuity of $597. The Admiralty, as has been seen, had not sanctioned any pension provision for the Dockyard Policemen, and when the Widow's and Orphan's Pension Act was passed in 1892, Turnkey Nolan, like many of those coming towards the end of their careers, realised that this complex scheme would carry little benefit for his family. The amount that would be received was naturally in proportion to the amount contributed, which, at 4% of the salary, would not be very much by the time he planned to retire. Nolan had not left a will, but with George Hennessy's help, probate was granted on the money, amounting to $1200, that he left. At some point a further sum was granted: perhaps the Electric Company shares had been overlooked and were then realised. In total Margaret Nolan inherited a little under $2400, around £250, which, it might be imagined, covered the cost of Rockview.

Employing the usual method whereby citizens could appeal to the Administration upon any subject, a year after her retirement Margaret submitted a petition to London through the Governor for some additional financial help. An elegant piece, written, one suspects, by her very literate older son, it lays out the careers of the couple, together with splendid testimonials from Nolan's superiors in the regiment, the Naval

Base and the Gaol. Mrs Nolan is grateful for the gratuity awarded her, but regrets that she cannot find further work herself and "*in consequence of the increased cost of living in Hongkong your petitioner finds it difficult to maintain herself and her family respectably*" on her sons' salaries, $100 and $4.60 per month.[268] She quotes other widows who have been granted a gratuity upon their late husbands' service, and prays that she might be treated similarly, given her husband's long and meritorious service. The Governor, Sir William Robinson, however, was not moved by the appeal. The other cases she quoted, he believed, were in very destitute circumstances, and she, after all, has already had an *ex gratia* payment. The appeal was submitted to the Colonial Office in London, but effectively the decision was made. Whilst it may seem that her application on the grounds of financial need was rather tongue in cheek for her eldest son's salary was, after all, a reasonable one, about £15 per month, reading between the lines, it is more recognition for her husband's service for which Margaret Nolan is asking. However, with widowhood still such a frequent occurrence in the colony, the Administration could only afford to ensure its employees' dependents were saved from destitution, and were not accustomed to give posthumous monetary awards for merit.

It was as well that the various government departments did not communicate too fully with each other, for what the Governor would have made of her application, fifteen months later, to purchase the land between Rockview and a neighbouring property can only be imagined, and perhaps would have done her son's career little good. Her application prompted a survey of the land and its release by auction 'on the spot' at 3pm on Thursday, 25th May 1899.[269] The lease came with the condition that a European style house valued at a minimum of $5000 was built within 18 months, and Margaret successfully purchased the 4500 sq. ft plot for $2480, the price having been bid up from an initial $1820.

But she was not destined to see the completion of the large property that was planned, and would become both 157 and 159 Wanchai Road. Margaret Nolan died some eight months after the building started, on

268 Petition of Margaret Nolan, ibid. p. 22.
269 *Hongkong Government Gazette*, 6th May 1899

4th July 1900.[270] The circumstances of her death are rather mysterious, for she died exactly four years to the day after her husband, and in the Lunatic Asylum. Was it worry about having overspent her resources and the prospect of raising a mortgage to finish the work, continued grief for her husband, or a depression brought on by the fatigue of a hard life in a harsh climate? The European Asylum, a small hospital with only two dozen beds or so (for most patients would be deported back to Britain), had quite a good record for care, and one hopes that, having received such commendations from the medical establishment, she there received gentle treatment in her last months.

More Newmarket matches

Nicholas George Nolan was, by 1903, Interpreter at the Magistracy, and at 28 years old was earning a salary of $1500, just under that of a 1st Class Police Inspector.[271] He was thus in a position to make good the agreement between his mother and Bridget Hennessy back in 1885. Arrangements for leave for civil servants outside the police appear to be a little more flexible, thus for this, his first leave since joining the service in 1891, he took a year, departing on 29th April, and journeying to Newmarket to claim his bride. May Georgina Hennessy had just turned eighteen when she married Nolan at the Catholic Chapel there on 14th July 1903. It can be assumed that the young couple spent some time travelling around the British Isles, but returned to Newmarket at the end of the year, brought back by the news that her sister Cissie, always delicate, had become very ill. Sadly Cissie died at the beginning of the following year, and the Nolans started their return journey, choosing to depart from Southampton, where on 22nd March they boarded the *Bayern* from a tender in the Solent, and made swift progress to arrive in Hongkong on

---

270 The house, *"Summersville"*, was completed the next January, but with $8000 owing to contractors, Nolan had to raise a mortgage, from J. J. Francis K.C. The death of both Queen Victoria and Francis in 1901 caused some problems with his acquisition of the lease (on completion of the property) and the mortgage, but these were eventually resolved the following year. HKRS 58/1/14(48).

271 As the first man promoted through the Student Interpreter scheme, there was no established pay structure: Nolan's salary had been increased in 1902 by recommendation. *Hongkong Government Gazette* 11th July 1902.

26th April. For the new Mrs Nolan this was a homecoming, having left only six years earlier and with plenty of friends still in the colony. By all accounts this was a most happy marriage, and the couple were soon joined by a clutch of healthy children.

Not all marriages were arranged and organised by the parents, but policemen, with only a few months every five years back in their native homes, had little use for protracted engagements and long distance romances. A sweetheart left behind would have to be a remarkably patient woman. Since the entitlement to married quarters only applied for full sergeants, for most this would mean that only on their second leave could they hope to return with a bride. The long romance of Edmund O'Sullivan and Maria Armstrong is an exception to the rule. Although through swift promotion already a full sergeant by the time of his first leave, even with the extra remuneration he received as a member of the Fire Brigade, and his language allowance, he had scarcely time to establish himself financially, especially as, like so many, he regularly sent money home. So he left Hongkong towards the end of February 1900, taking with him the ticket for the future Mrs. Lysaught, but with no intention of returning with a Mrs. O'Sullivan. Much of his leave was spent in and around Newmarket, for, like all the returning bachelors, he was expected to help around the farm as soon as he was home. Edmund spent time, of course, with his brother-in-law, George Hennessy, and his family in Kanturk. That Easter May, Cissie and Margaret were glad to be collected from school in Crosshaven, and brought back on the train by their beloved Uncle Eddie.

He also spent time with his older brother, Timothy, the entrepreneur of the family, who at the time was making a living through his ownership of a 'car', i.e., a horse-drawn taxi-cab, and had moved his family to Cork city to have sufficient business.[272] Timothy, also known as Tadhgy Tom, and his wife Bridget were living in King's Terrace, off the Lower Glanmire Road, a position convenient for the trade in more fashionable parts of the city, but in a house large enough to take in boarders to help the family

272 The first motor car had been brought into Ireland four years earlier, and the three dozen or so cars in the country by 1900 were owned by the most affluent.

coffers.[273] It was while staying here that Edmund met the Armstrong family. It is tempting to believe that he first met Maria, and was attracted to her, not realising how young she was, since she was tall for her 14 years. He came to know her family. Maria had six siblings, including two older sisters, but it was his friendship with Maria that flourished, and family memory has it that he promised to wait and return for her. The following year Michael Armstrong, the 64-year-old father, died, but evidently left his children, whose ages ranged from three to 23, sufficiently provided for. The younger ones were able to stay in school until 16 or 17, and later the family would move to a large house in Rotunda, central Dublin, where Mrs Mary Anne Armstrong, too, took in paying guests.

Edmund's gentle, attentive character, and the tales he could tell of life out east, seem to have made him popular with the next generation wherever he went. In Cork and in Newmarket with his brothers' families, both in 1901 and five years later, his nephews came under his spell and for the eldest two, Thomas Francis in Cork and John in Curraduff, this would shape the course of their lives. Thomas, at the time of the 1901 census was a boarder at St Colman's College, Fermoy, one of the most progressive schools in Ireland, but during the previous summer holidays would have met his uncle. On Edmund's next visit, he was able to help the two, now young men of 18 and 24, to put in their applications to join the Hongkong Police Force.

Edmund O'Sullivan made good his promise of marriage and at the end of his second leave, on 20th October 1906 the couple were wed in St. Patrick's Church, near the Armstrong's home in Cork, when Maria was 19 and Edmund 36. They travelled first to Newmarket, for Edmund to show off his young bride to his family, and from there to London where they boarded the *SS Nubia for* Hongkong. By chance Maria was introduced to her new life straight away, as travelling on the same ship was the returning Colonial Secretary and Edmund's former boss, Mr. May and his family.

273 With a plethora of shared surnames in the Newmarket area, the Christian name of the father is often affixed to a person's name. Thus Tadhgy (the Irish version of Timothy) Tom and Ned (Edmund) Tom. The author's father (Mortimer) is distinguished from his two Mortimer/Mortimor cousins of similar age by the same means, thus Murty Tom, Murty Ned and Murty Pat.

Sergeant Edmund O'Sullivan and Maria Armstrong
(courtesy O'Sullivan family)

The pictures that have survived of Maria show a very pretty woman, looking very young and gentle with her children, but presenting a more sophisticated, confident presence when in company. As a Detective Sergeant's wife, Maria spent most of her Hongkong years living in the married quarters of the Central Station, and when the couple arrived in December 1906, she, like May Nolan and Norah Murphy before her, found a ready-made circle of friends and relations, all with some connection to her husband's hometown.

Back in Newmarket, May Nolan's sister, Margaret, the youngest of Hennessy's three daughters from his first marriage had left school and during 1906 was tiring of helping her step-mother with her continual round of new babies and the confines of a very small town. The opportunity of returning to Hongkong with her Uncle Eddie and his new wife at the end of October was too good to be missed. She eventually persuaded her father to give her his blessing, and a small settlement, so she would not be a burden on the couple. With such a band of Newmarket men now there, and a fair number from other parts of Ireland, Margaret knew that she would be able to choose her husband and marry where her heart took her. That choice fell on Sergeant William Davitt, who had arrived with a group of men in 1898. As a young man in Co. Mayo, in the far west of Ireland, he had sent in his papers to apply for the Royal Irish Constabulary, but before an appointment came through, saw and responded to an advertisement for the Force in Hongkong. One imagines that George Hennessy heard of his daughter's forthcoming wedding with satisfaction: a family tradition was being built. In later years two of Hennessy's sons by his second marriage joined the police, one Hennessy's first force, the Metropolitan Police, the other An Garda Síochána, the post-independence police force of Ireland.

Margaret Hennessy and William Davitt were married at St Joseph's Church in Garden Road, Hongkong, by Fr. Augustine Płaczek on 25th February 1908. Missing only Patrick, who was still on leave, and William Lysaught, who was then over 70 and ailing, the wedding photograph of Margaret and William Davitt uniquely brings together the Newmarket contingent in Hongkong in the first decade of the twentieth century.

Chapter Eight

Policing the growing colony

The acquisition in 1898 by the Colonial Government of the land between Kowloon and the Shenzhen river, the 'New Territories', gave the Police Force a huge area to supervise: some 365 square miles, ten times the size of the existing colony. The skirmishes and battles that the British encountered here were overcome with comparatively little difficulty, but throughout the first decade, policing the New Territories was as near to a 'wild west' experience as could be found in Hong Kong. Initially the whole area was overseen and administered by one district officer, usually an assistant superintendent of police, acting also as magistrate. In 1909 the region was split into two districts: the mainland (North) and the many islands (South).

Widespread unrest was sweeping through China in the years around the turn of the century, with reformist and anti-reformist parties around the Qing government in Peking, the rise of the Boxers and severe drought in the north of the country all spreading disturbance south. For Hongkong, this resulted in an unprecedented number of migrants from Canton (Guangdong) and nearby provinces. Thus these earliest years of the new century saw another surge in population, from 262,000 in 1900 to 325,000 three years later. For most it was still Hongkong island, and to some extent Kowloon, that exerted its magnetic charm and the enlargement of the colony was immaterial. On the island, the completion of the Praya reclamation had created fifty-nine acres of new land, predominantly for commercial purposes but with some residential use. But even with this, the influx of people resulted in yet more congestion in the city, which could be expected to increase the likelihood of crime generally.

Since May's captaincy, the annual reports of the Captain Superintendent provided London with a very detailed picture of the level and type of crime in the colony, together with the Force's success, or otherwise, in bringing the perpetrators to account. They gave details of many of the more serious crimes committed and listed by month the numbers of crimes reported, and people convicted and discharged. Until 1907 two charts were included, 'Serious and Minor Offences' and 'Miscellaneous Offences', the latter list being the breakdown by crime of the 'minor offences' column of the first. The majority of these were still dealt with by the magistrate's court, with relatively few being referred upwards. Abstracted from both lists, examples are given below of the figures of reported crimes. Gross population figures are given beside the year, and the statistics for 1873 included for comparison. Changes in the way crimes were described and categorised lead to discrepancies, and make direct comparisons difficult.[274] In general, the conviction rate for the minor crimes, together with unlawful possession, gambling, common assault and disorder offences, i.e., crimes usually apprehended by the police, were naturally much higher than those reported by the public or discovered after the event. However, percentages of conviction are not calculable, since crimes are counted by event, but convictions by the number of persons involved.

Cases reported to the police[275]

	murder/ man-slaughter	gang robbery	larceny	kidnap, women & girls	unlawful possession	assault/ disorder	gambling
1873 122,000	5 / ?	?	938	103	232	1025	262
1898 254,000	1 / 4	4	2256	40	436	1765	265

274 For example, 'gang robbery' only appears in the later period, and the kidnapping of children came under the Protection of Women and Girls' Ordinance from 1889.

275 Taken from the reports of the Captain Superintendent for the stated years.

	murder/ man-slaughter	gang robbery	larceny	kidnap, women & girls	unlawful possession	assault/ disorder	gambling
1901 300,000	5 / 5	44	2754	22	388	1620	265
1904 361,000	4 /10	33	2622	90	427	1160	166
1907 414,000	14 / 7	6	2475	109	321	1119	315

	unlicensed hawker	street cries	suspicious character	vehicle ordinance	harbour ordinance	spirits/ opium	weights & measures	cutting trees	cruelty to animals
1873 122,000	604	353	266	71	93	24	11	64	7
1898 254,000	598	165	549	290	458	1234	560	121	39
1901 300,000	416	75	206	311	402	989	276	100	40
1904 361,000	548	86	273	399	563	2525	377	113	29
1907 414,000	1197	64	236	321	441	2129	145	103	16

What emerges from the figures, though, even if success rates cannot be identified, is no proportionate increase in crimes recorded (and here figures are for the whole colony at any date) to the growth of the population or territory. Crimes reported per head of population fell from 1: 24 in 1898 (total reported cases 10,596) to 1: 36 in 1907 (11,540). Whilst the figure fluctuated year by year, these (still high) levels present an erroneous picture of the criminality of the residents of Hongkong, since large numbers of the felons proved not to have a foothold in the colony, and were frequently banished to Canton after serving their gaol sentences. What does not come out of the figures is any diminution on those victim-less 'crimes' that were perhaps more about social control of the Chinese majority, i.e., being a rogue and vagabond, or a suspicious character, or unlawful possession.[276] It was the opinion of the outgoing governor, Sir Henry Blake, reporting on the proposed increase to the Police Force in November 1903, that the growth in both the numbers of people on Hongkong island, and in crime that had occurred that year was due in large part to the great number of steamers that now plied the routes from Macao and Canton. Competition between firms had pushed down the 2nd Class Chinese fare from Canton to 30 cents at the end of 1902, whereas it had previously been 60 cents.[277] The rich pickings of Hongkong, thought Blake, were now easily accessed by undesirable characters, who could just as simply slip through the net of detection back to their village. Annual figures also frequently recorded the value of goods reported lost or stolen and that of those recovered. All such records show a great discrepancy between these two figures and, back in 1870, Captain Superintendent Deane had lamented the establishment of a large pawn shop just over the Kowloon border, out of his jurisdiction.[278] There is no reason to think that the development of such a convenient outlet had been abandoned in the intervening years. The acquisition of the New Territories, it would seem, just meant that the thieves and their confederates had a longer land or boat journey to profit from their newly acquired assets.

On the island, police could walk between stations, take rickshas or travel on the newly opened tramline. To get to the south island stations of Aberdeen or Stanley ricksha or horse were the viable overland alternatives, or a boat journey of similar length. But in the New Territories the sole practical way to cover the miles was on horseback, using the very rudimentary road system.[279] Overall, the proportion of men employed

276 Unlawful possession was used rather indiscriminately to indicate that the person stopped was not able to adequately explain their possession of an article on their person. The link to any possible theft was not necessarily present. Such 'control' was not unique to Hongkong, for in Britain these same offences were used to manage the 'lower orders' of society.

277 Increase to the Police Force 6th November 1903, published Hongkong *Hongkong Government Gazette*, 22nd January 1904.

278 Report of the Captain Superintendent of Police, 1870, *Hongkong Government Gazette*, 24th June 1871.

279 In 1910 the Kowloon-Canton Railway was completed, linking Hongkong to the capital of the neighbouring province, but also between the intermediary stations in the New Territories.

there was not large: the *Blue Book* for 1908 is the first to record details: 15 Europeans, 112 Indian and 47 Chinese members of the Force, 174 out of the total number of 1,046, patrolled this area. With a greatly increased perimeter, the border was inevitably rather porous, although presenting nothing like the problems encountered by the Water Police, who, with only a couple of large steam launches at their disposal for speed, and a small steam pinnace in Mirs Bay, could exert little control over the frequent slipping in and out amongst the islands of members of the criminal confraternity.[280] However, with the crime figures returned from this area adding very modestly to those of the older Hongkong in the first years of the century, a large proportion of police time was spent collecting rents for the government, and acting as bailiffs.

The Police Force – its management and men

On 22nd April 1902, Joseph Badeley replaced the very sure hand of Francis May as head of the Force, the latter taking up the post of Colonial Secretary the following month. Badeley had taken charge in an acting capacity the previous year during May's absence on leave, and before that in 1900 when May had been Acting Colonial Secretary, so he knew his force as well as being an experienced leader. The previous year the management of the force had been enlarged by the creation of two Assistant Superintendent posts one for the New Territories; the other, designated as 'for Victoria' and based in the Central Station. This second had additional oversight of the enlarged Indian contingent, and was taken by the now almost fluent Urdu speaking P. P. J. (Pev) Wodehouse. Badeley's own elevation left a vacancy for the Deputy role, temporarily filled by Chief Inspector Mackie, until a 'suitable' man, i.e. cadet officer or similar, could be appointed. Men coming from the ranks were still considered socially ill-fitted for command, despite their superior policing experience.

In contrast to his rather new executive team, Badeley had a well established and experienced body of men totalling sixteen inspectors, 110 sergeants and lance sergeants (some in acting roles) and over 500

280 Report of the Captain Superintendent of Police, 1899, *Hongkong Government Gazette* 10th March 1900.

constables, the latter two figures including all at these ranks across the three contingents of the (land) Force. In the light of the growth of the colony in the first years of the new century, May had undertaken, and for once without too much objection from London, the most substantial single increase in manpower in the Force's history. He had enlarged the Indian contingent by 65% by recruiting 130 men, and promoted an additional five Indian constables to sergeants. The Chinese land force had seen an increase of sixty constables, a more modest 30% growth, but, unsurprisingly, a large number of men taken on in the Water Police, principally those involved in maintaining and manning the launches and rowing boats. The dozen or so European sergeant positions that had existed for over two decades were doubled and joined by a similar number of lance sergeant posts, bringing promotion to the longer-serving constables. However, at the turn of the century the distribution of roles between the contingents further reinforced the superior role of the European. For ambitious Chinese or Indian men in Badeley's Force there was just one (Indian) Sergeant Major post and seven Chinese sergeant posts in the land force and four in the Water Police.[281]

The Force's perennial struggle to replace the European men it lost did not abate with the new century, for just a handful each year prepared to make the journey to Hongkong from the British Isles. Thus, despite May's often repeated request for trained men, there was still the need to recruit locally.[282] For the first few years of the new century this remained as much an exercise of optimism as it had been thirty years earlier, for the men recorded as 'dismissed or deserted' were almost entirely already resident in the colony and whose association with the Force lasted only for the three months of their probation. As ever, many found better employment elsewhere, while a considerable number were shown the door at the end of this period, having proved unsuitable, usually through alcoholic excess.

281 Figures abstracted from the *Blue Books* of 1898-1902.

282 Hongkong was, of course, just one amongst a large number of dominions, colonies and protectorates of the British Empire all clamouring for able men. Throughout the period there are references to individual British Police Forces resenting the depredations made on their manpower by the Colonial Office.

Recruitment and losses – European contingent 1900-1914 [283]

	1900	1901	1902	1903	1904	1905	1906	1907	1909	1910	1911	1912	1913	1914	Total
Re-cruit-ed	9 *	11	36	15	45	25	17	18	13	21	18	41	31	21	321
From UK	1	7	7	6	17	9	10	12	2	10	8	10	25	18	
Local	8	4	29	9	28	16	7	6	11	11	10	31	6	3	
Died	*0*	*5*	*1*	*1*	*3*	*4*	*1*	*0*	*1*	*5*	*4*	*2*	*3*	*5*	*35*
Ill	*3*	*2*	*6*	*1*	*2*	*2*	*0*	*1*	*0*	*0*	*1*	*1*	*1*	*2*	*22*
Term ex-pired	*9*	*13*	*12*	*5*	*21*	*8*	*12*	*8*	*9*	*7*	*5*	*5*	*9*	*6*	*129*
Dis-missed	*5*	*2*	*11*	*17*	*12*	*4*	*10*	*8*	*2*	*4*	*4*	*1*	*6*	*3*	*85*
Total	*17*	*22*	*26*	*24*	*38*	*18*	*23*	*17*	*12*	*16*	*14*	*9*	*19*	*16*	*271*

The Police gain more Newmarket men

Family memory tells that Timothy Murphy, son of Daniel and Joanna Murphy of Island, Newmarket, and thus William Lysaught's eldest nephew, was one of the successes of local recruitment. Brought out by his uncle to help develop the family engineering and machinery business, and following his older sister, now Mrs. John Lysaught, the nineteen-year-old Tim Murphy (as he was always known) arrived in Hongkong late 1901 or early 1902. But although keen on engines of all types, perhaps his aptitude was not for heavy engineering and commerce. Certainly life with Uncle William provided no significant financial benefits and was all rather tame compared to his vision of life 'out east'. Thus, on 20th December 1903, using Lysaught's police credentials and supported by his fellow townsmen already in the force, Murphy enrolled as a constable. But the accuracy of this family memory may be questioned: is it just coincidence that a ship, the *Sungkiang* arrived from Manila on 20th

283 In addition forty Marines were recruited in 1900 for the Water Police, and seventeen, mostly Royal Navy Reservists, in 1904.

December 1903 carrying a number of passengers, amongst them one Mr. Murphy? His route out east remains undiscovered.

Thereafter the group of Newmarket men in the Force grew steadily. Recruiting from the British Isles usually had the advantage of providing ready-trained policemen, thus it is notable that the men who joined from Newmarket, whether in Hennessy's or Lysaught's 'line', were all raw recruits. The recommendation of the older men had been trusted and this trust had proved well founded. Thus future generations could rely on their Newmarket provenance for a sufficient introduction to the Force. Sergeant Edmund O'Sullivan's 'recruits' were the first to avail themselves thus when, in August 1907, Thomas Francis O'Sullivan enlisted as constable, and the following year was joined by his cousin John O'Sullivan. While most of his early years had been spent in Cork City and at school, Thomas nevertheless regarded himself as a native of Newmarket. However, he served only a single term in the force, then using his skills in shorthand, probably acquired at school at St. Coleman's in Fermoy, to move into a position in the Supreme Court as Clerk and Usher.[284] He took up this post in January 1912, slightly before his five years as a policeman were completed. In the normal way he would have had to buy his discharge from the Force, but since this role was one that had often temporarily been filled by a constable, it seems probable that the Court, valuing his particular skills, came to an arrangement with the Captain Superintendent. This was altogether an advantageous move for Thomas, for his Constable's salary of £100 p.a. became £140 p.a., and although he now had to find his own accommodation, he, too, could call on the assistance of his many kinsfolk in the colony. Of his cousin John little is known, except for his appearance in a few family photographs, and it would appear that he too served a single five-year contract. He was twenty-six years old when he joined in February 1908, above the statutory age of twenty-five, as was twenty-eight-year-old Richard Lanigan, a former RIC constable, who sailed out at the same time, and who served a full career in the Force.

---

284 Shorthand was a popular subject in some boys' schools at this period, including St Joseph's College in Hongkong, it being a requirement for those working in the Courts and increasingly used by clerks (male) in other branches of the civil service.

On the beat in Victoria and Kowloon

The newspapers of the time show that the regular day for the constable on the beat, with his station sergeant receiving his reports and even the inspector preparing paperwork for the Magistrate's Court consisted mainly of a multitude of small cases, most of which would have been quite familiar to the young George Hennessy and his colleagues, thirty or forty years earlier.[285] Their six-hour shift every twenty-four hours was still more likely to be at night than during the day and officially men had only one day off per month, but the increased number of European sergeants did allow men a little more flexibility than previously. Hennessy's successor might witness an acrimonious brawl and step in to find that the object was a small amount of rice whose ownership was contested. He could recognise the victim as a hardworking local camphor shop owner, and his adversary as a regular loafer. With law on the side of the established resident, the loafer found himself arrested and then given the option of paying a $5 fine or taking up residence in Victoria Gaol for seven days. The constable who was assaulted by a drunk Chinese Post Office employee had good reason to be surprised, for criminal incidents involving liquor were generally still the preserve of the Europeans in Hongkong. The relatively well-paid clerk had to forfeit $10 for his misdemeanour, which amounted to a week's wage. Random vandalism, as in earlier days, could often be laid at the door of the military: it was a private from the regiment that smashed up a showcase in a shop whilst he was drunk. His commanding officer had already made restitution to the shopkeeper, from the private's wages. The Magistrate relieved him of another $4 by way of deterrent. Hennessy might have been surprised to find that beach-combers, generally destitute Americans and Europeans, were rather less common in the early twentieth century, so much so that the report in 1912 is of one such man not being thrown into gaol, but placed in a house of detention, where he was to be fed and given the wherewithal to clean himself up and look for employment.

But life itself does not seem to be held very much more dear than in earlier times: the report of the raid on a suspected gambling den in

285 Cases quoted here all come from *Hongkong Telegraph, Hongkong Daily Press* and *China Mail* between 1900-1910.

Yaumatei which proved to be a wild goose chase, makes no mention of any inquest on the man who fell forty feet to his death in the course of the raid. The six week gaol term given to a Japanese man who stabbed and severely wounded a fellow-countryman seems light, especially when compared with the gravity with which any offences connected with opium were regarded. Six weeks, or the option of a stiff $70 fine was given to a man found in possession of a quantity (not stated) of the drug, whilst another found guilty of selling twenty cents worth found himself serving a two-month term, should he not be able to find the $100 fine. But the constable had to become inured to death: one particular period of four days saw a haul of sixteen corpses found by them in various states of decomposition on the inclines and slopes around the town and on the shoreline. The bodies had to be sent to the public mortuary and, if possible, the cause of death recorded, together with identity, or more likely, just approximate age and gender. Typically, of 200 found in any year, 50 of those were adults, mostly men, whilst of the remainder, two thirds (i.e., about 100), split fairly evenly between the sexes, would be under five years old. Plague still made annual appearances, and accounted for some of the deaths, whilst at this time tuberculosis was becoming more frequent in the Chinese community of Hongkong, as well as amongst the Europeans. Suicides and murders could be hard to distinguish from unlucky accident, and given the generally limited success of enquiries when there was no name or address for the deceased, there would have to be very real marks of violence to prompt a murder enquiry. Whether the Sanitary Department coolies who were detailed by the police to remove these bodies were the same as appeared before the magistrate charged with taking a purse from a dead woman, is not clear, but this crime was viewed with sufficient severity to warrant them being sent to stand trial at the criminal sessions. Given their position as Government servants, they were allowed bail, but each had to find $25, i.e., two months' salary, for this.

Hennessy would have remarked on the increase in women, both European and Chinese, coming before the Magistrate. Through the last quarter of the nineteenth century the Gaol Matron had charge of eighteen women prisoners on any day, predominantly but not exclusively, Chinese.

Margaret Nolan, who had taken that role in 1887, saw that number grow slightly in the last years of the century. With the gradual increase in the proportion of women to men in the colony, this figure was to double in the first two decades of the twentieth century. But, as with the male prisoners, most were only confined for periods of days or a few weeks, with very few serving terms in excess of one year. Three women appeared before the Magistrate of the Marine Court, charged by a town constable of mooring their sampan so as to obstruct other craft, and paid $5 each for the offence. Mrs. Parsons of Beaconsfield Arcade brought a charge of assault against a shoemaker, Mr. Pan Shing, who promptly brought a counter-charge against her. Since his 'assault' was to grab her arm as she left his shop without paying, and hers to hit him on the head with one of her shoes, drawing blood, it was she who left with a fine to pay. The rowdy Mrs. Amy Gillan made frequent appearances in front of the Magistrate, charged on various occasions by Detective Sergeant O'Sullivan for failure to adhere to the conditions of her bond to keep the peace. More seriously, women frequently appeared as instigators and actors in kidnapping cases, for example the Chinese woman found guilty of kidnapping a servant girl, and who had been caught just before she dispatched the girl to Macao to be sold, was given six months imprisonment with hard labour.

Towards the end of the nineteenth century various methods of categorising and recognising fingerprints were being developed throughout the world. The first police force to use prints to solve criminal cases was in Argentina, but it was the method developed, in 1898, by Indian experts Azizul Haque and Hem Chandra Bose, working for Sir Edward Henry of the Bengal police, that was adopted by the Metropolitan Police in Britain in 1901. Henry's system, as it became known, was circulated around the colonial police forces in 1900, and that year the Administration in Hongkong authorized prints to be taken from prisoners, although it was not until 1904 that it was possible to be effectively used. The great number of transitory visitors to the colony from the mainland provided the police with many problems of identification. The usual method of ascertaining whether a suspect had previous convictions was to take him into the Gaol to see if any of the guards could recognise him. Almost immediately upon use the fingerprint system proved itself a more exact method and within a year a dozen men had been additionally identified as having been in gaol before, or having been banished, beyond the 100 or so that had been recognised there. Prints were taken when the suspects were charged: by 1906 the collection amounted to almost 7000 sets, and the number of suspects identified increased proportionately.

The press greeted this new development enthusiastically, and copied articles published by the home papers celebrating the increased efficiency achieved. The Hong Kong Daily Press told its readers in 1902 that already *'many thousands of identifications"* had been made, whilst the Weekly Press published a long article explaining how fingerprint identification worked, and its place as both a science and an art.[286] That the method had a reliable history of use in India was reassuring, since from now on, juries might well be asked to convict a criminal on the basis of fingerprint evidence alone. Indeed, just the previous week a man had been arrested on a charge of theft and his fingerprints had found him to be someone banished earlier under a different name. The man had admitted truth of it, and was suitably dealt with.[287] Whilst the press focused on the use of the method in solving crime, the main benefit to the colony's administration was the increased control it could provide over those it saw as potential criminals, and whose presence in Hongkong it was keen to limit.

Many of the crimes and situations encountered were those that presented both victim and culprit to the police, without necessitating too much enquiry or digging about. Others had elements of detective work for the ordinary constable, where either on his own initiative or, more likely, through direction from his sergeant, he would seek to enquire deeper into the matter. A minority of cases, though, lacked an obvious perpetrator, or motive, or even chain of events, and required closer investigation.

Uncovering crime: the Detective Branch

The 'Plain Clothes' Branch, as the early papers often called the Detective Branch, had been established at the request of the Enquiry of 1871 and in response to increases in crime levels that threatened the security of

286 *Hong Kong Daily Press,* 30th October 1902.
287 *China Mail,* 8th January 1906.

Members of the Detective Branch, early 1914. Front row, 2nd from left Sgt. Bob Wills; 4th-6th from left Insp. Murison; Chief Det. Insp. Collett; Insp. Terrett. Second row, from left Sgt. Tim Murphy; Sgt. H.G. Clarke. Sun Tai and many of the other Chinese detectives must also be pictured, but a list of names does not exist (courtesy Simon Clarke and Clarke family)

Europeans. It appears to have been arranged very much on an *ad hoc* basis, without a fixed personnel or structure. Only a few mentions of it, or of individual detectives appear until the mid-1890s, when it was especially credited for some excellent work solving kidnapping cases. Men received a small extra allowance, nominally in lieu of uniform, to cover the cost of clothing. Few references were made to this allowance in the annual returns, and it is not until 1896 that two Inspectors, William Stanton and William Quincey were identified as being in receipt of a yearly allowance of $96 (a little under one month's wage). May saw the value of this Branch, and on 21st April 1897, just days before information about the Wa Lane gambling scandal reached his ears, he applied to create the post of Chief Detective Inspector and appoint Stanton.[288] The latter's enforced departure, along with that of Quincey and many of their colleagues, did not shake May's belief in his plan. Although he was not initially able to prise extra funding out of the colonial treasury, from 1st January 1898 Hongkong had two Chief Inspectors: John Hanson being the first occupant of the detective post. Later that same year May successfully put

288 Robinson to Chamberlain, 21st April 1897, CO129/275 pp. 380-386.

the case for better allowances to be made to the men engaged in detective work, and the total sum spent on this Branch was increased the next year from $1056 to $2124.[289] $900 of that was to be spent on additions to the allowances of Europeans and $168 would provide an additional $2 per month to each of the seven Chinese detective constables. Such sums were necessary, he explained, because the Branch needed to attract Hongkong's best policemen, but these men would then not be able to earn the extra allowances that were available to their colleagues, e.g., through service in the Fire Brigade and from theatre duty. In most other countries, he added, there was a differential between the regular pay and that of the Detective Force.

From 1900 the *Blue Books* start to record the numbers of men involved, but not the amount of allowances received. Two inspectors, eleven sergeants and forty men received Detective allowances, the numbers of lower ranks gradually increasing to twenty-three sergeants and fifty-five men in 1904 and then thirty sergeants and 134 men a decade or so later. These figures included the Chinese constables, whose allowance had by 1904 increased to $60 per annum, taking a first class constable's pay from $15 to $20 per month. There seems to have been no special training given, although no doubt senior officers would have been well aware of which of their men were sharpest in the solving of crimes and would have recommended them to their chief. The Europeans appointed generally held the second or third certificate in Cantonese. Aside from Hanson, who continued to receive the lower (clothing) allowance of $96, it is not until 1910 when another man, Edmund O'Sullivan, is recorded as having a $360 detective allowance, by far the largest of the various amounts available to inspectors in return for additional duties.[290]

However, such official identification of detectives lagged far behind the colony's recognition of its crime-solvers. One crime that showcased the Branch's skill occurred in 1907. Conversation in the clubs, bars, drawing-rooms and street corners through the late summer and autumn of that year followed the painstaking investigations of Chief Inspector Hanson and Detective Sergeant O'Sullivan. Nightclub singer Gertrude Dayton

289 Legislative Council, Meeting 10th October 1898, *Hongkong Hansard.*
290 All information here comes from the *Blue Books*.

had been murdered, and the suspect was former United States Marine, William Hall Adsetts. The story had all the elements of a best-selling 'penny-dreadful': women of the demimonde; brothel owners and cheap 'champagne'; gold and diamonds; a chase by sea and train up and down the China coast and a body crammed into a small trunk, decomposing in the heat of a steamer's baggage room.

The papers gave many column inches to the affair, from the discovery of a woman's body on 7th August 1907, reported first two days later, through to the execution of Adsetts on 13th November, and even, a month later, the story of the theft of the hanged man's clothes from the United States Consulate. From the outset, the police had been hard at work, discovering first the identity of both victim and suspect, and then the chain of events that resulted in the death, in the early hours of 4th August, of Gertrude Dayton in Room 184 of the Hongkong Hotel. Information was then gathered about the disposal of the trunk and Adsett's flight later that day. Sightings of the man were reported throughout Hongkong and the treaty ports, until he was tracked to Shanghai, but there evaded capture. On 13th August his arrest was made in Chefoo by the British Consulate Constable and a constable sent specially from the (British) Shanghai Municipal Police. The latter, 'Billy' Bellew was a well-known prize boxer, with whom Adsetts, also a pugilist, had fought. However, Adsetts escaped from the Consular gaol, only to be recaptured by the two policemen later that night, and put in the charge of the United States Navy. From Chefoo he was taken to Manila, since an American citizen could not be extradited from a Treaty Port.

Edmund O'Sullivan, who had had charge of the majority of the investigation was despatched along with Constable Perkins to Manila to receive the prisoner and escort him back to Hongkong. The choice of the second man was not random, for he also was a prize fighter, who had trounced Adsetts in a match earlier that year. Adsetts had made well-publicised threats to kill both of his guards during the course of the voyage, and although he was manacled at wrists and ankles, the two policemen had no sleep during the seventy-two hour passage. They seem not to have been armed with any guns, but O'Sullivan was reported as having "*toyed with a belaying-pin - a 'sleep inducer'".*[291] Whilst their prisoner appeared fresh and nonchalant leaving the steamer, the Sergeant and Constable were reported to be extremely glad to see their fellow officers take over the charge of their man when they reached Hongkong harbour on the evening of 23rd September.

The trials at the Magistracy and then the Supreme Court were closely followed by the whole colony, and both Hanson and O'Sullivan were witnesses at each. The evidence amassed by the Detective Branch was such that the jury took just five minutes to find Adsetts guilty. O'Sullivan spoke to the papers of his disgust at the murder, saying, in the language of the time, that "*it was one of the most cold-blooded ever committed in Hongkong by a white man.*"[292] Even the Hongkong Telegraph, which was not averse to criticising the police for any apparent failings and frequently spoke out against the death penalty, was full of praise for them and had no argument with the sentence on this occasion.

Political crime

The unsettled situation of its nearest neighbour in the first decades of the twentieth century occasionally brought political agitation into Hongkong, in the form of outbursts of anti-foreign feeling, which saw boycotts against firms of different nationalities. In 1905 American shops and businesses were targeted, whilst in 1908 it was Japanese establishments which came under attack, and, anxious that such actions should not lead to a more general disorder, the Administration ensured that they were closely policed. In the New Territories such xenophobia produced only limited and brief skirmishes, for the terrain and structure of the society here meant that outbreaks were frequently contained within one village or group of villages, and posed little threat of escalation.

However, some isolated acts of violence did spill over into the colony, one such being the murder of Yeung Kui-wan (Yang Quyun), a reformer

291 *China Mail*, 24th September 1907. A belaying pin is part of the rigging apparatus of sailing ships that often did duty for a weapon of discipline on naval ships, and was capable of concussing a man with a single blow.

292 *Hongkong Telegraph*, 23rd September 1907.

working for the overthrow of the Qing dynasty.[293] In his early life he had been an apprentice engineer in the Naval dockyard at Hongkong, moving from there to work in the commerce of the colony. Like many at the time, he saw China being left behind in all areas by a world dominated by Europe and America. He believed the problem to lie with the stagnating Qing rule, which was perceived as too acquiescent to foreign influence, undermining proper Chinese pride, and thus continuing the country's subservience. With some common ground with reformer Sun Yat-sen, Yeung was involved in the planning and execution of two (unsuccessful) attempted uprisings, and it was in the aftermath of the second, in 1900, that the Acting Viceroy of Canton and Governor of Kwangtung put a price of $20,000 on his head.

The Mandarin Li Ka Chuk, in charge of the military guard at Canton, was instructed to organise the capture or killing of Yeung, and fairly swiftly recruited Lau Chui *alias* Li Kwai Fan to head the gang of 'braves' required. Lau had more problem, though, putting the rest of the group together, and had asked many people, both in Canton and in Hongkong, especially in the Yaumatei area, so the plot was widely known, although fear of Qing forces ensured that it did not get to the ears of the police. Eventually, however, three men were found, and the gang assembled in Hongkong, together with the secretary of Li Ka Chuk and other representatives of the Viceroy, on 7th January 1901 to finalise arrangements.

At this time Yeung had rented the first floor of a house in Gage Street, which was very close to the Central Police Station, running parallel and between Hollywood Road and the Praya. The ground is so steep here that at the rear of the house the first floor was almost level with the back lane, making for easy, inconspicuous entry. Here Yeung ran an evening school, teaching English to young men and boys, with his family occupying the rear cubicles. After a thorough reconnoitre of the area, the gang were ready. On 10th January Yeung's class started at 6 p.m.; at 6.30 p.m., with the rest of the gang keeping watch and covering him, one of the group,

293 *Hong Kong Daily Press,* 21st and 22nd May 1903, Holdsworth & Munn, *Dictionary of Hong Kong Biography,* and papers from May Holdsworth: Central Police Station Project.

Chan Lam-tsai slipped unobtrusively into the schoolroom. He crept very close to Yeung, who was reading to his class from an English book at the time and shot him four times, in the head, shoulder, chest and abdomen, and then left without a word being said by either man. Yeung's wife and daughters heard the shots and found the teacher slumped over the desk, still conscious but obviously mortally wounded. They alerted a Chinese constable, who with commendable speed, organised Yeung's removal to the hospital and then ran to the Central Station to make his report.

Yeung Kui-wan made his 'dying depositions' to Dr. Bell and Chief Detective Inspector Hanson, but beyond the reach of medical aid, died the next morning. Detective Sergeant Edmund O'Sullivan was put in charge of the case and in the subsequent twenty-seven months, together with the Chinese detectives assigned to him, amassed the whole trail of evidence and found witnesses to testify, so that, at the trial of the gang leader Lau in May 1903, his own appearance in the witness box was very brief. Yeung himself had known of the ransom on his life, and told Dr. Bell of this on the evening he was shot. Very shortly after the murder, O'Sullivan had been able to learn the names of all the gang, and through trips to Canton and extensive discreet questioning of residents of Yaumatei, had been able to present the sequence of events to the Acting Attorney General. At the trial much of it was told through the statements of witnesses, crucially a man who had worked for the prisoner, Lau and the brother of the gunman Chan. On their return to Canton after the shooting, all the gang had received their rewards and been promoted to Mandarins of the 5th class, but the Hongkong Force's pursuit followed them there. Letters were written to try to lure them back to Hongkong, and it was when Chan was found to be the possessor of two letters, at least one of which came from *Mui,* the soubriquet by which the (then) head of the Hongkong police, Mr. May was known, that he was summarily beheaded, presumably because the trail implicating the highest levels in the murder had been exposed. Two of the other gang members were not found by the police, but their leader had returned to Hongkong in April 1903, whereupon Detective Sergeant O'Sullivan had the satisfaction of arresting at least one of the malefactors.

At the Supreme Court on 20th and 21st May 1903, Lau's only defence was that he had not committed the murder. However, since the charge was one of being concerned with the murder, and the prosecution had made a strong case for considering all those involved as culpable of the crime itself, it took the jury only ten minutes to find him guilty, whereupon the judge, Acting Chief Justice Sir Henry Berkeley, passed sentence of death by hanging.

But what of the witnesses who had been brought, much against their will, by all accounts, to the court and so had implicated the Qing dynasty in the case? Surely their lives might now be in danger? The Attorney General, noted that no one had been prepared to voluntarily go to the police, and commented that

> *"... it was not surprising that they were afraid to do so since the deceased himself was not safe in the Colony. It appeared that the Colony was full of spies, and knowing that the Chinese Government was the instigator of the murder it was only natural that the men would not have the courage to do anything to prevent it."*[294]

No mention is made of any arrangements for the protection of these men, but attention was paid, however, to the security of the jury, eight European men who were kept under guard in the comfortable rooms of the Hongkong Hotel on the night of 20th May. Such a step was extremely unusual, but not without precedent; but when the annals of legal history, as related by Norton-Kyshe, were consulted, it was found necessary to go back as far as 1868, when the jury had been accommodated in the Hotel d'Europe over night, narrowly avoiding the defence barrister's recommendation (surely tongue-in-cheek) that the Gaol would be the most comfortable place for them. The Attorney General (Mr. E. H. Sharp K.C.) had been impressed by the thoroughness of the evidence Edmund O'Sullivan presented, and asked for a commendation for him from the Bench. Sir Henry Berkeley, though, saw this as just police work thoroughly done,

---

294 *China Mail*, 21st May 1903

> *"... but he took it from the Acting Attorney-General that the Sergeant's conduct was such as deserved worthy commendation and he commended him accordingly."* [295]

Just before the arrest of Lau the press had complained about the inefficiency of police, stating that the colony was apparently full of spies and criminals, over whom there was no control.[296] Often in such political murder cases the police could not expect to make a prosecution unless the criminals happened to return to Hongkong, whilst those which did come to court could easily collapse due to lack of corroborative evidence through intimidation of potential witnesses. This case stands out in the legal history of Hongkong partly because the police had at least a measure of success under these conditions.

The Constables' sleep-disturber: Fire Brigade duty

The Fire Brigade, whose origins dated back to 1856, was staffed by roughly equal numbers of European Police volunteers and Chinese professional firemen.[297] Whilst the Chinese might be the full-time men, it was the Europeans who occupied the senior roles, providing most of the engine-drivers, and all the foremen and assistant foremen. The last named two roles were generally taken by sergeants or lance-sergeants, and these men were responsible for coordinating and directing the management of fires tackled, leading the Chinese firemen and the constable-firemen. Most constables would at one time or another do a stint of Brigade duty, often being roused from their beds having only just retired after taking the 'first watch' of Police night duty, since most fires in the colony seemed to occur in the small hours of the morning. Individual service at this rank was not recorded, but three of the Newmarket men regularly feature at the higher ranks. Until their promotion to the inspectorate, Edmund and Mortimor O'Sullivan served as foremen, and Tim Murphy usually as an

---

295 *Hong Kong Daily Press*, 22nd May 1903

296 *Hong Kong Daily Press*, 8th April 1903

297 Government Notification no. 138 of 24th December, published *Hongkong Government Gazette,* 27th December 1856; the personnel so described in the *Report of the Superintendent of the Fire Brigade for 1921.*

engine-driver, with William Davitt and Patrick O'Sullivan appearing on the lists for just a few months.[298]

The nature of the city meant that a fire, once it had hold, was apt to be particularly destructive, with an almost unlimited supply of flammable buildings so closely packed. During the last decade of the nineteenth century losses from fire had run at about $200,000 per year, whilst the next ten years saw that figure rise to close on $600,000 p.a. Arson was frequently suspected and sometimes convictions were possible, as in the case of the fire in Hollywood Road in 1905, in which ten people lost their lives. Two men received life sentences for the crime, but no one could be brought to justice in the case of the exploding godown in 1899, when a fire that started in some matting of a warehouse then spread to ignite huge numbers of stored fire-crackers, which blew off the roof and did damage reckoned at half a million dollars. Twice that amount was lost by local Fire Insurance firms three years later, when a fire starting on the north side of Queen's Road was fanned by inconvenient breezes across the road and up the hill, destroying forty-seven houses in its wake.

Gradually Hongkong was furnished with public fire alarms (four at the turn of the century, rising to twelve by 1915), and the Brigade with better communication, including access to private telephones, first aid resources, stronger pumps and motorised engines. The war years, however, saw the European section severely diminished by the departure of many of the police for army service, resulting in the formation of a small but successful Volunteer Fire Brigade from 1916 to 1920. However, it was an enquiry after two dreadful fires in 1920 which made the Administration realise that Hongkong had outgrown the rather haphazard system that had served since the earliest days. Thirty-four people had perished in a fire in Kennedy Town and twenty-seven houses destroyed by another in Aberdeen that year, and the Brigade had struggled to get enough man-power or engines to either. Thereafter eighty professionally trained, full-time Chinese firemen were recruited, under the command of Mr. Henry Brooks, formerly of the London Fire Brigade, the number of engines and fire-posts greatly increased, and the new Fire Station, originally requested

298 Lists of the Civil Establishment, annual *Blue Books.*

by Mr. May back in the 1890s, finally built. By 1923 the days of the Policeman-turned-Fireman-turned-First-Aider were over.

New fire engine at City Hall on the Praya, March 1916. Long awaited, it was made by Merryweather and Co. and cost Hongkong £1,300, arriving in one huge container from Britain. *China Mail*, 22nd March 1916. (O'Sullivan family photograph)

A slight diversion for Constable Murphy

Earlier in 1906, the Sanitary Department experienced real problems maintaining its effectiveness due to a lack of suitably qualified European men to fill the role of inspector. Their duties included inspecting the watercourses and drainage systems, markets, food shops and stalls, bathhouses and public latrines. It was essential that they spoke Cantonese with some fluency as the department employed over 120 local coolies, most with only a smattering of English. In addition, the inspectors had to be able to communicate with the residents, shopkeepers, market-stall traders etc., since they had powers of arrest. The sanitary inspector would also frequently receive tip-offs about infractions of the regulations from irate or inconvenienced townspeople. For the more outlying stations one of the police sergeants or inspectors would double as sanitary inspector, but the greatest need was in Victoria itself. To fill the gaps in what was an increasingly important department, given the inexorable growth of the city, the government authorised the full-time deployment of men from the Police Force, the Medical Department and the Public Works Department. It would seem that the men so seconded had little choice in the matter.

Four men were thus moved from the Police, of whom Tim Murphy, with two certificates in Cantonese under his belt, was the first, joining the Department on 26th November 1906. The Captain Superintendent, keen not to lose experienced policemen, managed to find enough recent recruits with sufficient Cantonese: Constables Sutherland, Willis, Hynds and Murphy. He had to hope that the men would return when their period of secondment was over, for whilst in the Sanitary Department they would come under its regulations in terms of leave, years of service and resignation, which were not so stringent as those of the Police Force. The regular 2nd class Sanitary Inspectors were paid £210 p.a., about the pay of a 2nd class police inspector, but without the benefit of quarters. The transferred men, from all departments, took that rank but were paid at a lower rate, £165 p.a. No doubt the Administration did not want to create too attractive a move for these young men, so an additional pay of £65 to the constables' £100 was deemed ample to cover the lodging, light and fuel costs. Murphy was in the fortunate position of having comfortable quarters provided for him with his uncle's extended family, and he lived for a while with his sister and brother in law, Nora and John Lysaught at 139 Wanchai Road. The department did not provide its own language school, so he was given an allowance to hire a teacher to further improve his Cantonese, and was even able to take the opportunity of a holiday in Macao, spending a couple of months away from crowded Hong Kong streets with Lysaught's relations there. However, his sojourn in this department did not last long, as the correspondence that appears in the Public Record Office in Hong Kong shows.[299] He rejoined the police on 1st January 1908, along with George Willis. Thomas Hynes had already been promoted in the Department and with his new salary of £240 p.a.,

299 Correspondence between the constables and the Captain Superintendent of Police, from 13th September 1906 onwards, HKRS 202-1-19-31.

was not prepared to leave. Sutherland also saw great opportunities for himself, and the two successfully petitioned to stay. Willis and Murphy, however, were happy to return but could see that men junior to them, and without any language qualifications (Willis had the highest, 4th, certificate in Cantonese) had been promoted to lance sergeants or acting sergeants. Their petition to this effect was favourably received, and they were assured that the Captain Superintendent would put them back in position as if they had not left the Force.[300]

Working conditions: challenges and compensations

In the summer months, the uniforms of all the contingents were made from drabette, a rather heavy type of linen, and whilst the Chinese had looser fitting tunics, the fastenings of hooks and eyes and a multitude of buttons on the traditional Indian and European outfit made no allowances for the climate. Thus attired, the men coped with the draining humidity, frequent soaking thunderstorms, persistent flies and ever present perspiration. The drying rooms were in constant use through summer and winter, when the fires in the barracks seemed woefully inadequate to the task of warming men who were shivering from nights made bitter by winds from the north. The stench from the uniforms must have pervaded the living space of each station, and, since deodorant and antiperspirant only became readily available after the Second World War, the men themselves were hardly less odorous. However, perhaps in this heavily congested and generally malodorous portion of the earth's surface, this was a challenge to which European nostrils rapidly became inured.

This was a period of station building. Necessarily the most pressing need was to construct permanent Stations in the New Territories, replacing the matsheds hastily put up and the village houses that had been commandeered as temporary bases. These, which generally housed

300 The Civil Service (and Police) examination for the first certificate in Cantonese was based on a working knowledge of Dyer Ball's *How to Speak Cantonese.* That for the second certificate included translating sentences from Bunyan's *The Pilgrim's Progress.* By the time of the fourth certificate the candidate could be asked to translate any passage from this work. *Civil Service List 1904* (General Orders).

a small team of Indian police, led by a (European) sergeant, were built or refurbished cheaply, and little thought seems to have gone into making these remote outposts at all comfortable for the men who would live there for one to three months at a stretch. In the existing stations, hurried adaptations and additions would give problems for years to come, e.g, the conversion of the former Sailors' Home into West Point Station (no. 7) was shoddily done and needed repairs before two years were out.

In November 1903 the Governor, Sir Henry Blake, petitioned London for permission to erect an additional storey on the main building of the Station. Blake, himself a former member of the Royal Irish Constabulary, had taken a particular interest in the Force throughout his governorship, and wanted them to benefit from the rash of public building that was happening in the colony in the first years of the new century. This new floor of the Station was sorely needed, as twenty-five Chinese constables had to live in matsheds in the compound and there was nowhere to put the additional men needed for the Central area. Developing methods and record keeping called for additional storage space, and P.P.J. Wodehouse, the Assistant Superintendent in charge of Victoria, would be able at last to have an office. Keen to get on with this during the dry season, Blake received the Secretary of State's permission to spend the £28,000 needed by telegraph on 14th December 1903. It appears, however, that the poor men bivouacking on the compound had to endure those rough conditions a while longer, since the storey, which used the original roof materials, was not completed until 1906. Earlier, the extension of Pottinger Street that led to the compound itself, in the Central Police Station, was incorporated into the site, and between 1904 and 1908 quarters for married sergeants and single inspectors were built behind the existing senior officers quarters that fronted onto Hollywood Road. These new buildings were two and three storeys high, divided by central staircases, and half-circled by open verandahs on the sides facing the compound. These verandahs gave a resting area with some privacy, and access to the small, projecting W.C. towers on the corners of the building, which housed drop toilets, surrounded only by a small wall. This design, used on both government and military buildings, led to a number of fatal accidents over the years, including here. Despite requests for suitable cookhouse facilities that date back as far as Captain Superintendent Deane's time in the 1870s, the kitchens remained in a much-patched temporary structure between the barracks and the magistracy, and in front of the latrines.

There are few references to the actual living costs a policeman would incur, but one short article in the *Civil Service List for 1904* provides some figures. The cost of messing for an unmarried constable or sergeant, excluding anything he might spend on liquor, was put at about $23 per month, if he was part of the large mess of the Central Station. At smaller Stations it would be higher, upwards of $30, and even $35 at some. The constable's basic pay was still $50 per month, but with E.R.C.S. added, whilst a lance sergeant received $60 and a full sergeant $70.[301] The article points out that the policeman had the benefit of alcohol and some canned goods available from their mess at cheaper prices than could be found in the town. The monthly cost of living for a married sub-ordinate officer, e.g., the sanitary officers, revenue inspectors, teachers etc., as well as married police might well come to $60-$70 for food, $20 for servants (probably houseboy and an amah), $10 for fuel and light, and a rent of $40 - $60. The latter two items were, of course, for the police, covered by their terms of service.[302]

It was through the petition of the Governor of the Straits Settlements that, midway through 1902, the Colonial Office in London had to consider and finally countenance provision to alleviate the problems caused for the Civil Service by the continuing fluctuations in the value of silver. The London government aimed to treat the administrative employees of Hong Kong, the Straits Settlements and the Federated Malay Straits as one unit, as far as it could, partly because all three used the silver ('Mexican') dollar. As silver continued its slide, salaries reckoned in it depreciated year by year against sterling, affecting not only the various police forces, but all departments of the Administration. Those in the courts, the hospitals and government schools, the Botanical Department and the Harbour Master's Department all saw their salaries

301 There were some at each rank on higher pay, and many with their salaries recorded in sterling, but these rates applied to the majority at each rank. Source: *Blue Books* 1896, 1904.

302 *Civil Service List and General Orders, 1904*

dwindling compared to those they might obtain in Britain or other parts of the British Empire. Having, some nine years earlier, authorised the principal of exchange rate compensation for these colonies, London now instructed the Governor of Hong Kong, Sir Henry Blake, to present its "Sterling Salary Scheme" first to the Councils and then to the public.[303] Under instruction from Joseph Chamberlain, then Secretary of State for the Colonies, there was little for Hongkong to do other than to finetune the various salary scales proposed.

However, the local Administration had long been aware that measures were needed, as tried and trusted employees were being hard pressed and not infrequently tempted into more lucrative commercial posts, but suitable new candidates were failing to materialise. Accordingly, at the end of 1901, it had taken steps to remedy the situation independently. The Exchange Rate Compensation Scheme (supposedly a mere stop-gap but now a fixture, voted in year by year) was revised to become 'Double Compensation', i.e., the supplement was paid on the whole salary, aside from particular allowances.

The Sterling Salary Scheme was put to the civil servants of the colony, and those who had joined before August 1901 had a free choice to either to accept this or to remain on a dollar salary, with double compensation, for the rest of their employment in Hongkong. Many of the more senior police officers chose the latter course, not least because those who had joined before July 1897 received their leave pay at four shillings to the dollar and their (future) pension at 3s/8d., both very advantageous rates, which could outstrip immediate losses when the prevailing rate of the dollar was well below two shillings. The majority of the junior men in the Force, whose retirement was very distant prospect and who had pressing immediate need for some fixity of income, agreed to transfer to the Sterling Scheme.

With the perversity of 'Murphy's Law', within eighteen months of the introduction of the sterling salaries, the dollar, having fallen for twenty-five years, started to rise, in most part pushed up by changes in world trade. By 1905 this was causing widespread problems, both in the Civil Service and in the many commercial firms that had also adopted a similar system.

303 *Hongkong Government Gazette* 13th June 1902.

The cost of living and prices in general had not decreased sufficiently to compensate to any real extent, and there was a general feeling, kept alive by vigorous press comment, that 'something had to be done'. At the end of 1906, and with the support of the Governor, Sir Matthew Nathan, petitions for relief were sent to London, signed by all departments of the service, including one from all the European contingent present in the colony. Lord Elgin, the successor of Joseph Chamberlain, initially refused to accede, but, pressed by the Straits Settlements employees too, finally changed his mind in June 1907, and agreed to fix the rate of exchange in connection with salaries to two shillings to the dollar.[304]

Out of hours

The growth of both the colony and the force resulted in a real increase in the options for entertainment and relaxation when the policeman had completed his duties. Cheap alcohol was still readily available, especially once a man 'knew his way around', and still resulted in the hospitalisation and dismissal of some European and Indian constables, but at least now there were options other than just Bible-reading groups to claim the men's attention away from the bottle. Sports were now better accommodated and teams had a higher profile than when the Scottish and London men had arrived. A Police Pavilion had been built just north of the Race Course, close to the Wanchai Gap Road, and not far from the Civil Service and Craigen Gower Pavilions. This Pavilion (which in a later incarnation became the Police Recreation Club) and its associated grounds filled an urgent need for pitches for football, hockey, rugby, cricket and lawn bowls. The latter was a very popular sport in Hongkong, since it required less flat ground than many others. The Pavilion also provided a venue for 'sports days', which always featured events for the wives and children as well as the famous tug-o'-war between married and unmarried officers. Police dances, too, were now relocated here from the run-down Nos. 7 or 8 Stations. With a large enough room to accommodate dancing, there was also space for a supper to be laid out. The annual Christmas children's party, with a great decorated tree and a visit from Father Christmas, could be more easily accommodated here

304 Meeting of the Legislative Council, *Hongkong Hansard* 16th July 1907

than at the Central Station. However, whilst there were many Chinese Police families, no mention is made in the papers of any Chinese New Year festivities for the many who had to stay in Hongkong on duty and could not return to their birthplaces for the season.

The Newmarket men, together with their Lysaught, Dixon and Nolan relatives, organised shooting parties, excursions and picnics into the hills on Hongkong island, and more adventurous ones into the New Territories. The family celebrations of this community, the baptisms, confirmations and weddings, would at some point or other involve most of the unmarried men, as they were called to stand sponsor or witness, such events bringing them often into closer contact with the Portuguese/Macanese of Hongkong than was the case for most of their colleagues. The church, specifically St. Joseph's Catholic Church, was prominent in their lives, since even if their faith was rather lukewarm, they attended mass each week, duties permitting, and Fr. Augustin Płacek, the Parish Priest and chaplain, was a close friend of most of the men. One particular religious devotion, that to Thérèse of Lisieux, which persisting through the generations in the Murphy, Nolan, Davitt and O'Sullivan families, had its roots amongst these men. A French Carmelite nun who had died, aged twenty-four, of tuberculosis in 1897, in these early years of the twentieth century clergy, St. Thérèse, as she was to become in 1923, was perhaps one of the first saints to have their cause taken up by popular worldwide devotion, made possible by the mass-media. Prayer vigils were held for the canonisation of 'The Little Flower', regularly attended by these policemen.

One social setting, though, was not open to the Newmarket men. Freemasons had early established a series of Lodges in Hongkong, with many of the prominent and rising men of the day amongst their membership. Members of the police belonged to the United Service Lodge as well as to others, and it was not uncommon for a man to receive an invitation to join soon after his promotion to sergeant or lance-sergeant. But joining a lodge was (and is) not an option for the Roman Catholics of the Force, since Masonry's principles and rituals are contrary to and incompatible with the Church's doctrine and beliefs. Membership would incur his automatic excommunication from the Church, which would mean the man was barred from receiving the sacraments, including the last rites and from a Catholic burial. In the small and highly reported world of Hongkong, clandestine membership was not an option either, since attendance lists of Masonic meetings, as well as personnel, was frequently reported in the newspapers of the day. No man could have such a secret for long in Hongkong.

Newmarket's pioneers depart

As the first decade of the new century drew to a close, so too did the lives of the two men responsible for starting the small 'dynasty' of Newmarketeers in this part of China. After almost fifty years, during which time he did not leave Hongkong, except for an occasional trip to Macao, William Lysaught succumbed to heart failure in the early hours of 21st June 1910. Having weathered the illnesses that frequently afflicted westerners throughout his working life, he had started to have heart problems six years earlier, and was more or less housebound for the last three. The final property transaction that can be traced is for I.L. 1584, once more on Wanchai Road, and which consolidated his ownership of the southern side of the road, out towards the Bowrington Canal. Five and a half thousand square foot cost him $5,420 in August 1902, and on it he built No. 153, called Homeville, which indeed became his home and was where he would die.

Grave of William Lysaught
(courtesy Murphy family)

Lysaught had made his will a year earlier, and this long document serves, of course, as a final record of his property. His eldest son, John Joseph, is not mentioned but rather than any family rift, it would appear from the Rate Books of 1905-6 that he had already transferred ownership of 135, 137 and 139, Wanchai Road to him soon after his marriage, as well as put the engineering business into John's name. It seems to have been assumed that the various families would live in

Homeville and the next door house, Killadoon; then the five properties in Cross Lane, together with the two houses next to John Lysaught's, were put in trust for his wife and his daughters. Specific provision was made, as was common at the time, that the women would hold rights in their own names, and could not transfer these to their husbands. No. 8, Burrows Lane went to Lysaught's younger son, James Patrick whilst Henry Dixon received both 5, Arsenal Street and 129, Wanchai Road. The family homes were left to his two unmarried daughters, Caroline and Margaret, who were also the residuary legatees. His executors, the Italian (Catholic) Mission and St Vincent de Paul Society received $1,500 each, (then about £150), whilst the Italian Convent was granted twice that sum. Whilst there is no definitive figure put on the value of his estate, this farmer's son from an out-of-the-way part of Co. Cork had amassed wealth sufficient to allow his daughters Caroline and Margaret, to travel frequently between houses in Hongkong and London, and regularly to enjoy the season at Cannes after they had finished their service as auxiliary nurses in France during the First World War.

In Newmarket George Hennessy received a welcome visit from his daughter Margaret when she and her husband, Sergeant William Davitt, took leave in 1911. The pair left Hongkong in February with their two children, May, aged two and George Neil, aged nine months, going first to Newmarket, where they stayed with Margaret's cousin, Timothy and Bridget O'Sullivan. The couple, who were Thomas Francis O'Sullivan's parents, now returned from Cork city and had a large house in the town. With only two children at home, they could accommodate the Hongkong family more easily than the Hennessy's, who by this time had six children.[305] Doubtless there were numerous visits for the Davitt's to pay in the area for not only did Margaret have to introduce her husband and children to their many relatives, but would have to relay news of her sister, May Nolan, of Norah Lysaught née Murphy and the Newmarket men 'out East'. One imagines that, as she was the first woman to return on leave, the Newmarket mothers were keen to hear firsthand news of

305 The family appears in the Census of Ireland, taken on 11th April 1911, at house 33 Scarteen Street, Newmarket, along with Timothy O'Sullivan and his family and four female boarders.

how their sons were keeping, rather than the perfunctory information that might be gathered from the letters they received. If so, then 1911 was a bonanza year for news since May and Nicholas Nolan were also were on leave from August of that year, and, hearing that May's father's health was failing, they too travelled first to Newmarket. Thus George Hennessy had the satisfaction and pride of seeing for himself that both his eldest daughters were settled into happy and comfortable marriages, before he died the following September.

Another Newmarket Detective

Tim Murphy, who possessed the rare distinction of being a local recruit who progressed to a career in the police, came early to the attention of his superiors for his dynamism and initiative. With their local knowledge and spoken Cantonese significantly enhanced by their service in the Sanitary Department, and the St. John's Ambulance certificates acquired, in accordance with the promise extracted from the police, both he and George Willis were promoted to Lance Sergeant on their return to the Force in 15th April, 1908. Murphy was moved into the Detective Branch very shortly after this and his experiences of the last two years were useful preparation for an aspiring detective.

Whilst F.H. May had campaigned for increased allowances partly because detectives were precluded from service in the Fire Brigade, this is not borne out by the records. In September 1908 Murphy was able to return to those duties, as one of the Assistant Engine Drivers, occasionally "driving", that is to say, working one of the engine pumps. At this point the machinery was still pulled manually by coolies through the streets, but Murphy, who had a great love all things vehicular, and had worked as an engine driver on the Kanturk to Newmarket Railway for a short time before he travelled east, approached his Brigade duties with great enthusiasm. He remained in the Fire Brigade until his promotion to the inspectorate, taking on different roles. The *Blue Book* of 1917, for example, shows that there were many vacancies caused by the depletion of the regular Police Force during the First World War, but Detective Sergeant Tim Murphy is a Foreman, whilst fellow Detective Sergeant

(A87) Henry Goscombe Clarke was Foreman and Engine Driver of the floating fire engine, both receiving an extra $300 p.a. for their duties.

Chapter Nine

The three Inspectors O'Sullivan

The careers of the O'Sullivan brothers, Patrick and Mortimor, ran along similar lines, and, in a force that still promoted primarily on seniority of service, just a year or two behind that of their cousin Edmund. Back in 1901 they had taken their first leave together, and were promoted to sergeants on their return. Both men were making their mark in the colony, and thus when they departed for their second sojourn in Newmarket in 1907, the *Hongkong Telegraph* reported the event thus:

> "*Three well-known police officials - Sergeant Pat O'Sullivan, late of Hunghom Police Station; Detective Sergeant M. O'Sullivan, of the Central Police Station, and Sergeant Kendall, of No. 7 Police Station - left for the Homeland today on nine months' leave, on board the English mail steamer Macedonia. A large crowd of friends accompanied the departing officers on board ship, there to wish them 'bon voyage'.*"[306]

The *China Mail* of the same day, which did not mention the departure of the policemen, but recorded a number of prominent citizens also departing on that ship, mentioned that the press of well-wishers on the vessel was such that it had been hard to make out who was sailing and who was staying when time came for the ship to cast anchor. They arrived in London on 27th April, a speedy five week journey, perhaps made more possible because the ship only took on passengers at Singapore and Bombay. There is no memory of whether the men spent time in London before returning home, or when there, if any of the local girls caught their eye. Doubtless their father, now over sixty, welcomed their help on the

306 *Hongkong Telegraph*, 23. 03.1907.

farm that summer and autumn. But all too soon it was time to return and Mortimer O'Sullivan boarded the same ship, the *Macedonia* in London on 5th December, arriving in Hongkong on 8th January 1908.[307] However, he made this journey alone, as his brother did not return until 14th April, significantly exceeding his allotted nine months. The reason for this is not recorded, but perhaps the malaria that was to dog Patrick O'Sullivan for the rest of his life was particularly troublesome that winter. If that was the case, however, it might have called into question his fitness for continued service in the colony. Alternatively, a pressing matter of family business for the eldest son to deal with might have been the grounds on which he was granted an additional three months leave.

Shortly before Patrick's return, on 21st March 1908, his cousin Edmund was appointed as Acting Third Class Inspector. He was standing in for Inspector Warnock, who had taken pre-retirement leave, and when he started to draw his pension, on 25th June, the substantive post became available for Edmund. As if in a reverse domino game, a series of men were 'bumped up' a rank on that day, including Patrick, who took over the Acting role vacated by his cousin. In this case, rather than covering for one particular man, it was deemed a 'temporary' post, helping to cover for leave and sickness, and he had to hold this until 20th March 1910, when another round of promotions allowed him the permanent position. An examination also had to be passed before the substantive post could be granted, which some men took whilst still sergeants, others when acting inspector. A year later another domino game on 10th June saw Edmund move to a 2nd Class appointment, whilst his younger cousin Mortimor became a Third Class Inspector. One imagines that three Inspectors O'Sullivan in the Force was occasionally a recipe for confusion.

Joining the permanent inspectorate came at a price for the unmarried amongst the men. The starting salary was £180 p.a., just £20 higher than that of a Sergeant; but now the man was precluded from earning a little extra from Fire Brigade service, etc., and nor did he automatically retain his detective allowance. Some time earlier, finding that married men were struggling to manage on their pay, a raft of allowances, mainly

307 *Civil Service List* 1914.

culled from other departments of the government, were granted, especially when they were in charge of a more outlying station. Moreover, posting married men to such stations relieved the pressure on married quarters around Central Station, and was felt to lend stability to the outpost. The opinion of the women about life half a day's journey away from the civilisation of Victoria was not considered. But in 1910 the three unmarried Third Class Inspectors found that they were earning less than many of their sergeant colleagues, and now no longer part of that mess, but quartered in separate accommodation, had greater outgoings than before. William Murison, Robert Fenton and Patrick O'Sullivan petitioned the Government, via their Captain Superintendent, asking that the rank of 3rd Class be abolished, and they be promoted to Second Class Inspectors, which brought with it a pay of £200 p.a., reminding the Government that men in their position had, almost always, already served fifteen years in the Force.[308] The machinery of administration moved in a stately fashion: the petitioners letter of 4th January 1911 was forwarded to the Governor on 6th March. Captain Superintendent Badeley added his recommendation for a favourable response, noting that a similar measure had been adopted in the Sanitary Department a few years earlier. From the Governor the letter then was transmitted to Lewis Harcourt, the Secretary of State for the Colonies in London on 8th April. On the 18th May approval was given for the rank to be abolished at the beginning of 1912, but Murison

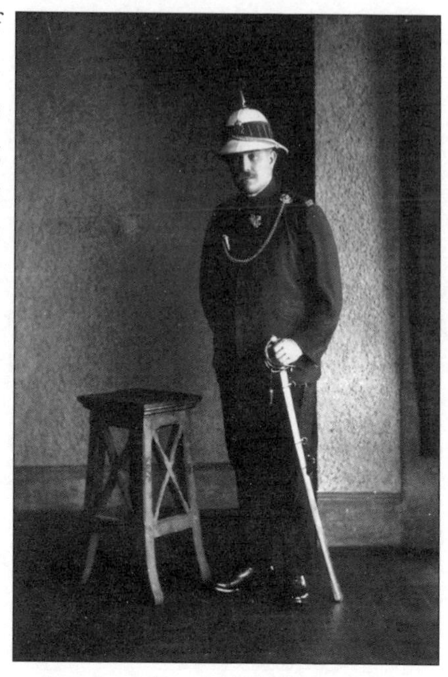

Inspector Patrick O'Sullivan, 1911
(O'Sullivan family photograph)

308 Petition of Third Class Inspectors and associated correspondence, 4th January 1911, CO129/376 p. 286-7.

and Fenton had already received their promotions in the ordinary way, so the beneficiaries were Patrick and Mortimor O'Sullivan, Detective Inspector Watt, and Alexander Gordon, the latter two of whom were married already.

While his brother and cousin would frequently be working over a period of time on large, complex cases, it was Patrick O'Sullivan, remaining in the uniformed branch, who, in his thirteen years as an inspector, handled hundreds of cases. Only occasionally had he the opportunity to investigate a case from beginning to end, for more generally an incident would be reported to him by a junior officer, after which he had only to direct any necessary enquiries and bring the case to court, if necessary. Many were trivial and mundane, but although they were quickly dealt with by the Police Court, it was their sheer volume that meant that the Inspector would spend the best part of his 'court' day there. The growth in population had required, as seen, a great increase in the size of the Force, but whilst the number of subordinate police officers had doubled since Hennessy's last years (about 500 in 1896 becoming 988 in 1914), the inspectorate now numbered just eighteen, compared to the twelve of earlier years. It can be surmised that the inspectors were, therefore, commensurately more busy. From the newspaper reports it is evident that the four-day scheme May described in 1897 was still in operation, doubtless, though, now with longer hours for the inspectors.

Various types of thieves were staple fare at the Court, for example the lad whose attempt to snatch an ear-ring, value five cents, from a baby carried on its mother's back earned him a good hiding; the man who made off with a bag of tree bark or the pickpocket who shadowed a man emerging from a bank and relieved him of $500.[309] Opium was still the downfall of many, be it smuggling, selling or buying illegal supplies, and on the day that the Armistice was declared, while the rest of Hongkong started to celebrate in earnest, the Courts kept busy, and Patrick O'Sullivan prosecuted a ship's 'boy', who was found with six taels of opium which he had agreed to take to Kongmoon in return for one dollar. The venture

---

309 *Hong Kong Telegraph,* 4th November 1918, *Hong Kong Daily Press,* 17th January 1918 and 23rd January 1914.

cost him a $20 fine, or three months in Victoria Gaol.[310] Alongside being a suspicious character and vagrancy, 'unlawful possession' was an offence that was still frequently used as a means of social control: keeping the 'order' more than the 'law'. One of his constables arrested a Chinese man who could not account satisfactorily for the bundle of twine he was carrying, whilst another, who claimed to be going to work (at 4 a. m.) had a chisel in his socks and was carrying a lock-pick, that might be used for house-breaking. The magistrate asked the Inspector to find the man's employer, if possible, whilst the former man was fined $3 for unlawful possession. A market trader and his *foki* (assistant) made a complaint that the latter had been robbed of a basket of cocoanuts (sic) by a gang of ten men. One of the alleged was found by a constable, but this man claimed that it was the others who had sneaked up behind the *foki* and grabbed the fruits. They had thrown them around a good bit, and given him one, whereupon he had eaten it. Once more, unlawful possession was the verdict, with a stiff $10 or fourteen days hard labour as a reward.[311]

Alcohol featured, although perhaps less frequently than thirty years earlier, for example the drunken Chinese man who declared that he wasn't very drunk, it was just a few drinks that he had taken, but since O'Sullivan reported that the police had had to send him to the hospital at 2 a.m., as he could scarcely move, he later found himself being taken to the Gaol for seven days.[312] This was still an unusual case because of the ethnicity of the culprit: more typical was the case of two rather intoxicated Russian sailors whose non-cooperation with a police constable meant a fine of $7 each or a fortnight behind bars.[313] Violence did not need alcohol to be fired up, since there was plenty of guild and trade rivalry for gangs to exploit. In 1915, Inspector O'Sullivan brought three members of a rattan guild to court, charged with seriously injuring five members of a rival guild, probably with a chopper that was found in their possession.

---

310 *Hongkong Telegraph,* 11th November 1918.

311 All three cases were reported in *Hongkong Telegraph,* 12th September 1918.

312 *Hong Kong Telegraph,* 2nd October 1918.

313 *Hong Kong Daily Press,* 23rd January 1914.

At first called a 'fight', it became apparent that it was a premeditated and unexpected attack, the five having no chance to defend themselves.[314]

Although Edmund and Mortimor O'Sullivan spent the greater part of their years of service engaged in detective work, regular police duties also made up part of their daily life. Just as errant Chinese could slip easily over the border into mainland China, until the restrictions on European movement imposed during the war years there were many possibilities for non-locals to quickly flee the *locus* of their crime. But increasing cooperation between forces meant that more were brought to book, as when Edmund O'Sullivan was sent to make the arrest of Vincente Sotto upon his arrival in the colony. He had eluded a sentence passed four years earlier in the Philippines for the abduction of a girl, skipping out of that colony when he was on bail pending an appeal hearing. The conviction (in his absence) was upheld, and his punishment in fact increased, so when O'Sullivan brought him to Court, the lawyers of Hongkong engaged in a lengthy consideration of the legality of his position in this colony, but without the need of any further police involvement.[315]

During his time as Inspector of Wanchai Police Station, Mortimor O'Sullivan encountered the captain of the *On Lee,* one William Hudson, in the early hours of the morning when the latter was brought in, charged with refusing to pay a ricksha fare. Apparently the mariner had been at the bridge since noon the previous day, and had gone ashore in search of tobacco. He had instructed the ricksha driver to take him to Sincere's (department store), but the man, perhaps knowing the opening hours of that place better than the captain, took him to Wanchai, which annoyed the Hudson a good deal, who refused to pay him. He only had a few cents on him - probably not enough to even pay his fare, but knew that he could buy tobacco by giving his name and ship. By the time he reached the Station he was in a high temper, using abusive language and calling one of the constables 'a dirty pig'. He was then put in a cell for the night, presumably to cool down. He used his appearance before the magistrate, Mr. Melbourne, later that morning to accuse the police of treating him

314 *Hong Kong Daily Press* 14th September 1915 and *Hong Kong Telegraph* 1st October 1915.

315 *China Mail* 6th June 1913.

'like a dog'. Inspector Mortimor O'Sullivan told the magistrate that the defendant was abusive and insulting, whereupon Hudson berated the Inspector for his treatment, whilst his counsel tried to quieten him. But the Captain would not be silenced, declaring that 'I may as well be fined for a sheep as a lamb.' The magistrate, however, was not going to allow him to vent his ire in court, and advised him to make any complaints to the head of the Police, but first to pay 60 cents to the ricksha driver. The paper called this a serious complaint against the police, but took it no further. It would appear that Hudson had received the same treatment as many a British seaman before him, and rather better than any dubious-looking Chinese man would, but it was his *amour propre,* rather than his physical self, that had been injured.[316]

Should life for the police become too humdrum, occasionally a more curious case came their way. One such was that of the man brought into the Central Station one Tuesday evening by a Revenue Officer, who had seen him with a bundle of letters tied up in a handkerchief. It would seem that the man was trying to run a little private postal service, since these were unstamped. Patrick O'Sullivan prosecuted him with bringing twenty-two letters into the colony without paying postage, and he duly received a fine of $30. The relatively high level of the fine (the postage due on each letter was just two cents to addresses in Hongkong and Canton, and 5 cents to the rest of China) showed the need to deter such enterprise, since too many 'assaults' on the Post Office of this nature could quickly undermine its operation.[317] That same day the *Hongkong Telegraph* also reported that the Inspector had prosecuted a man for cruelty to animals, after receiving a report from one of his Indian Sergeants. The policeman had noticed two coolies struggling to carry a basket for its owner, who walked behind them. Suspicious, the Sergeant asked to see inside, and found a huge number of live chickens. He took them to the Station, probably having to give the coolies a hand, for when the basket was opened 106 poor adult chickens were released. Mr Gibson, the Head of the Sanitary Dept said that it was a real act of cruelty to pack so many birds into such a crate, and the magistrate imposed a fine of $25, or a

316 *Hong Kong Daily Press* 19th March 1914.
317 *Government Gazette* 28th December 1901.

month's hard labour, if the owner preferred. One hopes that the coolies had received their wage, for the full crate, according to the weight of the chickens given by Mr Gibson, was about 140 kilo, or 22 stone.[318] Another man appeared before the magistrate where his story was that he had just got off the ferry and seen a basket lying on the Praya apparently unclaimed. In some fit of civic pride, perhaps, he decided to pick it up and carry it to the rubbish dump, where he left it, not realising, he said, that there was the dead body of a smallpox victim inside it.[319]

No policeman could become completely inured to the depth of misery endured by many in the colony, however frequently he encountered it, but he had to conserve his sympathy for the living. O'Sullivan might only have given a passing thought to the provenance of that body in the basket: we learn no more from the papers. The registration of births and deaths had been in place since the 1860s, and whilst the former was a reasonably well-established custom, amongst Chinese and non-Chinese alike, (there being a fine for non-registration, as in the British Isles), that of deaths was always a more difficult matter. Amongst the residents of Hongkong, whether living with families or workmates, it was sometimes still difficult to ascertain the cause of death, and amongst the more transitory population often even the identity of the deceased was not known. Indeed, as late as 1920s the tables of dead bodies found by the police include those whose gender could not be ascertained.

But there were many who managed to eke out an existence at the margins of society, and, then as now, the courts frequently dealt with these people. By twenty-first century standards their treatment by both police and magistrates can appear racist and harsh, but just occasionally a different sentiment is seen, as in the case of a former junk master who had lost his craft in a typhoon. One of Patrick O'Sullivan's constables had arrested him for hawking goods without a licence, but the Inspector recognised him as someone who had been similarly charged before. On that occasion the magistrate, Mr. Wood, felt that something should be done for the man, who had been made all but destitute through the typhoon. He had asked O'Sullivan to make enquiries, with the intent

318 *Hong Kong Telegraph* 2nd October 1918.
319 *Hong Kong Telegraph* 22nd December 1916.

to give him a licence paid for from the poor box. The enquiries were made, but the man had not reappeared to claim his licence. The Inspector was further convinced of his good character, for he had let him out the previous evening without bail, and the man had turned up at court at the appointed hour. O'Sullivan reminded the magistrate of all the circumstances, and was instructed to get the man a hawkers licence, thereby helping him to get back on his feet.[320] But whilst the magistrate had acted humanely, the press were not uncritical of the situation that criminalised such people. Under the headline '*Our "Hell for the Poor." Old woman must pay licence to make cakes and sell 'em*', the *China Mail* of 9th July 1920 told the pitiful story of an elderly woman, who had lost her daughter, her only means of support, and had been brought in for selling little cakes she had made, trying to earn a few cents to keep herself. She had earlier been refused a licence. Inspector Willis supported her story, and could arrange one for her if the magistrate thought that fitting. The latter very magnanimously offered to pay half the four dollar fee from the poor box, if she could raise the other half. The old woman thought that she could borrow the money, and wept tears of gratitude for the goodness of the Court.

The case of the young woman who posed as the sister of the owner of Wing Luk store, Mr. Wong Sui Wi, in order to accumulate a good store of stationary items from a shop in Queen's Road Central, attracted great public interest over the days when it was heard in Court.[321] After a number of occasions when sixteen-year-old Wong Kin Man had called at the shop with a list of requirements, the stationer became suspicious and telephoned Wing Luk shop. Eventually the girl explained that she had acquired the items for her husband in Macao, but was adamant that they would be paid for. Magistrate Mr. Wood and Patrick O'Sullivan tried to understand what her real situation was, and the Inspector uncovered that as a child she had been sold for the first time by her mother to one of the wives of Mr. Wong, who had treated her harshly and then sold on again when she was twelve years old. She had run away from this family

320 *Hongkong Telegraph*, 17th December 1917.

321 Between 10th and 17th September 1918 the case appeared in all the newspapers.

a year earlier, since they had also mis-treated her, and claimed to have married a Eurasian man in the Macao Government Service. Miss Pitt, a Sunday School teacher, was called to attest for her, and said that she had found Wong Kin Man, described as *'respectable-looking'*, wandering the streets and had taken pity on her. O'Sullivan certainly had his doubts as to whether she was actually married, but offered to write to her husband for her, since Wong Kin Man could not write English and her husband apparently could not read Chinese. All the items, valued at around $200 and including boxes of nibs, pencils, inks, calling cards, notepaper as well as inkstands and a gold penholder, were recovered, and Mr. Wood, obviously rather baffled as to what to make of the whole case, put the girl on remand, and placed her in the care of the *Po Leung Kok*, the organisation that sheltered and looked after the many rescued women and children who had been trafficked into the colony.

Unsolicited presents could be the bane of a policeman who desired to maintain his integrity. The usual custom of offering gifts to ease the passage of commerce was extended by the criminal classes in the hope that he might be persuaded to turn a 'blind eye' upon their next nefarious activity. However, there would also be quite innocuous gifts, frequently homemade sweet-meats or cakes, given with no ulterior motive, other than, perhaps, thanks for help rendered. But, with always an element of doubt, the wisest course was to refuse all, sometimes causing offence in so doing, but at least preserving the policeman's authority. Some gifts, though, O'Sullivan never declined. Throughout his years in Hongkong he had many occasions to find a small baby in some gully, slope or hillside and he would carry the child, almost always a tiny girl, to the nuns at the Italian convent in Caine Road or to those at L'asile de Sainte Enfance in Wanchai. Such abandoned children were one of the saddest and most persistent features of life in the colony: few survived, despite gentle and careful attention at the convents, for most had been born to weak and malnourished mothers, and abandoned often within hours of their birth.[322] Years later, and more especially when he had married, one of the

322 Back in the 1880s the number of such rescued children had been about 1500 each year, with 85-90% of those dying, often on the day of their admittance. (Correspondence respecting deaths in Italian and French Convents, November 1887 *Sessional Papers*).

Sisters would accompany a girl in her early teens to present Inspector O'Sullivan with a gift of a lace table cloth or lacework handkerchief she had made. She was one of the fortunate girls who had survived her sad infancy, and came to thank the man who had saved her.

Financial crime – a Hongkong 'growth industry'

The papers show that another type of crime was coming to the attention of the Detective Branch with increasing frequency. Although by no means unknown in the previous century, with the many financial and commercial businesses in the colony, there were now more frequent cases of financial misconduct and fraud brought to the Supreme Court. The police role in this was sometimes just one of making the arrests and attending court, with the investigation being conducted by external auditors or government departments. This can be seen in the case that led to Henry Dixon taking over from Mr. Barradas in the Money Order Office, or in Detective (Lance-) Sergeant Mortimor O'Sullivan's arrest of Hugh Carmichael, a director of the big engineering firm, Carmichael and Co., who was charged with defrauding his company.[323] Occasionally there was more to do, in collecting the physical evidence, tracing suspects and constructing the outline of the case for the prosecution. In the forgery case involving the Asiatic Petroleum Company, Mortimor O'Sullivan arrested the suspect, Frank Castlemain, and had been responsible for the seizure of some documents and some incriminating blank company notepaper amongst the man's effects.[324] The *'Hongkong Bank Case'*, however, saw greater police involvement with Inspectors Terrett and Mortimor O'Sullivan tracing the letters and taking statements which provided all the initial evidence of a large scale fraud by a number of Portuguese and Chinese clerks in the Hongkong and Shanghai Bank. The case opened in June 1914 at the Magistracy, and with the subsequent trial stretched out through the summer, often confused by the series of false names and profusion of codewords used by the principal defendants, Gutierrez and Remedios. Two other suspects, Pomeroy and Ribiero, had disappeared

---

323 *Hongkong Daily Press,* 24th December 1900. (The first reference to Mortimor O'Sullivan's service with the Detective Branch.)

324 *Hong Kong Daily Press,* 21st February 1917.

from the colony, the latter had been arrested in Colombo, Ceylon (Sri Lanka) and brought to stand trial, but again absconded. The principals eventually received three years with hard labour for their efforts, and the law caught up with the other two in 1916, when Pomeroy received an eighteen month sentence in April, and Ribiero appeared in Macao, where the authorities there decided to try him. Mortimor O'Sullivan and Detective Sergeant Tim Murphy appeared there for the prosecution, and the man was transported for six years to Timor.[325]

Living conditions, working conditions

The living conditions for the constables had declined further during the course of the new century. The growth in numbers of the Force and the continuous deterioration of the fabric of the stations, whose inadequacies had been patched over and rarely properly repaired, combined with more space that was once dormitory accommodation being taken over for administration purposes meant that men were crammed together. In the top floor dormitories of the Central Station there was still no ceiling to protect the men from the leaking roof, and the sleeping spaces were sectioned off between races with flimsy partitions, thus the Europeans complained that their food had to come to their quarters via the Chinese dormitory. The toilets and the kitchens were still in close proximity, and despite the earlier efforts of then Captain Superintendent May to ensure that men could have a hot bath when needed, the three bathrooms were only supplied with hot water for two hours twice a week.[326]

At No. 5 Station, the Fire Station, the situation was as bad as ever, but additionally there was a lack of space for the men when off-duty, who, as firemen, were obliged to remain on site. Now Governor, May, in his accompanying letter to London, acknowledged the truth of all this, but expressed confidence that the plans already sanctioned for the development of the Central Station site would alleviate the problems there and, exhibiting a distinct lack of urgency, suggested that he would

325 The case appears in many papers of the period, commencing in *Hongkong Daily Press* 5th June 1914, with the verdict reported in the same publication on 21st August, and the trial at Macao in *China Mail* 5th July 1916.

326 Petition of European Crown Sergeants, Lance Sergeants and Constables to the Governor, Sir F.H. May, Spring 1915 CO 129/422 p. 216-221.

put forward a proposal for No. 5 Station when the former was well under way.[327] The healthy state of the government's coffers (due in large part to the unhealthy opium monopoly) did now allow for the building and renovation of stations, which would continue throughout the war; but the construction of the Central Police Station administration building, begun eventually in August 1916, was hampered by lack of steel. By the end of 1917 just the main floor level had been completed, and it would not be until 1920 that it was finished and fully occupied. Little seems to have been achieved in this period for the stations to the immediate west of the Central Station, but more attention was given to the conditions for the men housed in stations elsewhere on the island and in Kowloon as the century progressed. What had been the makeshift improvements of the 1890s were incorporated into the design of the building or refurbishment. The renovated station at Hung Hom, for example, started in 1913 and completed the following November, included 3 new bedrooms for inspectors and sergeants, a new storey with good sized dormitories, adequate bathrooms and a drying room and kitchen as well as an enlarged charge room and new cells.

The chronic shortage of married quarters in and around Central Station began to be addressed, too. A number of the more junior inspectors, and most of the sergeants not posted to outlying stations had to rent a couple of rooms in Wanchai, or share small houses in Kowloon. Therefore, when the first phase of nine married quarter flats on Caine Road were finished in 1915, each with two or three bedrooms and with up to date bathrooms and kitchens, they were soon snapped up. In highly class conscious Hongkong, it was still the case that the elevation of your home was seen as directly correlating to your social standing, and thus Caine Road, in what is now the area called Mid Levels, was highly desirable. Electricity had been commercially generated in Hongkong since 1890, and quickly its use spread from street lighting to the lighting of shops, offices and private houses. Nevertheless, the Caine Road flats were some of the first police buildings to enjoy this new facility.

327 Sir F.H. May to Rt. Hon. Lewis Harcourt, M.P., Secretary of State for the Colonies, 19th May 1915 CO129/422 p. 207-8.

Group at Central Police Station, c. 1914. Tim Murphy standing on far left; John Murphy 2nd row, third from right (courtesy Murphy family)

Recruiting from home again

William Lysaught had brought out to Hongkong his niece and nephew in the first years of the new century. Back at his family home in Island, Newmarket, at the farm run by his brother in law, Daniel Murphy, were left three or four older girls, most of whom married, and three sons, the eldest of which was James, two years younger than Lance Sergeant Tim Murphy. John and William Lysaught were the youngest members of the family, born in 1892 and 1894, so James had to wait until August 1912 until he could be spared from the farm, and sail out to join his brother in the Hongkong Police.[328] There appear to be no records existing concerning James' recruitment, nor that of his brother John later that year, but since the Civil Service List for 1935 gives the date of John's service commencing as 5th October 1912 and his arrival in the colony as 16th November 1912, it seems that their joining was organised through the Colonial Office in London, almost certainly at the instigation of their elder brother. The youngest brother, the namesake of his uncle, was destined to be the one who never sailed east, and ran the farm with his father. Their cousin, Patrick Murphy, whose family had a smaller holding just along the road in Island, followed in 1914 and yet another cousin,

328 James Murphy's month of enlistment is derived from the re-engagement papers signed whilst he was on military service in France.

from another branch of their large family, Michael Murphy, the same age as William Lysaught Murphy, joined in March 1915. Michael's family lived just over the county border, in Brosna, Co. Kerry. The Murphy family were to serve the colony well, for three of these five rose to senior rank and were awarded the Colonial Police Long Service Medal for their work in the Force.

Constable Maurice Kenneally (left) (courtesy Mary O'Keeffe)

Travelling out on the same ship as Michael Murphy was another Newmarket man destined for the Force, Maurice Kenneally, who came from a large family living in the town of Newmarket itself. His parents, Maurice and Julia, both came from the area, but had moved to the United States, and it was there that they married and had their eldest two children, Ellen and John. Maurice was born in 1895 after they had returned to Newmarket, where Maurice senior kept a public house. The father and some of his six sons were passionately involved in the independence cause for Ireland, while their eldest sister, Ellen, was a member of the Gaelic League, a nationalist organisation promoting the use of the Irish language. Maurice, though, did not share the more radical views of some of his brothers, and saw the advantage of a career in a distant colonial police force at a time when members of the Royal Irish Constabulary were starting to come under attack from political groups who considered them traitorous representatives of oppressive imperial power.

Six months at home to find your girl, woo her and wed her

In Hongkong, the O'Sullivan brothers were due another leave in 1913, and determined between them that this one would see them return with a bride apiece. They left on 12th April, together with Inspector and Mrs. Gordon and newly-retired Chief Inspector Baker and his three daughters. Mrs. Baker had died of a heart affliction some three months earlier, indeed, Baker had booked the whole family's return passage just a few days before she died.[329] The group sailed first on *Assaye* to Colombo, and there changed to the *Mongolia,* arriving in London just five weeks later on 17th May.[330] As had been the case for all returning farmer's sons, the day after their arrival in Newmarket they found themselves engaged with the routine of the farm, but thankful that they could spend time with their ailing father, examining the new cattle and the changes made to the farm, leaving the heavier work to their three surviving younger brothers and the farm hands. Used to work at all hours of day and night as inspectors, Patrick particularly enjoyed the peace and gentleness of early mornings in the milking parlour.

Wedding photographs of Patrick O'Sullivan and Ellen Kenneally, taken Co. Cork, October 1913 (left) and Hongkong, January 1914 (O'Sullivan family)

329 *Hong Kong Telegraph,* 15th January 1913.
330 *China Mail* 12th April 1913 & passenger list of *SS Mongolia*.

Mortimor and Hanora O'Sullivan (courtesy O'Sullivan family)

Mortimor O'Sullivan courted the pretty Nora Ahern, one of seven daughters of Patrick Ahern, a publican turned shopkeeper in New Street, Newmarket, but Patrick's choice was perhaps both a little more cosmopolitan and unexpected. Ellen, daughter of publican and republican Maurice Kenneally, had been born in Orange, New Jersey, and still had family links in the United States, so, as a young woman, had returned there to work. Having become engaged to an American (so the family story goes) in 1912, she came back to Newmarket for a leave-taking, but broke off the arrangement when Patrick O'Sullivan started his pursuit of her. Having led an independent life in the States, Ellen was alive to the advantages of marrying a man already well established in his career and undaunted by the idea of a long separation from her family. By marrying a Barnacurra man, she was also sealing a union between neighbouring families. As Julia O'Donoghue, her mother had been born on the farm next to the O'Sullivans in the townland. It was certainly through her influence that her younger, more peaceable brother Maurice would join the force eighteen months later, along with Michael Murphy.

Patrick was the first to marry, on 7th October, with the brothers witnessing each other's marriage, and his sister Maria as the second witness, whilst Mortimor's wedding took place on 18th November, with Sarah Ahern, Nora's sister being the other witness. Ten years later Sarah herself would marry Thomas, another of the O'Sullivan brothers, and live in the farm house he built close to the original Barnacurra homestead. The Inspectors had earlier passed the medical examination, and been deemed fit to enlist for a further five year term, and on informing the Colonial Office of their marriages, had been provided with passages for themselves and their wives on the P. and O. steamer *Maloja*, leaving London on 12th December 1913.

A sad arrival

It had also been arranged that they would be accompanied by Detective Inspector Edmund O'Sullivan's wife, Maria, who was returning after the birth of her fourth child. Having sailed back to Hongkong with her husband after his leave in January 1913, Maria found herself pregnant with their fourth child, and it was considered better that she be at home for the confinement. Accordingly she and her children had left Hongkong on 8th April, travelling first to San Francisco or Vancouver, and then made the train journey across the American continent, followed by the transatlantic crossing to Queenstown (Cobh, Co. Cork). This route was becoming increasingly popular as the reliability, speed and comfort of American trains was improving all the while, and it was cheaper than the large steamships and more comfortable than the small ones. Maria stayed with her mother, now moved to Dublin, where her new son, George, was born in August 1913. A week or so later George was christened, and Maria had a photograph of herself and the children taken, which she sent back to Edmund. Whilst in this picture the children look slightly bemused, Maria gently smiles out, an expression rarely found in photographs of this time, and so obviously a smile for her husband. In November she had heard by letter from Edmund that he had been taken into hospital in October because of a particularly heavy cold. What he had not disclosed to his wife was that the doctors there had realised that he was suffering from severe tuberculosis, at the time referred to as phthisis. Now she was anxious to be in Hongkong, for her husband's subsequent letters had brought no news of returning health, and she was aware that his diabetes made him susceptible to illness.

Thus the ship carried a party of nine O'Sullivans, who changed at Bombay on 31st December onto the *Devanha*, and arrived in Hongkong on the morning of Friday, 16th January. However, at Singapore five days earlier, the Colonial Secretary of the Federated Malay Straits had sent a

Maria O'Sullivan and children, 1913 (courtesy O'Sullivan family)

message to the ship for Maria, informing her that her husband was very dangerously ill. Those final days of the voyage must have been acutely distressing to the party, and one can imagine that Maria left her children and her luggage in the care of her cousins' wives and flew to the Civil Hospital as soon as they made port. Edmund, always a devout man, had been heartened by the frequent visits from his priest and friend, Fr. Augustine Płaczek, and by the hope of seeing his wife before he died, but the disease had taken severe toll on him, and he was far from the strong, robust man of Maria's memory. Having once more waited for his Maria, it was with her and his priest at his side that Edmund died quietly from heart failure on Sunday evening, two days later.[331]

His funeral the next evening was attended by almost all his fellow inspectors and many sergeants and constables, including a large number of the Chinese constables of the Detective Branch.[332] The cortege through the streets from the hospital to St. Michael's Catholic Cemetery at Happy Valley was led by Captain Superintendent Messer and the senior police officers. Edmund's body was borne into the cemetery by his cousins helped by fellow Detective Inspector Watt and the recently returned Inspector Gordon. The funeral rites of the Catholic Church, longer and more elaborate than those of the Church of England, meant that the service started in the Cemetery Chapel, with prayers and the funeral hymns, and continued at the graveside, where Fr. Augustine gave a moving eulogy for his friend. In accordance with the custom of the time few women were present, the newspapers record only Mrs Nolan, the former Miss May Hennessy, with her husband, but her sister, now Mrs Davitt, was probably also with this party, Sergeant Davitt being amongst the police contingent. The Hennessy girls would not have missed the opportunity to say a final farewell to their dear Uncle Eddie, who had continued to support and watch over them since they returned to Hongkong.

The Inspectors' wives – married life in Hongkong

On their return from leave the Inspectors had first to report themselves to the Captain Superintendent and receive notice of where they were now posted, and to where they were to take their new brides. Thus Patrick and Helen settled first into one of the older married quarters at the Central Station, moving to No. 7 station in Taipingshan two years later, whilst Mortimor and Nora were sent to No. 2 Station on the junction of Wanchai Road and the Praya. Neither couple had much luggage: the men travelled to and fro with their trunks containing all their possessions, for not until he had passed the medical examination would a man know for certain that he would be returning. The women had little aside

331 Medical report J. Bell Superintendent Government Civil Hospital 19th January 1914, CO129/409 p.55.

332 Reports are found in *China Mail* and *Hongkong Telegraph* 20th January 1914.

from their clothes and personal possessions.[333] Newmarket and nearby Kanturk were well served by shops that could supply all that was required to set up home in Ireland, and much would be handed from mother to daughter, but not knowing what would be needed, they came with only a small 'bottom drawer' of linen and tableware, and a little money of their own. Having worked in New York, Helen was perhaps better placed to cope with creating a home in a new environment, but Nora was relieved to find Norah Lysaught and May Nolan living close by, and although neither were really known to the new arrivals, it was to them they naturally turned for advice in those first weeks.

But the immediate task was to look after their cousin Maria, whose eldest child had only just turned six years old. She might have four children and be the same age as both Helen and Nora, but Edmund had provided everything she needed in terms of domestic help and family organisation, such that she could not cook an egg or wash her babies clothes, much less deal with grocer's bills. Although Edmund had been a witness to the wills of a number of his friends and colleagues, he had not made one himself, and Tim Murphy stepped in to help sort out the situation. Maria stayed in their quarters until the end of that month, when she was provided with passage back to Ireland, boarding the *Devanha* on 31st January, which was passing through Hongkong on its return journey. One can imagine that with no amah and no relative to help her on the return journey, Maria had struggled to look after her four children, and returned to her mother's Dublin home with relief. She learnt that she was to receive £48 6*s* 10*d* per year from the Widows and Orphans' Pension Fund, and too soon realised that, with the little money Edmund had left, this was a very meagre income for one in her position. The scheme was funded by compulsory deductions from all married civil servants, rather than coming out of the colony's coffers, as did the regular pensions. Drawing a comparison from records in the annual *Blue Books* of 1913-1914, Inspector Alfred Dymond, who retired in 1914 on the same salary (£240 p.a.) and with similar length of service to Edmund

333 A man who wished to reenlist after his first or second term had to apply and seek the agreement of his Captain Superintendent; after this point he was deemed to have security of tenure, provided always that his medical examination proved satisfactory.

O'Sullivan, received a little over £112 p.a. Maria's pension, amounting to 18 shillings per week, gave her a similar income to that of an unskilled Dublin labourer.

Quite quickly the family had to be split up, with some of the children sent to live with Maria's maternal aunts, who were in Dublin and nearby Bray, Co. Wicklow. Maria made unsuccessful application to the Crown Agents for a small increase in pension, and, with no training of any sort beyond the schoolroom, and not in robust health, made equally vain attempts to obtain light work as a sewing maid. She too moved to Bray, and on 14th June 1919 she made one last attempt to improve her lot, appealing to her parish priest, Fr. Richard Colahan V.F., outlining her situation, telling him of her husband's long years of faithful service and begging him to use his influence on her behalf. He duly forwarded her letter to the Crown Agents, who in turn passed it to the Colonial Office, who then transmitted it to the Governor, Sir Reginald Stubbs in Hongkong. By the end of the year, Maria had received a polite but very final refusal. Maria did not remarry; the family were further split up, and although she was in receipt of the pension (slightly increased during the 1930s) until at least the outbreak of the Second World War, she sank out of view from that time.

A proper study of women's lives in Hongkong at the period is yet to be written,[334] but for purposes here, an examination of photographs, family memories (with the passage of time 2nd and mostly 3rd hand), newspaper advertisements, price lists and occasional mentions of domestic life in the records held in the National Archives, together with comparisons to the situation in the United Kingdom and the United States, a few indications about the external factors that concern the daily life of women can at least be drawn.

The new couples inherited some furniture from the out-going occupants of their quarters, and more could be obtained for a reasonable price at the frequent auctions of effects, advertised in the papers. New pieces could also be made up quite reasonably, and whilst initially these would all

334 Susannah Hoe's fascinating *The Private Life of Old Hong Kong* tells the stories of a number of individual European and Eurasian women from the earliest days.

appear as very unfamiliar 'oriental' styles to the wives, in later years they would be the prized pieces, to be taken back to Ireland and to occupy pride-of-place in their homes. Doubtless the established Newmarket community in the colony gave them some useful wedding presents of the fine locally produced table-linen and crockery. Again, some of this would become mementoes of *"our time in Hongkong"* when their husbands had retired.

With their husbands immediately back to work, juggling night and day duties, and hours of service that were frequently much longer than that required from their constables, Ellen and Nora O'Sullivan relied on the Hennessy sisters, and the Lysaught family, as well as other police wives, for advice on which shops to use, and where to instruct their cook to purchase fresh produce. For Nora in particular, the European-style department stores were rather exotic, but both felt like tourists when they ventured into the smaller streets and markets, and encountered quite unknown fruits and vegetables. However, most of the actual food and provision shopping was done by sending orders to the stores or by sending out the houseboy or cook. They soon learnt that whilst most items in a British larder could be purchased here, the varieties or brands would be different. Fresh foodstuffs were produced locally, but frequently tinned, imported substitutes were available, generally from America or Australia. Bacon and potatoes, so important in the Irish diet, were a case in point. Rather than being able to buy a side of bacon, the bacon available for the European market was generally imported in large four to eight pound tins from the United States. Potatoes were a perennial problem, for those grown in China were too wet for the Irish palate, and the American ones were prohibitively expensive. Ellen eventually abandoned the quest, and followed her husband's prompting to adopt rice as the basis of meals. Butter, which would be made at home even in Newmarket town houses, although on sale in the shops there too, was now dearer than cheese, and had to be imported from Australia. Some of the European vegetables, too, were only available in cans. However, such difficulties could be set against some improvements to their life. Here, both gas and electricity was available for domestic use and, as Norah Murphy (now Lysaught) had found before them, the low price of labour meant that their husbands were able to afford two or three servants to attend to the housework, which did compensate for other privations.

It was as well that they did not have to spend too much time on household chores, for the women of Hongkong kept up with the changes of fashion, mostly through magazines and papers from the United States. But little adaption was made to the very different climate, beyond a tendency to use lighter cloth, especially for outer garments. In Europe corsets were becoming straighter, with less pronounced curves in the boning, and the gradual use of elastic fabrics. For many years lightweight 'tropical stays' were produced for women in British India, and these corsets were a relief during the humid summer months in Hongkong. In the early decades of the twentieth century ordinary day dress was an A-line ankle length skirt in heavier cotton or linen, perhaps a light wool in winter, together with a cotton blouse, which would need to be changed frequently in summer. Strong ankle boots were needed if venturing out of doors into the dirty, uneven streets, and the fashion for a little heel made walking in these conditions harder, but did keep the skirts clear of most of the detritus. Hair styles, though still worn 'up', were much simpler than they had been at the end of the previous century, but still very few women would cut their tresses, and the damp air meant frequent adjustments and rearrangements if the woman was to go out. Many years later Ellen O'Sullivan recalled that her head was never dry in all the years she was in Hongkong.

A changing world – Europe

Conflict in Europe had been looking inevitable throughout the summer of 1914, so Hongkong was not unduly surprised when it woke on the morning of 5th August to the news that, a few hours earlier, war had been declared between Britain and Germany. At such a distance from any hostilities, this initially gave rise only to a spate of official pronouncements the Governor had to make on behalf of the British government, the formation of new committees, some movement of troops and more activity in the Volunteer Defence Corps. Little asides in the newspapers of the day convey the excitement the news brought, e.g., the sight, which must have been seen world over, of small boys, here Chinese paper boys, lining up and marching up and down, all of them wanting to call out the orders. There was, too, anxiety for what this might mean, expressed in the churches' calls for prayers for peace. But the main effect of the war in those early days was to give continued excuse for huge price increases in many imported foodstuffs. A similar situation existed in London, and especially in Paris, and was considered to be nothing other than blatant profiteering by greedy firms. Action was taken by some of the larger manufacturers who publicly committed their retailers to a fixed or capped price, Nestlé Milk being one such in Hongkong, but with limited success.

Throughout the years of the conflict efforts were made to find ways to support both the British war effort and the organisations providing relief for the civilian casualties. All sectors of the population were generous in their support of these war charities, with the Chinese community donating very substantial sums throughout the whole time. Almost every organisation in which women were involved set up working parties to produce all manner of knitted and sewn items, from leg warmers and balaclavas, pot holders and babies' dresses for the troops and their families. Lists of items sent were printed in the papers, and there was a distinct air of competitiveness, especially between the different denominations of churches.

Lady Helena May, perhaps the most socially engaged of all the Governors' wives to that time, organised the annual "Our Day" events, which saw the entire community come together in festivities, port illuminations and a great fundraising effort, centring on the sale of flowers. It became more or less obligatory for every man in Hongkong to purchase one or more blooms from the flower-selling ladies, and thousands of dollars were then sent to help the war effort. The Newmarket women appear in lists of those manning the Police Stall at the annual bazaar also instigated by Lady May, and would have been contributing to the St. Joseph's Church sewing circle. Along with the "Our Little Bit " society, these efforts resulted in thousands of bandages rolled, and hundreds of garments sent to the troops at the front.

However, in the first days of the war both Helen and Nora O'Sullivan were more occupied with the arrival of their first children, Julia born to Helen on 20th July and Catherine to Nora on 24th August. The girls were baptised two weeks after their birth by Fr. Augustine, with the couples standing sponsor for each others' child.

A changing world – Ireland

The English language newspapers had, from their beginnings, kept the colony up to date with happenings in the British Isles, from reports on major events and new legislation, the state of the economy and the movements of the royal family, to county cricket scores and curious or amusing snippets culled from local papers. During the European conflict, news was telegrammed every few hours to the offices of all the papers, and each edition had at least a page, and often considerably more, devoted to these dispatches. But one topic of news that had started long before the War and continued all throughout was *'The Irish Question'*. From Westminster's perspective, this was whether or not Home Rule for Ireland, a limited self-government, but still with substantial constitutional links to Great Britain, should be enacted. This long-debated issue had considerable support within the island of Ireland, excepting in the province of Ulster, but there was also general dissatisfaction over the grindingly slow process of the reform. The then Prime Minister William Gladstone had brought the first Home Rule Bill to parliament way back in 1886, and scant progress had been made since then. However, in the months before the outbreak of the War, momentum had gathered, and it really seemed as if a Bill could soon be passed. With the declaration of war, however, the matter was put on hold, with a promise of its resurrection at the conclusion of hostilities.

Ireland had a long history of groups, some of a paramilitary nature, calling for independence from Britain, and although not enjoying popular support, these were growing in strength in the first years of the century. In part this was in reaction to the increase in opposition to any form of Home Rule from many in Ulster. With the postponement, and many thought abandonment, of the promised reforms, this impatience turned into direct action, culminating first in the Easter Rising of 1916, when the Irish Volunteers (later the Irish Republican Army) launched an attack on the centre of Dublin, and declared an independent Ireland. The Rising was summarily put down by the British Army, with brutal 'justice' meted out to its protagonists, and the destruction of large parts of the capital. This specifically military response had the result of turning the tide of public opinion in Ireland to the cause of full separation from Britain. In doing so, it helped legitimise direct action against the 'occupying enemy', the Crown forces, including members of the Royal Irish Constabulary. The situation remained at a high level of tension throughout the rest of the decade, with continued violence from both sides, and into the 1920s when *The Troubles* became a civil war, as the British handed control to the provisional government of *Saorstát Éireann* (Irish Free State), and factions fought within Ireland for supremacy.

All this was reported, often daily, by the Hongkong press, which, of course, took its material from the British papers, and although not slavishly uncritical of Westminster, the tenor of the reporting in *The China Mail, et al.* presented only one side of the story. There was little sympathy for the rebels, and the reports of the murders and ambushes of soldiers and police hardened attitudes in Hongkong. That, in 1916, the leadership of some of the factions in Ireland had allied themselves with Germany and accepted help in the form of a shipment of weapons, ignoring the 150,000 Irishmen presently fighting for the British Crown, could only elicit the strongest censure from public opinion and was not easily forgotten.

For the Irish in Hongkong during this period, then, the only alternative slant on these reports came through news from home carried by letter, and the Irish community shared round the fragments thus learnt. Munster, and especially County Cork, saw high levels of involvement at both political and paramilitary level. Popular support from the town and country people increased in the wake of the Easter Rising, and Newmarket had its own company of the Volunteers, later to become the Newmarket Battalion. This group of local men, whose supply of arms had been increased by its quota from the German shipment, took part in many ambushes and forays, sometimes resulting in fierce reprisals from the British forces. The Battalion was led by Seán Moylan, who would later serve in the Irish parliament, and included Joe Kenneally, Helen O'Sullivan's younger brother.

The attacks on the police and on R.I.C. barracks were obviously particularly disturbing. The 17,000-strong force was seen as the first arm of an oppressive Crown by nationalists, no matter that the vast majority of constables were Irish Catholics. The R.I.C. policy of not stationing men in their own locality allowed them to be seen as strangers, and therefore as enemy targets. Although still sporadic, and not at the level that it would reach during the Anglo-Irish War (1919-1921), the killings cast a pall over the retirement hopes that Mortimor and Patrick O'Sullivan and William Davitt, amongst others, were starting to formulate.

The perennial problem of money

Back in Barnacurra at the time of their departure in November 1913, the brothers had known that they were unlikely to see their father again , thus it was not a shock when news reached them that Mortimer O'Sullivan had died on 1st April, 1914. His wife and four of their remaining children still lived and worked on the farm, whilst the eldest child, Margaret, was now a religious sister in the United States. They had hoped to keep up at least some of their remittances to the farm after their marriage, but quickly they found that married life, especially when babies started arriving, precluded this. So with unfortunate timing, the Inspectors had to curtail the help they sent home, generally only managing a remittance at Christmas time thereafter.

Aside from their own increases in expenditure, the war continued to push the cost of living ever higher for Hongkong residents. An examination of the market prices reported every Saturday in *The China Mail* before the start and towards the close of the war suggest that the price of locally sourced meat and fish rose in some cases by 25%, and from the frequent comments in the newspapers, it would seem that foodstuffs imported from Europe or North America rose between 25-33% in the same period.[335] The police had petitioned for an increase in pay to help cover rising costs in January 1912, which resulted in a stop gap measure whereby Sergeants received an additional £15 p.a. and Lance Sergeants £10, with no increase for any other rank. Indeed, a number of the small extra allowances available were actually curtailed and the work

335 *China Mail,* 19th January 1914 and 5th March 1918.

for which they had been allowed subsumed into regular duties. This was unsatisfactory all round and the men reckoned that the Government had saved in allowances what it spent in increased salaries. Thus, 1915 saw another round of petitions, one from the inspectors and a second from the junior ranks, and on this occasion the entire European contingent signed one or the other. The sergeant and constables' petition asked for an immediate rise of £30 p.a. across the board, pointing out that not only were they not able to support relatives back home now but were often short for their own upkeep. Both petitions refer to the better terms that now existed for the home forces, both in pay and pensions, to the extent that instead of improving their situation by coming to Hongkong, the men showed how they were disadvantaged compared to their less adventurous brothers. The inspectors felt the injustice of the level of their pay compared to the men who had left the Force after a very few years service and found better remunerated employment elsewhere within the colony's government. Many examples were quoted of men only eight to ten years in Hongkong who were earning as much as if not more than the inspectors, who, for the most part, had served seventeen years or more. The recent allowance of free quarters to other departments removed yet another differential from the police.

Henry May included a detailed analysis of the petitions from the Captain Superintendent, Mr. Messer, but made only passing reference to it in his covering letter. The Governor obviously felt himself still the real head of the Force, and eminently able to recommend to London the correct response to the petitions. Admitting the need for new accommodation, as seen, he also granted that the pay was relatively low in comparison to other departments. These disadvantages, however, he considered outweighed by the earlier entitlement for pension (after 15 years service) plus the provision of up to four full passages paid when the men went on leave. The latter meant that a man could take his wife and up to four children (each travelling at half fare) without incurring extra expense, whist other departments were limited to two and a half free passages.[336] Thus he dismissed the request for an increase in pay, but did

336 Second class adult return passage cost c. £50 in 1911 (Free Passage Scheme for Subordinate Officers, Sessional Papers 23rd February 1911): thus not until a

recommend that on their second leave (i.e. after ten years service, and during which men were most likely to marry) they should receive full pay for the six months that they were at home, and the half pay now limited to their journey time, when there was not the expense of paying for the family's food or lodging.

So the men had to manage the best they could on their salaries, for it was not until a major restructuring of the ranks in 1920 that their situation would change. At that point the distinction between first and second class inspectors was removed (one of the petitioners' requests), and their pay at that rank increased from £240-260 to £400- 450 p.a. All full sergeants then became Sub-Inspectors with a doubling of their pay, and constables and lance sergeants were each promoted up a rank with a similar increase. However, the figures present a rosier picture than actually existed, for now on sterling salaries, drawn in Hongkong dollars at the prevailing rates, they were in precisely the reverse of the situation that had beset the men at the turn of the century. The dollar stood at one shilling and eleven pence in 1915, but had risen to a value of four shillings and ten pence by the end of the decade, consuming in one gulp any advantage of which the men might have dreamt. The problems with the dollar's relationship to sterling meant that the pay of the Indian and Chinese contingents was not deemed to require increases to anything like the scale seen by the Europeans. In general the salaries of constables and sergeants here rose by between thirty and sixty dollars per year, although the lowest grade constable in both contingents was expected to work for less than four dollars per week. Two Indian inspectors appear in the *Blue Books* from 1918, and two from the Chinese force two years later. Significantly, although the specific good conduct allowances earned by the particular holders of these posts are noted, their names are not recorded at this point. Their salaries, listed in dollars, were two fifths (Indian) and one third (Chinese) that of the European inspectors.

The impact of the European war on the Hongkong Police

At the outbreak of war in Europe in August 1914, the Hongkong newspapers, in common with many of their Home counterparts,

---

policeman had four children would he reap the full advantage of his position.

expected this 'spat' to be of only short duration, and give the impression that the general populace felt that this was a conflict with little relevance to them. The business of the administration was initially little troubled by events. One of the few measures it needed to take was the enlistment of 352 special constables, allowing Indian police to be withdrawn to assist the regiments in the colony, who in turn had sent men to Europe. When these police returned to their normal duties the next month, it was noted at the Legislative Council meeting how successful the operation had been, and that members of the public, Chinese, Portuguese, Indian and European had served readily and competently. An Ordinance was put forward to allow for the development of a Police Special Reserve in the light of this success, but without the assumption that this would be required either semi-permanently or imminently.[337] But as the cables from Europe began to bring ever more frequent news of atrocious losses, the mood in Hongkong changed, and by February 1915 the Reserve started recruiting in earnest, with the young barrister, Mr. F.C. Jenkin, taking able command, having managed the earlier experiment with credit. Described as 'tactful and energetic', he ensured that the Reserves became an efficient and effective body, and worked cooperatively with the regular force, without creating too much of the friction that might have been anticipated. Arranged on lines of ethnicity, the companies comprised British and Indian; Chinese; and Portuguese, with a largely Chinese ambulance corps and a Portuguese band added later, together with a mounted corp that took over the direction of traffic. In 1916 a Police Reserve School was established, with Chief Inspector Kerr, and Inspectors Garrod, Gordon, Patrick O'Sullivan and Grant acting as lecturers.[338] The Reserve Force was well received in the city, and the war effort as a whole was supported by many of the prominent Chinese residents, with war charities benefitting from their generous support.

---

337 Legislative Council Meeting minutes, 1st October 1914, *Hongkong Hansard.*

338 The newspapers carried frequent notices of the days and times of classes. Patrick O'Sullivan taught class IV, *e.g. Hongkong Telegraph,* 5th January 1917, when this class was called to sit for examination at 5.30 p.m. on Friday 12th January.

Party leaving for European War, February 1917. First row, 2nd from left John Murphy, 3rd from left Donald Burlingham. Third row, 3rd from left James Murphy (courtesy Murphy family).

Meanwhile, Hongkong was starting to see a steady stream of its civilian menfolk leave to join the troops in Europe. Fifty-six had left by the beginning of March 1915 and Mr. Messer was aware that many of his men were anxious to offer their services.[339] By July 1915 the work of the Reservists enabled the first dozen regular police from the European contingent to be released to enlist. The progress of these men through the permissions and necessary medicals was followed with interest in the press, and they were given a reception by the Governor at Government House. With their increasing frequency in the months and years to come, however, these police departures attracted less comment. Primarily for reasons of economy only single men were permitted to join, since separation allowances would have to be paid to remaining families, and there was a long-winded debate between the Colonial Office and the colonies in the far east as to who would be responsible for this and for repatriation of any widows that might result.

The Irish amongst the Police shared the same desire to be of service to the nation: they had, after all, sworn allegiance to the Crown in

339 *Hong Kong Telegraph* 1st March 1915.

their present role, and with so many of their countrymen serving in the British Army, any sympathy they might have for the republican cause in Ireland was put aside for the greater good of defeating the German foe. The Police went in parties, twelve, fifteen or more at a time, and so in February 1917 two Newmarket men, brothers James and John Murphy sailed for home alongside seventeen of their colleagues, initially under the authority of Assistant Superintendent Donald Burlingham, who left them at India for military service in the form of a temporary attachment to the government there. Soon after their departure, the crossing via Suez and the Mediterranean became too dangerous for regular use: mail came by the Siberian route, but as the situation in Russia collapsed, this ceased to be a possible passage route. Thus later contingents of men were sent to Britain via Vancouver and then the transatlantic crossing from one of the eastern American ports. The last, and smallest, Police party also included Newmarket men, and arrived in Liverpool on 5th September 1918. Michael and Patrick Murphy, and Maurice Kenneally, the brother-in-law of Inspector Patrick O'Sullivan, had enlisted, together with five other colleagues. Whether this group stayed together is not clear, although since Michael Murphy told his family that he only got as far as Catterick (the training camp in North Yorkshire), it is probable that they did. The military careers of John and James Murphy have been difficult to trace, given the abundance of men by those names serving in the Army, but fortunately re-enlistment papers for the Hongkong Police have survived. These were signed by the men at a military prison-in-the- field in Le Havre late in 1917, corroborating family tales that they were deployed as military police. John Murphy would talk very little to his sons in later years, only saying that his time as a military policeman were the worst years of his life. After the Armistice the men were gradually repatriated, and all the Newmarket men rejoined the Force in Hongkong. Thirteen of their comrades did not return, however, twelve having lost their lives in the conflict and one dying in the influenza pandemic of 1919.

Throughout the war years the work of the police continued, with strong support from the Reserves. The involvement of so many more of the community in keeping law and order in Hongkong allowed the British to 'do their bit' for the war effort, and helped raise the status of the police amongst the Chinese. Alongside all the petty crimes, the smuggling of opium, kidnapping and sale of girls into prostitution, illicit gambling occupied as much police time as forty years earlier. Many of the crimes brought to the magistrates by Inspector Patrick O'Sullivan, recounted earlier in this chapter, date from the latter years of the war. Violent gang robberies, usually in the streets nearer the waterfront in Sheung Wan or Wanchai, were becoming more frequent. Murders were still relatively rare, but seem, during the War years, to have attracted a greater level of outrage when they did occur. Noticeably murders within the Chinese community were now treated in a less cavalier fashion by the English papers than in earlier times.

But as the war entered its final year, it was to be a crime against the Detective Branch itself which would shatter the world of the older Newmarket men, and to hold to account a police force that was perhaps beginning to think itself inviolate.

Chapter Ten

One morning in Wanchai

It was during the early hours of Sunday 13th January 1918 that an Indian Constable on patrol in Queen's Road East saw someone lying awkwardly on the pavement near Landale Street, close to the army barracks. Even before he had reached the crumpled figure, he realised that it was that of a colleague, a Lance Sergeant, who appeared to be dead. He swiftly summoned help, first with his police whistle, then by calling from the nearby police phone-box, before returning to try to staunch the man's profuse bleeding. Acting Lance Sergeant Norman G. Johnston had been shot at close range, and was unconscious when he was transported to the Hospital, where he died at 7 a.m. that day. He was twenty six years old, and had transferred from the Dundee Force two and a half years earlier. The Constable had not heard any gunfire, but a shop owner nearby had come out when he heard the shots and seen someone running off.[340]

At first the Police had no indication as to who had committed the crime, but then they received information about the possible motive a young sapper from the Royal Engineers, William Bloomfield, might have for the crime and that Bloomfield had been seen behaving strangely in the area. He was brought before the magistrate two days later, charged with being connected with Johnston's death. But as one newspaper reporter noted, although he told Mr. Wood, the magistrate, that he understood the charge, the soldier did not seem to understand the seriousness of the matter and appeared very relaxed. The case was remanded for the police to collect evidence, and Bloomfield was scheduled to appear at Court again at 10 a.m. on 22nd January.[341]

340 *China Mail*, 14th January 1918.
341 *China Mail*, 15th January 1918.

A search warrant

Shortly after 10 a.m. on Tuesday 22nd January, Inspector Mortimor O'Sullivan, Detective Sergeant Henry Goscombe Clarke and Principal Chinese Detective Sun Tai received the information that the police had been hoping to acquire for weeks.[342] During the early hours of that day there had been a break-in at a lime merchant's on the Praya in the area of Ship Street, the owner being found gagged and bound. Colleagues from No. 2 Station, a quarter of a mile down the Praya, who had investigated had unearthed the information that the gang responsible used a cubicle in a house on Gresson Street, just a hundred yard's distance or so from the lime merchant's property. This crime had the hall-marks of a gang who were responsible for numerous robberies in recent months, including, it transpired, that from a military property on Kennedy Road. The gang had been a thorn in the side for the Police, but now was opportunity for the Detective Branch to swoop on them.

Obviously this property must be searched, and, if the right cubicle could be found (for surely finding contraband from previous robberies would supply the proof of that) the people there should be arrested. Thus just before 10.45 a.m. the Constable summoned seven others attached to the Branch and ordered his men to take revolvers and handcuffs. O'Sullivan, Clarke, Sun Tai and some of the rest of the party were in plain clothes. Early in the course of the journey by tram to Gresson Street, the nature of the job was communicated to the constables, O'Sullivan carrying the search warrant himself.

Gresson Street had been laid out around 1909 on Marine Lots Nos. 29 and 30 and named after William Jardine Gresson, a partner in the powerful trading house of Jardine Matheson. On a 1909 map it appears as the only road (although unnamed) connecting Praya East (the harbour-side) and Queen's Road East between Ship Street to the east and

342 The events of the day were reported by the newspapers: *South China Morning Post, China Mail* (English and Chinese editions), *Hongkong Telegraph and Hongkong Daily Press* on 22nd- 24th January, 1918, and the trial at the Magistracy by the same papers on 4th - 7th March, 1918. Full accounts also appeared in the Chinese language papers, including the *Chinese Mail* for the same dates. I am grateful to Prof. John Carroll and members of the History Department of Hong Kong University for sourcing these papers, and especially to Mr. Ernest Chu of the Hong Kong Police for his meticulous translation.

Arsenal Street to the west.[343] About ninety yards long, Gresson Street comprised of three storey tenements of the usual narrow fronted, deep variety occupied largely by working Chinese, but with a sprinkling of other nationalities, including Eurasians and Europeans. No. 6 was on the eastern side of the road, on the ground floor of which was a concrete arch encasing a wooden shop frontage, with a narrow front door to one side. Lun Fat Street came into existence in 1912, parallel to Gresson Street, some forty yards further east. Between the two ran, for at least part of their length, a gated back lane, with access from the yards of individual properties and out into the two streets at the rear of the corner buildings on Queen's Road East. On the western (Praya) corner of Gresson Street stood the Seamen's Institute whilst the opposite corner where formerly had been the French Hospital was now occupied by a Japanese house.

Floor plans (now lost) were produced for both the Magistrate and the Supreme Court. Extrapolating from the newspaper reports, it would appear that the door opened almost immediately onto the staircase to the first floor, while the ground floor was occupied by a building supplies merchant and contractors, Chang Loong & Sons. The stairs were evidently steep, narrow and necessarily dark. On the the first floor there appears to have been a short passage, giving access to the front section of the house, but leading also to a 'bridge', a connection across an air shaft, with a door to the back portion of the house. This itself was divided into a room at the front, and two cubicles and a kitchen. One of these cubicles and the kitchen ran along the back wall. Cubicles in this style of house were typically eight foot in depth and ten to twelve foot in width, with the exception of the back one, which was rather smaller on account of the kitchen. It may be that the front room of these had a window onto the air shaft area, for frequent criticism of the practice of building very deep, narrow buildings which had to share air and light coming only from the outermost cubicles had begun to result in some modifications to building design. At the very front of the building that there was a verandah, which jutted out over Gresson Street.

343 Held at the National Archives, London CO 700/Hong Kong and China 48.

Alighting onto the Praya at the entrance to Gresson Street, some of the party made straight for the back portion of the first floor of No. 6. Both O'Sullivan and Sun Tai detailed the constables to their individual roles within the house, with one man, Constable Li Kum Yau, sent to guard the back gate into the alleyway. Three men went up to the second floor with Clarke, where after a brief search Constables Kwong Wa, Ng Fu and Chang Tim were stationed to keep watch over the only occupants of this floor, a group of women and children and to guard the potential exit points. On the first floor Constables Cheung Kam and Lo Hoi guarded the passage way and the stairs, while Kwong Kui covered the kitchen at the back. Constables Kwong Sang and Sun Tai went to the rear cubicle with the Inspector.

The officers anticipated that this would be a routine search, no different to any other in the daily fare of a policeman. Crimes committed with the aid of guns were few in proportion to overall crime, and tiny if compared with London or the cities of the USA. Criminals had perhaps less need of guns in the colony than in China, for 'soft' British justice meant that capture would involve a brief stay in Victoria Gaol, with a reasonable diet provided free. Here they did not have to fear the dreadful gaols of China, let alone the usual summary justice of beheading. More especially, though, the lanes, alleys and interconnecting houses provided perfect cover and they could rely on at least the neutrality of the local population in any contest between themselves and their colonial masters. On the other side, general confidence in the police was now so much greater than it had been in the earlier days of Hongkong, when no gentleman would step outside of an evening without suitable firearm protection. The earlier murder of Johnston was seen as an aberration, and that it might be the work of a gang was not even considered. By this point in the European war, the police may have had difficulty acquiring their usual stock of ammunition and guns, as there is some suggestion in the aftermath that insufficient amounts were available for the men.

No. 6, Gresson Street

Detective Sun Tai had not checked to see who had followed his orders concerning firearms: in the event, just three of this party: Sun Tai himself,

Lo Hoi and Cheung Kam collected revolvers, although meeting and co-opting the armed Constable Kwong Sang on the way made a fourth. That neither of the Europeans thought it necessary to similarly arm themselves was evident; none of the constables recalled seeing their officers with a gun. O'Sullivan, and perhaps Clarke, carried a walking cane, but this was more a sartorial accoutrement than a weapon. Certainly there was no anticipation of resistance, either to the search or to potential arrest. Although it was armed men, Sun Tai and Cheung Kam, who initially led the way, closely followed by the Europeans, their guns were not out and no calling out or shouting was reported. Indeed, one witness recalls how quiet the house was: perhaps this should have aroused suspicion.

The police who went through to the back cubicle passed first two men smoking opium, one of whom was said to be a medicine man, So Yui Chee. On a spare bed in the passage a man, two women and a small girl were sitting and Lo Hoi caught sight of a second man underneath this. Entering the last cubicle, O'Sullivan and his colleagues found the one bed pushed up against the back wall, underneath the window which opened onto the back yard. Two men were lying across the bed and one sitting on it. There seems little doubt that this was where O'Sullivan expected to find the contraband, and that the men in the cubicle were immediately under suspicion. However, initially, all did go as the police might have hoped, with no resistance from the men. They stood up and moved to one side of the cubicle when so ordered by Constable Sun Tai, and gave the information that they were from Swatow when questioned. The three men were then searched, brothers Ng Ming and Ng Ling by Sun Tai, the third man by Kwong Sang. No weapons were found. Ng Ming, dressed in European style trousers, asked for his coat, a dark blue European jacket, which was hanging on a hook on the cubicle partition. O'Sullivan assented to this, having first had the garment checked.

The other two men then made the same request and their Chinese long coats were searched and handed to them. Sun Tai called out for the handcuffs, which were with Cheung Kam, who was in the passage. At about that point Sergeant Clarke entered the cubicle and was followed immediately by another of the gang. This man, a tall man, was not one of the two smoking opium in the front, but came from somewhere else in that back portion of the house. Meanwhile at least one of the men had been allowed to sit on the edge of the bed to put on his shoes. Ng Ling, the only man who stood trial said that they sat side by side on the bed to do this. It was at this time that Sun Tai, having searched the new man, stepped into the passage to take the handcuffs from Chang Tim, where upon he became aware that in a low voice and in Cantonese the Inspector was saying *"Don't move, don't move your hand."* Turning around, he saw Ng Ming reach out into a black box on the bed and straightaway start firing a revolver.

Immediately, O'Sullivan, Clarke and Kwong Sang grappled with the men in an attempt to prevent them gaining more firearms. Guns were quickly passed, however, between Ng Ming, the tall man and the other man, and despite the greater height and strength of the Europeans, it is apparent that, in the very cramped confines of the cubicle, the gang had had the advantage of surprise, and, for the policemen, the battle was soon over. Sun Tai, who at this time was hit in the left hand, maintained that shots came both from the bed and from under the bed, whilst gang member Ng Ling, who Sun Tai was attempting to hold at bay, was also shot in the chest. The box was packed with guns and ammunition and the situation in the cubicle descended into mayhem amidst a barrage of bullets. Of those, just three came from the gun of Constable Kwong Sang and none at all from Sun Tai, who could not get his revolver out in time. Lo Hoi and Chang Tim, the other armed constables, hearing the volume of fire, did not venture into the cubicle. Kwong Sang was hit in the lower stomach and the leg and at some point rolled under the bed. Of the Europeans, Clarke fell first, receiving bullets to the neck, chest and shoulder, fired from above and fatally injuring him in the heart, lungs and liver. O'Sullivan was killed by a bullet into his brain, but he had also been shot in the chest, back and the groin.

Sun Tai was shot again, this time in the thigh, before he got out of the cubicle, across the bridge and down the stairs. Reaching the pavement he only just had time to warn Cheung Kam and for both to take cover in the doorway of No. 10 before Ng Ling came out. This man was not trying to escape, indeed the policemen gave evidence that he was '*walking fast*' to where they were. He later proved to be unarmed, but at the time the police were unaware of this, and, having failed to get his gun to fire, Sun Tai gave instructions to Cheung Kam to shoot Ng Ling, who fell to the ground. But they had to swiftly turn their attention to another of the gang, who had followed his fellow down the stairs and was continuously firing a revolver at them. Cheung Kam returned fire and the man clambered back up the stairs in retreat. Early on, reports appeared about men who had been seen running away from the scene, down Gresson Street and eastwards along the Praya. If correct, these men may have been connected with the gang: in any case, it is easy to imagine how the two policemen in the busy and noisy street, fully occupied by these immediate events and Sun Tai's own wounds, might have failed to notice other men slipping out.

Meanwhile, Lo Hoi, who had been instructed by O'Sullivan to watch the entrance to the kitchen, had seen nothing of the action, and only caught sight of Sun Tai when he emerged to claim the handcuffs from Cheung Kam. However, when the firing started, he saw a man emerge from under the bed in the passage and attempted to arrest him. Either this man or one of the brigands in the cubicle fired a shot which missed Lo Hoi and whilst trying to get his revolver from out of its holster, found himself under more fire from some of the robbers who made a rush down the stairs. During a lull in the firing he '*peeped*' into the cubicle, but as some of the gang were on the staircase, his instinct for self-preservation took over, and he made a hasty dash back to the kitchen. Here he found Constable Kwong Kui, crouched behind the stove, armed with a chopper for self-defence, as well as an old woman, who cowered in a corner. Lo Hoi tried to bolt the door, and lent against it to hold it firm, but the noise this created was noticed by the gang, who were soon back up the stairs and trying to get in. Kwong Kui then started to climb out of the window to escape, but hearing this, too, the gunmen went back to the cubicle. Some fifteen minutes or more after the events Lo Hoi was able to leave the kitchen and tumbled down the stairs, landing somewhat ignominiously on the pavement.

The beginning of the response

It was not until Chang Tim, who had been guarding the second floor, came out with his colleagues some minutes later, and after the firing had stopped, that the alarm was raised. The constable went to the nearest telephone, in the Seaman's Mission on the Praya and got through to No 2 Station where Sergeant McWalter received the message to send all available help, armed, to the Ship Street area. Meanwhile, Chang Tim's colleagues from the top floor, who had followed him out into the street, blew their whistles to bring other police in the vicinity to their aid.

Events had occurred so rapidly inside 6 Gresson Street that it was still not even 11.15 a.m. when the whistles alerted those in the neighbourhood who had not already been alarmed by the sound of gunfire, and the street started to crowd with onlookers. Just at this time Inspector George Sim, who had been travelling back to No. 2 Station on a tram following a session at the Magistrate's Court, noticed a Chinese man (gang member Ng Ling) lying on the pavement and jumped off to investigate. He then met Cheung Kam, and whilst the constable was in the process of explaining what had happened, shooting resumed, and a bullet fired from No. 6 staircase flew between the two men. Cheung Kam returned fire, probably with his last rounds, and the men took cover while Sun Tai made his report to the Inspector. Sim asked for Cheung Kam's revolver, but the constable is recorded as refusing to give it to him. Probably he told the Inspector that the gun was empty, and he then urged Sim not to go into No. 6. The warning was heeded, and Sim went to call for help, having instructed Sun Tai to be taken to hospital and Ng Ling to No. 2 Station. At the Seaman's Mission, Sim was not initially able to get through to the Central Police Station, and first repeated the request for help to the Interpreter at No. 2 station. On his third attempt he found the Central line free, and gave as full a report of the situation as he was then able to the Captain Superintendent.

Sim, leaving the Mission, met the armed Sergeant McWalter hurrying up the Praya, and the two men went into the first house, No. 19, on Lun Fat Street, via the alley that ran between it and Gresson Street. Here, from a vantage point high at the back of the house they could cover the windows and exits at the rear of No. 6. Initially, Sim left McWalter there and went back to ground level to deploy the other police who were beginning to arrive. He met a group of four Indian constables returning to No. 2 Station from '*up town*'. Since these men were all in plain clothes and carrying revolvers, Sim stationed B410 Mullah Singh at the archway where Lun Fat Street joined Queen's Road East, with B332 Tara Singh at the Praya end of that road, whilst the other two, B267 Magher Singh and B265 (unnamed in reports) accompanied him. Back into Gresson St, where firing yet again came from No. 6, the inspector managed to get a revolver from a Chinese constable. Sanitary Inspector Allan, a member of the Police Reserve, had taken position on the roof of the Seaman's Mission, from where he could cover most of Gresson St and particularly the entrance to No. 6 with his volunteer service rifle, and so, leaving the Indians on guard, Sim returned to Sergeant McWalter.

In pursuit of the gunmen

At about this time the '*desperadoes*', as they were frequently called in the press, made to escape from the back of the building. Clambering out the kitchen window onto a ledge, they started to climb down the waterpipe between Nos. 4 and 6. McWalter could see that they were heavily armed, with a pistol in each hand and two each hanging by string from their teeth. Their descent was precarious, particularly as they were firing their guns and being shot at all the time, as more police arrived on the back verandahs of Lun Fat Street and took aim at them. A shot of McWalter's caused one to lose his footing and drop heavily into the yard. The escapees' bullets hit and seriously wounded Constable Tung Wai, in No. 3 Lun Fat Street. A third man was seen peering from the kitchen window but thought better of the risk and retreated. Sim reached his sergeant too late to see the descent, and was told that the men had run down the alley in the direction of Queen's Road, at which news the Inspector rushed back down the stairs to the street once more.

The two men, Ng Ming (in European dress) and the tall man in a long dark coat, whose name was never learnt, reached Lun Fat Street before Sim, and fired at him when he came out. At this stage they were about twenty yards from him, in the direction of Queen's Road. Sim returned the fire, and believed that he had hit one of the men. As they approached the archway, Mullah Singh was able to get a clear shot at the long-coated man, but almost immediately Ng Ming was upon him and fired at near point-blank range. The Constable managed somehow to duck and avoid that shot. They were joined by Constable Tara Singh, who had rushed up Lun Fat Street, and the chase then continued a short distance along Queen's Road East, which was crowded with shoppers. In consequence the police stopped shooting and lost some ground when the brigands turned south into Ship Street, a steeply rising road giving onto a network of small lanes and alleys above main thoroughfare. This street was less crowded, and the firing recommenced from both sides, whereupon the people in the road hurried to take cover. Sim thought that it was the first shot fired here by the man in European clothes that killed a small boy sitting on a stool outside his home, while the second wounded a Korean gentleman, '*a mere spectator*', standing close to the junction of the two roads. The Indian constables were ahead of Sim by this time and when Chinese police ran to report to him, Sim instructed them to continue to follow the gunmen.

The maze of stepped alleys opening into streets, little more than passage-ways between buildings and frequently having no access to other roads except via the steps, ideally suited the purposes of the fugitives. Hau Fung Lane was just such an alley, running parallel to Ship Street to the east, and thus very steep. Schooner Street, a winding and rather ill-defined passage above and parallel to the main road, linked the top of Ship Street to the head of St Francis Street to the west, and the Catholic Chapel and the Italian convent. The gunmen split up at this point, with the man in European clothes diving into Schooner Street and the tall man rushing up the steps that led him eastwards and into Hau Fung Lane. Since Constables Tara Singh and Mullah Singh were by then close by that alley they pursued this man, eventually confronting him in 6 Han Fung Lane, a Japanese brothel. It may well be that the encounter took place in the back yard of this house, into which the gunman had run, for it was here that Mullah Singh died, shot through the head, whilst Tara Singh staggered into the house and collapsed in the front room. The gunman, meanwhile, slipped back out into the streets and was seen flying up the steps and into the scrubland below Kennedy Road, where he then had excellent cover and made good his escape.

It was the gun fire that woke Sergeant Marriott of the Naval Dockyard Police. The noted prize boxer, Henry 'Kid' Marriott, who lived at 3 Hill Terrace, part of Schooner Street and adjacent to the wall of the back yard of the Italian Convent, had been on night shift at the Yard. The noise of the chase was heard by his wife, who hurried to alert her husband. Swiftly pulling on his trousers, jumping into his shoes and picking up his service rifle, he went into the lane where Inspector Sim was labouring up the steep hill, and shouted out to him, *"Armed robbery, get your gun, prepare to shoot"*. The Dockyard Sergeant returned to his house, and went to an upper window from where he could see the ringleader, whilst his wife stood at the front door, from where she kept him informed of the gunman's movements. At this point Ng Ming became aware of both Marriott and his wife, and made a sign as if to silence her, but then shot at her, fortunately missing by a whisker. Marriott lost sight of him for a short time, but then saw him very close by, as Ng Ming jumped onto the Convent wall, almost below his verandah. This proved to be the gunman's fatal error, for although Marriott had only four rounds of ammunition, at that distance, and with a clear sight of him, it took just a steady aim to seal Ng Ming's fate, and he was felled instantly.

Inspector Sim, once more out of ammunition, had to leave the chase to younger and better armed men. His chief, Mr. Charles Messer had arrived by one of the police cars, and joined Sim in Queen's Road East. Here some of the Chinese constables told them of the events in Hau Fung Lane. They hastened there and found Tara Singh in the front sitting room, severely shot and wounded, with the worst damage to his thigh, and arranged for him to be taken to hospital. Going through the house, they came to the backyard, and found the lifeless body of Constable Mullah Singh.

With the chase for Singh's killer now abandoned, Sim and Messer returned to Ship Street, and were soon hurrying, together with their colleagues, to Schooner Street. Here they received Marriott's report and examined the body which lay at the foot of the Convent wall. On it they found four revolvers, including two tied to the wrists and eighty-six rounds of ammunition, together with a parcel that included shoes. Ng Ming had obviously been profiting from his trade, as he wore a gold watch, and his shirt sleeves were held together with gold cufflinks.

6 Gresson Street – a state of siege

The party arrived back in Gresson Street shortly after midday, and found that all was by no means over there. Whilst the action on the other side of Queen's Road had occupied Sim's attention, there had been sporadic fire from different rooms and floors of the house, giving rise to speculation that there were still quite a few of the gang inside. There were suspicions that a hole had been knocked through to No. 4. Sergeant McWalter had stayed at his post in the house in Lun Fat Street, on the lookout for more of the gang. Indeed, not long after Inspector Sim had left him in pursuit of the two gunmen, a third man made a dash for the back gate, but meeting with fire from McWalter and his Chinese colleagues posted further along, made a hasty retreat back into the house. After a lapse of some minutes this more cautious man poked his head and gun round the back door. A single shot from McWalter was enough that time to send the desperado back indoors. He reappeared some minutes later, but McWalter lost sight of him, and although sure that he had not escaped down the back lane, was not certain that he was back in the house either. Unlike those from 6 Gresson Street, McWalter didn't have an unlimited supply of ammunition, and at this point, about 12.10 pm, had to return to his Station to rearm himself.

Meanwhile in Gresson Street itself, the police, aware that there were still many women and children inside the house, repeatedly called for them to come down, but with gunshots heard throughout the building, and perhaps also from the house next door, the occupants showed a natural reluctance to put themselves at risk. Police were also stationed in houses on the opposite side of the road, from where they could fire into No 6. With little information as to how many gunmen remained in the house, the temptation must have been to treat any movement within the house as suspicious. The road had by this time been cleared of onlookers and the occupants of the other houses ordered to stay indoors, but great crowds, hundreds, if not more, were gathered at either end of the road, attracted by the almost incessant sound of gunfire. The number of police, meanwhile, both regular, Dockyard and reserve, grew steadily, joined by members of other government departments. The police who were arriving from Central and No. 2 stations were all armed, as were, perhaps more surprisingly, the Reservists and Revenue and Sanitary Officers.

Carnage revealed

Gradually, though, it became evident that the remaining gang members were confined to the ground floor, and, very cautiously, a search was made of the upper floors. Revenue Officer Inspector Watt led a party comprising Sergeants Cockle and Tim Murphy, a Chinese detective and two members of the Reserve force up the stairs. They found a five chambered revolver on the stairs, and a trail of blood which led them to the back cubicle. Here they found an horrific scene: pools of blood on the floor and more splattered everywhere, walls and furniture heavily scarred by bullets. On the floor lay the bodies of the two Europeans, Inspector O'Sullivan's lying across the head of his Sergeant, Henry Goscombe Clarke. Life was obviously extinct.

As the party were leaving the cubicle to search other parts of the house, Police Reservist Henry Hanson caught sight of two feet moving under the bed. Alerting the others to this, both he and Watt fired, but a voice from under the bed called them to stop, and Watt realised that the man was in fact one of the detectives. They lifted him out, and Kwong Sang, in a very weak state, told them, "*They shot me and I shot them.*" Had the police shots injured him? No, he said, he was already hurt. He was carried downstairs and a car was procured to take him to hospital, where he was admitted at 12.30pm. Constable Kwong Sang died an agonising death two days later, with the postmortem examination revealing that his intestines had been ruptured in nine places.

Out in the street, the party met Doctor Baleen, who, hearing of the affray, had come to lend assistance. He was led up to the cubicle where he confirmed what was obvious to the first party, that both men were dead. They then made a search of the other cubicles on that floor and the floor above, persuading some of the women and children to leave the building, and calling a halt to the police firing as these occupants came out. Meanwhile, with shooting still coming from the ground floor of the building, a very large body of police were present in Gresson Street, with not only Mr. Messer, but also the Deputy and Assistant Superintendents, Mr. Philip Wodehouse and Mr. Thomas King, together with the Assistant Superintendents of the Reserve Force, Mr. Hough and Mr. Franks. The Army Ordnance Department, led by Major Robertson, were called in, and two teams of St. John's Ambulance were standing by. With the other houses successfully evacuated, the scene became one of siege, as the police and army considered how to best regain the ground floor and flush out the remaining desperadoes. Although it would later become obvious that there was only one man of the gang remaining in the house, in the hours immediately after the original events this was not at all apparent, since this one man, with command of a large arsenal, and the run of the floor, gave the impression of a coven of gunmen holed up with no intention of surrender. Accordingly, with the arrival of Governor May, a 'Council of War' was held, with various options considered and some tried. The fire engine was brought along, with the intention of flushing the gang out, but it was too large to get down Gresson Street and the water pressure from the standpipe in Queen's Road was not even sufficient to break the windows, let alone have any effect on those inside. Rumour went around and was duly reported in the newspapers of that day that bombs had been thrown into the house and that burning the gang out had been considered; certainly the army threw smoke bombs into the house, but only with the effect of bringing six terrified women to the second floor verandah. Meanwhile, Police Sergeant Bob Wills scouted round the back to find if anything more could be seen from there. Presumably entering the backyard, he was shot in the thigh, and hobbled back into Gresson Street, from where he, too, was taken to the hospital.

Inspector Sim then had the grim task of leading a small party including Captain Superintendent Messer and the Governor back up to the first floor cubicle, where Sir Francis May remained for some minutes surveying the scene. Perhaps he recalled how, twenty-two years earlier, he had travelled to Newmarket to interview the senior man who now lay dead before him. Certainly May, who had found his *metier* as the head of the police, was unique in the gubernatorial history of Hongkong in attending and taking charge of such a crime scene.

If ever it was in doubt, an examination of the cubicle showed the scale of the cache at the disposal of the brigands. The box on the bed still contained 300 rounds of ammunition, along with eleven revolvers. Spent cartridges were everywhere, and an empty automatic magazine showed that it was not only revolvers with which the gunmen had armed themselves. The floors, walls and furniture were all peppered with bullet holes, and the nefarious activities of these men were attested to by the complete set of house-breaking implements, as well as a crowbar, choppers, masks, wire gags, Chinese ammunition, slings, and electric torches present. The handcuffs, which ought to have bound these men, lay abandoned on the floor, and underneath the bed Kwong Sang's revolver was discovered. He had used only four rounds and one of those had misfired.

Meanwhile, the remaining women and children on that floor, including the elderly So Yuet Ching who was found in the kitchen, were escorted downstairs and taken to No. 2 Police Station for questioning. Returning to the ground floor, the party gave their attention to the situation there. The firing was now only coming from the out-house in the backyard, thought to be the water closet, and from this, and the evidence of Wills, it was realised that only one man remained. A little after 1.30 p. m., the party made their way through the ground floor, finding here the proprietor of the shop, Chang Loong, with severe bullet wounds to the stomach and in a very bad condition. He, like so many that day dreadful day, was transported to the Government Civil Hospital with the help of the St John's Ambulance volunteers, while the gunfire coming from the outhouse continued. Eventually a break in the shooting allowed the police to speak to the occupant. Later identified as Ah Leung, he asked, in Mandarin, whether he would be shot if he came out. The answer in the negative, however, did not convince him, as he refused to give himself up when Ho Hung, one of the chief Chinese detectives, spoke to him. After a period of stalemate, it was proposed that Excise Department Officer and former policeman Charles Wilden would enter the water closet to reason with the man; however, when told of this the gunman threatened to shoot Wilden if he entered. The latter then fired a shot through the door, but to no avail. Major Robertson, who had organised the smoke bombs, was then called, and he suggested that a bomb could be thrown into the backyard sufficient to blow open the toilet door. Two such were prepared and thrown, but simultaneously a loud shot resounded in the cabin. As the cloud of dust cleared and the police entered, the brigand was found, just alive, belligerent to the last, feebly waving his revolver and threatening the men who lifted him out of the rubble. Wilden's bullet had grazed his cheek, but his own bullet through the temple had caused much more damage. Taken to hospital, he died a few hours later. Attention was then drawn to another body in the backyard, which had been seen earlier from the windows of Lun Fat Street houses and was thought to be one of the gunmen. Now examined, the police realised that this was yet another of their colleagues, Constable Kwong Kui, the luckless man who had tried to make his escape via the kitchen window, and who had been shot by the gang from the window of the cubicle. He had many broken bones from the fall, but, riddled with bullet wounds, he was probably dead before he hit the ground.

With the house now clear of all occupants, whether criminal or not, a final search was made. After the tension of the preceding hours the mood, both amongst the police in Gresson Street and of the hundreds of onlookers gathered at either end of the road became very sombre as the scale of the day's carnage was reckoned. Inspector Sim had the unenviable duty of organising the removal of his two colleagues. *'Heads were bowed and jaws clenched'* as the bodies of Detective Sergeant Henry Goscombe Clarke and Detective Inspector Mortimor O'Sullivan were brought down the stairs and into the street, and that of Detective Constable Kwong Kui carried out through the shop.

Gresson Street was kept closed for some hours more that afternoon, as investigations proceeded, but in the dreadful quiet of those hours, the toll of life could be assessed. The Inspector and the Sergeant both shot dead in the house, whilst Constable Kwong Kui lay dead in the backyard. Constable Kwong Sang, shot in the stomach and intestines, as well as a wound to the leg, was, at that time, just hanging onto life. Constable Mullah Singh, one of 'reinforcements', had lost his life in the chase of the gunmen. Also in the Hospital were the gang members Ng

Ling, alias Kwang Kwong, with a severely fractured palate and a bullet lodged in the chest cavity, and the dying Ah Leung. Of the other known gang members, Ng Ming had been felled by Sergeant Marriott's bullets, whilst his companion had escaped, and would by now be out of reach, on Chinese territory. Of the other desperadoes possibly involved, nothing further was ever known.

A small boy had died, caught in the crossfire during the pursuit of Ng Ming, as had a Korean or perhaps Japanese gentleman earlier in that same chase. In common with the injured bystanders, these people remain shadowy characters, only meriting a clause in a sentence in the (English) newspaper reports. An assistant in an unspecified shop, but probably that of 6 Gresson Street, was shot in the thigh, whilst the proprietor Chang Loong was reported to be in a very serious condition, and not expected to survive. Wounded members of the police force came mostly from the rescue party, but of the original search party, Principal Chinese Detective Sun Tai was shot in the hand and the leg, and taken to hospital. Constable Tara Singh had sustained the worst injuries when he had been shot in the thigh. The following year his injuries proved too severe for his continuance in the Force, and he had to be retired, aged thirty-five, on a special pension.[344] Sergeant Bob Wills had also been wounded in the leg, but not so severely and Constable Tung Wai had been shot in the arm when he was firing at the escaping gunmen from a house in Lun Fat Street. Thus it came about that of the four police and four gunmen who were in the cubicle at 11 a.m. on 22nd January, there was just one man to bring to trial, and just one witness to the actual events.

The colony in shock

In a time when the newspapers had a complete monopoly on the dissemination of news, and journalists had to speedily write vivid, lucid accounts of events still unfolding before them, what does not appear is sometimes telling. Two men are, to the modern reader, conspicuous by their absence in these reports. But at the time the reader, however, would have been deeply shocked, almost disgusted, had reference been made in

344 Report of the Captain Superintendent of Police, 1918 and pension records in the annual *Blue Books*.

the day's reporting to Inspector Patrick O'Sullivan and Revenue Officer Samuel Clarke, brothers of the two European victims. Together with their respective brothers-in-law, Acting Lance-Sergeant Maurice Kenneally and Sergeant Marks, they only appear in connection with these events during the reports of the funerals. But it is inconceivable that they did not rush to Gresson Street, for the news was all over Kowloon as well as Victoria before the siege had played out. It is tempting to think that fellow detective Tim Murphy had made sure that he was on the scene, and perhaps counselled the surviving brothers as to whether they, too, should go up to the cubicle to see the awful sight. Nothing was ever said about the details of that most painful day in the O'Sullivan family; neither has memory of any such conversation come down to the Clarke family.

Local knowledge and understanding of the events came primarily from the accounts in the various newspapers, published on that day and the next, as the subsequent trial did not take place for two months. Due to the immediacy of reporting, all the evening papers, both Chinese and English language, ran the story that day. Indeed, almost before the siege was fully over, the happenings in Wanchai were brought into many living rooms, with what might now be seen as an almost televisual impact. In the days and weeks following comparison was often made between the affray here and the Sidney Street shoot out in London in 1911, where the police had been involved in a siege-like situation, with suspected anarchists as the protagonists.

The *Hongkong Telegraph*, one of two English evening newspapers, sold out minutes after publication on the day, and had to rush out a single page edition with just the War news (received daily by telegraph) and the account of the affray. But even before any account had been published, the thoughts of the colony were with the families of the murdered policemen. All were married men, and donations were initially brought to the newspaper offices, amounting to some $3000 before the end of the day. In a short time these were put on a formal footing: the head of the Police Reserve opening the Gresson Street Fund at the Hongkong Club, whilst a Chinese subscription list was run by Legislative Council members Hon. Mr. Ho Fook and Hon. Mr. Lau Chö-pak. The separation of the accounts was only for purposes of collection, for all the victims' families, and that of Lance Sergeant Johnston, were beneficiaries of each. Within a week the Chinese community had collected over $12,000 (a little over £1,800) and when the Police Reserve Fund closed it stood at $15,600 (about £2,350).[345] Cash payments were then made to Kwong Sang's, Kwong Kui's, Mullah Singh's and Norman Johnston's families, and trusts were set up for the children of the Europeans, whilst the wives would receive about £60 per year.

The funerals

The evening papers of 22nd January and those of the subsequent days gave many column inches to the murders, but it was at the funerals of the victims that impact made by this violence upon the whole community was unequivocally displayed. Having the furthest to travel to his final resting place, the first funeral was that of Constable Kwong Kui early on the 24th. With full honours his coffin was escorted by detachments of Chinese and European police from the mortuary to Salt Fish Lane, where, after a short ceremony it was placed on a junk. Accompanied by some of his fellow officers, Kwong Kui's body was taken to Kongmoon, his birthplace, for burial. Sadly many of the same officers had to repeat the procession, ceremony and journey the following afternoon, when Constable Kwong Sang, also from Kongmoon, succumbed to his injuries. By comparison to the funerals of the other police, the Euro-centric papers give very few details of these funerals, but the Chinese Detective Branch, which numbered around sixty at the time, had certainly suffered a considerable blow.

With still high levels of Force mortality and the need for swift burial, the police were very experienced at organising impressive funerals at very short notice, as they had for poor Norman Johnston less than ten days earlier, but the funerals prepared for Singh, O'Sullivan and Clarke were on a scale never before seen in Hongkong.[346] The Inspector's body was taken on the evening before to the Catholic Cathedral, where it was

345 The total sum today equates to c. HK$3 million or £325,000. (2016).

346 The funerals were reported by all the newspapers the following day, 25th January 1918.

Above: Funeral of Henry Goscombe Clarke, procession, 24th January 1918.
Below: Funeral cortege, with Samuel Clarke and Robert Marks at head.
Behind, in grey coat, is Sir Henry May (courtesy Clarke family)

received and watched overnight, with a Requiem Mass celebrated the following morning. By 3.30 p.m. Queen's Road, from the junction of Wellington Road to the Monument had been cleared of traffic, and, with the coffins of Clarke and Singh brought to No. 5 Station and placed

Funeral of Henry Goscombe Clarke – burial at the Protestant Cemetery (courtesy Clarke family).

on gun carriages, the solemn procession began.[347] Great numbers of constables and sergeants of all three contingents escorted their colleagues, with relays of volunteers to pull the heavy vehicles, coming to a halt at Garden Road. Here the party coming down the hill from the Cathedral, consisting of O'Sullivan's fellow inspectors, and all the senior officers of both the regular and reserve Forces joined the procession, the Inspector's coffin on a horse-drawn hearse.[348] As the procession fully assembled, all the streets and lanes along the Queen's Road route began to fill up, particularly those on the south side, which, by virtue of their steep gradients, gave an excellent view. The contemporary estimate was that of the half million population, one half of that, 250,000 people, were on the streets to see this. The papers attributed this to respect for the men concerned, and for the Europeans on that afternoon in January 1918,

347 The Monument was at the junction of Queen's Road East and Wong Nei Chung Road. The newspapers would frequently advertise the time of a funeral by reference to when the procession passed the Monument, as from here those paying their respects to the deceased would join the mourners following the hearse to one of the cemeteries on Wong Nei Chung Road.

348 The gradient from the Catholic Cathedral on Caine Road to Queen's Road would prohibit the use of a gun carriage for the Inspector's coffin.

there was more than a hint of tribute to their fallen country-men on the other side of the globe. But many more must have been drawn by the sheer grandeur and spectacle of the event, for when fully formed, the procession stretched well over half a mile.

Procession list

Mounted Police under Mr Jenkin DSP and Insp. Gregg Band of the HK Police Reserve Buglers and Drummers of the HK Police Reserve Band of the 25th Middlesex Coffin of Inspector Mortimor O'Sullivan on horse-drawn hearse Inspectors of Police and Police Reserve Relatives and Friends Body of Sergeant Clarke on gun carriage drawn by Sergeants of Police Relatives and Friends Body of Constable Mullah Singh on gun carriage drawn by Indian Police Principal Police Officers including CSP Hon. C. McI. Messer Mr TH King ASP Mr TF Hough ASP Dr Jordan and Dr Lindsay Woods (surgeons attached to HKPR) Naval and Military Officers Members of Hong Kong Police Members of Hong Kong Police Reserve	Volunteer Fire Brigade Warders of Victoria Gaol Naval Yard Police Warrant Officers and Men of the Royal Navy Royal Marines Dockyard and Defence Corps (RNVR) Garrison Military Police Military detachments including: Royal Engineers, Royal Garrison Artillery, Middlesex, Royal Army Medical Corps, Army Service Corps, Army Ordnance Corps Indian Police Indian Warders of Victoria Gaol Naval Yard Indian Police Indian Watchmen (in large number) Pupils of St Joseph's School (100) Members of the Police Reserve (lining route from Wanchai Market, falling in as guard of honour as procession passed them)

Just before the Monument was reached, the procession came to halt at Morrison Hill Road, where, at the Sikh Temple, the Constable's body was met by detachments of Indian soldiers from the Royal Engineers, the Ordnance Corps and the Garrison Artillery, and escorted in. The Temple was covered with beautiful flowers and a huge number of wreaths, from all sections of society, were presented. The funeral rites were conducted, and Mullah Singh's body was cremated, accompanied by the chanting of the prayers and the sounding of gongs, in the presence of many of his colleagues from the three contingents, Mr. Messer and his staff, and some of the members of the Executive and Legislative Council and prominent Indian members of the community. Although Singh was married, no mention is made of any relatives here.

At the conclusion of this ceremony, the procession moved on to the Monument, where the Governor and the rest of the Council members joined for the short distance to St. Michael's Roman Catholic Cemetery.[349] The cortège was swelled here by a large number of Chinese constables bearing wreathes, and the fire engine was parked at one side, laden with more flowers. The papers assiduously printed lists of those who had sent floral tributes to each funeral, eventually running out of space. There were hundreds upon hundreds of wreathes that day, and the florists of Hongkong must have laboured night and day to fulfil this sudden huge demand.

At 5 p.m. the burial party and the principle members of the procession followed the bearers, Inspectors Brown, Garrod, Gordon, Grant, Gerrard and Brazil, up the steps to the first terrace of St. Michael's cemetery, the area where the Police buried their men. Thousands more filled the terrace and the paths below, with yet more outside the gates of the cemetery, unable to get in. At the graveside the choir of St. Joseph's School sang a full choral interment service, conducted by the Force's 'own' priest, Fr. Augustine Płacek, together with the Bishop's representative (Bishop Pozzoni being in Canton at the time), and many other priests. Fr. Augustine's eulogy, reported in full by the papers, moved many, including O'Sullivan's fellow officers, to tears. The priest had arrived in Hong Kong just two years after the Inspector and the two had been good friends,

349 Since the Governor and his party must have travelled down Kennedy Road to join the procession, it seems perhaps surprising that May did not attend Singh's funeral. Nor did he send a wreath. This could be put down to May's racial chauvinism, more evident in his gubernatorial time than when he was head of the Force, or to the rank of the deceased, since he had neither attended nor sent a wreath to Johnston's funeral, a week earlier. To be more generous to him, he was in poor health, having already had to cancel some engagements, and would leave the colony for good in September of that year, after a mild stroke.

so this was a particularly difficult moment for him. Of O'Sullivan's worthiness for the promised heaven, however, he had no doubt.

> *"In him, Erin has lost a faithful son; the Empire a faithful member and the Colony a gallant officer and an honest citizen. We have lost a friend who was sincere, and at the same time acceptable to everyone, and the Catholic Church has lost a faithful son. … People say that when a man passes the Canal*[350]*, morals and principles are left behind – it was not so in the case of our dear friend."*

Mortimor O'Sullivan was buried next to his cousin, Edmund.

Returning to the gates of St. Michael's, where Sergeant Clarke's body had been guarded by the Reserves, the procession regrouped, and the many mourners and well-wishers were marshalled along to the Protestant Cemetery. Here a team of eight sergeants bore the coffin up to the Police section, where Clarke was interred beside the still-fresh grave of his colleague, Norman Johnston. At the graveside the principal mourners were joined by the Bishop of Victoria who, along with supporting clergy, led the shorter Anglican burial service, with dusk falling around the huge numbers present.

In common with all European funerals, by far the greater part of the crowds attending that day were men. During the first hundred years of the colony's existence, most burials were of necessity attended only by colleagues and friends of the deceased. But on this day, Clarke as well as O'Sullivan had family members at the graveside, with Samuel Clarke, and Robert Marks. As propriety dictated, and understandably, neither Mrs. Clarke nor Mrs. O'Sullivan were present, nor were Clarke's sister, Ethel Marks, or O'Sullivan's sister-in-law, Helen O'Sullivan. But the Clarke family had been in touch via telegraph with his father and sister at home, and a wreath represented them. At O'Sullivan's graveside his brother, Inspector Patrick O'Sullivan was the principle mourner, together with his Hennessy cousins and their spouses, Mr. and Mrs. Nolan, and the newly

---

350 Suez Canal.

promoted Inspector and Mrs. Davitt, and Mr. and Mrs. T.F. O'Sullivan.[351] At each grave Governor May and Captain Superintendent Messer were present, together with most of the government and senior figures from all branches of Hongkong life: legal, military and commercial. The list of wreath donors gives a more telling glimpse into the lives of the men. Both bereaved families sent wreathes to the other, whilst the many branches of the late William Lysaught's family sent tributes to O'Sullivan's graveside. Both men were keen lawn bowls players and members of the Kowloon Bowling Green Club which sent wreaths.[352] Clarke played cricket at the Craigen Gower Club, and although O'Sullivan did not, the Club sent wreathes to each. Both had done Theatre Duty occasionally, and were remembered by the management of the Victoria Theatre. The list for Inspector O'Sullivan finishes, perhaps wryly, with "… *eloquent tribute, two from hawkers of Stanley Street.*"[353]

Hongkong reflects

In the days following the outrage, the police worked assiduously but fruitlessly to identify and find the escaped perpetrators, and to investigate whether the current occupants of the house had any connection with the gang. Statements were taken from all the police who had been on the original search, including that from Chief Detective Sun Tai, who was in hospital, as soon as he was able. All suspect residents had been initially held at No. 2 station and questioned, but beyond finding out that Ng Ming, the leader of the gang, and his brother had been seen in the house over the last few months, this really yielded little of help. Ng Ling, alias Kwang Kwong, spent six weeks in hospital, where his severely fractured palate

351 The harsh world of bureaucracy intruded on the grief of the Davitts when William was promoted to Inspector, 3rd class, as part of the general rearrangement necessary following Mortimor O'Sullivan's death. *Blue Book* for 1918.

352 A few years later a lawn bowls competition was inaugurated between members of the different government departments for the Goscombe-O'Sullivan Cup. In 1929 the *Hongkong Daily Press* ran an article recalling the events of Gresson Street to explain to its newer readers the significance of the Cup (27th September 1929). Matches were played for the Cup until the Japanese occupation during World War Two. It is assumed that the cup itself fell into the hands of looters or the occupying army.

353 *South China Morning Post,* 25th January 1918.

The graves of Inspectors Mortimor (right) and Edmund (left) O'Sullivan, taken in 1921 (courtesy O'Sullivan family)

The graves of Detective Sergeant Henry Goscombe Clarke (left) and Lance Sergeant Norman Johnston (right) (courtesy Richard Morgan)

had been reconstructed; but it had been established that the bullet in his chest was not endangering any organs, so no further surgery was undertaken.

The investigation into another murder in Yaumatei showed that this man was almost certainly implicated, and as soon as the doctors permitted, he was charged with that, which allowed him to be transferred to the Gaol hospital and held there, pending his appearance at the Magistracy in connection with the Gresson Street affray. With so little in the way of eye-witness accounts possible, and a suspect who had been the first away from the scene, there was no option but to wait until both he and Constable Sun Tai were fit enough for the trial.

With the events of 22nd January in the minds of so many, it was not surprising that the papers were soon receiving and publishing letters critical of the handling of the original search. Decorum required that Inspector O'Sullivan was not censured by name, but the writers were aghast that these men had set out when, they claimed, Wanchai was currently known as a hotbed of violent gun crime. The Government also carried a share of the blame, for obviously, these men were not supplied with adequate weapons. Even with the conflict in Europe, it was the Administration's duty to ensure that all police had easy access to firearms and ammunition, and the training to use them effectively. In its editorial of 24th January, the *Hongkong Daily Press* considered that

> *"although …. serious resistance was not anticipated that is no excuse for neglecting reasonable precautions."*

and, noting that it was practically by chance that the situation came to the notice of a senior policeman (Inspector Sim) who could take charge, suggested that men should be posted outside a house that was being searched, to raise the alarm if necessary. There was also criticism of the lack of control of gun and ammunition smuggling which, it was (incorrectly) thought, had allowed such a huge cache to be amassed.

The anonymity that was customary in the Hongkong press meant that serving officers could write equally energetic ripostes. Thus "*Policeman*" wrote to the China Mail:

> *"The 'job' which the late officers were performing, i.e., the searching of a suspected house, was, in itself, a very ordinary one for the average policeman. … Now, every police officer is armed, i.e., he has arms supplied him by the Government, but experience has taught most policemen that it is only on exceptional occasions he need to go armed to the teeth. The use of fire-arms has to be exercised with caution … especially in dwelling-houses. Seldom is serious trouble anticipated. The rule is otherwise, and the Gresson Street case proves it, because it is an exceptional case which stands out by itself in the whole history of the Colony. Does anyone … imagine that these two unfortunate officers knew that they were to strike such a gang of ruffians? Neither I, nor any other policeman, will ever believe that the mere possession of arms … would have saved their lives.*
> *There are risks to be borne in all trades and professions. Inspector O'Sullivan and Sergeant Clarke were policemen, and both took the attendant risks of their profession. The question whether they were*

> *armed or unarmed is, therefore, as I have endeavoured to show, one of little importance.*"[354]

Governor May, at the short meeting of the Executive Council on the morning of the funerals, made a statement about the affray which was strongly critical of the Europeans for both allowing the men to get their weapons from their coats (as was then thought) and for not being themselves armed. He put this all down to *"carelessness, due to the immunity of the Police through long years."*[355] The angry statement perhaps tells more of his shock and grief than his considered opinion, as later, when in possession of more information, he was to alter his views, although he would recommend that police were discretely armed on a more regular basis.

The Police Reports presented a rather different picture to that of the complainants as regards violent crime in the colony. In 1917 the figures for murder (11) and manslaughter (9) had fallen slightly compared to the previous year with a significant reduction in gang robberies reported.[356] The situation would reverse in 1918, but there had also been remarkably few attacks on the police, who felt that they had the confidence of the community, and, although not stated, a wary sort of respect from the criminals. Johnston's earlier murder had been put on the soldier Bloomfield, for it was far more likely that this was an argument between two young British men than an attack by local Chinese on the Force. That January morning in Gresson Street was the moment when this chauvinistic complacency was challenged and shown wanting. Rather than being exceptionally cavalier in not going armed with the search warrant, O'Sullivan, Clarke and their team were following usual practice on what should have been a routine operation. Of course, had they at that stage known that the recent robbery at the military property had included the theft of guns, they would have no doubt acted differently. Even so, given the amount of weapons the gang had at their disposal, it is, as *"Policeman"* suggests, difficult to believe that the outcome would have

354 *China Mail*, 26th January 1918.
355 Minutes of Executive Council Meeting 24.1.1918 CO 131/54.
356 Report of the Captain Superintendent of Police for 1917.

been very different. The events subsequent to the initial shootings showed how unprepared the police were to react to this scale of operation, for time and again individual officers ran out of ammunition; there was only one telephone line into the Central Police Station and the whistle was the only really sure way of raising the alarm. The rigid ethnic hierarchy did not encourage the development of initiative amongst the Chinese contingent, and so, once deprived of their senior officers, the remaining men could hardly be blamed for just running for their lives.[357]

Bloomfield's trial, which had again been pushed back another week, was dropped. He was summonsed to the Magistrate and informed that in the light of recent events in Wanchai, the Police did not intend to pursue charges against him, and that he was fully exonerated of any involvement in the murder of Lance Sergeant Johnston, which was now presumed to be the work of the Gresson Street gang.[358]

Yet further grief, both private and public

After the magnificent and moving funerals on 24th January, the colony was in a sober mood the next day. The papers still carried more information about the siege, together with reports and photographs of the funerals and the procession. But life and death went on, and for one of the families affected there was still more heartache to come. Patrick O'Sullivan was stationed in No. 7 Station on the corner of Queen's Road West and Pokfulam Road, and lived in the Inspector's quarters above the station. The early months of 1918 saw an outbreak of cerebro-spinal meningitis that was particularly virulent through the poorer Chinese community, where lack of ventilation and sanitation gave the bacteria the ideal moist, warm conditions it required to spread easily from person to person. The regular influx of people from Canton and other parts of the mainland also provided a ready source of recipients with no immunity to the disease. The findings of the government specialist Lieut. Dr. P. K. Olitsky reporting the next year pointed to the overcrowded and unhygienic conditions and the absence of any attempts to isolate

357 At the Supreme Court the judge, perhaps harshly, criticised P.C. Lo Hoi for running away from the scene when he had looked into the cubicle.
358 *Hong Kong Telegraph*, 26th January 1918.

sufferers. In the first six months of 1918 over 1000 Chinese died, many in the notoriously overcrowded area bounded by d'Aguilar Street (east) and Pokfulam Rd (west). In that period just five Europeans died.[359] Police Station no. 7 lies on the western edge of this area, and Inspector O'Sullivan had, amongst his tasks, to lead and co-ordinate the work of his men in an attempt to control the spread of the disease. Just four days after his brother was killed in Wanchai his second child, two-and-a-half-year-old Peggy, who had been sickening some days, succumbed to the disease. The announcement of her death appears in the papers of the day, immediately beneath the *in memoriam* card of Mortimor O'Sullivan and the acknowledgement note of the two widows. Her small grave lies at the end of the row containing her uncle and cousin. Aside from her grieving parents, particularly hard hit by this was her maternal uncle and god-father, Lance-Sergeant Maurice Kenneally, who had kept vigil beside his little niece.

Aside from this epidemic, the year had already proved to be a bad one for fires, with three major and expensive conflagrations, which had destroyed houses in Cheung Chau, warehouse matsheds in Cheung Sha Wan and a business in Burd Street. Worse was to come, though, the next month, as on 26th February 1918 the most devastating fire that Hongkong had ever seen occurred. Fine weather had encouraged a more than usually large crowd to the second day of the Races at Happy Valley, not that much encouragement was needed. This was one of the most eagerly anticipated events on Hongkong's social calendar, with people from every walk of life attending. Many of the stands were matsheds, often three tiers high, and inevitably overloaded with more spectators than should have been possible. Food stalls were everywhere, with charcoal fires cooking all range of snacks and meals. Just before 3pm it was sparks from one such stove, underneath a three-tiered matshed, that ignited the highly flammable structure. The fire had no difficulty getting a good hold, and had spread within minutes to neighbouring matsheds. In the ensuing panic many were crushed to death, aside from all those who perished in

359 The records of meningitis-related deaths commenced in February 1918, and four Europeans were noted as having succumbed. It seems likely, therefore, that, occurring before the epidemic had really set in, Peggy's death was not included in this figure.

the fire or through asphyxiation. The final death toll reached over 600, with dozens who remained unaccounted. The Chinese race goers suffered most severely, but, reflecting the constituents of Hongkong, people of every nationality perished that day.

As Inspector-in-Charge of No. 2, Wanchai, Station, it was yet again George Sim's sorry duty to oversee the removal of the bodies and to prevent looting from those corpses. Having suffered the loss of one of his own men in Johnston's murder, then identifying and bringing down the bodies of his colleagues in Gresson Street, the man was, after this fire, almost numb with trauma. In that condition he volunteered, some days after the fire, to personally open around one hundred as-yet-unburied coffins to try to identify the body of a prominent Chinese gentleman.[360]

---

360 George Sim had transferred from a Scottish force the year after the O'Sullivan brothers joined and had steadily risen to 2nd class inspector. Now aged forty-four, married and with four children, he lived in the quarters above No. 2 Wanchai Station. In the words of Captain Superintendent Messer, crime seemed to concentrate in his district during 1918, for along side Johnston's murder, Gresson Street and the Race Course fire there were at least two other murders as well as a series of violent robberies and a number of gruesome accidents involving the trams. The whole station was severely overworked, Sim himself often starting at 6 a.m. and finishing well after midnight. He had not told his superiors that, following the Gresson Street affray, he had received three anonymous letters threatening to kill him. His work was appreciated by his superiors, and Sim was under consideration for a second medal for his labours. On Sunday 10th November 1918, the wife of a suspect in a murder that had been committed in Pennington Street was being kept in the station as a witness. At 9 p.m. that evening, Lance-Sergeant McWalter found Sim's youngest girls on the stairs asking for their father, who they said was in the Chinese mess room with a Chinese lady. McWalter looked into this room from the verandah where he saw Sim having sex with the prisoner's wife. The following day as rumours of the Armistice were coming through, Sim was out on police business, and, that concluded, was having lunch with a friend when a Frenchman showed them a telegram about the imminent peace. Soon, drinks were being stood all round, and although it would seem that he did not have a great deal of alcohol, in the depressed mental condition he was in, it was enough to render him beyond reason. He returned to the Station, repeated the incident with the woman, this time forcing himself on her, whereupon his junior officers took charge and transported the raving man to hospital. He was swiftly diagnosed as having a severe mental breakdown, and watched to ensure that he did not try to do away with himself. Initially, it was proposed to prosecute him, but the doctors persuaded the government that in his medical condition no such charge would be upheld. He was quietly compulsorily retired, with a 25% reduction in pension, and returned with his family to Scotland, to a farming life, and, one hopes, some peace of mind.

The inquest into the fire, which was well underway at the time of the Gresson Street trial, saw the Police and Public Works Department criticised for not anticipating the possibility of such an outcome when there was no control exerted on the number of people who attended the races. The scale of the fire was kept in the forefront of people's minds, as the papers had printed daily updates of the enquiry which became more a harrowing account of the suffering than an investigation. Witness statements came from the whole range of the Hongkong community, and indeed, on the second day of the Gresson Street trial, the Hongkong Daily Press printed the inquest statement of one Job Witchell, manager of the King Edward Hotel, the same Job Witchell who had fallen foul of the Police gambling scandal more than twenty years earlier.

At the Magistracy

On the afternoon of the 4th March, the Gresson Street suspect, Ng Ling, though still recuperating, was brought from the Gaol Hospital the short distance to the Magistracy, where he was to be indicted by Magistrate Mr. J.R. Wood. The Assistant Crown Solicitor, Mr. Leo Longenotto, prosecuted, and at this hearing the prisoner was not represented. The events had caused such a level of anxiety and outrage in the colony that although in magnitude of loss of life and impact on the whole community it was greatly overshadowed by the Racecourse fire, there was still a very large crowd in the public seating of the Chamber.

The charge brought against Ng Ling was that he was concerned in the murder of Inspector O'Sullivan, Sergeant Clarke and Police Constable Kwong Sang. Singh's murderer could not be identified, and was almost certainly now in China, and it had not publicly been established (nor enquired into) who fatally shot Kwong Kui. During those three days in the Police Court the story gradually unfolded and the public were able to learn for the first time, not just more precise details of all the incidents that happened in the lanes around Gresson Street, but the events within the house itself, as far as they could ever be known.

The court heard about the number of people in the house, and of how, aside from two men smoking opium in the front of the rear portion of the house, there were two or three others, with possibly some hiding beneath beds. The quietness of the house suggested that the gang had received some warning of the approach of the police. The box of weapons was on the bed, but why had O'Sullivan or the constables not been suspicious about it? Were the men lying on the bed initially hiding it or was it well concealed in some other way? As the only policeman to emerge alive from the back cubicle, Sun Tai's evidence was crucial for understanding the sequence of events, although he had left the scene on two occasions to get handcuffs from a colleague. The Inspector certainly did become suspicious as Ng Ming started towards the box. Sun Tai saw Ng Ming reaching into the box at this point, whereupon the firing started. The shots brought Lo Hoi to the entrance of the cubicle, from where he could see O'Sullivan and Clarke trying to restrain Ng Ming and the other man (Ah Leung) while Constable Kwong Sang was grappling with the tall man. Sun Tai gave evidence that he had grabbed at Ng Ling when he made a lurch towards the box, but could not prevent him from extracting a revolver. Lo Hoi stated that the man Sun Tai was holding did not get a gun from the box, but the fourth man to join the group certainly had. What of Sun Tai's assertion that shots came both from the bed and from under the bed? Was this simply the direction from which shots were fired in the fight that ensued, or was there indeed someone concealed? There was no conclusive way of knowing. Of all the bullets fired there just three came from the police. The prisoner was hit in the chest by a bullet fired by another of the gang. It had been thought at the time that the gun found on the stairs by the rescue party, which had two bullets discharged, had been dropped by Ng Ling in his flight. But now, with hindsight, could this not have been in the possession of another of the gang members as they initially flew down the stairs? There is no suggestion that fingerprint evidence was used in this trial at all.

Ng Ling asked to give evidence, and although it was explained to him that if he went into the witness box he could be questioned, he persisted in his request. He stated that he was a 23-year-old businessman from Shun Tak, a fishmonger. He had come to Hongkong only three days before the incident, and was living in 6 Gresson Street with his elder brother when the police came in. The men asked for their coats, and Ng Ming for his shoes.

"The Inspector asked them what they had. Ng Min (sic) made a motion with his hand and said nothing. The Inspector struck him down with a stick. The third man, who had got up from the bed, put his hand into a black box and fired a shot outside. The bullet struck Sun Tai's hand. Ng Min sprang to the box to take possession of it. The Inspector also attempted to take possession of it. Sun Tai caught me by my collar and I was then shot in the chest by a shot which came from the direction of the bed. Sun Tai ran and I followed him."[361]

Under questioning, he went on to say that he had not seen the Inspector shot, and had not seen Sergeant Clarke at all. Sun Tai was lying, he said, when he maintained that he had taken a revolver from the box, for he had not been able to move when the constable was holding him.

Ng Ling was committed for trial at the Criminal Sessions later that month, with the Yaumatei murder case remanded week by week.

The verdict

The trial of Ng Ling at the Supreme Court was for the murder of Inspector Mortimor O'Sullivan, and commenced on 19th March.[362] Sir William Rees Davies, K.C. presided, with the Attorney General Mr. Joseph Kemp K.C. prosecuting and Mr. Alabaster defending. As was usual in Hongkong, a seven man jury had been selected, who were cautioned by the judge to put aside the still fresh emotions and feelings that the affray had caused. So much evidence, he said, that could be desired in such a case was unavailable because the lips of those who could best provide it were now closed in death. Gaps in evidence, he hoped, would not be filled by making a scapegoat of the one man who stood trial, but only by '*fair and legitimate inference*'.

The jury then heard a resumé of the events of 22nd January, pieced together from the welter of evidence given at the Magistracy, and

361 *China Mail,* 7th March 1918.
362 Once more, the events at the trial were closely followed by the press, and appear in all the papers between 19th and 22nd March 1918.

specifically how Detective Sun Tai had tried to catch hold of Ng Ling as the man went to put his hand into the box to draw a revolver. The Attorney General admitted that there was no grounds for saying that Ng Ling had planned or intended to kill the Inspector, rather, that he would show by inference that the prisoner was part of a gang who would use murder as the first resort to avoid arrest.

> "*If you think that these people were prepared, that they intended to resist the Police in their lawful arrest; if you think that the prisoner's action in making a rush for the revolver at the same time that the attack was made on Inspector O'Sullivan and Sergeant Clarke, then even if he did not fire a shot it will not relieve him from being guilty of the murder.*"[363]

He was challenged by the defence counsel that he would have to prove both common intent to resist arrest and that Ng Ling's intention was not to obtain a weapon for self defence but to attack the police.

Proceedings on the second day, however, were abruptly adjourned, and the following day took a significant change of direction. The judge had examined the statements given by witnesses immediately after the events, and had found that Detective Sun Tai's differed in a number of points from that which he had made at the Magistracy. Feeling that justice would be better served if the defence counsel were fully informed, the Detective was recalled and the Attorney General allowed to cross question him. Amongst other discrepancies, Sun Tai had not mentioned seeing Ng Ling pull a revolver out of the black box in the statement he gave to Inspector Terrett whilst recovering in hospital. Questioned about this, his explanation was that he had been tired and the matter had not occurred to him at the time. This earned him a stiff rebuke from the bench, for, after all, twenty years of service in the Police Force should have taught him not to overlook such a matter.

Ng Ling acknowledged that he was in the cubicle with his brother and a tall man when the police arrived. He was standing near the door, the others sitting on the bed. After the men were given their coats,

363 *Hongkong Daily Press,* 20th March 1918.

Inspector O'Sullivan struck Ng Ming with his cane and the tall man started shooting. It was the second shot that hit Ng Ling, and his brother 'stooped over' the black box, he had not rushed to it, nor had he drawn a gun from it. He denied that he had said at the Magistracy that Ng Ming had done so. The suggestion that it was a shot from the defendant that had hit O'Sullivan in the back, and so contributed to his death, had been early dropped by the Crown. It now seemed increasingly difficult to prove that he had acted 'in concert' with the others in the cubicle, or had even rushed to the box to snatch a weapon. Surely Lo Hoi had had the better sight of the situation? Unlike both Sun Tai and Ng Ling, he was uninjured at the time, and recalled seeing the fourth man, and not the prisoner, take a gun from the box. The prisoner's change of evidence could be put down to an attempt to distance himself from the attack on the police in the light of his impending trial for the murder in Yaumatei. More damagingly for the case, though, was that chief defence witness had developed his evidence, the inference being that the Constable was trying to ensure a conviction.

After just a quarter of an hour's deliberation, the jury found Ng Ling not guilty of the charge of O'Sullivan's murder. However, still on remand for the murder of Chan Leung, he was not released. The next month he was convicted of being concerned in this murder, and deported to Canton, where he was handed over to the Chinese authorities. Three months later, in July, a report was received that he, along with another deported criminal, had been tried and shot by order of the Tuchun. Ng Ling, it was stated, was an infamous robber in the Shun Tak region, and was wanted for many crimes.

The aftermath

In the months that followed reference was often made to the affray. Perhaps the only benefit to the colony was that it had disposed of the gang thought to have been the most prolific robbers seen in recent years. There had been nothing heroic in the deaths of the policemen in No. 6 Gresson Street, mown down as they were by bloodthirsty criminals. It was rather those who risked their lives in attempts to bring the murderers to justice who were the heroes: the murdered Constable Mullah Singh;

Constable Tara Singh; others of the rescue party; Sergeant Marriott and perhaps, too, Mrs. Marriott, boldly keeping watch as to where the absconding killer was running, despite an attack on herself. When he was released from hospital Tara Singh was awarded the 4th class medal in recognition of his bravery, before having to retire unfit the next year. Sergeant Henry Marriott, D.C.M., being of the Dockyard Police could not be so decorated, but the feeling both within the police and the community at large was that he should be publicly honoured for the part he had played, shooting the gang leader.[364] Accordingly, on 8th May a ceremony was held at the Central Station, attended by a very large number of the Force, at which Mr. Messer presented him with a gold watch and chain, the former engraved

> "*Presented to H. Marriott by the Community and members of the Police of Hongkong for his courageous conduct in the Gresson Street Affair on 22nd January, 1918*".[365]

All the murdered policemen were married men with families: details in the Chinese language "*The Chinese Mail*" for 16th February 1918 note that of the $13,000 raised by the Chinese community to date, it had been decided that the families of the two Europeans should receive $3,500 each and the two Chinese and Indian constables' families $2,000 apiece. Each family would also have received money from the fund collected by the Police Reserves, and from the Widow and Orphan's Fund, into which all serving and retired officers paid. Whilst the European families received regular payments from the latter fund, it appears that the two Kwong families and the Singh's were made, or perhaps opted for, a lump sum payment, thus, sadly, no more is known about the future lives of these families. Both European women returned to the British Isles with their children, first Mrs. Alice Clarke, who was pregnant with their third child, Kathleen, with her two young sons, Goscombe Goddard and Henry Philip. Hanora O'Sullivan remained in Hongkong for another fifteen

364 Henry Marriott had served in the Boer War, in the Sherwood Foresters, 1st Battalion Derbyshire Regiment, for which he had been awarded the Distinguished Conduct Medal.

365 *China Mail*, 9th May 1918

months, perhaps whilst her financial situation was sorted out. Certainly she was able to attend the laying of her husband's headstone, which, rather than being the standard Police type, with helmet and belt as part of the insignia, is, perhaps fittingly for the man Fr Augustin described, a simple cross. The following year, with her two daughters, Kathleen and Hannah, she did return to her father's family in Newmarket. After a few years both women remarried: Alice stayed in the England whilst Hanora emigrated to Chicago with her new husband and family, only to be widowed again within a decade. The elder of Henry Clarke's sons would return later to Hongkong, and take up his father's profession.

Chapter Eleven

A changing world: the interwar years and beyond

The Force came together on 27th March 1919 for the first medal presentation after Great War, although not all the men who had joined the Army had been repatriated to Hongkong by that time.[366] The salute was taken by Mr. Claud Severn, C.M.G., administering the colony in the absence of Sir F. H. May, who had left some months previously and retired on the ground of ill-health at the beginning of March. Although not Hongkong's most popular or successful governor, for the Police there was a real sense of sadness that the man so intimately concerned with their work for over twenty-five years should not be with them at this rather poignant moment. This was particularly felt by some of the oldest members there who received medals that day, including Patrick O'Sullivan, who gained a third class medal for meritorious work during the previous four years.[367] Inspector William Davitt was awarded a fourth class medal for '*long and faithful service*', whilst Patrick Boulger, god-father to O'Sullivan's third daughter, received this medal for '*exceptional services during the past four years*'.[368] At this ceremony Constable Tara Singh, now out of hospital, was called out for special mention by Mr. Severn, and awarded the fourth class medal for '*pluck and zeal at Gresson Street*'. The injuries to his leg, although superficially healed, had left him with less than full mobility, and doubtless some pain as well. Thus he

366 *Hongkong Telegraph,* 27th March 1919; *Hongkong Daily Press,* 28th March 1919.

367 Since both he and his late brother, Mortimor, gained the 4th Class medal in 1915.

368 Back in 1912, when based on Cheung Chau, the then Sergeant Boulger and his wife had both narrowly escaped serious harm when the station was attacked by pirates.

At St. Joseph's Terrace, early 1925. From left: Tim Murphy, Henry Dixon, Mary Murphy, Fr Rigianti and Margaret Murphy (courtesy Murphy family)

was to be retired on pension, and soon to to return to his home, and Severn wished him well on behalf of the Colony. Referring to the war years, he complemented the Force for the work done with such reduced numbers, congratulating those who were fortunate enough to be able to go to the front, and commiserating with those who volunteered but were not permitted to leave Hongkong.

1920 saw the long awaited completion of the new building at the Central Station. To become primarily an administration building in later years, this initially housed many facilities for the men, including a mosque and a Sikh temple, the gymnasium and recreation rooms on the lower floors, with dormitories, kitchens, mess-rooms and bathrooms for the Indian and Chinese contingents on the top floor. Only the floor at the station compound level, two floors above Hollywood Road level, was given over to the offices of the executive team and for record keeping. One newspaper report of this announces that plans were afoot for "*the early erection on the site behind the Central Station .... This proposed new building which will be three-stories, will contain kitchens, bathrooms, lavatories and drying rooms for the use of Europeans on the top floor, Indians on the first floor, and Chinese on the ground floor .... connected ... by means of bridges.*"[369] The police had long learned not to hold their breath when improvements to their living conditions were proposed. Like the kitchen and bathroom courtyard of 1862, this building did not materialise.

Life as a Detective

Tim Murphy's career as a detective had started quietly enough, although in his first year in the Branch he received a commendation from the Governor for his investigative skills which had helped ensure a successful outcome in three cases of larceny and robbery. But in 1914 he received his first medal (fourth class) for his work on a number of cases. A brief attachment to the water police followed, and it was during his time here that the *SS Tai On* was attacked by pirates, a particularly brutal incident which claimed the lives of over half the crew and passengers, in excess of 200 persons. In what was at that time a rare joint effort between the police forces of Hong Kong, Macao and China, survivors were rescued from the subsequent fire and pirates captured. Murphy's involvement in this event earned him the third class medal for bravery.[370] Little mention is made, but it was an exceptional achievement to gain two medals within the same year, and perhaps gave intimation of the direction of his future career.

Thereafter the newspapers reported Murphy's successes and prosecutions. An issue of the *Daily Press* on 21st January 1914 records him arresting one Li Miu who was trying to cash a forged cheque for $8136. The same issue tells how butter worth $420 had disappeared from a Kowloon godown, and, although a separate item in the paper, it was perhaps not unconnected that Detective Sergeants (H.G.) Clarke and Murphy had arrested a man for the unlawful possession of 338 tins of margarine butter.[371] In 1916 he was commended for arresting the culprit of a jewellery robbery from a house in Caine Road, and recovering the jewels as well; two years later he prosecuted a man in very dubious possession of a gold watch, just before the miscreant tried to pawn it.[372] He was again

369 *China Mail,* 10th February 1920.

370 *Hongkong Telegraph,* 24th October 1931.

371 *Hongkong Daily Press,* 14th January 1914.

372 *Hongkong Telegraph,* 24th October 1931, 29th January 1918.

commended by his Captain Superintendent for his 'plucky conduct' in arresting two armed men in a teashop in Mong Kok and had later that year what can only be called a 'lucky break' when investigating the mysterious case of the disappearing kerosene. An oil trader's servant apparently tried to abscond (by sea) with 308 barrels of the fuel, and might have been successful had he not remembered that he needed to get some milk, and returned to port to buy this.[373] Murphy's appearance (in plain clothes) in the famous photograph taken after Assistant Superintendent Donald Burlingham had shot the Sheung Shui Tiger in 1915, suggests that his detective postings were not confined to Kowloon and Hongkong Island.

Probably because he was by then well established in the Detective Branch, he alone of the Murphys did not volunteer, or was not permitted to leave, for service in France during the Great War: there was enough crime in the colony to keep him fully occupied. Tim Murphy used his fluency in Cantonese and his local knowledge to help unearth the truth in many investigations, including finding well-hidden killers, such as, in 1920, his arrest of the murderer of Lau Tam, a West River travelling trader, from photographic evidence he gained.[374] He was becoming well known in the colony, and provided good copy for journalists, even when he was not on the scene at the time of the action, as in the case of a long night watch of a house in St Francis Yard, Wanchai, when, in the early morning, after Murphy and Sergeant Kelly had left for their Station, the remaining Chinese constables had the satisfaction of surprising and overpowering a gang of heavily-armed criminals.[375] In that same year he was awarded the second-class medal, "*for skill and untiring energy in searching for and tracing criminals in a dangerous locality*".[376] He became a Sub-Inspector in the reorganisation of ranks of 1920 and almost

373 *Hongkong Telegraph,* 24th October 1931, *Hongkong Daily Press,* 12th November 1918.

374 *Hongkong Daily Press,* 26th August 1920, and the case widely reported in other papers of the time.

375 *China Mail,* 1st December 1920. The police must have wished, sometimes, that the pressmen were a little less assiduous in their reporting. This account states that the intended victim of the planned robbery was a wealthy Chinese gentleman, known to have $2000 and much valuable jewellery in his house, which was No. 1, St Francis Yard.

376 *Hongkong Telegraph,* 24th October 1931.

immediately was appointed as Acting Inspector. He did not, it seems, spend much of his 1922 home leave in Newmarket, preferring Cork city where he was able to help his recently widowed sister, Norah Lysaught, who was finding life hard in Ireland. Without much difficulty Murphy persuaded her to return to Hongkong, where she really had many more relatives than were left in Newmarket, and he booked a passage for her family to travel that December, using the trans-American route. Murphy himself, though, did have some business in Newmarket, marrying Miss Mary Sheahan on 12th September.

The Canton Road affray

Back in Hongkong, the following year brought Detective Inspector Murphy the case for which he would be most celebrated. At ten past eight on the morning of Saturday, 29th December 1923, a resident of 206 Canton Road ran the hundred yards or so down the road to the new Yaumatei police station, where Sergeant Kelly and Inspector Murphy were on duty. He reported that he and the other occupants thought that there were robbers on the second floor, as they had heard such unfamiliar noises, things being dragged around and some sort of violent search. The two policemen went to investigate, and on confirming the story, Murphy left the armed sergeant to guard the stairs whilst he rounded up as many colleagues as he could. With little time to explain what was happening, a couple of sergeants jumped on their motorcycles, thinking that there was a distance to travel, only to have to abandon them almost immediately. However, even if the police were not fully briefed, it is notable that all, detectives staff and regular police, Chinese, Indian and European, were now both armed and better-trained to use their weapons.

Towards eight thirty, when the police were assembling in front of the house (there fortunately being no rear door to the building), Canton Road was thronged with Saturday shoppers, with more, of course, attracted by the 'event' that was obviously about to happen. Creating further obstacles for the police, the road had been taken up in front of the house in question, whilst opposite was a building site. With about twenty-four police in the street positioned to cover the door, and the side road onto which the house overlooked, Murphy and Kelly, together with

Sergeant Fender crept into the house. Fender guarded the stairs while the others hid near the door of the suspect apartment. Hearing no sounds from within, Murphy blew his police whistle, which brought three men to the door. To the surprise of the officers, they appeared to be unarmed, but were not prepared to be questioned or arrested by the police, two of them making a dash for the stairs, a third dodging back into the flat. The police then opened fire, and as the men started down the first staircase they were met by bullets from Fender. One of the men was hit at this point, and remained in Hospital at the time of the trial, some five months later. Fender was also hit, taking a bullet in the arm, possibly from one of his colleagues. Murphy then released the residents of the apartment from the cubicle where they had been locked, whereupon a small boy found another of the robbers sitting on his bed on the verandah. This man was searched, and an automatic pistol found near him, but with only the two police in the flat and Fender out of action on the stairs, the gang were able to retrieve at least some of their weapons, and Murphy and Kelly could not prevent their escape. One got out via the verandah, whilst a further man, who had until that moment eluded their notice, was the first out of the main door of the house. He was followed by the man who had opened the apartment door, who risked heavy fire from the officers, as they pursued him down the stairs.

The street, meanwhile, was filling up dangerously, for there had been insufficient time to create any sort of cordon around the area. The police outside thus had to attempt to keep up fire on the emerging robbers whilst avoiding the onlookers. Perhaps miraculously there were no reports of bystander casualties, even as the gang-members dispersed. Two sergeants, Robertson and Magher Singh were shot at close range by the first man out, who, it would seem, subsequently escaped, whilst the second engaged in a running gunfight with Sergeant McEwen. The latter, running out of ammunition, grabbed the wounded Indian Sergeant's revolver and pursued the gunman, who had run further down the road and into a deportee shed, presumably unoccupied and unguarded at the time. Shooting between the pair continued, until McEwen again ran out of bullets and not knowing for certain whether the robber was still armed, had to engage him in physical combat. Overpowering him finally,

Officers involved in the Canton Road shoot-out. Tim Murphy (centre, in plain clothes) and new dog (courtesy Murphy family)

he pulled the man out of the shed, but the latter suddenly collapsed, and McEwen realised that he was riddled with gunshot and in a very serious condition. He instructed his colleagues to lift the injured man onto his, McEwen's, back and took him thus the short distance to the police station. Meanwhile, the man who had dropped from the second floor verandah into Pakhoi Street had dived to cover into the building site opposite where he was pursued, and eventually cornered and caught by Detective Constable Mak In. Inspector Murphy's loyal dog, almost as well known as the man himself, was killed as he ran up the stairs of the house in pursuit of his master.

When brought to court in May 1924, only three of the gang of five stood trial. One had escaped, and the man shot on the staircase was to spend many more months in hospital. It had become clear, both from evidence found and the initial statements of the prisoners, that this was an organised robbery, whose plans had been worked out in a tea house. Having tied up and imprisoned the unfortunate occupants, the gang had ransacked the apartment, with jewellery and money found on two of the men. They had come well armed: aside from loaded automatic pistols, they had cigarette packets of spare ammunition, much of it with the top of the cartridge case cut off, making it the particularly lethal 'dum dum' type. Although at the trial all three pleaded innocence, and one man even claimed not to have been in the house, the evidence against them was overwhelming. The three were found guilty, receiving each a sentence of 15 years hard labour, with the man who had fired at Sergeant McEwen given an extra 10 years.[377]

When the injured police had returned to duties, those concerned were gathered for a presentation at the Central Police Station on 11th June the following year. Murphy had been recommended for the highest honour, the King's Police Medal. It had not come through by the time of the presentation, but he had the satisfaction of seeing the bravery of all the men under his command recognised that day, with what must have been a record of two third and nine fourth class medals awarded for a single event. One of the third class medals was earned by Detective Constable Mak In for his brave work capturing the armed escapee in the building site. Injured Sergeant Maghar Singh received his first medal, but Sergeant John Robertson, who, being shot in the abdomen, had been the most severely wounded of the group, was not able to pursue his duties long, and went home, invalided, on pension on 17th September. He died early in 1926, aged thirty, of complications related to the wounds he had received.

Hennessy's line between the wars

In 1920 the Newmarket community in Hongkong were deeply saddened when, not long turned forty-four, George Hennessy's eldest son-in-law, Nicholas George Nolan succumbed to a brain tumour, diagnosed only three weeks earlier. He had worked until just a week before his death, when he had to go into the Civil Hospital, where he died on 22nd January. His career had truly been one of the Irish community's success stories in Hongkong, as his gift for translation had bought him the prize appointment of Chief Interpreter of the Supreme Court in January 1909.

377 The events and trial received wide coverage in the local press, including *Hongkong Telegraph, 29th December 1923, Hongkong Daily Press, 31st December 1923 and 20th May 1924.*

According to the obituaries, his skills as a linguist were almost without compare in the colony, as he was fluent in Cantonese, Fukien, Hakka, Hoklo, Portuguese, Spanish and Tagalog, with a working knowledge of Hindustani and French. He filled a number of other posts in the colony, for example as a Commissioner for Oaths, and was particularly useful to the Administration as part of the cable censorship team during the War. When the Supreme Court sat on Monday 26th January, three days after Nolan's death, the entire senior legal community gathered and stood to pay their respects, with many attestations of his merit not just as a translator but as an interpreter, able to find the right nuance and shade of meaning. *'An artist in interpretation'*, Mr Justice Gompertz said of him, who had known Nolan for over twenty years.[378] His funeral that evening was attended by many from the Courts, with the chief mourners Inspector Davitt, the Murphy men and others of the Irish police community, alongside Nolan's eldest sons, twelve-year-old Nicholas John and nine-year-old Henry.

By all accounts a quiet, modest man, his family life had been very happy, with eight children born to the couple, living in one of the Wanchai Road houses that he and his mother had built. His salary, of £500 p.a., was twice that of a police inspector, and had allowed him to set money aside for his children's education, and helped the very modest pension due to May Nolan from the Widows' and Orphans' Fund. The family returned to Ireland, and settled in south Dublin, where they kept close contact with both the Davitts and the O'Sullivans, when these two inspectors retired, and with Nolan's sister, Maria Jones, known to the family as Paupis. Sadly, May Nolan also died young, but with the children provided for, they, in due course, made their own contributions to the world.[379]

Patrick O'Sullivan had been first appointed to the Inspectorate, albeit in an acting role, in June 1908. Having climbed rapidly to that position,

---

378 *China Mail,* 26th January 1920.

379 The eldest two boys, Nicholas and Henry, became respectively politician and priest. Nicholas J. Nolan served as Cabinet Secretary in the 1960s and was the speech writer for Eamon de Valera, whilst his brother entered the Jesuits, and spent much of his later life at the Vatican, where he became the (English language) 'Voice of Vatican Radio'.

really by virtue of vacancies created by the Wa Lane Scandal, he moved up to become a First Class Inspector on 23rd May 1914. He was thus next in line for promotion to Chief Inspector, the highest position a man from the ranks could then achieve, and of which there was only one post. This would, of course, have meant a larger salary, but more significantly, a far better pension, and O'Sullivan was determined to achieve this. But James Kerr, then occupying the role, showed no signs of retiring, despite, at 51 years, being well over the usual age.[380] O'Sullivan and his family left Hongkong on leave midway through 1919, when, rather than travelling the Mediterranean route, they had chosen to cross America, stopping to visit Patrick's eldest sister Margaret, now a religious sister working in the administration of St. Michael's Hospital, Grand Forks, North Dakota. However, the family story tells that when the O'Sullivans arrived at the hospital, the Mother Superior of the order refused to let Margaret, now Sister Benita, see her brother since they had not sought prior permission. They had to travel on to Montreal, from where they took the short ten day crossing to Liverpool.[381] Passports had been obligatory since 1916, and the family's travels can be tracked by the stamps on this document.[382] Henceforth, he was under increasing pressure from his wife to return to the British Isles, for they had already lost one child, and the fourth daughter, born in Newmarket during that last leave, had been left with her sister there, rather than take an infant back to Hongkong with all the inherent risks that posed.

---

380 Kerr did, in fact, relinquish his post in August 1922, but only to join the executive staff. (He had been first appointed as inspector in 1903.) In 1921, a month after O'Sullivan's departure, he had served as Acting Assistant Superintendent for a month, during one of the periodic temporary shuffles of personnel, when Captain Superintendent E. D. C. Wolfe had acted as Colonial Secretary. It would appear to be this period that confirmed him as fit material for the executive role, the first such case. He eventually retired in 1926.

381 It was another ten years or so before brother and sister were reunited, when some of the Order paid a visit to Ireland.

382 *Defence of the Realm Regulations* published in *Hongkong Government Gazette,* 28th January 1916 required all people not of Asiatic ethnicity travelling to or from the colony to have a passport not more than two years old, and with a photograph of each adult.

For both O'Sullivan and Davitt, though, there was a more pressing concern connected with a move back to Ireland. The escalation of attacks against the police and all Crown forces, especially in Counties Cork and Clare (Davitt's birthplace) made settling back in their hometowns most inadvisable. In October 1920 the ambush of soldiers in Kanturk, just a stone's throw from Newmarket, had shut the town down for a few days for fear of reprisals, and early in 1921 one R.I.C. constable was murdered in Newmarket and two in Mallow, not twenty miles away. The papers at the end of September 1920 were full of the capture of Mallow military barracks by *Sinn Feiners,* the only such successful operation in the War of Independence. The reprisal was swift and harsh, when the town was set a-blaze the next night, destroying many of the principle buildings. Under curfew orders, the Fire Brigade could not turn out to fight the fires.[383] Similar miserable reports came from most parts of County Clare, and, more generally, the "*Irish Problem*", with details of these attacks and counter-attacks almost daily front-page news in Hongkong. Although Newmarket itself, partly because of the high esteem in which the land-owning Aldworth family had been held, was quite a moderate place, it nevertheless contained many with strong republican views, and a number, including Brigade leader Seán Moylan, who turned those views into action against the British forces. Lance-Sergeant Maurice Kenneally, returning in 1919 after a single five year term, which had been extended because of his service in the British Army, found life in Newmarket difficult, surrounded as he was by his republican brothers, and chose to depart for a farming life in Oregon, U.S.A. within a few months.

Passport of Patrick and Ellen O'Sullivan (courtesy Conor O'Brien)

383 *China Mail,* 1st October 1920.

Patrick O'Sullivan had signed for another five-year reengagement before arriving back in Hongkong in March 1920, but with his 45th birthday the following February, eventually decided that he could not wait for the Chief Inspector post any longer, and bowed to his wife's wishes, going on pre-retirement leave on 29th April 1921, drawing his pension a month later. William Davitt left Hongkong with his family the following February, and having considered London, in the end both families settled in comfortably suburban south Dublin, which provided them with a level of anonymity. Only during the Second World War did Patrick O'Sullivan move his family back to Newmarket, when he purchased *'The Cottage'*, the dower house of the Aldworth's former estate; the Davitts did not return to Co. Clare but remained in the capital.

William Davitt, who had arrived in Hongkong a couple of years after the O'Sullivan brothers, had been promoted to Sergeant in 1905. Married to George Hennessy's youngest daughter, he was frequently posted to the Island's southern stations and to Kowloon, where his police role was joined to that of Acting Sanitary Inspector. He stood next in line for promotion to Inspector at the outbreak of the war, for he had been close to the tail end of the recruitment that had filled posts left vacant by the Wa Lane scandal at the end of the previous century, so that there were a large number of men with slightly more seniority of service. As a married Sergeant he was not permitted to enlist for military service, and there was a general stasis within the inspectorate for the duration of the conflict. In 1916 the one post that did come available was given to Edward Browne, who had superior Cantonese qualifications to Davitt but a year of less service, so that, as seen, Davitt's elevation was brought about only by the death of Mortimor O'Sullivan in January, 1918. Like O'Sullivan, he also had leave due shortly before his retirement, but due in part to the situation back home, at the end of October, 1920 the family departed for Sydney for a vacation in Australia, where his wife had many cousins, the families of George Hennessy's siblings who had emigrated fifty years or so earlier.

The mysterious case of Thomas O'Sullivan

With the departure of Inspector Patrick O'Sullivan in 1921, and those of George Hennessy's line also soon back in Ireland, only one of the five O'Sullivan men remained in the colony. Thomas Francis O'Sullivan, who had started life as a constable, had moved swiftly into the post of Clerk and Usher at the Supreme Court five years later, in 1912, probably on account of his knowledge of shorthand. Chief Interpreter Nicholas Nolan was at that time away on leave, and his cover had involved a number of moves of staff, including the promotion to 1st Bailiff of Joseph Leonard, who had also joined the Courts after a term as a policeman. The younger man struck up a friendship with Leonard, and at any rate became acquainted with his young daughter, Mary Frances, possibly at a Christmas party given that year by Leonard at his Kowloon home. Perhaps the twenty-six-year-old O'Sullivan seduced the girl, or maybe, not quite sixteen years, she was anxious to escape the family home and saw in this man a way of achieving that. At any rate, they were hurriedly married on 19th February 1913 at the Rosary Church, Kowloon, which required a dispensation because the bride was just sixteen years and one month old.

Since Thomas O'Sullivan was a government official who was already quite well known in Hongkong, the wedding was well reported in the press, but with no mention, of course, of any slight irregularity. However, maybe it was for decorum's sake that the passenger list of the *SS Sardinia,* on which they sailed back to the United Kingdom that day, gave Mary's age as eighteen. One might imagine that the couple would not want to have to run the gauntlet of disapproval from other passengers. Leonard, of Irish stock but born in Liverpool, had himself married and raised his family in Hongkong, and so this was Mary's first trip to Europe.[384] Her son was born in Newmarket, Co. Cork towards the end of September, thus ensuring that she had spent all her pregnancy away from the eyes of Hongkong, and with the hope that, returning with a very young babe in arms, no one would enquire too closely about his exact age. Three years later O'Sullivan was promoted to 2nd Bailiff, a position which became

384 Since Government servants of O'Sullivan's rank normally had to give six months' notice when submitting a request for leave, there was here apparently a discreet waiving of this requirement.

vacant on the death in service of his father-in-law. His pay increased to £200, and the position came with free quarters and a range of allowances, for shorthand, conveyances and language which added another $600 (then about £90) per year to his income. The civil service salary increase in 1920 saw his pay rise to £360, although, as the police had found, this increase only served to restore some of the losses incurred with the currency fluctuations of the war and post war years. This family were perhaps the most assiduous in keeping their contacts with Newmarket, and they appear at frequent intervals on the passenger lists, taking leave in the small town. For all that, no memory of the family has yet been unearthed there.

The couple went on to have four or five more children, and were able to rent a house on Robinson Road, within walking distance of the Botanical Gardens and St Joseph's Church. It was in 1926, when O'Sullivan was just 40 years old, that he started to suffer from psychiatric ill health, possibly a very early-onset dementia or a severe depressive illness. He was treated by his family doctor initially, but in May 1927 had to take sick leave and entered the Mental Hospital. The government treated him well, first giving him the month's vacation leave he had earned, then allowing him nearly four months medical leave on full pay and a further six months on half pay leave. O'Sullivan was retired on pension on 9th March 1928, aged 42, and a year later he was allowed to be cared for at home, since it was considered that he was not a danger to himself or his family if kept under supervision.

At about 6.30pm on Thursday 8th May, 1930, he was returning from a visit to friends in St. Joseph's College, walking through the Botanical Gardens accompanied by his seven-year-old daughter. His illness had left him very short-sighted and frail, and the little girl had been charged with looking after her Daddy. They sat on a park bench for a short time, whilst Maureen fed the birds, but when she returned to the seat, she found that her father had disappeared. In distress, she sought help from two ladies who looked for O'Sullivan with the child, but eventually they had to return her home with the news that the man was nowhere to be found. Fearing an accident or even abduction, Mary O'Sullivan reported the matter to the police, who initially got the Park-keeper to institute a thorough search. This proved fruitless and news of the disappearance came to the ears of Assistant Superintendent Tim Murphy, who then took command of the search, and had forty of his men comb the hillside, including all the crevices and ravines thereabout, but with the same result. It was felt that since O'Sullivan was a well-known figure locally, some good might come from offering a reward, and a notice was circulated in all the papers, English and Chinese, offering $200 to the person who could lead the police to him, whether the former Bailiff was alive or dead. This notice, with a photograph, was also sent to Macao and Canton.

Mary O'Sullivan's life must have been one of deep anxiety at the time, but at least the colony did continue to pay O'Sullivan's pension for some months. Realising that the situation was unlikely to change, and that her husband must now be dead, wherever he might be, in August 1931 Tim Murphy helped her to prepare to appeal for authority from the Courts to apply for probate. Having heard the full story, and the extent of the search put out to find Thomas O'Sullivan, the Chief Justice, Sir Joseph Kemp, agreed that although fifteen months was a short time for a case of disappearance on land, that in this instance there could really be no doubt that the man was dead. O'Sullivan had insured his life for $1000 some time earlier, and when probate was granted on his estate the next month, his wife received a further $15,000 along with her Widows' pension on which to keep herself and her children.[385] Some years later, Mary remarried, to a Mr. Remedios, and lived in Seymour Terrace. She was not interned during the occupation of Hongkong, and died in July, 1957.

The mystery of Thomas O'Sullivan's disappearance was never solved, for no body was discovered, nor any ransom claimed. It has been suggested that perhaps, realising that the future held only further degeneration for himself, and knowing that his wife and family were provided for, O'Sullivan weighted his pockets with stones, took himself down to the

---

385 The story of O'Sullivan's disappearance is covered by the English language papers on 10th,12th and 17th May, 1930 and the court application of Mrs. O'Sullivan and the will on 4th August and 25th September, 1931.

harbour and boarded a vessel for Canton, slipping quietly overboard when out of Hongkong waters.[386]

The antecedents of Mary O'Sullivan (née Leonard) connect her both with the distant past of the Dockyard Police and the local community. Carl Jensen, a constable in the Dockyard when the list of those prepared to relinquish pension rights had been drawn up in 1869, had been promoted to sergeant by Inspector Lysaught. In March, 1872 he married Matilda Elisa, an eighteen-year-old who had been in the care of the Italian convent. Matilda had been baptised and recently confirmed in the Catholic church, so the wedding was at the Cathedral, although Jensen was described in the marriage certificate as an English Protestant. The couple appear to have had no children, but they adopted two Chinese orphaned baby girls from the Convent, Caroline Emilia in 1877 and her natural sister, Maria Josepha the following year. However, Jensen died in 1881, and his widow married her husband's former colleague in the Yard Police, William Godwin, who also adopted the girls. Godwin, who was one of the longer serving sergeants of Lysaught's team, and still there when the older man retired, then transferred, as noted earlier, to the Public Works Department in charge of the recreation grounds.

Joseph Leonard, from Liverpool, had joined the regular Police Force in 1890 and married the elder Godwin daughter in August 1895. This marriage was one of necessity, since the couple's first daughter, Elizabeth Agnes, was born just four months later. By the time of the birth, Leonard's first term in the Police had come to an end, and he had not been permitted to re-engage. He had, in the eyes of his superiors, committed multiple offences: not only marrying without permission, and before he was a sergeant, but his wife, Caroline Emila, was Chinese, despite her adoption. That she was pregnant some months before the marriage occurred might also have been a dismissing offence. Leonard had to look around for work for some months, maybe finding some temporary position, but on 1st August 1896 secured the post of Assistant Bailiff at the Supreme Court. The salary of just $480 per year was twenty per cent lower than that he had received in the Police, and the couple had to depend on

386 I am grateful to Jason Wordie for this, the most plausible explanation to date.

the generosity of Godwin and Matilda to some extent. He left in 1899 and appears on the Jury lists for 1900 as a runner for the Taikoo Sugar Refinery Company at Quarry Bay, living, probably with his in-laws, at 41 Queen's Road East. However, he was able to move back to the Courts the following year when the post of 2nd Bailiff became available, at the improved salary of $1,000 p. a. This was increased the following year by an additional $200, and from there on he seems to have had a secure and steady career. He kept his connections with the police: the godfather of his first son was William Davitt.[387]

Lysaught's line – the interwar years

Not a great deal of material exists about Tim Murphy's brother in law, John Lysaught, the eldest son of the late Dockyard Inspector. In 1906 he bought a site in Kowloon, in To Kwa Wan, a large waterfront plot close to Hung Hom, where he planned to build another machinery factory, and two years later his ageing father made the family firm over to him, whereupon it became John Lysaught & Sons. In the years following his father's death, he went into partnership with another engineer, Samuel Farrell, and eventually developed the Kowloon site, specialising in heavy marine engineering. It seems, though, that he lacked his father's sure hand with business, and, after Farrell's death at the end of 1914, Lysaught dissolved the firm, with not a lot to show for it. In 1917 his entry in the annual Jurors list describes him as an engineer for the China Metal and Mining Co., by which time he and his family had moved to Burnbank, a house in Tsat Tsze Mui, on the Shaukiwan Road. This was primarily a Chinese area, with many small shack-like properties and just three larger houses and the factories of Lysaught's new employers. Burnbank had been purchased in Norah Lysaught's name from Mr. Kynock, an overseer in the Public Works Department, on 5th February 1916: it is tempting to speculate that this was done to ameliorate the effect of any later financial problems.[388] However, the 1918 Juror's list gives John Lysaught's address

387 Material for this and the previous paragraphs comes largely from the Carl Smith cards, together with the Civil Establishment lists from the relevant *Blue Books.*

388 Rate Books 1916, *Civil Establishment List* 1916.

as York Buildings, behind what is now Alexandra House in Central. This was probably a business address for China Metal and Mining Co., but may also have accommodated a mess for engineers and similar. If the couple had indeed separated, John Lysaught returned to the family home later in that year when his health broke down. Suffering intense pain from cellulitis of the neck and scalp, with his system compromised by diabetes, he died in the French Hospital on 17th August 1918, leaving Norah and seven children, the eldest only fifteen years old.

When, in December of that year, following the Armistice, the government removed the restriction they had placed on women and children leaving the colony, Norah took her family back to Ireland, where they stayed in Cork city rather than return to Newmarket. She placed the letting and management of Burnbank in the hands of architect Charles Warren, who had owned property opposite William Lysaught's houses on Wanchai Road, and would also be known to her as a fellow Catholic. But the family did not settle to life in Cork, and she returned, with her brother Tim's help, in 1922. At the end of 1924, perhaps unable to sell what was now a rather isolated building, Norah surrendered the lease back to the Crown, and, having returned to Hongkong, purchased a newly built house in Somerset Road, in what is now Kowloon Tong. Two of the three daughters married, the youngest, Eileen, to American business man, Moritz Cunha, twice her age, with whom she emigrated to the United States, whilst the second, Kathleen, to Hongkong police man Sub-Inspector Arthur Dorling.[389] William Lysaught's daughters, half Portuguese (or Macanese) might have been too non-British to be potential mates for men from Deane or May's Force, but there was no such 'stigma' attaching to Kathleen, who was, of course, three quarters Irish. Her fashionable wedding was naturally held at St. Joseph's and just as naturally conducted by Fr. Augustin Płacek. Dressed in quantities of cream satin and orange blossom, with her bridesmaid sisters similarly attired, Kathleen was given away by her uncle, Tim Murphy. Norah Lysaught, though it was now some five years since her husband's death, was dressed all in black satin for the occasion.

389 *China Mail,* 31st October 1923.

As a young boy the couple's eldest son, William John, had received at least some of his education in the USA, and seems, from passenger, census and death records, to have been working there during his adult life. The death records show both his name and his mother's maiden name: given how unusual his surname is, this would surely suggest a correct identification. However, albeit many years later, his sister stated that he had died in Cork as a young man. He did not travel back with the family in 1922, and a William Lysaught is recorded as dying in Cork early in 1920, aged 16, but there is doubt if this would tally with the photograph of William with his Murphy uncles and cousin (*opposite page*). The second son, Edward St. Leger, held various posts in the colony, working in the Gaol at one time, and also managing a hotel in Kowloon. During the Second World War he signed for the Navy, joining *HMS Thanet* as a stoker. Immediately after the invasion of Hongkong, the *Thanet* sailed for Singapore, where it was used for escort duty. On 27th January 1942, it was attempting to intercept a Japanese troop convoy when it was targeted by enemy warships and swiftly sunk, with the lost of most of the crew, including Lysaught. Norah and her eldest daughter, Margaret, were evacuated to Australia in August 1940, but Norah became terminally ill with cancer three years later. Margaret, whose psychiatric health had always been delicate, had to be placed in a mental hospital, with little hope of any recovery. Sadly, another son had to be left in Hongkong. Henry had been committed to the Mental Hospital early in the 1930s. It was there that he died, of starvation and exhaustion, a year after the start of the Japanese occupation.[390]

The Murphys of Hongkong

Meanwhile, Tim's brothers and cousins were steadily progressing in their careers, with John, James and Michael attached to the Detective Branch, and Patrick in the regular Force. In 1924, James Murphy was a Sub-Inspector, working on anti-piracy duty, part of the operation to counter the great rise in attacks on vessels of all sorts that had come about since the unrest in mainland China. Much of his time was spent supervising

---

390 The records of this family appear in HKRS 41-1-1498, 41-1-3129, 41-1-1467, and cards at CO 1070/4 (National Archives, London).

John, James and Michael Murphy and William Lysaught, son of J.J. Lysaught (courtesy Murphy family)

and accompanying the Anti-Piracy Guards as they searched down in the holds of junks, launches and small steamships that came into the waters around the island and Kowloon. The work was dangerous and uncertain, with the pirates just as vicious as they had been almost a hundred years earlier. Towards midnight on Monday, 15th December, James Murphy had returned from duty and gone to bed in his room on the second floor of the officer's quarters, within the Central Station compound. About an hour later, clad in his pyjamas, he fell from the verandah adjoining his quarters onto the compound below. Quickly found by colleagues, he was losing consciousness as he was transported to the Hospital, where he was found to have severely injured his spine and to have broken a number of bones. The assumption was that he had been sleep-walking, a disturbance that had developed in him of late and perhaps a sub-conscious reaction to the particularly hazardous duties he was currently undertaking. The balustrade on the balconies was low, and similar incidents, often fatal, appear occasionally in the press. There was no suspicion aired in the papers that he had taken a little too much alcohol before retiring for the night. The press treated the police with due propriety, but nevertheless would generally couch in polite terms any such possibility than not report it. But rather than either rapid intoxication or stress induced sleep-walking, a call of nature, which would not, of course, be alluded to by the papers, may well have been the reason he was on the verandah. The notorious drop toilets were perched on the edge of these, and an unwary or drowsy man might easily sit down and then topple backwards over the low restraint. James Murphy did not regain consciousness, and died late on Sunday 21st December. He was buried directly behind Mortimor O'Sullivan, in what was all too rapidly becoming a small part of County Cork off the Wong Nai Chung Road.[391]

Tim Murphy received his King's Police Medal in May 1925, at the presentation and valedictory parade taken by outgoing governor, Sir Reginald Stubbs. Sergeant Fender was also awarded the fourth class medal his part in the Canton Road operation had earned him here, having been on leave the previous year. In June of the following year, in advance of some longer serving colleagues, Murphy was promoted to Acting Chief Detective Inspector, substantiated in November of that year at the conclusion of the pre-retirement leave of his predecessor, John Grant. This also meant a move from Yaumatei back to the Central Station, and to the Inspector's quarters on Caine Road. Built relatively recently (1915 and 1922), these were of a superior construction to the earlier ones, and are remembered as comfortable flats for a family, with two or three bedrooms, a large living room and a (well balustraded) verandah. But he had to move without his wife, Mary, who had struggled with poor health, probably tuberculosis, for some months. This had finally become too much for her, and she had agreed to go into Victoria Hospital, on the Peak, in May. Here she died in the early morning of 7th July, and Tim Murphy's happy marriage was brought to an untimely end.

In a similar fashion to Nora Lysaught née Murphy a quarter of a century earlier, another Newmarket woman, Margaret Fitzpatrick, travelled to Hongkong to marry John Murphy, almost sight unseen, fulfilling an arrangement made, this time, by Tim and James Murphy. In 1922 these two, together with their cousin Michael Murphy, had taken leave delayed by the war, journeying home accompanied by the soon-to-retire Inspector William Davitt and Sub-Inspector Bob Wills, who had been injured in the Gresson Street siege. It seems that, already planning to commute the leave that would be due to him the following year, John Murphy had asked his brothers to look for a bride for himself. Tim and James had sung Margaret's praises when they returned at the end of that year, and so, after a correspondence over the next two years, the 23-

391 Murphy's fall, death and funeral were reported by the English language papers between 17th and 24th December, 1924.

Above: The wedding of Tim Murphy and May Colbert at St. Joseph's, 15th September 1928.

Below: The wedding of John Murphy and Margaret Fitzpatrick, January 1925. From left: Miss ? Lysaught, Margaret Lysaught, Tim Murphy, Margaret Fitzpatrick, Michael Murphy (behind), John Murphy, Mary Murphy, Nora Lysaught, Patrick Murphy, Henry Dixon (courtesy Murphy family)

year-old Margaret used the return from leave of Court Usher Thomas O'Sullivan and his family to travel with them on the *Kashmir,* leaving London just before Christmas, 1924.[392] She married Sub-Inspector John Murphy at St. Joseph's Church early in February, 1925.

The same church saw another Murphy marriage two years later when Chief Detective Inspector Tim Murphy remarried, on 15th September 1928, his bride also arriving from Britain a few days earlier. That Murphy had met May Colbert whilst on leave in Newmarket at the beginning of the year was perhaps unsurprising: her father was a engine driver of the local railway, and given Murphy's enthusiasm for engines of all sorts, he renewed his association with the railway whilst at home. Without, as yet, relatives in Hongkong, she was given away by Murphy's colleague, Assistant Superintendent Walter Kent, (recently promoted, formerly Murphy's opposite number in the uniformed force) and since her bridesmaids were Kent's daughter and Eileen Lysaught, (Murphy's niece), it is likely that she stayed with the Kents for the few days before her marriage. Newmarket, or more likely Cork City, had done its best, providing the bride with a fashionably knee length dress of white georgette, trimmed with pearls and roses, and a veil of best Brussels lace.[393]

The still perilous nature of motor travel in Hongkong caught up with the newly married couple and made front page news when, in March 1929, they and sister-in-law Mrs. Margaret Murphy (née Fitzpatrick) went for a drive, taking Margaret's young son, Kevin. They were returning from Stanley in a hired car, but the road, which rose steeply before it joined the main road, was being resurfaced, and one half of the road was a foot higher than the other. Just after a sharp turn, and with another fifty yards or so to climb before reaching the main road, the driver apparently tried to change down gear, but slipped the clutch, whereupon the car started to slide backwards. Murphy grabbed the steering wheel and directed it into the embankment, but the car quickly gained momentum, and, destabilised by the road conditions, hit the bank at speed and turned turtle. The driver, May and Kevin Murphy were thrown clear, Murphy

392 From the passenger list it would seem that the Crown Agents paid the passage of Murphy's fiancée.

393 *Hongkong Telegraph,* 13th September and 15th September 1928.

was briefly trapped underneath but Margaret took a little longer to extricate. With some help the car was righted, and the party were able to return in a friend's car. Cuts and bruises were found to be the extent of the injuries, but Margaret Murphy was soaked in petrol, and the ladies were prescribed complete rest for a few days. A rather stiff and achy Tim Murphy returned to duty the next day; of the shaken-up driver we hear nothing more.[394]

Detective Inspector Tim Murphy, mid-1925, wearing, from left, King's Police Medal, 2nd, 3rd and 4th class Merit Medals (courtesy Murphy family).

Margaret's husband, John Murphy, had become a Sub-Inspector at the very end of 1923, and continued to work primarily in the Criminal Investigations Department, receiving his next promotion in 1929.[395] From the reminiscences of his son, it would appear that his work in this department kept him based at the Central Station for all the latter part of his career, with occasional attachments to the Secretariat for Chinese Affairs. Little has yet emerged of his cousin Sub-Inspector Patrick Murphy's career. A quiet man, and closer in age to Tim Murphy than the others, he remained unmarried. It is believed that on retiring in 1932, aged 46, he was one who did return to Newmarket, and possibly back to his family's farm in Island.

394 *China Mail,* March 18th 1929.

395 The Legislative Council, on 12th October 1922, had budgeted for an additional Deputy Superintendent, to be in charge of the Detective Sub-Department, now renamed the Criminal Investigation Department. The first officer in charge was James Kerr, promoted from the post of Chief Inspector, to which he had so tenaciously stuck. *Hongkong Hansard,* 12th October 1922.

Ability rewarded – Newmarket's highest ranking Police Officer

During his tenure as Chief Detective Inspector, and while Assistant Director of the Criminal Information Department, Murphy had acted as Assistant Superintendent of Police on a few occasions. In July 1931 he was appointed to that rank on his own account, a promotion which required the Secretary of State's approval, granted in October of the same year. Following in James Kerr's footsteps ten years earlier, Murphy was one of a still very small group of men to rise from constable through to the directorate of the force. He was part of a changing scene, as both the Hongkong Administration and the colonial forces in general realised that the demands of twentieth century policing required experienced policemen rather than competent civil servants as leaders. Sadly, because on retirement the returning Newmarket men had dispersed, together with the lingering hostility towards forces of the British crown, news of Murphy's achievement, the only man from the town to make such a rank, did not reach the local press back in Ireland. Indeed, whilst Newmarket knew that it had a number of men in the Hongkong Police Force, it does not seem to have been seen as a 'tradition', nor was there awareness that the majority of the men had enjoyed successful careers.

Not the least of the benefits that this rank conferred was an increase in pay. Murphy had received £700 as Chief Detective Inspector, this now became £780 and rose to £830 the following year, without the loss of most of his allowances. The improvement in the Murphy family fortunes was welcome as the family itself grew. In terms of health, as in so many other ways, Hongkong was a very different place to fifty or even twenty years earlier, with improved hygiene, better (if still erratic) water supplies, widely available good medical care resulting in lower mortality, particularly infant mortality, better containment of disease and a final disappearance of the dreaded plague. However, three years before Tim Murphy's retirement, shades of one of the tragedies suffered by the O'Sullivans visited his family, when, on 22nd May 1934 his little daughter Colleen died of cerebro-spinal meningitis. The *China Mail* reported the funeral the next morning, taking almost a full column to relate the many friends and colleagues who came to support Mr. and Mrs. Murphy, and the numerous wreathes that were sent, attesting to both the popularity

Coleen Murphy (standing) with amah and brother in Cork, 1933 (courtesy Murphy family)

of the police officer and the esteem in which he was held. Five priests were present for the chapel service and the burial, and most of the remaining Newmarket contingent attended.

Continuity

There were Newmarket men in Hongkong for close to ninety years. William Lysaught had arrived in 1864, and taken the first forty-five years. As the generations of these men from north Cork arrived, pursued their careers and took their leave, it was a Newmarketeer by adoption, Lysaught's step-son, that remained the constant presence almost to the end of this long period. Henry Dixon regarded as his closest family the Murphys, O'Sullivans, Davitts and Nolans, and took an active interest and share in their lives. Following the early death of his wife, Severina, in 1905, he had devoted himself to the upbringing of his children, aided by his step-sisters, particularly the youngest, Kathleen. Dixon did not remarry, so Kathleen's marriage in 1909, and the departure for Europe of his two unmarried step-sisters, Caroline and Margaret in 1910 meant that his children spent more time with their Amah, and the Nolan and John Lysaught families, who were very close neighbours in Wanchai Road.

He continued in his post as Superintendent of the Money Order Office, and his dedication was rewarded with a good salary and, later, a comfortable pension. On 3rd June, 1927, he was granted the Order of Companion of the Imperial Service, a decoration usually given to civil servants at their retirement after a long and meritorious career, but in Dixon's case, awarded some six years in advance. He finally retired in 1933, aged sixty-eight years, this unusually late retirement probably arising through lack of a suitable successor, as his post was unoccupied for some years thereafter. He served in various capacities in the Old Boys' Association of St. Josephs, and was considered one of the leading Catholic laymen in Hongkong, continuing to be deeply involved in church life, and was connected with St. Margaret Mary Church in Happy Valley from its beginning in 1923.

His eldest son, Philip, who seems not to have married, remained in Hongkong and worked for many years as a manager and merchant for T.E. Griffith Ltd., a firm trading in fabrics from China. Of his other children, one daughter married a prominent Portuguese banker, whilst Dermot made his home in north London and the youngest, Edith, entered an Augustinian convent in England and became Sister Chrysostem. Dixon himself continued to manage the estate of his step-father, holding onto the Arsenal Street property he had inherited until at least 1930, but eventually selling all the Wanchai properties, and moving first to Nathan Road and then to No. 6 Hart Avenue in Kowloon. It was here that he and Philip somehow managed to eke an existence during the Japanese occupation, and here, too, early in 1945, that Henry Dixon died. For all the world as if nothing in Hongkong had changed, his death was recorded by the *Hong Kong News,* the Japanese controlled English language newspaper published during the occupation, thus:

> *"Henry Dixon passed away peacefully at his residence No. 6 Hart Avenue Kowloon at 9 a.m. on 21st February. Funeral will take place in the Roman Catholic cemetery, Hongkong, on Thursday 22nd at 4 p.m. (Macau papers please copy).*

With little as yet written on the life of 'third nationals' in Hongkong at this time, this, plus the announcement that there was to be a solemn Requiem Mass for the repose of his soul on 28th February at the Catholic Cathedral offered by the St. Vincent de Paul Society, offers a rare glimpse of a time, relatively close and yet so inaccessible. Neither did Philip

Group at Central Police Station, early 1930s. Pat Fitzpatrick front row, 1st on right (courtesy Murphy family)

Dixon live to see the liberation, for he died in hospital, aged 50, some three months before the end of the war.

The last intake of Newmarket men

With four of the Newmarket Murphy clan serving in Hongkong, the 1930s brought renewed contact between the Irish town and the Hongkong Police Force itself, as three more men joined. Patrick (Pat) Fitzpatrick arrived in February 1931, at the instigation of his sister, Margaret, now Mrs. John Murphy. The 25-year-old joined as a Lance-Sergeant on 10th January 1931, sailing out with a few young recruits from Ireland. He was followed by his younger brother Michael, who served a single term, and on 2nd September 1932, by the Hongkong-born George Neil Davitt, the eldest son of William Davitt. Another police son joined in December of the following year: H. G. Clarke's eldest son Goscombe Goddard (G.G.) Clarke, who remained in the Force until August 1942. Whilst it is not the intention of this study to cover this period in any detail, a few notes will perhaps show both the growth and change of the Hongkong Police Force at this time, as it pursued the development of more modern policing methods and reacted to the changing world of the interwar years and beyond. The Force they joined had, reflecting the wider population growth, expanded to almost twice its size during the course of the

1920s, with a total of 1,854 men in the land force in 1932 compared with 921 in 1903 and 631 in 1896 when, respectively, Tim Murphy and Patrick O'Sullivan joined. The senior management had increased from two men in 1896 to fourteen in 1932, which now included one Assistant Superintendent from the Indian contingent. The personnel was a lot more stable than it had been in previous times. Dismissals and desertions now ran at about 4% per annum, and many of these were men who were let go whilst still at the Police Training School. Indeed, the School was now fully established, based in its own building in Kowloon, at the northern end of Nathan Road and akin to that which would be recognised today, rather than the couple of classrooms squeezed into the overcrowded Central Station of earlier years.

The crimes the men investigated had shown a similar pattern, doubling in the years from 1903 to 1932 to around 20,000 reported crimes, of which 5,700 were ranked as serious. Some were apparently perennial, whilst others developed or increased in significance. Piracy continued to challenge the colony, and in 1930 the police took over responsibility from the Army for providing the Anti-Piracy Guards, whilst the detection of smuggled arms and ammunition required painstaking work in a port becoming busier by the year. The newly established Political Bureau responded to increasing attacks from the rival forces on the mainland, from Russia and from Japan. Boycotts and anti-Japanese activity increased as the decade progressed, and occupied much police time. The work of the Traffic Branch grew, too, with over 1,500 cars on the road, alongside 3,000 rickshas and chairs in this decade, whilst that most unpleasant duty of the police, to record and deal with the abandoned dead bodies discovered, continued as ever, with frequently 1,500 being found in any one year, the majority now in Kowloon.

By the late 1930s retirement was approaching for the remaining Murphys, although it was their niece's husband, Arthur Dorling who left on pension first, returning to the United Kingdom with Kathleen (née Lysaught) and their children in September 1936. Reflecting the still 'civil service' nature of the executive staff of the police, men here regularly continued in post beyond the policeman's statuary 45 year age limit, thus Tim Murphy went on pre-retirement leave in May 1937, aged

55 years. At the same time Peter Grant, another former police constable who had travelled through the ranks, to be, first, Chief Inspector of the regular force, then Assistant Superintendent also retired: the departure of the two men thus causing another round of promotions similar to that which, two years earlier, had seen John Murphy promoted to the rank of Chief Detective Inspector. The period 1934 - 1938 was another of those times of exodus in both the Indian and the European contingents, when a long-serving group of men who had joined in the years before the First World War reached retirement age and left something of a void in terms of experience and service. In this situation able men had their chance, one such being Michael Murphy, who, having served 19 years as a constable, sergeant and sub-inspector, was promoted to Inspector in 1934 and became Chief Detective Inspector just four years later. This latter raise was due to the retirement of his cousin, John Murphy.

The story of the war years is well told in the histories and memoirs of the period. In the first years the police soon realised that, should Hongkong suffer a similar fate to that of Canton, they, together with the military, would be the land defence force of the colony. Only scraps of information have come down to date about the work of the Newmarket men in this period. Michael Murphy had frequently chosen to commute his leave, earning a bonus but remaining in the colony. However, in 1937 he had returned home, where he had married, bringing his bride back later that year. From 1940 onwards the danger to Hongkong from Japan became more apparent, and the evacuation of European women and children to Australia commenced: in late 1941, Chief Detective Inspector Murphy was permitted to accompany his wife and children to Sydney, due to return after a few months. Thus it was that he was far away when, on 10th December, the day after attacking Pearl Harbor, the Japanese began their assault on Hongkong.

Sergeant George Davitt was part of the regular force, but, as was the pattern in the pre-war years, having gained experience in the Water Police was frequently posted back into this section. It is thus likely that he was involved in the many patrols that had to be made during the attempts to secure the free passage of Hongkong shipping against the aggression of the Japanese navy, whose indiscriminate attack of all Chinese craft resulted in many civilian casualties in the months and years leading up to the occupation. With the island of Hongkong seen as a safer haven than Kowloon, the Water Police then became involved in the evacuation of many across the harbour, after which they scuttled their vessels in the face of the inevitable advance of the Japanese. The Europeans of the Water Police became part of the main force for the remaining days of liberty, and were thus involved in the fighting to try to hold off the enemy's capture of the island.[396]

Sergeant Pat Fitzpatrick was based at Aberdeen Police Station, and his part in leading a groups of about ten police in the evacuation, reoccupation and eventual retreat from that station is partly recounted in Crisswell and Watson's history. It is there described how, less than twenty-four hours after the landing of the first Japanese troops near Quarry Bay, the enemy had managed to reach the southern side of the island. The hills and valleys and often dense vegetation here made for a very different battle situation from that which was going on in the built-up north side. With reports coming in that the Japanese were advancing toward Aberdeen, in the morning of 19th December 1941, A162 Sergeant Williamson, unable to contact Headquarters, made the decision to evacuate the Police Station there, sending the men off in two parties, under the charge of A55 Sergeant Fitzpatrick and A145 Lance-Sergeant Goldie. Told to go to the Dairy Farm Hill, from where the whole group would seek instructions and move to one of the nearby stations.

However, as the record of the 'Police Situation War Diary' makes somewhat clear, there was a deal of misunderstanding between the officers, and Fitzpatrick seems to have overridden Williamson's orders to act on his own initiative.[397] He, and some of his party, boarded a passing army lorry, and whether they went first to the Dairy Farm Hill or the University remains unclear. They certainly left behind a Police Interpreter and a Chinese detective constable who were 'straggling', who would later claim that Fitzpatrick had boarded the lorry by himself, leaving behind

396 This is a very short synopsis of the story much better told by Iain Ward in his *Sui Geng The Hong Kong Marine Police 1841-1950.*

397 This extraordinary document of reports made while interned at Stanley and immediately afterwards is held at CO129/592/4.

all his men. That afternoon Fitzpatrick brought his men to No. 7 station, from where he went to the Upper Levels Station and reconnected with Goldie. Statements from all the men were taken by Senior Superintendent Calthrop whilst in Stanley Internment Camp, some thirteen months after the event. They arrive at no definite conclusion, but whilst Williamson's suggestion that Fitzpatrick was acting out of cowardice had he actually abandoned his men seems unfounded and is not pursued, the latter's actions in not fully following Williamson's orders did leave him open to censure.

The next day it was necessary for Aberdeen Station to be re-occupied, as reports of Fifth Columnist activity, including the burning of hillside houses came in, and Williamson, Fitzpatrick and Goldie returned with their parties of men. The enemy intensified their assault on Aberdeen, and on December 24th the Station was heavily shelled, and orders were once more given, this time from the Commissioner of Police, to evacuate. Having found themselves in a para-military role in those tense weeks, it soon became clear that they needed to revert to something more akin to their normal policing role as the British nationals were rounded up from the various points where they were initially corralled, and Stanley Prisoner of War Camp established. As men from Ireland, which was by this time an independent country and not part of the United Kingdom, they were officially third nationals, and as such might have remained at 'liberty' within Hongkong, as, for example, did Henry and Philip Dixon. However, their employment as Crown Police Officers made them an enemy of the Japanese Emperor, and thus liable to imprisonment.

Barbara Anslow, fellow-internee and veritable trove of information on both life in Stanley Camp and the occupants thereof, sadly does not remember coming across Pat Fitzpatrick, but George Davitt she recalled seeing often, both at Mass and in his role of 'runner' for the camp hospital. After liberation in September 1945, both men returned to Ireland for rehabilitation. Fitzpatrick, six foot tall but lean and wiry rather than robust, had been reduced to just over six stone (about 40 kilo) in weight, and was retired with pension on medical grounds. With the troubled times of the 1920s now overtaken by the poverty of the 1930s and the difficulties of the war years, he returned to his hometown without fearing for his life, and there, in the depressed conditions of post-war Ireland, his modest colonial pension was considered quite a handsome income. Davitt's rugby player frame perhaps masked the level of damage done to him by the severe privations of the camp: certainly his family felt that he should have received more help and treatment. Chief Detective Inspector Michael Murphy's family returned to Ireland but he resumed duties in Hongkong, where, in the immediate aftermath of the Japanese surrender, it was necessary to establish some level of law and order as swiftly as possible. However, at fifty-one years of age, he was at the end of his career, and retired back to Ireland within eighteen months.

George Neil Davitt (courtesy Marjorie Davitt)

Davitt, however, was still only thirty-six and was pronounced fit to resume his engagement in late 1946. Now promoted to Inspector, in May 1950 he was working from Kowloon police headquarters when he became very ill. He had previously been seen by the doctor for depression and nightmares, likely stemming from his time during the occupation, but had hopes of marrying a particular young lady when he next had leave in Ireland. He was still a keen sportsman, particularly known for his skills on the rugby and hockey fields, and whilst he enjoyed a drink, he was considered to be one of the more sober men in the force. Therefore the acute outbreak of an underlying renal complaint, with which he was diagnosed in Kowloon Hospital, was thought to be probably due to the many diseases, including beri-beri, typhoid and dysentery prevalent throughout the time of the camps, and scarcely fully eradicated in the colony five years later. The medical team did not get a chance to begin real treatment, for he died just two days after he had been admitted to hospital, on 2nd June, 1950.[398]

398 *Hongkong Telegraph,* 2nd June 1950.

George Neil Davitt was the last of the Newmarket men in the Hongkong Police Force, and with his death, quietly, unobtrusively, the lines of succession that started with William Lysaught and Davitt's grandfather, George Hennessy, came to an end. His funeral the next day was attended by many of the force, including the Commissioner, Mr. D.W. McIntosh, and a guard of honour comprising of 51 constables. The papers report, as ever, the attendees at the funeral, and the donors of the wreaths and tributes, but not one name from the 'old brigade' of Newmarket contacts remained. Chief Detective Inspector Tommy Cashman, a Corkman and friend of the Murphy brothers provided the only link.

Because of this, it would seem, little was known by his family back in Ireland of Davitt's life, either in Stanley camp or when back on duty. Barbara Anslow recollected him as a great tall man, always helpful around the hospital, very quiet and rather shy, which perhaps aligns with the rather serious man who looks out from both his portrait photographs and the rugby team pictures. In the summer of 2011, over sixty-five years since the days of Stanley camp, it was the author's rare privilege to recount Barbara's recollections to Davitt's youngest sister, Marjorie, just a few months before the latter's death. That her brother, now so long gone, should be thus remembered moved her deeply.

Epilogue

In the summer of 2009 I visited my ninety-year-old aunt in Dublin. The child of Patrick and Ellen O'Sullivan and born in Newmarket during the couple's last leave, she had been left with Ellen's youngest sister rather than be taken back to Hongkong, and was restored to her parents two year's later, upon Patrick's retirement.

As we looked through photos, and Aunt Ann got down on her knees to drag further boxes of such treasures from under the sideboard (eschewing any offers of help from me), the subject of the uncle she'd never met arose. "Patricia, you're good at that googly thing, you go on your computer and find out what happened to Uncle Murt in Gresson Street. My parents were such Victorians that they never really told us."

This book is the result of that request. Getting started was made possible by an article in a contemporary police magazine, available online, which recorded a visit by Henry Goscombe Clarke's grandsons to the sites involved in the Gresson Street story. Contact with one of those grandsons, Dennis Clarke, then head of the Conrad Hotel in Hong Kong, brought an invitation to stay at the Conrad as his guest. Needless to say, I had scarcely finished reading his email before I had booked my flight! Then a wealth of material, gathered over years of research, from the then-serving Hong Kong policeman, Richard Morgan, started me on a course where it became obvious that it was not just my grandfather and great uncle who had been in the police, but a large group of their kinsmen from Newmarket, Co. Cork. Hence the story of a group of Irishmen who travelled 10,000 miles to find employment between 1864 and 1950.

Bibliography

Primary sources

Great Britain, Colonial Office, Original Correspondence: Hong Kong, 1841-1951, Series 129 (CO 129), National Archives, Kew.

Great Britain, Colonial Office, Executive and Legislative Council Minutes: Hong Kong, (from 1844), Series 131 (CO 131), National Archives, Kew.

Great Britain, Colonial Office, *Hongkong Blue Books*, 1844-1940, Series 133 (CO 133), National Archives, Kew.

Great Britain, Home Office, Irish Constabulary records, general register, Series 184 (HO 184/16).

Hong Kong Civil Service List and General Orders, Hong Kong, Colonial Secretary's Office, from 1904.

Hongkong Government Gazette, (from 1853).

Hong Kong, *Staff List Hong Kong,* Colonial Secretary's Office, 1932.

Metropolitan Police, Office of Commissioner, *Police Orders,* London, (MEPO 7), National Archives, Kew.

Metropolitan Police, Office of Commissioner, Correspondence, (MEPO 4), National Archives, Kew.

Newspapers: *China Mail* (from 1866).
Hongkong Daily Press (1864-1941).
Hongkong Weekly Press (1895-1909).
Hongkong Telegraph (from 1881).
South China Morning Post (from 1903).

The Chronicle and Directory for China, Corea, Japan and the Philippines, etc., Hong Kong, Hong Kong Daily Press Office, from 1866.

Empson, Hal, (ed.), *Mapping Hong Kong: a historical atlas,* Hong Kong, Government Information Services, 1992.

Unpublished sources

Kerrigan, Austin, *Policing a Colony: The Case of Hong Kong, 1844-1899,* PhD thesis, Cardiff Graduate Law School, University of Wales, 2001.

Christine M. Thomas, (compiler), *Almost Forgotten - A Researcher's Guide to the Past Members of the Hong Kong Police Force*, Force Historical Records, Royal Hong Kong Police Force.

Christine M. Thomas, (ed.), *In the Days of Tiffin, Being an Account of Life in the Hong Kong Police Force as related by Inspector James Dodds.* Force Historical Records, Royal Hong Kong Police Force, 1991.

Unknown, *Police History 1851-1955,* unpublished manuscript in Hong Kong Police Archives, restored May 2006 by Chris Bilham, Force Archivist.

Web-based sources

Index to CO129, Great Britain, Colonial Office, Original Correspondence, compiled by Dr. Elizabeth Sinn, maintained by Rev. Dr. Louis Ha, http://sunzi.lib.hku.hk/co129/.

Gwulo: Old Hong Kong, built, developed and maintained by David Bellis, http://gwulo.com.

Hong Kong War Diary: built, developed and maintained by Tony Banham, http://www.hongkongwardiary.com

Secondary sources – books and articles

Allen, D. H., *Ath Trasna. A History of Newmarket, County Cork,* Cork, Cork Historical Guides Committee, 1973.

Andrew, Kenneth, *Hong Kong Detective,* London, John Long Ltd., 1962.

Annieson, Anthony, *The One-eyed Dragon. The Inside Story of a Hong Kong Policeman,* Moffat, Scotland, Lochar Publishing, 1989.

Bandon, Mandy, *Administering the Empire 1801-1968. A Guide to the Records of the Colonial Office in the National Archives of the UK,* London, Institute for Historical Research, London, 2008.

Bickley, Gillian (ed.), *A Magistrate's Court in Nineteenth Century Hong Kong. Court in Time,* Hong Kong, Proverse Hong Kong, 2009.

Bickley, Gillian, 'Early Beginning of British Community (1841-1898) British Attitudes toward Hong Kong in the Nineteenth Century,' in Cindy Yik-yi Chu (ed.), *Foreign Communities in Hong Kong, 1840s -1950s,* New York & Basingstoke, Palgrave Macmillan, 2005.

Cameron, Nigel, *An Illustrated History of Hong Kong* Hong Kong, Oxford University Press, 1991.

Carroll, John M., *A Concise History of Hong Kong,* Lanham, MD., Rowman & Littlefield, 2007.

Carroll, John M., *Edge of Empires. Chinese Elites and British Colonials in Hong Kong,* Hong Kong, Hong Kong University Press, 2007.

Chiang Hai Ding, 'The Origins of the Malaysian Currency System (1867-1902),' *Journal of the Royal Asiatic Society, Malaysian Branch*, vol. 39 No 1, July 1966 pp. 1-18.

Chu, Cindy Yik-yi (ed.), 'Catholic Church between Two World Wars' in *Foreign Communities in Hong Kong, 1840s -1950s,* New York & Basingstoke, Palgrave Macmillan, 2005.

Clear, Catriona, *Social change and everyday life in Ireland, 1850-1922.* Manchester, Manchester University Press, 2007.

Crisswell, Colin N., *The Taipans Hong Kong's Merchant Princes,* Hong Kong, Oxford University Press, 1981.

Crisswell, Colin and Watson, Mike, *The Royal Hong Kong Police (1841-1945),* Hong Kong, Macmillan Hong Kong, 1982.

de Courcy, Anne, *The Fishing Fleet: Husband Hunting in the Raj.* London, Weidenfeld & Nicolson 2012.

Eitel, E. J., *Europe in China: The History of Hong Kong from the Beginning to the Year 1882,* Hong Kong, Kelly and Walsh 1895 reprinted Hong Kong, Oxford University Press, 1983.

Emmett, Chris, *Hong Kong Policeman,* Hong Kong, Earnshaw Books, 2014.

Emsley, Clive, *The English Police. A Political and Social History,* Harlow, England, Longman, Pearson Education, 2nd edition 1996.

Emsley, Clive, *The Great British Bobby. A history of British policing from the 18th century to the present.* London, Quercus, 2009.

Faulkner, R. J., and Field, R. A., 'Vanquishing the Dragon: The Law of Drugs in Hong Kong - Part 1,' *Hong Kong Law Journal,* vol. 5, no. 2, 1975, pp. 134-177

Faulkner, R. J., and Field, R. A., 'Vanquishing the Dragon: The Law of Drugs in Hong Kong - Part 2,' *Hong Kong Law Journal,* vol. 5, no. 3, 1975, pp. 277-335.

Faure, David, 'The Common People in Hong Kong History: their livelihood and aspirations until the 1930s' in Pui-tak Lee, ed., *Colonial Hong Kong and Modern China: Interaction and Reintegration,* Hong Kong, Hong Kong University Press, 2005.

Faure, David (ed.), *Society. A Documentary History of Hong Kong,* Hong Kong, Hong Kong University Press, 1997.

Ferriter, Diarmaid, *The Transformation of Ireland 1900-2000,* London, Profile Books Ltd., 2004.

Greenwood, Walter, 'John Joseph Francis, Citizen of Hong Kong, A Biographical Note,' *Journal of the Royal Asiatic Society, Hong Kong Branch* Vol. 26, 1986, pp 17-45.

Hamilton, Sheilah E., *Watching over Hong Kong. Private Policing 1841-1941,* Hong Kong, Hong Kong University Press, 2008

Harland, Kathleen, *The Royal Navy in Hong Kong since 1841,* Liskeard, Cornwall, Maritime Books, 1985.

Herlihy, Jim, *The Royal Irish Constabulary: A short history and genealogical guide with a select list of medal awards* Dublin, Four Courts Press, 1997.

Hoe, Susanna, *The Private Life of Old Hong Kong. Western Women in the British Colony 1841-1941,* Hong Kong, Oxford University Press, 1991.

Holdsworth, May and Munn, Christopher, *Dictionary of Hong Kong Biography,* Hong Kong, Hong Kong University Press, 2012.

Hong Kong Police Force, *The Police Museum (Guide)* Hong Kong, 2008 and Royal Hong Kong Police, *The Police Museum (Guide)* Hong Kong, 1994.

Howell, Philip, 'Race, Space and the Regulation of Prostitution in Colonial Hong Kong,' in John M. Carroll and Chi-Kwan Mark (eds.), *Critical Readings on the Modern History of Hong Kong, vol. 1.,* Leiden, Brill, 2015.

Hyam, Ronald, *Understanding the British Empire,* Cambridge, Cambridge University Press, 2010.

Kirk-Greene, Anthony, *On Crown Service. A History of HM Colonial and Overseas Civil Services 1837-1997,* London, I. B. Tauris & Co., 1999.

Lau, Chi Kuen, *Hong Kong's Colonial Legacy. A Hong Kong Chinese's View of the British Heritage,* Hong Kong, Chinese University of Hong Kong 1997.

Lee, Rance P. L. (ed.), *Corruption and Its Control in Hong Kong: Situations Up to the Late Seventies,* Hong Kong, Chinese University Press, 1981.

Lee, Vicky, *Being Eurasian: Memories Across Racial Divides,* Hong Kong, Hong Kong University Press, 2004.

Lethbridge, Henry J. ' Caste, class and Race in Hong Kong before the Japanese Occupation' in John M. Carroll and Chi-Kwan Mark (eds.), *Critical Readings on the Modern History of Hong Kong, vol. 1.,* Leiden, Brill, 2015.

Lethbridge, Henry J., *Hong Kong: Stability and Change: A Collection of Essays,* Hong Kong, Oxford University Press, 1978.

Lethbridge, Henry J., *Hard Graft in Hong Kong: scandal, corruption and the ICAC,* Hong Kong, Oxford University Press, 1985.

Levine, Philippa, *Prostitution, Race and Politics: Policing Venereal Disease in the British Empire,* New York, London, Routledge Keegan Paul, 2003.

Miners, Norman, *Hong Kong under Imperial Rule, 1912-1941,* Hong Kong, Oxford University Press, 1987.

Miners, N.J., 'The Hong Kong Government Opium Monopoly, 1914-1941,' *Journal of Imperial and Commonwealth History*, 11:3, 1983, pp. 275-299.

Munn, Christopher, *Anglo-China. Chinese People and British Rule in Hong Kong 1841-1880,* Richmond, Surrey, England, Curzon Press 2001.

Munn, Christopher, 'The Hong Kong Opium Revenue, 1845-1885,' in Timothy Borrok and Bob Tadashi Wakabayaski (eds.), *Opium Regimes: China, Britain, and Japan, 1839-1952,* Berkeley, University of California Press, 2000.

Nebbs, Adam, *The Great Fire of Hong Kong,* Hong Kong, Bonham Books, 2010.

Norton-Kyshe, James William, *The History of the Laws and Courts of Hong Kong,* (2 vols.) London, 1898, reprinted Hong Kong, Vetch and Lee, 1971.

Platt, Jerome J., Jones, Maurice and Platt, Aileen Kay, *The White Wash Brigade: The Hong Kong Plague of 1894,* Dix Noonan Webb Ltd., London, 1998.

Pope-Hennessy, James, *Half Crown Colony. A Hong Kong Notebook,* London, Jonathan Cape, 1969.

Reynolds, Mr. A. N., Looking Backwards, *The Hong Kong Police Magazine,* Hong Kong, 1951.

Ryan S.J., Thomas F., *The Story of a Hundred Years: The Pontifical Institute of Foreign Missions (P.I.M.E.) in Hong Kong 1858-1958,* Hong Kong, Catholic Truth Society, 1959.

Sayer, Geoffrey Robley, *Hong Kong 1862-1919 Years of Discretion,* Hong Kong, Hong Kong University Press, 1975.

Schiavo, Alessandra, (ed.), *500 Years of Italians in Hong Kong and Macau, Essays by Gianni Criveller and Angelo Paratico,* Hong Kong, Societá Dante Algheri di Hong Kong, 2013.

Shepherd, Bruce, *Kelly and Walsh's Handbook to Hong Kong,* reprinted as *The Hong Kong Guide 1893,* Hong Kong, Oxford University Press, 1982.

Sinclair, Kevin, *Asia's finest marches on: policing Hong Kong from 1841 into the 21st century,* Hong Kong, Kevin Sinclair Associates, 1997.

Sinn, Elizabeth, *Power and Charity. A Chinese Merchant Elite in Colonial Hong Kong,* Hong Kong, Hong Kong University Press, 2003.

Sinn, Elizabeth, 'The Strike and Riot of 1884 - A Hong Kong Perspective,' *Journal of the Royal Asiatic Society, Hong Kong Branch,* vol. 22, 1982, pp. 65-98.

Smith, Carl, *A Sense of History: Studies in the Social and Urban History of Hong Kong,* Hong Kong, Hong Kong Educational Publishing Co., 1995.

Starling, Arthur E. ed., *Plague, SARS and the story of Medicine in Hong Kong,* Hong Kong, Hong Kong University Press, 2006.

Sweeting, Anthony, *Education in Hong Kong Pre 1841 to 1941: Fact and Opinion. Materials for a History of Education in Hong Kong,* Hong Kong, Hong Kong University Press, 1990.

Tak-Wing Ngo (ed.) *Hong Kong's History: State and Society under Colonial Rule,* London, Routledge, 1999.

Taylor, Alice, *To School Through The Fields. An Irish Country Childhood,* Dingle, Co. Kerry, Brandon Book Publishing Ltd., 1988.

Ticozzi, Sergio, 'The Catholic Church and Nineteenth Century Village Life in Hong Kong,' *Journal of the Royal Asiatic Society, Hong Kong Branch,* vol. 48, 2008, pp. 111-149.

Tsang, Steve, ed., *Government and Politics: A Documentary History of Hong Kong,* Hong Kong, Hong Kong University Press, 1995.

Turner, J. A., *Kwang Tung or Five Years in South China,* London, 1894 reprinted, Hong Kong, Oxford University Press, 1982.

Ward, Iain, *Sui Geng: The Hong Kong Marine Police 1841-1950,* Hong Kong, Hong Kong University Press, 1991.

Welsh, Frank, *A History of Hong Kong,* London, Harper Collins, 1997 (revised edition).

Wesley-Smith, Peter, *Unequal Treaty 1898-1997: China, Great Britain and Hong Kong's New Territories,* Hong Kong, Hong Kong University Press, 1980.

White, Barbara-Sue, ed., *Hong Kong: Somewhere Between Heaven and Earth,* Hong Kong, Oxford University Press, 1996.

Index

Page references in bold refer to photographs. Police ranks are given when the man appears in the text only or predominantly at that rank.